STATIC FORMS

MODERNIST LATITUDES

MODERNIST LATITUDES

Jessica Berman and Paul Saint-Amour, Editors

Modernist Latitudes aims to capture the energy and ferment of modernist studies by continuing to open up the range of forms, locations, temporalities, and theoretical approaches encompassed by the field. The series celebrates the growing latitude ("scope for freedom of action or thought") that this broadening affords scholars of modernism, whether they are investigating little-known works or revisiting canonical ones. Modernist Latitudes will pay particular attention to the texts and contexts of those latitudes (Africa, Latin America, Australia, Asia, Southern Europe, and even the rural United States) that have long been misrecognized as ancillary to the canonical modernisms of the global North.

Mat Fournier, *Dysphoric Modernism: Undoing Gender in French Literature*

Nergis Ertürk, *Writing in Red: Literature and Revolution Across Turkey and the Soviet Union*

Cate I. Reilly, *Psychic Empire: Literary Modernism and the Clinical State*

Adam McKible, *Creating Jim Crow America: George Horace Lorimer, the Saturday Evening Post, and the War Against Black Modernity*

Hannah Freed-Thall, *Modernism at the Beach: Queer Ecologies and the Coastal Commons*

Daniel Ryan Morse, *Radio Empire: The BBC's Eastern Service and the Emergence of the Global Anglophone Novel*

Jill Richards, *The Fury Archives: Female Citizenship, Human Rights, and the International Avant-Gardes*

Claire Seiler, *Midcentury Suspension: Literature and Feeling in the Wake of World War II*

Elizabeth Outka, *Viral Modernism: The Influenza Pandemic and Interwar Literature*

Ben Conisbee Baer, *Indigenous Vanguards: Education, National Liberation, and the Limits of Modernism*

Aarthi Vadde, *Chimeras of Form: Modernist Internationalism Beyond Europe, 1914–2014*

Eric Bulson, *Little Magazine, World Form*

Eric Hayot and Rebecca L. Walkowitz, eds., *A New Vocabulary for Global Modernism*

Christopher Reed, *Bachelor Japanists: Japanese Aesthetics and Western Masculinities*, 2016

For a complete list of books in this series, see the CUP website.

Static Forms

WRITING THE PRESENT IN THE MODERN MIDDLE EAST

Shir Alon

Columbia University Press
New York

Columbia University Press
Publishers Since 1893
New York   Chichester, West Sussex

Copyright © 2025 Columbia University Press
All rights reserved

Library of Congress Cataloging-in-Publication Data
Names: Alon, Shir (Professor of Middle Eastern studies) author
Title: Static forms : writing the present in the modern Middle East / Shir Alon.
Description: New York : Columbia University Press, 2025. |
Series: Modernist latitudes | Includes bibliographical references and index.
Identifiers: LCCN 2025011676 | ISBN 9780231215947 trade paperback | ISBN 9780231215954 hardback | ISBN 9780231561051 ebook
Subjects: LCSH: Arabic fiction—20th century—History and criticism | Hebrew fiction—20th century—History and criticism | Time in literature | Time—Philosophy | Politcs and literature | Modernism (Literature) | LCGFT: Literary criticism
Classification: LCC PJ7577 .A426 2025 | DDC 892.43/09—dc23/eng/20250521

Cover design: Chang Jae Lee
Cover image: *The Body of Film*, 2017 (detail). Based on the negatives of the Jerusalem-based photographer Antranik Bakerjian at the Arab Image Foundation, Beirut. © Akram Zaatari. Courtesy the artist, Sfeir-Semler Gallery, and Thomas Dane Gallery.

GPSR Authorized Representative: Easy Access System Europe, Mustamäe tee 50, 10621 Tallinn, Estonia, gpsr.requests@easproject.com

CONTENTS

Introduction 1

Chapter One
Reverb: Literature's Absent Present 36

Chapter Two
Scratch: The Present Out of Work 69

Chapter Three
Routine: The Present of Reproductive Labor 104

Chapter Four
Threshold: The Limit of Correspondence 142

Chapter Five
Touch: The Present of Crisis Ordinariness 147

Conclusion: Civil War 178

ACKNOWLEDGMENTS 189

NOTES 191

BIBLIOGRAPHY 229

INDEX 249

STATIC FORMS

INTRODUCTION

وأين نَحْنُ، السائرين على خُطَى الفعل
المضارع، أين نحن؟ كلامُنا خَبَرٌ
ومُبْتَدأٌ أمام البحر، والزَّبَدُ المراوغُ
في الكلام هُوَ النقاطُ على الحروف،
فليت للفعل المضارع موطناً فوق
الرصيف . . .

> And where are we, the marching on the footpath of the present
> tense, where are we? Our talk a predicate
> and a subject before the sea, and the elusive foam
> of speech the dots on the letters,
> wishing for the present tense a foothold
> on the dock . . .
> —MAHMOUD DARWISH, "A NOUN SENTENCE"

Mahmoud Darwish's poem "Hiya jumla ismiyya" ("A Noun Sentence"), published in 2004 at the height of Darwish's long and celebrated poetic career, is part of a cycle titled *Fi shahwat al-iqaʿ*, which Fady Joudah sensually translated as "In the Lust for Cadence."[1] The subject matter of this cycle is what Huda J. Fakhreddine calls the "chemistry of the poem" because it prods poetry's elementary particles: letters, sound, rhythm, image, and metaphor.[2] In this metapoetic sequence, Darwish interrogates the defining forms of poetic craft. "A Noun Sentence" opens with a grammatical definition followed by a demonstration:

> A noun sentence, no verb
> to it or in it: to the sea the scent of the bed
> after making love . . . a salty perfume
> or a sour one. A noun sentence: my wounded joy
> like the sunset at the foreigner's windows.
> My flower green like the phoenix.[3]

The opening lines are composed of a series of verbless "noun sentences," which propagate meaning through figurative tropes: description (*waṣf*), simile (*tashbīh*), and metaphor (*istiʿāra*), none of which require verbs. In classical Arabic linguistics, a noun sentence (*jumla ismiyya*) is simply a sentence that begins with a noun, but in modern use, the term often refers, as Darwish does here, to a sentence that has no verbs ("no verb / to it or in it").[4] Darwish can write an entire poem using no verbs, a feat that Fady Joudah can only partially accomplish in his translation, because the Arabic verb "to be" (*kāna*) is normally not used in the present tense. The noun sentence is bereft of action or temporal signposts, establishing an evanescent static situation, a present made of images and figurative constructs. As a poem, "A Noun Sentence" offers not merely a lesson in grammar but a lesson in poetry: it defines a poem as a series of images suspended in the present, having no need for action or verbs. Nevertheless, against the definition offered in the opening lines, the poem's latter part expresses an insistent desire for a verb in the present tense (*al-fiʿl al-muḍāriʿ*) as a guide or companion for movement: "Wishing / for the present tense a foothold for walking behind me / or ahead of me, barefoot."[5] The poetic voice then shifts from the singular to the plural: "Where are we, the marching on the footpath of the present / tense, where are we?"

Darwish's status as the Palestinian "national poet" is such that this metapoetic reflection is inevitably read as a statement about a Palestinian temporality: a condition of temporal instability, a threatened and delicate present without a solid foothold in time's flow. The static noun-images that open the poem are replaced by lost paths, roads, and stairways, spaces that promise movement, both directed and aimless. Without a firm foothold (*mawṭaʾ*) for the present tense, movement becomes a desired impossibility. In the conclusion of the poem, quoted in the epigraph at the beginning of this chapter, speech becomes "a predicate / and a subject before the sea," with no verb between them. This is also the moment in which speech becomes poetry: the word *baḥr* means both sea and poetic meter. The "elusive foam / of speech," so precarious without a verb to sustain it, becomes the dots differentiating Arabic letters, and so the letters also risk evaporating into senselessness. Without a foothold for the present tense, the static figures of the poem are also dodgy (*murāwigh*) and prone to slippage.

INTRODUCTION

The Hebrew poet Dan Pagis's poem "Targilim be-'ivrit shimushit" ("Exercises in Practical Hebrew") similarly stages itself as a lesson in linguistics reflecting on an absent present. The poem adopts the form of a schoolbook in Hebrew grammar:

שָׁלוֹם, שָׁלוֹם. בְּעִבְרִית יֵשׁ עָבָר וְעָתִיד,
אֲבָל אֵין הֹוֶה, רַק בֵּינוֹנִי.
עַכְשָׁו נַעֲבֹר לַמִּשְׁפָּט.

> Shalom, shalom. In Hebrew there is past and future,
> but there is no present, only *beynoni*.
> Now we will move on to the sentence.[6]

These lines contain, on a literal level, technical grammatical information—the *beynoni* form (meaning middle or intermediate, but also mediocre), which acts as the present tense in Hebrew, is not considered to be a proper verb but rather a grammatical article between a verb and a noun, hence its midway name. Yet the lines are meant to be read also as a statement about Israeli temporality, which forsakes the present for grandiose visions of the past harnessed to a no less grandiose future. There is little to say about the intermediate present beyond its absence, which merits moving on to the "sentence." The "sentence," in Hebrew as in English, is both a grammatical object, the next topic in the language lesson, and a juridical-evaluative conclusion. The denotation of "sentence" as judgment resonates with the questions that serve as the poem's epigraph, ostensibly taken from a high school grammar book as neutral examples of the interrogative: *ha-shalom lekha?* (Are you well? Literally: Have you peace?) *ha-ratsaḥta ve-gam yarashta?* (Hast thou killed, and also taken possession? [1 Kings 21:19]).

In both of these poems, the grammatical idiosyncrasies of Arabic and Hebrew are highlighted as a means of commenting on a collective temporal dimension. What is the experience of the present if it lacks a present tense? What would it mean, after all, for the present tense to have a stable foothold? The following chapters of this book trace a series of literary forms engendered by such a strangely embodied present, when a gap manifests between the expectation of the present as a stable transition between the past and the future and its actual experience as an absence or an impasse. The "noun sentence" is one such static yet fragile form, defining a poem and its temporality as a series of similes, transpositions, and displacements. As Darwish's series of questioning charges demonstrates, the present may be experienced as an existential problem (What and when is "my" present and how does it relate to "ours"?), but it manifests as a problem of aesthetic and literary form. This is the case in poetry and even more so in the novel, a genre often tasked with narrating the modern present, its own contemporary. *Static Forms: Writing the Present in the Modern Middle East* examines the literary forms that emerged in Arabic and Hebrew letters as solutions to the problem of writing the present, a particularly troubled and challenging tense for languages uncertain about their own temporality within a universalized literary modernity. Examining the present as a literary problem, *Static Forms* sets up a framework for reading Arabic and Hebrew literatures together, based on their shared narrative of modernization. Moving away from a conception of modernist literary form as a preexisting commodity that travels from the West to the Middle East, it demonstrates how particular formal solutions emerge in relation to the lived experience of the modern present.

This book's central argument is that the present, in its various modalities, is written in *static forms*. Static, as the following pages will clarify, can mean several things: from fixity and cessation of movement, through parasitical or excessive interloping, to distortion and sedition. Reading form as static allows us to identify what literary form *does* and how it mediates the affective present, which is always also historical and collective.[7] My use of the word "form" is therefore deliberately flexible: as a set of relations, form can function at a variety of scales and contexts, from the unit of the sentence or a narrative text to a social structure or an experience of lived time.[8] Static forms assemble several hermeneutic registers that together constitute an aesthetic theory: *thematic*, as a trope in the fictional, diegetic world of the text; *affective*, in the lived experience of the historical moment in which the text appears; and *metapoetic*, theorizing the practice of literary writing as well as literature as a particular mode of textual engagement. To return to the "noun sentence" in Darwish's poem, as a static form—a linguistic construct lacking a verb—it reflects on an experience of unmoored and precarious temporality marked by displacement, but also articulates and performs a poetic theory: the poem as a site for images held together by figuration rather than by action. In the following chapters, I identify and analyze a series of static forms that emerge as organizing tropes in key historical-political moments in Arabic and Hebrew literary modernities, moments in which the question of properly inhabiting the present became particularly fraught. The overarching historical narrative outlined in these chapters traces a parallel trajectory, beginning with discourses of cultural awakening or revival, moving through the harnessing of Arabic and Hebrew literatures to projects of nation building (albeit through postcolonial praxis in the former and a settler colonial one in the latter), and culminating in the emergence of the institution of the state as an organizing frame for temporal experience. Another way to look at this trajectory is as a series of moments in which Arabic and Hebrew literatures grapple with a set of questions that modernity poses to the Orientalized and racialized Arab or Jewish subject: Can it truly be modern? Can it *properly*, which often simply means *efficiently*, inhabit space and time?

The term "static form" may seem redundant: Isn't form, by definition, a static, rigid structure? Although structural narrative theory may have bequeathed us the idea of form as synchronic rather than diachronic, forms themselves are often dynamic, implying progression in time or space: consider forms such as causation, entropy, or most common narrative structures.[9] Static forms, as I define them in this book, are relational structures without direction in which movement, if and when it happens, goes nowhere. Checking the ongoing flow of past-present-future, static forms are suspended in the present, yet they rarely denote a simple cessation of movement. Stasis, the condition of suspension within a static form, is variegated: the tense immobility of waiting is different from the repetitive, cyclical gestures of daily routine, and those are distinct from the compulsive-obsessive motion of picking at an open wound or the ecstatic luminosity of transcendental timelessness. Each of these states has its own rhythm or internal movement, its range of associated affects, and its correlating sociopolitical significances. *Static Forms* expounds on four such static forms: *reverb* is a mode of accumulation through repetition that creates the effect of simultaneity; *scratch* refers to random, aimless, and compulsive movement; *routine* denotes self-devouring repetition; and *touch* maps contiguity and seamless continuity. Reverb, scratch, routine, and touch each become meaningful in particular historical moments in Arabic and Hebrew literary modernity, mediating between the aesthetic, the political, and the affective.

THE PRESENT PREDICAMENT

No genre better illustrates the stakes of writing the present than the literary review. Unlike novels that might imagine their audience in posterity, the book review is a presentist genre, always written to and about its present moment. Appearing in ephemeral periodicals responsive to recent events and shifting public moods, the book review addresses the present through reflection on one of its products, a literary work. I begin, therefore, with three literary reviews that appeared in the Arabic or Hebrew press in the early teens of the twentieth century and demonstrate, through their intersections, how the present first appeared as a problem for Middle Eastern writers. From there, the introduction proceeds to unfold how static adjoins four key concepts: *the present, form, modernism*, and the comparative scope embodied in the term *Middle East*.

Mohammed Hussayn Haykal's novel *Zaynab* was published in Cairo in 1913 without much fanfare. The so-called "first Egyptian novel" was certainly not the first to appear in Cairo's thriving book market and arguably not very different from its contemporaries.[10] Only a single review of *Zaynab* appeared before the novel vanished from the public eye for fifteen years, a gushing, somewhat schizophrenic essay published without a byline in the October 1913 issue of *al-Bayan* (*Communique*), a journal that had featured a number of Haykal's essays previously.[11] Seeking to establish a broad cultural context for the novel, the review opens with a long lament for the "shameful deficit" of novelists in Egypt, a humiliating indicator of the weakness of the entire literary field. This lack, the anonymous reviewer stipulates, might have to do with the Egyptians' failure to notice "concrete minor details" of their surroundings, such as the number of windows in their house or steps in their staircases (supposedly necessary details for establishing a proper literary realism). It certainly should not, the reviewer adds, be blamed on Egypt's "orderly and dull landscapes, which fail to inspire novelists" because novels should not at all be limited to the sublime or awe inspiring. Quite the contrary. "We want novels," the reviewer proclaims, "whose materials come from our existing present [*ḥālnā al-ḥāḍira*]: our ailments and deficiencies; the adherence to the archaic, which is deeply rooted in the souls of our elders and some of our youth; the circumstances faced by our fathers, both their good and their corrupted habits. Such topics shape novels according to the principle of *realism* [*mabdaʾ al-riyālīzm*]."¹²

The deficiencies of the present, indicated by the shameful and humiliating lack of novels, must be depicted in a novel form. There is an attractive circular logic here because the existence of a "novel of the present," depicting the present's sad state, would already be a step toward overcoming this shameful deficiency. The realist novel is called to perform a double task: on the one hand, it must depict the shortcomings of the present; on the other hand, its very existence would be evidence that these shortcomings have been overcome. At this point, the reviewer concedes that novels should not merely confine themselves to the inadequate present: "There is no harm in writing imaginary novels, which align themselves with rightly guided principles, refine the [readers'] emotions, and satisfy their moral needs. A novel guided by the principles of *romanticism* [*mabdaʾ al-rūmāntizm*] is no less useful than a novel based in reality." The distinction between "al-riyālīzm" and "al-rūmāntizm," used here for the first time in a literary review in the Egyptian press, marks the reviewer's departure from the critical vocabulary of the time, which differentiated between didactic, socially beneficial novels and those read for mere entertainment, instead adopting aesthetic categories as a mode of literary classification.¹³ Both the realist depraved novel and the romantic righteous novel, he claims, are socially and individually beneficial. But novels are not merely utilitarian: a realist novel of the present, in and of itself, is an indicator of a "healthy" cultural sphere.

Only following this general introduction does the reviewer introduce *Zaynab* as the herald of "a new literary age." Depicting "the chastity, virtue, purity, and honor" of the peasantry (*rīfiyyīn*), the reviewer summarizes, Haykal has written a contemporary novel (*riwāya ʿaṣriyya*) in which everything is, nevertheless, honorable and lofty. Haykal's achievement, therefore, is that he found the alchemy of realism and romanticism: a novel about the present that manages not to be overwhelmed by the present's corruptions.

Debates on the health of the Arabic novel extended beyond the Arabic press. In October and November 1911, the Jaffa-based Hebrew journal *ha-Poʿel ha-tsaʿir* (*The Young Worker*) featured a long review of modern Arabic literature composed by Yitzhaq Shami (1888–1949), a young Hebron-born Jewish writer.¹⁴ In 1911, Shami was based in Damascus, teaching Hebrew in the small local Jewish community, and was closely following debates on the cultural revival known as the Arab *nahḍa*.[15] Although in those years Damascus seemed much closer to Jaffa than it does today, the review takes the form of a "dispatch from afar," as the majority of the journal's readers, Eastern European settlers in the Zionist colonies, neither spoke nor read Arabic and had little knowledge of Arab literary culture.

The overarching narrative that Shami recounts in this review was a common one: Arabic literature, once the greatest and most appreciated art form among the Arab people, has been neglected, forgotten in slumber for hundreds of years. Only recently, after Egypt came into contact with other "civilized nations," did life begin flowing again in the arteries of Arabic literary culture, extending beyond Egypt to the regions of Syria and Iraq. This narrative of golden age, decline, and awakening is rife with Orientalist stereotypes, but this is not simply due to Shami's external gaze, as he has carefully translated the historical narrative as it appeared in the revivalist Arabic press since at least the mid-nineteenth century. Egypt is now the center of a new period, Shami continues, which the Arabs call "the recent revival" (*ha-tkuma ha-aḥrona*, his Hebrew rendering of the term *al-nahḍa al-akhīra*). The Arab present is a period full of events; changes and influences come at it from all directions. The Arabs had "realized that they are losing their ground, that everything must be mended and renewed.... And so the Arab buckled down and started performing strange leaps, absorbing everything with no discrimination, devoted to everything without informed judgment."[16] The literature produced by these shifting and unstable times, Shami writes, is still embryonic, in a fragile and unformed state, not yet having found its own bearings: "Not only does it lack sufficient time to discover new horizons, or destroy what must be destroyed of the old ones, but it is also not yet fully free of them: the secular and the sacred, religion and enlightenment, realism and romanticism, nationalism and assimilation, all of these are mixed together, and a thick fog covers it all."[17]

There is one exception, Shami writes, towering above this hodgepodge: the work of the writer Jurji Zaydan. One of the most influential agents of the *nahḍa*, Zaydan (1861–1914) was a Cairo-based Lebanese novelist, journalist, and editor. He had written a cycle of serialized novels on Islamic history, which with their accessible language and suspenseful plots proved to be extremely popular. For Zaydan, the historical novel form was primarily didactic, an attractive vessel to familiarize audiences with the Islamic past.

Yet Shami loathed the didacticism of Zaydan's novels; he found the significance of the historical novel elsewhere. Zaydan's genius, Shami claims, is that he instinctively realized that the Arab present, in all its chaos, simply could not be written. In such a confused period, it is "impossible to find complete and healthy protagonists [ṭipusim bri'im u-shlemim]" that could hold up a literary text.[18] Instead, Zaydan turned to Islam's glorious past as a setting for his characters. Historical figures such as Harun al-Rashid and Fadl Ibn al-Rabi' are not only well-grounded in their relatively static environment, Shami claims, but also exemplify what has been established as "the Arab character"—a character obscured in the turbulent times of revival. Shami argues that the Arab present does not live up to any solid literary genre and therefore cannot be properly represented. This judgement can also be reversed—modern genres such as the short story or the realistic novel, which are most often tasked with narrating the present, are mismatched to the current moment. The past, however, offers itself readily for narration.

Two months before Shami's article came out, in August 10, 1911, *ha-Po'el ha-tsa'ir* featured an essay of literary criticism by the writer Yosef Haim Brenner (Y. H. Brenner) under the title "ha-Janer ha-erets yisra'eli ve-avizarehu" ("The Land of Israel genre and its accoutrements").[19] Brenner was a well-known, influential, and provocative agent of Hebrew literary culture who had joined the Zionist settlement in Palestine in 1909. Merely a year later, his article on Jewish conversion and assimilation—essentially a polemicist call for the secular-national Hebrew Zionist culture of the colonies to cut itself off from international Judaism—had almost gotten the journal discontinued.[20] "Ha-Janer" was no less consequential. Initially appearing to be simply an apologetics in defense of *Mi-kan u-mi-kan* (*From Here and There*), Brenner's recently published novel, it became one of the most influential and analyzed critical essays of modern Hebrew literature. There is much to say about this essay, and I return to it in chapter 2, discussing it in relation to Brenner's own prose and Zionist settler-colonial ideology. Suffice to mention here that Brenner's standing at the time was such that this article was said to cause a "chilling effect" on Hebrew literature, as writers refrained from writing about the Zionist colonies for fear of Brenner's criticism.[21]

In "ha-Janer," Brenner sets out to defend the fragmented chronicle style of *Mi-kan u-mi-kan*, arguing that fragmentary notes and memoirs are the only literary form fitting to describe the Zionist settlement in Palestine. Literature, he claims matter-of-factly, should be the "revelation of inner life and their essence within a recognizable time and a recognizable environment."[22] Thus the Yiddish writer can write about the Jews of Russia, or the German writer can write about the people of Berlin. These sites have a stable and recognizable existence that lends itself to literary depiction. But the Zionist colonies, Brenner writes, are still "a new and shifting environment." And because there is nothing recognized, specific, or typical about them, it becomes impossible to write proper stories—"genre stories," as Brenner calls them—about them. As an example, Brenner mentions "Raiza the innkeeper," a fictional but typical character of Yiddish-Russian literature that all Jewish readers could immediately conjure in their minds. The Zionist settlement does not have such "character types" available for the writer, and hence the writer should suffice, at the moment, with quick dynamic sketches, rather than false depictions of "pastoral Jewish-peasant life."[23] Brenner clarifies that the problem is not writing in Hebrew per se: "There is no problem for the Hebrew writer to write about Jewish life in Russia or Poland, since it is clear, though somewhat uncomfortable, that he is not writing in the spoken language."[24] The ongoing project of vernacularizing the language, in and of itself, poses no challenge for the writer. The problem emerges when the Hebrew writer attempts to write the culture of Hebrew revival in the messy midst of the revival efforts, in and of the Hebrew present.

These three reviews articulate a similar predicament. On the one hand, they echo a normative demand for a literature *of* and *about* the present. On the other hand, they are deeply skeptical that the present—specifically a present that conceives of itself as a moment of revival—can be properly represented at all. The present appears as a problem of genre and form: romanticism or realism, historical fiction, documentary fragments—all of these are conjured as provisional solutions, even compromises, used to address a present that demands representation but fails it. The reviewers offer diverse solutions. The anonymous reviewer of *al-Bayan* advocates a turn away from the city to the countryside, a location where contemporary changes can be contained within a romantic framework. Rather than writing the urban present, in which colonizers, industrialists, reformists, workers, and migrants collide, setting a novel in the countryside is a means of writing the end of a way of life now considered (at least by the urban

INTRODUCTION

intellectual milieu) to be static and hence outdated, a handy workaround.²⁵ Shami's solution is not very different. Arguing that the novelist should avoid the present altogether and write the historical past, with its archive of established characters, he similarly recommends choosing a setting that is familiar, recognizable, and relatively static. Brenner posits that the only way to stay with the present is to give up on narrative arcs and claims to objective representation and instead limit oneself to quick subjective sketches. As in the two other reviews, this is not an aesthetic ideal but a temporary fix, a solution to be utilized until the messy process of revival successfully concludes. Then the proper literary genres of the present—chief among them the realist short story and the novel—can materialize and take their rightful place in Arabic and Hebrew writing.

Before considering these solutions, I want to linger on the problem they point toward, the crisis that they aim to address: the simultaneous *necessity* and *impossibility* of writing the present. What is it about the conditions of the present that makes it appear as a *literary problem*? Is there anything unique about these writers' predicament, or are these problems simply a built-in, intrinsic feature of the dictate that modern literature's role is to narrate the present, the most elusive of tenses? And what can we make of the fact that this predicament is articulated so similarly across concurrent Arabic and Hebrew literary debates?²⁶

The narrative of modernity as an overwhelming, even traumatic, encounter with radical change and novelty is by now familiar; its most emblematic articulation, Walter Benjamin's paradigm of "modernity shock," linking Baudelaire's urban explorations in 1860s Paris and Freud's investigation of trauma in the 1920s, has been the basis of countless accounts of the modern experience.²⁷ Yet, the temporal structure described in these three reviews is markedly different. Their complaint is not merely that the present is suddenly moving too fast for processing, comprehending, or keeping up—outpacing established forms—or that an unfamiliar future is at hand. These literary reviews were written with the horizon of the proper genre of the present in sight: they already *know* the form of a modern literature emerging from an established national modernity. It is against this predefined future novel that they can judge the Arabic and Hebrew attempts to write the present as lacking.

Rather than a "shock of the new," the temporal structure these reviews describe is aligned with what Moroccan philosopher Abdallah Laroui has called *le futur antérieur*, the "prior future" or the grammatical tense known in English as the future perfect. It is the tense that refers to something that lies ahead and yet that is already complete, what "will have happened." Modernity is a future already outlined elsewhere, Laroui notes, that we are not at liberty to refuse.[28] Laroui underscores that modernity is not simply a condition or a time frame but is the culmination of a predetermined process of modernization, a teleological process that dictates a particular future on its subjects: the future of the nation-state and its social, economic, theological, and aesthetic logics. Within this structure, Laroui continues, the non-Western subject can do two things: he can accept this future as inevitable and work to accommodate it, or he can claim this future is not valid and assert a return to a so-called authentic self. Either option cannot bypass an engagement with Western histories of domination and the "prior future" they have established.[29]

A decade after Laroui's French publication, the Lebanese writer Elias Khoury echoed his reading of the implications of a predetermined modern future on the temporality of the present in a special issue of the Beirut-based journal *Mawaqif* (Positions) dedicated to the question of modernity. The journal's editor, the poet Adonis, had asked several of its regular contributors to reflect on Arabic modernity—or modernism, as the Arabic word *al-ḥadātha* refers to both—in literature and thought. Shifting constantly between the two meanings of *al-ḥadātha*, as a historical period and set of circumstances and as an aesthetic movement, most essays in the April 1979 issue define modernity as a form that emerged in the West, before manifesting (or not) in Arab culture. Khoury's contribution to this volume, however, rings different, as he declares in its opening sentences that Arab modernity has its own form that is markedly different from Western modernity. "Arab modernity came as a revival modernity [jā'at al-ḥadātha al-'arabiyya ḥadātha nahḍawiyya]," Khoury asserts. Revival modernity is experienced as a cultural, social, and political break, for which the solution must be sought from outside by latching oneself to a future that is already known in advance.[30] For if, as the Moroccan philosopher Mohammed Abed Al Jabri observed around the same period, the European renaissance was named in retrospect, the Arab *nahḍa* was named while it was ongoing. It was a project based in the desire to depart from one's own present.[31] The premodeled future that the *nahḍa* aims itself toward, which Khoury explains is delineated by Western capitalist hegemonic expansion, becomes in itself a kind of memory, replacing a historical-cultural memory that has lost its legitimacy in the present and has become a museum artifact. Between the obstructed cultural memory of the past and the modern memory of the future, the present is absent, external to both. According to Khoury, the Arab writer must resist this movement and reinstate himself (*sic*) in this absent present as a witness.[32]

WHAT IS THE PRESENT?

What does it mean to write the present? There is nothing obvious about the grammatical object in the phrase "writing the present," nothing certain or fixed about its scope, boundaries, or contours. The present will accept whatever we say about it.

For example, the present is the most ephemeral, ungraspable of times. The past extends back to time immemorial, full of myths, tragedies, and glories, individual as well as collective. The future (especially if we conceive of it as independent of human existence) extends to no end. In between them, the present is fleeting, impossible to hold on to. The present is a speculative point in time that has no volume or substance of its own. It is a mere medium of transition, gone whenever we try to seize it.

Yet the present is all that we have. The past is gone, the future is yet to occur, and the present is all that is. Anything we have of the past or the future exists solely in the present, in the form of experience, memories, ruins, hopes, projections, and expectations. We need the fullness of the present to mediate those other times that do not actually exist. The modern terms referring to the present, the Arabic *ḥāḍir* and the Hebrew *hove*, both carry the same semantic baggage as the English: the present is what is present, what exists, what *is*.[33] The present, then, is not merely a temporal but an ontological site.

The present is both nothing and everything. This is illustrated by the multiple scales and modes in which the present is asked to perform: as a solitary "moment in time"; as an embodied, unfolding experience; as a historical period in which one's life is enmeshed; and as a grammatical tense. This inconsistency makes the present an inherently unstable object of representation because we can never decide, once and for all, what it is that should properly be represented. When did the present start and how long does it continue? What, in the mess of experience, gets to be counted as the present, and what is labeled a living emblem of the past, an outdated infiltrator or harbinger of the future that breached its proper temporal boundaries? Rather than an objective physical datum, the present is "a convention, imposed on a physical and physiological reality that is much more fluid."[34] It is a sociopolitical form, a conceptual construct that shapes and is shaped by social life, constantly made and remade in discursive practice; it is "inseparable from the historically determined and politically motivated ways we choose to divide the present from the past," writes Theodore Martin in his study of an overlapping concept, "the contemporary."[35] The present is not a self-evident unit but the result of a critical and discerning practice, or as Lauren Berlant writes, it is "something given back to us by those who reflect on it."[36] As such, the present is often articulated in retrospect, and its immediate experience is often inconclusive. This inevitable belatedness has been translated in literary debates into an anxious tension between the story and the telling of it (the *fabula* and *syuzhet* of Russian formalism) and to a common normative assumption that the past tense is the natural medium for storytelling whereas the present tense is a provocation or interruption.[37] This, in turn, relies on the supposition that novels are first and foremost vessels for narrative dynamics and that they have a "story" that is creatively and productively distorted by the method of its narration. *Static* moves away from this approach to consider the modern novel as a text charged with giving the present an aesthetic form, rather than as a retroactive narrative unfolding. The problem of the present as I approach it here has less to do with a melancholy desire for an impossible immediacy or authenticity and more to do with knowing what to do with the present once it is given to us as an overburdened sociopolitical site. Although some modernist strands ideologized the fleeting present as a heroic site of immediacy and spontaneity, what Paul De Man calls "the facticity, in modernity, of a present that is ruled by experiences that lie outside language and escape from the successive temporality, the duration involved in writing,"[38] the present as I approach it here is always already acknowledged as a mediated site.

The modern present, by its very definition, is an especially fraught terrain. It is difficult to say precisely how the quality of the present has changed in modernity, but it is clear that the stakes of the present have been altered: in discourses of modernity, the present is a site of heightened significance and concern.[39] Modernity is defined, in this study, as a set of global economic and political relations but also, more significantly, as a discursive category or a narrative act: it is a declaration of the new breaking itself from the past, a celebration of the autonomy of the present. "A writeover of capitalism," as Harry Harootunian calls it, modernity constitutes a global historic phenomenon proclaiming the advent of new time, a time administered and controlled by new technological tools bringing immense distances into simultaneity and a promise of synchronicity.[40] Cut off decidedly from the past, the modern present flows only in one direction, toward an ostensibly unknown future.[41] It is precisely the "openness" of this future that is obstructed by revival modernities' temporal structure.

This kind of present, the modern historical present, is necessarily about sharing time with others. "No one has this kind of present alone," Michael North notes.[42] When the reviewer of *al-Bayan* calls for novels "of our current present" (ḥālnā al-ḥāḍira), he designates an imprecise temporal duration extending around the time of publication, but whether it implies one year or twenty is not as significant as the fact that this present is communal. Saying "our present" assumes a community existing in the same temporal medium, a temporal homogeneity. In Benedict Anderson's by now standard account, the ability to imagine such a national and/or global community rests on a notion of "homogenous, empty time," measured by clocks and calendars and spread through print capitalism.[43] The very feeling of being part of a present moment participates in the creation of a unified social subject, the by-product of technologies of recording and communication, from writing to clocktowers to telephones, that shape an increasingly organized society. These technologies allow people to feel their own lives as part of narrative sequences, tied to a past and a future that exceed their individual present.

Anderson's analysis of how technology participates in the creation of a shared objectively existing present is crucial to any account of modern temporalities, but it is good to keep in mind that the ideal of homogenous empty time has never been more than just that—an ideal of a secular capitalist globality, constantly confronted by countless other lived and imagined temporalities. The continuous "discovery" of other temporalities in philosophy and social sciences has accompanied empty scientific time's global spread: from Henri Bergson's interiorization of time, phenomenology's embodiment of it, and the Freudian unconscious's timelessness, through the Frankfurt School's critical investment in everyday life,

Walter Benjamin's willful insertion of messianic openness to the future, and Jacques Derrida's hauntology, and all the way to the most recent elaborations on queer temporalities and rejections of futurity. Postcolonial critique has been, from its incipience, a critique of the politics of colonial time.[44] The anxiety about making the present meaningful "again," through appeals to memory, authenticity, or the deification of the instant as the access to a lost eternity, is therefore just as characteristic of the modern present as the scientific empty time of the clock. If modernity is indeed, as North implies, a temporal period in which the present is seen to be always compromised, alienated, hollowed out, or cut off from time's natural flow, and if the novel is truly a genre of the modern present, then the novel is clearly in trouble by virtue of its subject matter.[45] What are the stakes for a literary genre wedded to such an unhappy tense?

STATIC FORMS AND THE AFFECTIVE PRESENT

In a rare yet oft-cited piece on Arabic literature, Edward Said echoes Khouri's assessment of the Arab writer's unique responsibility to write a present that has been obstructed through histories of material and epistemological violence. Whereas Khouri returns to the *nahḍa* and to colonial modernity as the moment when the present lost its foothold in Arab culture, Said associates the present's predicament with a later colonial moment, the war of 1948 in Palestine and the establishment of the State of Israel. In "Arabic Prose and Fiction After 1948," he points out that the loss of Palestine was conceived, even in its immediate aftermath, as a deviation, "a veering out of course, a serious deflection from a forward path."[46] While other nations were setting on the path of decolonization, Arab modernity had suddenly lost its future. The *nakba*, the experience of Palestinian dispossession and expulsion, made clear "the problem of the *present*, a problematic site of contemporaneity, occupied and blocked from the Arabs."[47] As a result, Arabic writing was tasked with the heroic duty of creating the Arab's obstructed present and insisting on Arab contemporaneity in the face of extinction. Said then highlights the prevalence of the episodic *scene* as a form in modern Arabic literature, replacing forms such as the historical period or the linear narrative, and ties it to the precarity of the Arab present. "The past is usually identified with loss," he writes, "the future with uncertainty. But as for the present, it is a constant experience, a *scene* to be articulated with all the resources of language and vision.... It is the *scene* as the irreducible form of the present which the writer must affirm."[48] For the Arab writer, Said asserts, "the present is not an imaginative luxury, but a literal existential necessity."[49] Writing the present, making it in language, becomes in itself a historical act, a provocation, an act of defiance against extinction. The Arab experience of the occupied present after 1948, according to Said, manifested in the literary form of the fragmentary, static scene.

Static Forms extends and elaborates Said's insight, identifying a series of literary forms, more specific than Said's *scene*, that emerged in modern Arabic and Hebrew literatures to narrate the experience of the present as an impasse or a blockade. Literary tropes such as echo (*reverb*), agitation (*scratch*), repetition (*routine*), and opacity (*touch*) articulate the historical present as it was experienced in a series of parallel moments in the histories of modern Arabic and Hebrew cultures, starting from shared narratives of revival, through projects of modernizing settlement and law-preserving violence, to the suspended historicity of neoliberal governance. Static literary forms are viewed here as an aesthetic and affective heuristic, a means to link between social or political forms, the lived present, and the literary text. The literary archive presented in the following chapters includes works in which the present is suspended, extended, interrogated, or fetishized, animated by the tension between the experiential, embodied present of the individual (the Arab body, making those impulsive "strange leaps" in Shami's account) and the historical, social present and its temporal form (the predetermined future of a cultural awakening, for example).[50] A conscious sense of the present may appear in the absence of active actions and in nonevental, static moments: daily routines of maintenance, phases of suspended waiting, or times of idle rest. Their affective register is boredom, nervousness, impassive indifference, or alternately, the impersonality of ecstatic transcendence. These moments of immobility foreground awareness of the body itself—how it occupies space or rubs against its immediate environment, its continuous sensorial input, and the minor gestures it performs by the force of habit.

The relationship between the affective, individually experienced present and the "historical present," the collective narrative about the shape and meaning of the current historical moment, animates Raymond Williams's search for "terms for the undeniable experience of the present," which he eventually names "structures of feelings."[51] For Williams, structures of feelings address those elements of the emergent, experienced present that cannot be reduced into recognizable, fixed forms. Neither personal nor private, they are "social experiences in solution" on the edge of semantic availability, linking the present of the sensing subject to already-formed social forms and institutions. "Structures of feelings" as a concept allows Williams to perform a surprising reversal of the standard account of the experience of modernity: suddenly it is not social reality or history that is changing and shifting so rapidly, while the astounded individual stands watching in paralyzed shock, but rather it is the experiential present of the individual subject that becomes the site where forming structures and changes are identified.

The question of change and movement in the experiential present, which is really the question of what kind of movement is worthy of attention, splits the prevailing theoretical approaches to literary affect. In the works of affect theorists who mark their tribute to Williams as well as to Spinozist vitalism, such as Kathleen Stewart, Lauren Berlant, and Erin Manning, to name a few among many, the present is not merely a moment of transition between the past and the future but is "weighted and reeling," "stretched out," composed of continuously "moving sheets," a rich, vibrant field of interconnected becomings.[52] This affective present is never static—it is busy and shimmering (a key word for the vitalist strand of affect studies) with potential. In the work of Fredric Jameson, in contrast, we find affect to be radically static. In *The Antinomies of Realism*, Jameson distinguishes between a narrative impulse, or *récit*, and a static or scenic impulse, which he names *affect*, based on their temporal forms. The narrative impulse—namely the plot—follows the regime of past-present-future. Affect, however, is marked by a reduction to the present, which is also a reduction to the body.[53] Jameson laments affect's overwhelming of narrative, a process that eventually culminates in modernism's "eternal present."[54] Whereas the narrative impulse ties "character" to destiny, history, and genre, affect, according to Jameson, rejects genre by its very definition: the singularity of the embodied present would be lost when associated with a prefigured or historical form.

Whether the definition of affect is of an ongoing, dynamically unfolding present or of a static detachment from history and narrative, both the vitalist affect theorists and Jameson accept the premise that affect, given its somatic and nonlinguistic nature, provides access to unmediated experience. Studies of affect-in-the-present promise to maintain allegiance to the evolving, not-yet-existing nature of Williams's "structures of feelings" by foregoing interpretation, representational thinking, evaluative critique, and other forms of abstraction that would reduce the singularity of affect to a mere symptom of existing "larger structures."[55] Although I am sympathetic to this turn away from reductive "paranoid readings," I refuse to accept the assertion of affect's formlessness.[56] Especially when it comes to literary affects, claims to immediacy and formlessness are of limited value. Language, publication, circulation—these are all social forms that inevitably participate in the formation of a literary text, myriad levels of mediation between experience and the ultimate reader (in their own affected body). More accurately, literary affects are modes of representation that present themselves as *nonrepresentation* or as immediacy. Rather than being genre-less, their generic convention is the immediacy and availability of the present. Static literary forms, in their attention to embodied habits, gestures, and routines, cling to surfaces of texts and of the bodies they write and resist depicting dramas of interiorities. They rub against the skin of the reader as well, causing—and not simply depicting—agitation, nervousness, or boredom. These textual surfaces, however, are never simply evident and available for consumption, as the last decade's manifestos for surface reading seem to assert.[57] Surfaces are textured, mediated, and call for interpretation.

Unpacking the denotative meanings of static may further elucidate how static forms function textually: static is common shorthand for "static electricity," a suspended electric charge that gathers on typically benign surfaces (sweaters, balloons) so that they act strangely, giving unexpected jolts or insistently clinging together or repelling each other. Static is also a feature of technology based on electromagnetic waves, such as radio and analog television: crackling and hissing that interfere with the broadcast. The French term for this kind of static, which has carried over to several Arabic spoken dialects alongside the Arabic word *tashwīsh* (confusion, derangement) is *parasite*: static is a parasitic interloper on the transmission—aural or visual noise that registers the materiality of the medium.[58] In modern communication theory, a noisy transmission is one that has a lot of dirt, or a lot of aural vibrations added to the signal that are unintentional and therefore redundant.[59] Although static is a technical feature of transmission, it inevitably introduces subjective parameters of value and intention. "The decision as to what constitutes noise in the signal and what constitutes its information is a necessarily subjective matter," Greg Hainge writes, "that assumes the absolute intentionality of the originary emitter to be the only defining characteristic of the information that needs to be considered."[60] What is significant information and what is interloping noise? Static noise on the radio may sound like formless crackling, but it is information as well: caused by atmospherics, or electromagnetic disturbances in the atmosphere, it is how atmosphere becomes information becomes sound.

Needless to say, literary static lacks the physical, measurable qualities that characterize electric static. *Acoustical* rather than *acoustic*, to borrow the distinction Julie Beth Napolin makes in relation to literary resonance, literary static is located between the materiality of language and its referential and relational qualities.[61] The forms for writing the modern Arabic and Hebrew present depend on figures that cut across these three meanings of static: forms of the present are suspended in time and space; they map charged surfaces of bodies rather than depict interiorities; and they interrogate the parasitic and hierarchical relation of dirt or noise to efficient communication. As such, static forms are often an interruption to the proper flow both of narrative and of politics. As the Arabic term *tashwīsh* denotes, they are a derangement of orderly conduct. The static forms I read here—housework routines, landscape descriptions, records of minor physical gestures and perceptions—often amount to what Franco Moretti calls "fillers," those sections of the novel in which nothing happens, filling up novels between one turning point and another.[62] Moretti, like Jameson, reads the history of the modern novel as the increased encroachment on plot by fillers until they take over books in their entirety. Both of these scholars view fillers as expressions of a bourgeois sensibility taking over: rational and ordered in the case of Moretti, antirevolutionary in the case of Jameson, and not particularly appreciated in either. This approach not only assumes that the (aesthetic and political) purpose of the novel is to tell a story but also willfully ignores the political potential of static forms, literary moments of absented interiority in which "nothing happens." *Static Forms* argues that in their departure from an interiority-based concept of character and subject and from a future-oriented mode of action, static forms denote a political intervention that challenges political ideologies based in principles of progress, productivity, and identification.

INTRODUCTION

This ambivalent political capacity is inherent to the notion of stasis. *Stasis* (στάσις) denoting a position, is derived from the Greek verb *istamai* or *istemi*, which can mean either to stand up or to be standing—either the movement upward or the state in which one finds oneself after the movement is completed.[63] Its meanings appear to alternate between two opposite poles—stasis can mean lack of movement as well as movement toward a state.[64] The contemporary use of the term *stasis*, and its prominent derivatives in Latin, English, French, or German, is associated with immobility and immutability, a notion of arrested movement or suspended time, as well as stability or equilibrium. This is the origin of words such as status quo, static, and of course the political institution of the state (I examine some alternative political vocabularies in Hebrew and Arabic and the different theory of state they suppose in chapter 3). In the Greek polis, however, *stasis* also meant a seditious dissent culminating in civil war, a denotation I return to in the book's conclusion. *Stasis* is both the state and its undoing. How can these two seemingly opposed meanings be accounted for? The classicist Nicole Loraux offers two possible explanations: the first, a historical-semantic speculation, suggests that the concept of *stasis* as "position" evolved to that of a party, particularly a party constituted for the purpose of sedition, which in turn evolved to a raging civil war.[65] Yet she also comments that the interpretations of this semantic evolution should be sought in Greek thought about the city itself. If the proper functioning of the polis and of politics is envisioned as a mobile flow, an ongoing process depending on friendship and agreement between the citizens, *stasis* as sedition or civil war represents an arrest of the flow of operative politics, a stoppage in circulation. Stasis as civil war not only introduces disorder but also halts the proper movement of the political. It is a civic restlessness that leads to stagnation; a restless standstill or dynamic inactivity; an arrest that is swarming and full of movement.[66]

In the following chapters, opaque characters and the static forms they inhabit offer a series of metaphoric figures for political gestures that depart from the much-heralded modernist tropes of resistance or break, invested in behaviors of minor adjustment, renunciation, divestment, and restraint. Performing a withdrawal from both work and actualization, static forms depart from instrumental or progressive logics of identity and community to inform an ethical and political horizon condensed to the immanence of the present.[67]

GLOBAL MODERNISM AS STATIC

As the earlier brief discussion of Jameson and Moretti insinuates, *Static Forms* is primarily engaged with literary techniques that are associated with the aesthetics of modernism. Several of the writers analyzed in this book are often explicit about the modernist masters who have shaped their literary sensibilities: Y. H. Brenner had translated *Crime and Punishment* into Hebrew, and his own self-disparaging protagonists owe an unmistakable debt to the proto-modernist Fyodor Dostoevsky of *Notes from the Underground*; both Yeshayahu Koren and Sonallah Ibrahim cite their encounter with Ernest Hemingway's short stories as a breakthrough moment, crucial to honing their own technique; and Elia Suleiman regularly plants references to Samuel Beckett's plays in his films. Nevertheless, I am reluctant to belabor the somewhat circular argument that claims these writers and their works' place within a global modernist movement. Having expanded modernism's geographical scope and highlighted its transnational, cosmopolitan, or global engagements, the new modernist studies, as identified by Douglas Mao and Rebecca L. Walkowitz, still grapple with the challenge of maintaining the moniker "modernism" while overcoming its decidedly Eurocentric associations and attributes.[68] Beginning with a predefined notion of modernism inevitably leads to a contested terrain of comparisons with what Jahan Ramazani refers to as "Euromodernist techniques" and to a host of disputations relating to periodization, origins, and influence.[69] Chapter 1 further elaborates on these foundational questions of world literature, mapping debates on changing literary form in relation to the politics of periodization as they appeared in Arabic and Hebrew literary theory and praxis.

Instead of beginning with a preconceived definition of modernism, *Static Forms* considers literary works through formal and relational categories, not bound to a chronology or a prototype.[70] It elaborates an apparatus for theorizing the development of literary forms in relation to the lived, embodied experience of the present as it is shaped in cultural discourse about time in specific settings and contexts, rather than as the outcome of "traveling forms," migrating from the West to the rest.[71] Identifying static form as a means of writing the present allows for a departure from a concept of modernism as a literary period, a movement, or a canon in favor of its designation as an aesthetic challenge—as a series of formal solutions to the problem of finding a genre for the present. As such, static forms are a heuristic to study and read works beyond the Middle Eastern context, whether they are already recognized as part of an established modernist canon or not. Static is the modernist novel's primary mode of writing the present.

In revival modernities, whether in Arabic or in Hebrew, the foothold of the present appears to be especially precarious. If, as Jameson argues, the historical category of "modernity" is itself primarily a self-referential narrative form, an exciting rhetorical trope that signifies a break with previous figuration, modernity is first and foremost an affective structure, an attachment to a set of expectations.[72] Yet the narration of modernity as *revival modernity*, in the tense of the *futur antérieur*, suggests that the global experience of modernity is not necessarily one of novelty shock, of speed, or of limitless horizons of expectations, but of impasse. In the global periphery (an economic rather than geographical denotation), the narrative trope of modernity is often experienced as "narrative fissures," which appear when "the emergent condition of globality grate[s] against the expectations" of what modernity should be.[73] Alberto Moreiras sums up the set of affects associated with peripheral modernities as "a sort of *negative globality*." "It is not that modernization has not happened or is yet incomplete," he writes. "It is rather that modernization has not happened in the sense it was supposed to have happened."[74] The many instances in which modernity's futures fail to align with the present may explain why we encounter so many moments of stasis, immobility, and impasse in global literary cultures far beyond the Middle East. They highlight a predominant experience of modernity not as novelty but as a structure of repeatedly thwarted expectations, a memory of a future to which one has no access. Static forms—literary forms that confine themselves to a plotless present—are among the many symptoms of negative globality's narrative fissures.

The literary works examined in this book all negotiate the relation between literary forms and the temporal forms of the lived present. For their writers, the pressing question is that of positioning oneself in time—not *where* am I, which is the question much literary criticism posits to global modernist literature (The East or the West? Home or away? Reality or symbol and sign?), but *when* am I (What is the time of literature and how does it relate to the historical present?). As such, this book turns away from the spatial focus of pioneering studies of world literature, which conceives of literary form as a preexisting commodity that travels from the

West to the Middle East. It also departs from the critical proclivity for spatial movement in both modernist and postcolonial literary studies, which tend to valorize concepts such as translation, border crossings, flows, and ceaseless change.

Arabic and Hebrew have their unique "present issues," which in turn produce a unique collection of static literary solutions. The set of static forms examined in this book—*reverb*, *scratch*, *routine*, and *touch*—is by no means exhaustive. They emerge from the texts themselves as central figures in which aesthetic, thematic, and political concerns coalesce in a solution to the problem of articulating the present. This elaboration of static form as a method rather than an archive also allows me to extend the corpus studied in this book beyond the midcentury moment that is considered the heyday of Arabic and Hebrew modernism, going back to the revivalist discourse of the 1910s and all the way to the sense of suspended historicity at the beginning of the twenty-first century. The books in this corpus are linked by their formal concern with the shape of the present.

THE MIDDLE EAST IN ARABIC AND HEBREW

The following chapters proceed with parallel readings of static forms in literary works in two Middle Eastern languages: Arabic and Hebrew. Needless to say, reading Arabic and Hebrew literatures together is not arbitrary or inconsequential. In the twenty-first century Middle East, Jews and Arabs are bound together through a system of partition, settler colonialism, and apartheid (what Judith Butler has called "the wretched forms of binationalism that already exist").[75] As I write this introduction, the genocidal obliteration of Palestinian lives in Gaza is maddeningly, inconceivably ongoing. The violence of Zionist settler colonialism, which continues to shape Palestinian and Jewish lives in clearly unequal ways, forms the backdrop of this study.

Nevertheless, Jewish-Arab or Hebrew-Arabic encounter is not the focus of *Static Forms*, which instead traces parallel temporalities and literary structures in these two literary corpuses. As such, this book departs from a burgeoning body of scholarship that established precedents for reading Hebrew and Arabic literatures in conversation. The past few decades have seen a plethora of scholarly, curatorial, and pedagogical projects challenging the nationalist logics of separation between Jews and Arabs in what Ella

Elbaz identified as a "redemptive" mode.[76] Whether engaging in recuperative archival projects that trace forgotten or disowned possibilities of joint Jewish-Arab existence within the individual or political body or reading Israeli and Palestinian literatures for transgressions of their contemporary boundaries, this scholarship is driven by a desire to critique and counter current logics and practices of partition.[77] The political import and influence of these projects notwithstanding, with their now familiar gesture of corrective coupling, they have, to some extent, narrowed the available examples and possibilities of Arabic and Hebrew literary scholarship to a particular set of encounters, contexts, and archives. Their project of destabilization has stabilized into a new orthodoxy, turning to literature to find fluidity, movement, and transgressions against the supposedly rigid identitarianism of political life.

Static joins a number of recent titles that move away from excavating literature for recuperative visions: Liron Mor's *Conflicts* traces conflictual modes in Israeli and Palestinian literatures that, although occasionally shared, do not gesture toward reconciliation or resolution but rather underlie a political reality of hostility and severance; and Kfir Cohen Lustig reads Israeli and Palestinian literatures not in relation to each other but against common political and economic processes of globalization.[78] Similarly, *Static Forms* reads modern Arabic and Hebrew literary corpuses as emerging from a parallel or shared narrative of integration into the modern world-system, a narrative that begins with a revival modernity and continues in projects of nation building and state consolidation.

To make a claim for parallel processes and epistemologies is of course not to say that the historical and material contexts of Hebrew and Arabic literatures are identical, but it is rather the basis for a historically informed analysis. Modern Hebrew literature, and the broader project of the "revival of the Hebrew language" (*t'hiyat ha-safa ha-ivrit*), emerged as part of Jewish modernization trends spanning Western and Eastern Europe as well as smaller communities in the Middle East.[79] It is conventionally divided into two roughly consecutive chapters: *haskala* ("education," often glossed as enlightenment) and *t'hiya* ("revival" or renaissance). Both involved projects of scholarly excavation of Hebrew texts alongside the language's adaptation for use in new written and spoken forms. Whereas the original *haskala* impulse was to integrate the Jewish community into nascent liberal European societies, later intellectuals and activists sought separationist nationalist solutions for the Jewish population facing antisemitic persecution. Hebrew vernacularization became central to the Zionist settler colonial project of establishing a Jewish nation-state in Palestine, a project that was consolidated in 1948 with the declaration of the State of Israel and the expulsion of the majority of the indigenous Palestinian population.

Arabic literary modernity traces its origins to the *nahḍa*, a term literally meaning "rising up" but usually glossed as revival or renaissance. The *nahḍa* was a series of cultural, social, and intellectual processes and debates across the Arabic-speaking world, and in conversation with modernizers far beyond it, arising in the context of a weakening Ottoman empire, increasing European colonial domination, and the intensified integration of the western Mediterranean and Egypt into capitalist circuits. Contemporary scholarship often adopts, explicitly or implicitly, Stephen Sheehi's positioning of the *nahḍa* as the basis for modern Arab subjectivity and for Arab national selfhood more broadly.[80] After the collapse of the Ottoman empire, the *nahḍa*'s intellectual and cultural activity was increasingly directed toward the nation-state as the locus of an anticolonial struggle for self-determination.

Can and should these two modernization movements be read together? Surveying the European discursive context in which Zionism emerged, Amnon Raz-Krakotzkin argues that "Zionism in its early stages emerged as what indeed should be considered an anti-colonial national movement resisting oppression and defending against measures similar to those employed in colonies." But the parallel ends here because, as he claims, "while in anticolonial national struggles the national model served as the basis for the struggle against European rule, in the Zionist case it was more a step toward joining—returning to—all that was envisaged by the concept 'Europe.'"[81] Zionism adopted colonial language and racialized vocabularies to define Jewish collectivity, and it did not wage its struggle against Europe but against the Palestinians. But what Raz-Krakotzkin identifies as the "anticolonial East" could not but also adopt and adapt to European forms of political modernity, be they literary forms like the novel or social forms, such as the nation-state as the organizing framework of political life. As Shaden Tageldin has pointed out, "the *nahḍa* unfolded in translation: it transported French and English into Arabic [and thus] appeared to 'preserve' Arabic—all the while translating it."[82] Arab modernity was a translated European modernity, even as it was fighting against British or French colonial rule and cultural imperialism.

Despite crucial divergences in their contexts and political trajectories, "the histories of both the *haskala* and *nahḍa* are fundamentally narratives of how a certain people—Jewish or Arab—came to be 'modern' in their own eyes and the eyes of others," Lital Levi explains.[83] In terms of cultural activity, both the *haskala* and the *nahḍa* produced similar projects and creations. "Language revival" manifested, in both cases, in a classicist drive toward extracting a "pure" idiom, purged of the degenerations that the language had accumulated through use, alongside a reformist zeal to adapt language to new genres and conventions, from scientific expositions to historical romances.[84] The comparability of the two literary movements was evident to early twentieth-century writers, appearing for example in another of the rare reviews of modern Arabic literature in the Hebrew press, composed by Yehuda Burla in 1922 in *ha-Tkufa* (*The Period*), a Moscow-based Hebrew literary journal.[85] Running over thirty pages, this decisively negative essay eventually concludes that "there is nothing here but flotsam and jetsam, complete chaos, lacking any vitalizing spirit of creation."[86] Much of this disparagement is grounded in typical Orientalist stereotyping. But surprisingly, it is Hebrew literature that Burla keeps evoking as Arabic's parallel. Throughout the essay, he compares Arabic and Hebrew writers and essayists along a developmental scale, assessing their ability to express the "national spirit" in the process of revival, and concludes that "the state of the new Arabic literature, at this point in its development, is equivalent and similar to the state of literature in the Jewish *haskala* period, sixty or seventy years ago."[87] This comparative measuring is typical of revivalist discourse: as the literary reviews read in the beginning of this introduction betray, both Hebrew and Arabic writers were concerned with civilizational comparison, assessing literature's "health" (read as a measure of national health) against that of European nations. When Burla places Hebrew and Arabic literatures on the scales, he is not trying to establish a link between Jews and Arabs, historical or contemporary, but is rather performing an exercise in self-positioning: taking for granted that Hebrew and Arabic cultures are navigating parallel systems of modernization, he concludes that Hebrew literature has simply "progressed" further on the literary evolutionary scale.

Burla's developmentalist paradigm highlights that the *naḥḍa* and the *haskala* shared a temporal structure. The discourse of revival was shaped by a colonial logic of civilizational hierarchies that had a distinct temporal dimension. If the world market was a mechanism for synchronizing temporalities, the *ideology* of modernity condemned large parts of the world to a lagging delay. In Dipesh Chakrabarty's useful shorthand, modern capitalism imposed on its subjects a global "transition narrative": a homogenizing narrative of transition from a decadent medievalism, what he memorably calls "the waiting room of history," to modernity.[88] Revivalist intellectuals often subscribed to this temporal ideology in order to argue their way out of it. Both Arab and Jewish processes of modernization were thus conceived as an awakening from a period of stagnant slumber, a return to history, as Raz-Krakotzkin has called it, and to time itself.[89] Revival modernity was grounded in the premise that Arabs and Jews were inhabiting the present wrongly: their contemporary appeared to be noncontemporaneous with modernity as such.

It is crucial to recognize this discourse as ideological: what was narrated as a "lag" in development is a built-in feature of the modern world system of combined and uneven development.[90] To continue utilizing the distinction of "new" and "old" temporalities is to merely replicate the revivalist discourse's conceptual vocabulary, rather than to examine it critically. In nineteenth-century Egypt, for example, as On Barak shows, everything that was fast was identified as Western (and hence modern) and everything that was slow was labeled Egyptian, authentic, and old.[91] The very notion of multiple, nonsynchronous temporalities was the result of the comparative context of a homogenizing progressive timeline, which differentiated cultures along temporal lines. "Local" temporal structures and rhythms, what Barak calls "countertempos," did not necessarily precede Western time but were formulated against it, and both were loaded with significance in a dialectical process.

Somewhat similarly, the struggle over the geopolitical goals of Jewish modernization was conceptualized as a battle over temporal priorities and allegiances. This manifested in an opposition that crystalized in early Zionist debates around the turn of the twentieth century between the concepts of ʿavodat ha-hove (labor of/for the present, *Gegenwartsarbeit*) and ʿavodat erets yisraʾel (labor of/for the Land of Israel), which implicitly became labor for the future. ʿAvodat ha-hove, conceived as a cultural civilizing mission, was initially popularized by philosopher Martin Buber. The term was then reformulated to the demand that the Zionist Organization should not focus solely on organizing mass Jewish migration to Palestine but should simultaneously work toward strengthening Jewish minority rights and forming Jewish autonomies in Russia and the Austro-Hungarian empire. Meanwhile, advocates of ʿavodat erets yisraʾel insisted that Zionism should work toward a national, majoritarian future. Placing themselves as the avant-garde, Zionist settlers rejected the diasporic present, and although both factions were futurist, settler colonial territorialism won semantic rights over the future.[92]

Static Forms begins with the shared temporality of the revivalist discourse in Arabic and Hebrew and proceeds to examine how labor ideologies in national and statist discourses impress upon novels from Israel and from Egypt. What does it mean that the cultural production of a settler colonial movement such as Zionism can be read in the same framework as that of a postcolonial nation such as Egypt? How is it possible to read Hebrew and Arabic together if in the present moment the two languages occupy such different positions in the global structure of power? Burla's essay demonstrates that comparisons such as these are never neutral or innocent. Comparisons are "inevitably tendentious," writes R. Radhakrishnan, "didactic, competitive, and prescriptive. Behind the seeming generosity of comparison, there always lurks the aggression of a thesis."[93] The "lurking thesis" of this book's comparative project is that reading the history of modern literary form in Arabic and Hebrew *together* is necessary in order to wrench the two traditions out of parochial national scholarly debates, in which particular roles and relations have become predetermined, and to allow them to take their place as central elements in the scholarship of global modernism's emergence. Clearly, the "comparison" of comparative literature is not the practice of evaluative ranking that Burla pursues, nor does it assume a "mirage of symmetry," in Liron Mor's phrase, by drawing connections.[94] Instead, *Static Forms* reads Hebrew and Arabic literatures side by side to see their divergent responses to the demands of modern temporal narratives, institutions, and labor regimes across the post-Ottoman region. Like any program of interpretation, which extracts an object out of what appears to be its "natural" context and casts it into a new one, this move might seem, at times, aggressive. Furthermore, like any other comparison, this one too risks overlooking contexts and differences in favor of establishing common ground, particularly the risk of disregarding or smoothing over the radically divergent constellations of power and exposure to violence in Palestine in the present and over the course of the twentieth century. I have aimed to signpost such rhetorical moments throughout the book, reminding the reader that any program of comparison is, to some extent, exclusionary and hence utilitarian and provisional. Ultimately, foreclosing the possibility for comparison due to the national and colonial structures within which both Hebrew and Arabic literatures operate is to ignore the many transnational and transcultural systems in which they were and are implicated, such as global capital and finance, racial hierarchies, or Orientalist imaginaries.[95] These are as integral to shaping the Middle Eastern present and its literary mediations as the colonial dynamics unfolding in Palestine.

STATIC FORMS OF MOVEMENT: THE STRUCTURE OF THE BOOK

Each of *Static Forms*' chapters centers on a static form for writing the present, offering a figure in which thematic-diegetic, sociopolitical, and metapoetic concerns coalesce. Together, they trace a parallel transition narrative of modern Hebrew and Arabic literatures: it begins with reinventions and revivals of "heritage" and continues in parallel histories of the making of political institutions and labor regimes—projects of nation building and state formation that are simultaneously revolutionary and repressive, productive and violent. The first three chapters identify analogs between Arabic and Hebrew texts in key moments in this history. Chapter 1, "Reverb: Literature's Absent Present," establishes the comparative program that follows, examining how modern Arabic and Hebrew writers negotiated the Orientalist legacies that underly literary periodizations that nominally distinguish traditional from modern texts. The problem facing these writers, I demonstrate through a reading of Leah Goldberg's shelved Hebrew novel *Losses* (composed 1936), is the impossible modernity of the Hebrew or Arabic text—its inability to be "of the present" or contemporary to itself. I then examine two works that elaborate a remarkably similar solution to this problem by theorizing literature as a static, timeless realm of reverberations. S. Y. Agnon (b. 1887 in Polish Galicia), writing in Hebrew, and Mahmud al-Masʿadi (b. 1911 in Tunisia), writing in Arabic, both professed to have no interest in literary innovation and composed mock-classical works that eschew the formal expectations of literary periodization. Reading their literary output as theoretical interventions in debates on modernism and world literature, I demonstrate how al-Masʿadi's novel *Haddatha Abu Hurayra qal* (*Thus Spoke Abu Hurayra*, written 1938, published 1973) and Agnon's novella "'Ido ve-'Enam" ("Edo and Enam," 1950) adopt a central Orientalist trope, the imaginary of timeless, primordial origins, and recast it as a plane of humanist literariness. In this static realm, all that is literary reverberates simultaneously, undermining the purchase of terms such as change or development, which sustain theories of literary periodization. Taking a cue from Gayatri Spivak, I call this construct "strategic anachronism" because, once they establish its contours, both writers proceed to divulge the gendered exclusionary mechanisms that necessarily underly the fantasy of a depoliticized and timeless literary realm. The melodies of primordial birdsongs echoing through the two texts turn out to be the mocking repetition of parrots. *Reverb* is a static temporal form, the simultaneous layering of repeating sounds without a clear origin, that characterizes the idealized realm of humanistic literary creation. And yet it is also a mechanized parasite that, in attaching itself as material excess to any transmission, puts its presumed unmediated authenticity into question.

Chapter 1 questions whether the Arabic or Hebrew text (and by extension, the Arab or Jewish subject) can be truly modern and of its time. Chapter 2, "Scratch: The Present Out of Work," considers whether this subject can properly settle and appropriately inhabit space. The static form organizing this chapter is *scratch*—a futile, random, and directionless movement that remains superficial and produces nothing. Scratching emerges in this chapter as an ethical and aesthetic alternative to national visions of productivity as the basis for a proper way of settling and inhabiting space. It becomes a figure for a mode of writing that steers away from the expectations for a nationally or collectively committed literature and from the demand that literature itself would be put to work. The texts discussed in this chapter, the Egyptian novels *Les Fainéants dans la vallée fertile* (*Laziness in the Fertile Valley*, 1948) by Albert Cossery and *al-Jabal* (*The Mountain*, 1956) by Fathi Ghanem, and two works composed in Palestine by Y. H. Brenner, "'Atsabim'" ("Nerves," 1910) and *Shkhol ve-khishalon* (*Breakdown and Bereavement*, 1920), all negotiate ideologies of productivity in their national context. Though Ghanem is concerned with a state-imposed modernization project of peasant resettlement and Brenner depicts a settler colonial project in its early days, both stage similar ideological and aesthetic challenges to the imperative of national productivity, to which both writers were nominally committed. Focusing on the depiction of embodied affects, desires, and repulsions, I identify two models of settlement at conflict in these texts. The first, which I name a "settlement of depth," appeals to a psychological narrative of rootedness and a productive symbiosis with the land in a national context. The second, which I call a "settlement of surface," is embodied in the gesture of scratching: a futile, nonproductive, compulsive movement that goes nowhere and remains bounded to the present, close to the skin and to the dirt at the earth's surface. Each of these models of settlement aligns with a different set of political identifications, as well as with divergent approaches to the labor of writing. The formal instabilities and contradictions of the texts eventually reflect their inability to reconcile these two conflicting fantasies of habitation and of literary production.

Transitioning from production to reproduction, chapter 3, "Routine: The Present of Reproductive Labor" inquires after the proliferating representation of housework and housewives in popular culture in the Middle East in the mid-1960s. What is the literary form of reproductive labor, specifically the nonaccumulative, noncommodified work of daily domestic maintenance, and why does it become so significant in this particular moment? Housework and the figure of the housewife became central in the Egyptian and the Israeli postindependence moments both as an allegory for the state's reproductive temporality and as an imagined solution to a perceived crisis of foreclosed progress. In a period experienced as static and stagnant, characterized by the lukewarm sense of concluded political battles and the waning of progressive narrativity, the "liberation of the housewife" allowed the story of time's progress to linger a bit longer. This was not unique to the Middle East or the postcolonial world—an entire discipline of "everyday studies" emerged, primarily in France, in the post–World War II period and peaked in the 1960s. In this gendered body of works, housework has a tendency to disappear precisely when it finally makes an appearance, as an empty form of (non)labor that produces nothing. Housework emerges as a mode of action that is indistinguishable from inaction, lending itself to a self-effacing literary form that conceals its own plot.

INTRODUCTION

In chapter 3, I focus on two novellas written in the mid-1960s, *Levaya batsohorayim* (*Funeral at Noon*) by the Israeli Yeshayahu Koren and *Tilk al-raʾiha* (*That Smell*) by the Egyptian Sonallah Ibrahim, both of which adopt housework and its rhythms of minute gestures and daily repetition as subject matter and as form. The self-effacing static form of housework creates the sense that "nothing happens" in these texts (even though much does). Departing from earlier readings that view these novellas' investment in everyday routines as symptoms of lack or ahistoricity, I argue that the reproductive form of housework novels is a means of engaging with the routine of state violence, which is similarly self-effacing. Law-making or productive violence is often a visible and celebrated aspect of a national liberation struggle, but the reproductive, ongoing violence of the state, embodied in spheres such as boundary surveillance, policing, and population management, remains hidden behind the narrative structure of everyday repetition and its attendant feeling that "nothing happens." Housework novels inhabit these structures while making their violent basis apparent. Their dissent, if it is to be found, emerges from the ground zero of housework, not through melodramatic fantasies of escape, but through inhabiting housework's minor affects as the necessary basis for any project that questions the injustices of the present.

Up to this point, *Static Forms* proceeds in a comparative manner, tracing parallel literary solutions in Arabic and Hebrew literatures that emerge in comparable presents of revival modernity, nation building, and state formation. The final chapter, which turns to the present of prolonged and ongoing crisis in Palestine, necessarily departs from this comparative framework. If chapter 3 explored the temporalities of "state time" and its self-effacing violence, chapter 5, "Touch: The Present of Crisis Ordinariness," turns to temporalities of statelessness and the structures of precarity and normalized emergency that it generates. Chapter 4, a short chapter titled "Threshold: The Limit of Correspondence," surveys the reasons for and implications of the departure from the comparative structure and highlights the potential pitfalls of reading Jewish-Israeli and Palestinian literatures together in the mode pursued in the book thus far.

Chapter 3's novels of housework feature characters whose emotional life and thoughts are barred and unreported. The works read in chapter 5 take this a step further, experimenting with characters who are scandalously neutral, having no internal life to report on beyond a chronicle of minute, textured perception. This chapter puts the oeuvre of Palestinian writer

Adania Shibli in conversation with the films of Palestinian director Elia Suleiman within the temporality of normalized violence of "the Ongoing Nakba." Shibli has repeatedly associated the experience of living under the sustained violence in post-Oslo Palestine with "practiced autism," and this chapter surveys the development of a detached yet embodied poetics in her work, concentrated in the figure of touch or haptics. This narrative mode, which provides jarringly intimate access to a character's somatic and sensual functions through attention to texture, rhythm, and form, produces a contiguous textual/textural terrain in which touch and contiguity take precedent over emotional and intersubjective content. It demands a haptic practice of reading from its readers—a careful unfolding of shapes and forms in lieu of interpretation.

Inadvertently, the trajectory of this book took on the structure of Franz Kafka's "Little Fable"—that dreary story of the mouse who finds the walls narrowing around him until he is caught between the trap and the cat. It begins with the wide literary and historical expanses of the mock-classicist texts of S. Y. Agnon and Mahmud al-Masaʿadi, whose timeless present is born of awesome erudition. Each chapter chronicles another closing of horizons, another withdrawal into the individual body. In the final chapter, the only available means of survival is adopting hermetic opacity, a complete externalization of affect. This trajectory is, to some extent, arbitrary and perhaps could have looked different had other materials been chosen—but I am not completely convinced it would. The horizons of the sensed present seem to be shrinking, if we are to trust these texts. The book's conclusion assesses these withdrawals, summarizing the shared characteristics of static form that recurred throughout the four chapters and considering their political affordances: the models and imageries of sociality that they offer in lieu of emphatic gestures of refusal or rejection. Finally, I return to the definition of *stasis* as civil war, the disruption that undoes the proper flow of politics-as-usual. Reading Elias Khoury's novel *Abwab al-madina* (*City Gates*, 1981), written in the midst of the Lebanese Civil War (1975–1990), I identify one last static form at the limits of narrative legibility. Khoury positions *ashlāʾ*, or dismembered flesh, as a prose form that writes the historical experience of the war's undoing. In *City Gates*, he documents affective experience directly in form, attempting to bypass the convention of a sensing subjectivity as well as the temporal logics put in place by a revival modernity that appears to be in ruins.

I identify *ashlāʾ* as the static form that Khoury develops during the present of civil war, but it is also a term that emerged in the present in which this book was concluded and sent to press, a present dominated by the eliminationist bombing of the Gaza Strip by the Israeli army and the intentional destruction of all infrastructure necessary for the survival of its population. In March 2024, Palestinian scholar Nadera Shalhoub-Kevorkian, working with an archive of online videos and testimonies from Gaza, began theorizing *ashlāʾ*, scattered body parts and dismembered flesh, as a colonial technology, as well as the site for unsettling "the totalizing perception of annihilation" by attending to and bearing witness to the scattered body, identifying flesh stripped from all identity markers, and bringing it to burial.[96] This mode of extreme disembodiment and impossible mourning is emerging as the form of our present, a time of carnage whose effects will persist long after the bombing ceases. It is making itself felt far beyond the Gaza Strip through chaotic and fragmented videos on social media platforms, documentary snaps by countless eyewitnesses and survivors, "poor images" circulating widely, wrenched from their immediate context, mutilated and degraded, yet creating in their materiality and plurality "a link to the present" and to reality.[97] The images and videos from Gaza, accessed in the algorithmically curated stream of phone-based media platforms, themselves take the form of *ashlāʾ*, scattered evidence of a once whole body, an attempt to bear witness and to collect. It is a form that requires new reading practices and methods developed in real time, none of them easy or obvious, all of them frustrating for the sense of simultaneous urgent proximity and impotent distance they evoke when watched from the United States. It is necessary that we learn to read these forms, so that we know this present, which is also ours.

Chapter One

REVERB

Literature's Absent Present

The protagonist of *Avedot* (*Losses*, 1936), a posthumously published novel by the Hebrew author and poet Leah Goldberg, is Elhanan Kron, a young Russian Jewish Zionist. It is 1932, and Kron is back in Berlin to complete his dissertation.[1] An Orientalist scholar specializing in Jewish and Islamic mystical traditions, Kron is also an occasional Hebrew poet.[2] In the beginning of the novel, we learn that he has just completed his greatest piece, by his own estimation, a poem written for his estranged wife, Lily. Yet for Kron, as for so many academics, scholarship and love life bleed into each other. Not only is the poem composed in the register of thirteenth-century Hebrew liturgical hymns, but Kron has also copied it, in scrupulously old-fashioned lettering, on an old parchment that he had found in Safed. The poem, "Brihat elohim" ("God's Abandonment"), imagines a final encounter between Judas Iscariot and Mary Magdalene after Christ's death (Lily's first husband, who was also Kron's good friend, was killed before the beginning of their romance). The hapless Kron manages to lose this masterwork shortly after its completion—it falls out of his pocket in a university lecture, as he hurries to catch up with an attractive German girl. Much later, after Kron has seemingly reconciled with the poem's loss, he suddenly encounters it again, published in one of the discipline's leading academic journals. But is this the same poem? Two of his Nazi-sympathizing colleagues at the Department of Oriental Studies had found the poem and published it as an original, recently discovered thirteenth-century Hebrew manuscript and, moreover, as an authentic piece of evidence of medieval Jewry's anti-Christian sentiments. As Allison Schachter concludes, "Kron's modernist Hebrew poems become the Orientalist object par excellence."[3] Helpless before such an appropriation, Kron stands "ashamed before his own poem, as if the poem was a living creature, much older and wiser than himself."[4]

The "losses" evoked in the novel's title are many, not least among them the loss of confidence that Germany, and Europe as a whole, could be a welcoming home to Jews and, by extension, to modern Jewish and Hebrew culture. By the end of the novel, Kron declares himself an "Oriental" and returns to Palestine. Kron's poem is lost and then found, but it is no longer the same poem: it becomes a historical text produced by the "Jewish Orient." The misreading that restores the poem as an Orientalist object of philological study illuminates a foundational problem: the modern Hebrew text, the product of a culture of secular Hebrew revivalism, always risks being read as an emblem of an ossified Jewish past. To be accepted as modern literature, Kron's poem needs to be extracted from both liturgical and Orientalist practices of reading and be read as "literature": a text emerging from a secular and dynamic modern temporality.[5] Kron's personal and iconoclast poem is emblematic of a modernist impulse, yet even he, facing his "much older" poem, appears to be asking: Can this Hebrew text truly be modern? Can it escape its identification as an object of philological study? And where lies the difference between the liturgical text, an object of study that marks the boundary between the German/Christian and the Jew, and the "modern" poem, read as a specimen of a humanist, secular, and national literariness? What distinguishes "the literary" as a modern mode of reading?

This chapter reads works by two writers whose oeuvres stage, explicitly and implicitly, the question captured so vividly in this anecdote from Goldberg's novel. In the first half of the twentieth century, both the Hebrew writer Shmuel Yosef Agnon (1888–1970) and the Arabic writer Mahmud al-Masʿadi (1911–2004) wrote erudite literary works that followed the linguistic and formal styles of premodern exegetical or liturgical texts. Toying with the risk of an anachronistic misreading, which was the fate of Kron's poem, these works remain unmappable according to conventional metrics of literary history and historiography, purposefully upsetting the expectations set up by what Emily Apter calls, after Arjun Appadurai, literary Eurochronologies.[6] The problem of Eurochronology, Apter explains, is that critical traditions founded in the Western academy contain inbuilt temporal categories and typologies deduced from Western literary examples. As a variant of modernization theory, Eurochronology assumes not only that European modernity is a global teleological exemplar but also that each historical stage in the development of the secular nation-state should have an appropriately corresponding form of literary expression (romanticism, realism, modernism, and so on). The works of writers like al-Masʿadi, Agnon, or the fictional Kron, which conjoin formal and thematic elements that appear to be chronologically incongruous, explicitly challenge a presumed literary chronology extending from a classical theological holism to a modernist break and, by extension, the modes of reading that define a text as modern, or "of its time."

In the introduction, I argued that "writing the present" was the crucial imperative and challenge for authors of the novel in Arabic or Hebrew, but I begin in this first chapter with texts that seem to purposely ignore this undertaking: their attempt to stage an alternative practice of literary reading, unburdened by the demand for literature to be either a site of dynamic progress or a record of the present, limns the contours of this prevalent demand. Both al-Masʿadi and Agnon mobilize an aesthetics of untimeliness, evoking what Hoda El Shakry calls an "extratemporal" setting[7]: their plots, characters, and chosen literary genres rarely rest securely in a historically identifiable moment, instead appealing to a timeless domain of tradition or myth. The recurring chronotope of their works is the site of primordial origins, a time before time, a static scene before history. They turn this quintessentially Orientalist chronotope into the stage of literature itself—a shared humanist realm of simultaneity and contemporaneity in which chronological considerations become insignificant. Both writers articulate a theory of literature as a timeless realm of reverberations, repetitions, and retrodden paths in which novelty is no longer a valuable currency.

Despite the different trajectories of their careers, al-Masʿadi and Agnon occupy somewhat similar symbolic positions in the respective Arabic (and particularly Tunisian) and Hebrew literary spheres. Al-Masʿadi's belles lettres are few and date primarily to his early career, but he was a towering public figure, serving in a variety of roles in Tunisia's postindependence government and as Tunisia's representative in UNESCO for ten years. Agnon, meanwhile, was a prolific writer, and unlike other prominent Hebrew Zionist writers of his generation, he abstained from any public political role. Both writers, however, seem to occupy a paradoxical position: celebrated as representative figures of the Arabic or Hebrew modern literary revival, they are also considered exceptional, not fitting with this revival's most characteristic aesthetic modes. Both are renowned writers who, because of their erudite and anachronistic literary registers, are not readily accessible to contemporary readers, and both have generated a cottage industry of specialized scholarship on their respective oeuvres.[8] For both, much of this critical literature is invested in positioning them in a stable position between tradition and modernity, authenticity and assimilation, or piety and secularism. Finally, both have been called out for their "sly irony," which upsets any attempt to cast them as successful embodiments of an ideal narrative of Arabic or Jewish modern national revival.[9] Reading al-Masʿadi and Agnon together allows stepping away from a verdict on the eventually futile question of their modernity in order to address their similar formal, thematic, and eventually ideological solutions to the problem of the Arabic or Hebrew text's impossible literary modernity, its inability to be of its time.

This first chapter, therefore, is somewhat different from the following ones, not solely because the texts reviewed here suggest an alternative trajectory for modern Arabic or Hebrew literatures, one less amenable to the model of a psychological-realist novel of the present. Whereas chapters 2 to 5 are organized around the affective experience of the present and how it produces a particular kind of literary text, this chapter performs some groundwork. First, it explores the conditions defining modern literature in a revival modernity through two of its untypical yet celebrated writers, whose mock-classical texts scandalously (and precariously, as the fictional fate of Kron's poem demonstrates) push against the demands for a literature of the present. Second, it solidifies the basis for this book's parallel approach to Arabic and Hebrew literatures, demonstrating how the aftereffects of Orientalist philology led to the emergence of strikingly similar literary strategies and theories in both languages, foremost among which is a definition of literature as a static and timeless space of contemporaneity, an atemporal humanist realm beyond history. The condition of the Oriental, unchanging and ahistorical, becomes the condition of literature itself.

The novels discussed here are about modernity's missing affective experience: the experience of transcending time itself. Can literary reading be this transcendental sphere?

The static trope that structures these texts is *reverb*. Reverberation, as aural phenomenon, is created when soundwaves reflect back and forth between close surfaces, traveling over very small distances. The reflecting sounds "pile on" one another so that reverberation is heard as a single continuous static sound, often classified as unwanted or parasitic noise. The two works anchoring this chapter, al-Masʿadi's novel *Haddatha Abu Hurayra qal* (*Thus Spoke Abu Hurayra*, written 1938, published 1973) and Agnon's novella "'Ido ve-'Enam" ("Edo and Enam," 1950), culminate with the same figure of the absolute song: a voice that reaches from the primordial timeless past and echoes through all of literary and poetic texts.[10] Formally, these two works operate as echo chambers, reverberating countless other texts, narratives, and tropes, offering their own theory of the literary as a noisy space of aural reverb.

THE PRESENT OF PHILOLOGY

> Indeed, it is only today (in the present of philology) that we can conceive of the loss of the gods. And since in foreign lands, as Hölderlin would say, we have almost lost our tongue—lost the language of the gods—we need philologists, obviously, in order to restore it to us. The philologists will give language back to us. No doubt about it: the mythological gods are philological gods. But to restore a language philologically is, for us, who have arrived late, to establish and confirm the loss of it. The native element of philology is plainly mourning.
>
> —MARC NICHANIAN, *MOURNING PHILOLOGY*

Over the past two decades, scholars of modernism have sought to elaborate alternative models to the developmental periodization of Eurochronology to accommodate a global landscape of literary production within its scopes. Susan Stanford-Friedman, for example, suggests that while modernism is simply the expressive dimension of modernity, modernity itself should be considered "polycentric, planetary, [occurring] in various geohistorical locations."[11] Periods of rapid change, such as the Tang dynasty in China, the Abbasid dynasty of the Muslim empire, or the Mongol empire, could be considered loci of modernity, producing their own modernisms. Syrian poet Adonis outlined a similar theory four decades earlier, in the four-volume study *al-Thabit wa-al-mutahawwil* (*The Mutable and the Immutable*, published between 1973 and 1978). Adonis argues that the Arabic textual heritage should be read as a site of continuous struggle between static and dynamic textual currents or between conservative forces and modernist ones dedicated to radical innovation in both form and content. His idiosyncratic definition of modernism is a direct reaction to the politics of periodization that placed European literary forms as the future of Arab writing: Adonis positions himself as the successor in a lineage of Arab poetic innovators peaking in the ninth and tenth centuries, rather than as the product of a newly established "modernity."[12] In an alternative approach, Eric Hayot suggests divorcing changes in literary form and style from a technological-progressive chronology and maps realism, romanticism, and modernism as "modes of relating" to the modern concept of the world—a definition that does not assume a narrative of development.[13]

These models' innovation and significance notwithstanding, they still skirt a crucial aspect of Kron's problem and of the Hebrew text's questionable literary modernity because they tend to leave unquestioned the very nature of "literature" as an all-engulfing category that can incorporate diverse textual artifacts. As Michael Allan argues, the modern category of "literature" denotes a set of practices and conventions of reading rather than a collection of texts that share some inherent characteristic or form.[14] The difference between a liturgical text on Jewish-Christian polemics and a modernist poem comes down to *how* the text is read, a practice that reflects back on what the text *is*. "Literature" as a worldly mode of secular, humanist reading emerged globally in the nexus of colonialism and Orientalist philology, as languages and texts from around the world were introduced into a model of literature conceived as a universal vehicle for national expression.[15] "Orientalism is, among other things, the philological institution of historical categories," Jeffrey Sacks comments on this history. "Philology in the colonies . . . is the institutionalization of the terms for the formation of national-historical, which is also to say Orientalist, literary institutions."[16] The modern Arabic or Hebrew writer is bound to what Marc Nichanian describes as being "in the present of philology": their writing must pass through philology and its shaping of literature as a shared humanist medium that expresses the national-ethnic ethos.[17]

From within the present of philology, al-Masʿadi and Agnon play with the conventions disciplining the historical legibility of the Arabic or Hebrew literary text by staging a return to a timeless realm—a primordial site of origins and of cultural authenticity. This realm is the essential site of Orientalist fantasy: the Muslim or Jewish Orient as static, unchanging, and composed in the tense of the "timeless eternal," in Edward Said's shorthand.[18] Al-Masʿadi and Agnon appropriate typology, one of the central tools of Orientalist philology, to stage a literary theory. In its theological context, typology provides a method of reading the Bible as a prefiguration of the New Testament, a central tenet of Christian approaches to history and textuality.[19] Typological readings consider the stories of the Bible as a pre-enactment, prefiguring the arrival and the sacrifice of Christ. Nineteenth-century philologists adapted the method of typological reading in order to write the relation of East and West: the discovery of Indo-European languages and the shared linguistic roots of the people of Europe and Asia inspired a large-scale typological narrative of the static Orient as the bedrock of civilization that remained suspended and frozen as civilization continued to develop and progress in the dynamic Occident.[20] Al-Masʿadi and Agnon stage a theory of literature that takes up this typological model, translating it from the historical to the literary realm. Literature emerges in their novels as an ahistorical timeless realm of reverberating figures and types, where nothing is truly new or original, every detail echoes a cohort of precedents, and all tropes resound simultaneously. If revival modernity's narrative of "returning to history" inevitably harnesses texts to a progressive national ethos, this alternate model adapts the same Orientalist discourse that deemed the Jew or the Arab ahistorical to begin with and formulates an alternative definition of literature that does not rely on the notion of progressive temporality.

A MOMENT OF DAWN: THE TIME BEFORE TIME STARTED

ṭalabtu al-mustaqarra bi-kulli arḍin / fa-lam arā li bi-arḍi mustaqarran

I sought the permanent in every land, but found residence nowhere

This epigraph to Mahmud al-Masʿadi's novel *Haddatha Abu Hurayra qal*, a verse from ninth-century poet Abu al-ʿAtahiyya (d. 847), captures a tension between a desire for permanence and inevitable change, between the static and the moving, through its repeated use of the word *mustaqarr*.[21]

In the second part of the verse, in its indefinite form, *mustaqarr* implies a concrete notion of settlement, dwelling, or residence. However, the definite form *al-mustaqarr* can be rendered more abstractly, as durability, stability, fixity, or permanence. The poem's speaker seeks more than a place to settle: he searches for intransience and an existence unchecked by time. Both searches are fruitless because the first conditions the second. The word's repetition betrays the notion that spatial restlessness on this earth (*arḍ*) is emblematic of a search for something that exceeds its transience, a search for an alternate temporality.[22]

As al-Masʿadi remarked in an interview with Mohamed-Salah Omri, quoted in the latter's monumental study of al-Masʿadi, *Nationalism, Islam and World Literature*, the mindset described in this line is emblematic of Abu Hurayra, the novel's restless protagonist.[23] It crystalizes the primary plotlines of the text: Abu Hurayra is a wanderer and questioner, part prophet and part fool, always on the move. As one of his companions testifies, "Abu Hurayra was like running water. Never during all his life did I see him but on the move. He was always as if about to leave, always with leaving on his mind" (*Haddatha*, 197). The novel, composed of a series of anecdotes told by or about Abu Hurayra, is set in the deserts extending between Mecca and Medina in a period that is vaguely evocative of the early days of Islam. In its opening chapter, Abu Hurayra, a pious and law-abiding man, joins a friend to view a marvelous primordial scene in the desert: a young couple, a man and a woman, singing in joy and ecstasy, dancing naked before the rising sun. The following day, Abu Hurayra discovers that his friend was inspired by this sight and disappeared with one of his young slave girls (58). Abu Hurayra names this moment "the first awakening" (*al-baʿth al-awal*): awakened to life's pleasures and freedoms, he embarks on a lifelong journey of discovery. Quite conveniently, just then his house burns down in a thunderstorm and his wife is struck by lightning, and so nothing binds him to his old life. In a series of loosely linked episodes, reminiscent of the classic Arabic picaresque genre of the *maqāmāt*, the reader follows Abu Hurayra's radical conversions: lecherous drunkard, romantic lover, self-flagellating ascetic, leader of a utopian commune, solitary philosopher, violent outlaw. Abu Hurayra abandons each persona as suddenly and inexplicably as he adopts it.

Nevertheless, this restlessness is motivated by a search for stasis, for a timeless, continuous present, in which the wonder of the moment of origin is not depleted. In an early episode, Abu Hurayra's lover Rayhana explains that he deserted her because "he was always longing for the sun and always afraid of its arrival. He used to say, 'if you can, make your entire life a dawn' [*ajʿal kāmil ḥayātuka fajr*]" (*Haddatha*, 105). Abu Hurayra is always searching for that initial moment of dawn of the first awakening, in which everything seems new. The temporality he longs for is a static moment of beginning whose promise is suspended rather than depleted: a day out of time, in his words (108).[24] His search leads him through a wide spectrum of experiences, but it follows a regular pattern: once the novelty of the experience wears away, he is compelled to move on and again embark on a search for a state of being that cannot be depleted by time.

The epigraph from Abu al-ʿAtahiyya could also describe al-Masʿadi himself, who notes in the introduction to *Haddatha* that the novel had emerged from a moment of disorientation and longing for his native home. Like the majority of al-Masʿadi's literary works, *Haddatha* was composed during a creative burst between 1938 and 1941, when al-Masʿadi was concluding his second period of academic studies in Paris and returning to his native Tunisia, awash with new ideas and theories. Although some excerpts of *Haddatha* appeared in journals throughout the early 1940s, the text in its entirety was published only in 1973, when al-Masʿadi's public persona in Tunisia was already established. In his youth, al-Masʿadi was trained in both Islamic and French institutions, including the prestigious Zaytuna Islamic University. He completed a doctoral degree in Arabic studies at the Sorbonne, where his mentors and teachers included preeminent Orientalist scholars such as the expert on Islamic mysticism Louis Massignon and the Arabist Régis Blanchère. Following Tunisian independence in 1956, he became the de facto architect of Tunisia's educational policy (1958–1968) and then served as the minister of cultural affairs (1973–1976) and speaker of Parliament (1981–1986).[25] Already well known as an anticolonialist trade unionist, educator, cultural editor, and government official, al-Masʿadi was through his literary publications enshrined as Tunisia's most renowned public intellectual.

In 1975, in his capacity as Tunisia's minister of cultural affairs, al-Masʿadi gave a lecture on the contemporary state of Arabic literature, in which he summarized a widely shared view on its predicaments and needs. Al-Masʿadi's starting point, an assertion seemingly shared by the speaker and the audience, is that Arabic literature is not doing well: it has not yet reached "the level of other World Literatures" and has not made its mark in the contemporary literary sphere. Al-Masʿadi attributes this shortcoming to Arabic literature's approach to temporality, or its misguided understanding of the relationship between the human and time, and its failure to integrate a historicist, dynamic view of man and the world: "For a long time," he states, "we continued to understand or imagine man as something given rather than evolving, static rather than developing, fixed rather than changing and transformed. But our modern literature has began to grasp the truth now, and to give us characters in which being acknowledges and integrates this temporal dimension, expressing itself in a sense of existential becoming."[26] Life is bound to time, and time is change and movement, al-Masʿadi contends. Arabic literature's historical "mistake," in this account, was its allegiance to a vision of man relative to the divine: unchanging, fixed, and timeless. The temporal orders of the worldly and the divine, al-Masʿadi claims, must now be separated: modern literature should consciously take into its scope of concerns the changing rather than the immutable. Arab writers have just started to acknowledge that man is not a static given or an unchanging ideal but is rather an ongoing and continuous process of becoming and evolution (*kaynūna wa-ṣayrūra*).

Al-Masʿadi creates a strict division between the modern and the medieval worldviews: the fluid and shifting definition of man in time is a distinctly modern one, he says, while the temporal structures and literary forms in which Arabic literature is still largely caught up have been inherited from the "Middle Ages."[27] With this act of periodization, al-Masʿadi differentiates himself from the medieval writer, who lacks both historical consciousness and a notion of time and change, and positions the recognition of dynamic time as the emblem of a modern literary and historical consciousness. Centuries of Arabic writing about history, historiography, and time are disregarded in this—admittedly common—periodization, which depicts Arabic culture, before its modern-day encounter with European culture and governance, as bereft of a sense of historicity.[28]

The indictment of the premodern as a period lacking a concept of time and history is a basic trope of European modern thought. As Kathleen Davis argues, such indictments persist, despite no lack of evidence to the contrary, as they usefully maintain the division between our supposedly modern, secular, and progressive age and the so-called medieval, religious, and oppressive past to justify claims to political sovereignty and colonial expansion.²⁹ After having differentiated itself from its own feudal, religious past, Europe cast the colonized world in that supposed Middle Ages constructed image—static and lacking in historical consciousness and a sense of time—and by necessary extension, positioned modern Europe as the colonized world's inevitable future.

The story of how the colonized Oriental intellectual often accepted this narrative of timeless existence to forcefully argue for his way out of the "the waiting room of history" and into historical modernity is by now familiar.³⁰ Both Arabic and Hebrew revival movements often shared the implicit assumption that modernization entailed *joining* history and recognizing its dynamic progress after a long period of slumber or denial. Al-Masʿadi was not immune to this mode of ideological periodization, despite his rich familiarity with the premodern Arabic archive. This archive, and particularly the poetic archive configured as the depository of pure and eloquent Arabic, is associated with a specific geomythical location: the Arabian Peninsula, also known as the Hijaz, conceived as an empty, ahistorical, and timeless landscape of blowing sands and nomadic vagabonds. This image of the pre-Islamic Arabian Peninsula remained impervious to modern drives of historicization well into the twenty-first century, as James E. Montgomery has demonstrated. Leading historical accounts of the Hijaz lose their historicizing drive when addressing the pre-Islamic period, depicting a "sense of timelessness, of nomadism as representative of population patterns in the peninsula, of the perduration of this precarious nomadic existence as somehow beyond time and impervious to change, like a Platonic idea or a philosophical universal."³¹ The reasons for such "perduration" are complex, but they emerge from the ideological functions that the trope of the timeless Hijaz performs in various distinct but correlated discourses. In the Islamic tradition, the myth of a timeless and static origin highlights the miraculous appearance of the Qurʾan in a culturally arid landscape, as well as the marvelously quick conquests of Islam, instilling civilization in the empty expanses of the desert. Islam, as Aziz al-Azmeh notes, appears in this narrative as "formed instantaneously at the moment of its miraculous inception."³² Arab secular nationalism, on the other hand, which established itself on the basis of a shared ancient tongue, could turn to this site of origins as a stable archive of authenticity to be mobilized in the present against an "inauthentic" and imposed colonial epistemology.³³ Finally, the notion of an Orient devoid of history and time, always persisting in sameness, was inherent to much Orientalist and philological scholarship: the West managed to progress from the Eastern "cradle of civilization," it seemed to maintain, but the Eastern Semite, "immobile in time as well as space," was still bound to this inherently static domain.[34]

THE AHISTORICAL NOVEL: A TEXTUAL LANDSCAPE

The timeless site of origins, Arabia in the early days of Islam, appears to be the setting for Abu Hurayra's wonderings, yet this environment is anything but historical. Despite the signposts that identify *Haddatha*'s setting with seventh-century Medina, the novel does not align with any of the conventions of a historical novel. To the contrary, it is an "un-historicizing" text, whose formal and thematic gestures aim to distort historicist temporalities and acts of periodization. Even referring to it as a novel is a matter of convenience. Rather than evoking a recognizable past period and fashioning it in the linear narrative form characteristic of the historical novel genre, *Haddatha*'s episodic structure mimics historical writing forms such as the *maqāma*. More specifically, it borrows from one of the most canonized literary forms of Islamic orthodoxy, the collection of *aḥādīth* (singular: *ḥadīth*): accounts of the deeds and utterances of the prophet and his companions transmitted through an oral chain of witnesses that offers guarantee of their authenticity.[35] Each of the episodes of *Haddatha*, some as brief as a single paragraph and some extending over a dozen pages, is narrated by a witness to Abu Hurayra's adventures, except for a few that are told by Abu Hurayra himself. The phrase "ḥaddatha Abū Hurayra qāl," literally translating as "Abu Hurayra related, saying," is a traditional *ḥadīth* introductory form (*isnād*), preceding the content or the story (*matn*) itself.[36] The *isnād*, or the chain of transmission, verifies the *ḥadīth*'s veracity, ensuring its authenticity and authority. Moreover, the linguistic register throughout the text follows classical Arabic syntactic structures and employs a vocabulary evocative of canonic theological, philosophical, and juridical writing, staging an ongoing conversation with the Quranic text and its exegetical traditions. Sufi terms and images serve as an important intertext, as several scholars have commented.[37] The structure of the book as a whole loosely follows the Sufi model of the journey of an individual who must pass through several stations on the way to perfection and annihilation in the divine.

To further complicate things, Abu Hurayra's historical namesake was one of the prophet Muhammad's illustrious companions and himself a prolific transmitter of *aḥādīth*. In fact, the excessive number of *aḥādīth* attributed to Abu Hurayra—the thirteenth-century scholar al-Mizzi counted more than 3,300 in the canonical collections—made him a suspicious source of dependable reports already in the eighth century, and debates on his reliability continue to emerge well into the twentieth century. Nevertheless, the historical Abu Hurayra is a figure that grounds stories about the prophet in historical temporality as events that took place in front of actual reliable witnesses. Although this makes the combination "ḥaddatha Abū Hurayra qāl" ring familiar to any reader acquainted with the Islamic canon, the two figures share little but a name. The licentious escapades of al-Masʿadi's Abu Hurayra and his dismissal of any form of religious authority except for his own spiritual search are hardly characteristic of the prophet's pious companion, as some enraged readers who "misread" the novel as a blasphemous and falsifying manuscript exclaimed.[38] The novel makes no attempt to identify between the two figures and simply "borrows" the historical figure's name for its periodizing effect.

But what is this effect? The narrative is set in the environs of Mecca and Medina in a period that is vaguely evocative of the early days of Islam, but although the geographical location of the narrative is clearly marked, its temporal dimension is much more difficult to pinpoint. *Haddatha* freely draws from an Arabic literary canon extending over hundreds of years, explicitly citing from or implicitly alluding to pre-Islamic poetry, the Qur'an and its exegetical traditions, works of philosophy and poetry from the Abbasid era, and Sufi accounts and traditions, without any periodizing distinction. It is not merely that the narrative is "virtually saturated" with references to *turāth* (the Arabic heritage, or textual canon), as Mohamed-Salah Omri claims,[39] but rather that the narrative is set within a *textual landscape*, composed entirely of carefully chosen elements from the *turāth* archive.

The confusions of an undifferentiated temporal realm are made explicit in the narration, which occasionally addresses its anachronistic citations in jokes for the learned reader. When asked, in "Hadith al-ʿama" ("The Story of Blindness"), about his journey to the East, Abu Hurayra enigmatically replies, "Were you to live in the future, you would read and enjoy Ibn Battuta's accounts of the East as though they were fairy tales" (*Haddatha*, 106). The famed traveler Ibn Battuta wrote his travel journals some seven hundred years after the supposed period in which *Haddatha* takes place. The name is evoked as a wink to the reader, highlighting the chronological infidelities of the text, as if somehow in his own travels Abu Hurayra managed to get access not only to new geographic information but also to future knowledge.

In a different episode, Abu Ghural, Abu Hurayra's occasional mentor, assumes a prophetic tone when he mentions Sibawayh (linguist and grammarian, d. 796) as "a man that will invent and create grammar" (*Haddatha*, 209). Beyond a mere chronological incongruence, Sibawayh's work is central to the canonization of Arabic's timeless origins. As the author of the first study of Arabic grammar, Sibawayh relied on three kinds of sources of language in its pure and uncorrupted form to extract Arabic's grammatical laws: the Qur'an, the Arabic poetic archive, and nomadic Arab informants. However, Sibawayh's informants were always suspected of corruption, either for ulterior motives or for simple mistakes. In contrast, he considered the language of poetry to be "fixed," stable and static, and thus could provide a depository for unearthing grammatical rules. As Georgine Ayoub points out, the most exemplary and extraordinary language of poetry and the Qur'an was at the same time considered the most "common," illustrating language's most general rules of use.[40] The rules of the pure language were set with its emergence. Eloquent and true expression (*faṣāḥa*) was therefore grounded, fixed and unchanged, in this miraculous feat of language emerging from the ahistorical desert.

MEETING IN THE FIELDS OF LITERATURE

The semimythical textual landscape serves as *Haddatha*'s setting, but it is also frequently interrupted by mismatching references and citations, which disrupt any appeal to a fantasy of authenticity or temporal hermeticism. The epigraphs introducing various chapters of the book include citations from Friedrich Nietzsche, Henrik Ibsen, and Friedrich Hölderlin. The body of the text is rife with implicit references to Goethe's Faust, Shakespeare's Hamlet, and Albert Camus's Prometheus, confusing any attempt to posit it firmly in one cultural legacy or tradition. These citations have a chaotic effect, upsetting the text's seeming allegiance to a notion of religious or national authenticity. Rather than remaining confined to the primeval, timeless realm of the desert and of the past, *Haddatha* extends this past all the way up to the present, weaving classic and modern works of European literature into its textual landscape.

Al-Masʿadi learned the skill of weaving old and new texts into one literary tapestry from his teacher and mentor at the Sorbonne, the renowned Orientalist and Islamic scholar Louis Massignon (1883–1962). An expert on Islamic mysticism, largely responsible for the introduction of Sufism as a field of study in France, Massignon presented an idiosyncratic model of Oriental scholarship, astoundingly erudite and yet frustratingly subjective and personal.[41] As Edward Said notes in *Orientalism*, Massignon had the admirable ability to refer "easily (and accurately) in an essay to a host of Islamic mystics and to Jung, Heisenberg, Mallarme, and Kierkegaard."[42] Massignon was particularly invested in exploring the confluences of gnostic and mystic traditions in Islam and Christianity (and to a lesser extent in Judaism). Such comparative work concentrated, in the post–World War II years, at Carl Jung's famous Eranos circle in Switzerland, where Massignon conferred with like-minded scholars such as Gershom Scholem, Mircea Eliade, and Henry Corbin—scholars and historians of religion who posited a symbolic and largely shared repertoire of mystical experiences at the center of the monotheistic religions.[43] The technique of weaving together a variety of sources and influences was therefore not just a style but an expression of a deeply spiritual, theological, and intellectual approach to history and philosophy. Massignon's interest in cross-denominational relations and influences left a distinct footprint on his scholarship of Islam and Sufism, as well as on al-Masʿadi's construction of the literary space of *Haddatha*.

Al-Masʿadi explicitly acknowledged this influence. "It may sound strange," he wrote, "when I say that I learned the deepening of my faith and religion from Massignon, because he revealed to me the horizons of al-Hallaj's experience and the greatest meaning, which is Sufism. Sufism is the summary of the human adventure."[44] Massignon introduced al-Masʿadi to al-Hallaj as a tragic existentialist figure with universal humanist significance. The ninth-century Islamic mystic Mansur al-Hallaj (858–922), who was famously executed for heresy, was the object of Massignon's lifelong scholarly obsession, the subject of his doctoral dissertation and first monumental monograph. But his fascination with the Sufi mystic far exceeded an intellectual passion. Massignon was a deeply devoted Catholic who for many years contemplated joining the missionary order. His religious and spiritual awakening occurred after a turbulent emotional and physical crisis, during which the spirit of al-Hallaj was revealed to him and called him to life.[45] The central tenant of his religious vision was the notion of witnessing as a practice and an act of faith: he viewed the history of the monotheistic religions as a "spiritual chain of pure witnesses" to the divine, starting with Abraham and passing through Isaac and Ismael, Jesus, Muhammad, and al-Hallaj, all the way to contemporary figures such as Catholic writers J. K. Huysmans and Charles de Foucauld. This theological approach shaped his view of history as a typological realm of repeating forms.

Nowhere is this clearer than in Massignon's depiction of the heretic mystic from Baghdad. For Massignon, the defining (and damning) characteristic of Orthodox Islam was its insistence on the absolute division between the earthly and the divine and its consequent rejection of the divinity of Christ. In the Sufi ideal of mystical union, however, Massignon found the counterpart of the Christian model of the embodied spirit.[46] Al-Hallaj, who "like Joan of Arc, died by the Law and for the Law which condemned him," set a personal and theological example for Massignon in his final act of martyrdom, which Massignon positioned as a cross-denominational ideal. In a classic example of typological reading and to the aggravation of some of his Muslim colleagues, Massignon rewrote al-Hallaj as a Christ-like figure whose martyrdom finally overcomes Islam's tragic rejection of the Incarnation.[47]

Al-Hallaj makes a coded appearance at the conclusion of *Haddatha*, and although he is not quite the Christ-like al-Hallaj created by Massignon, he is also not the teacher recorded in the Sufi tradition. Al-Hallaj had to be translated into French in order to return to al-Masʿadi's Arabic as a universal hero, seeking to overcome worldly limitations in death. The final episode of *Haddatha* is titled "al-Baʿth al-akhir" ("The Last Awakening"), concluding a trajectory that opened with "The First Awakening" of the first episode. In this final account, Abu Hurayra asks his friend Abu al-Madaʾin to join him for a ride in the desert at sunset. After about two hours of riding and conversation, they hear a marvelous voice singing:

> I am Truth, calling you
> I am Love, courting you
> I am longing, overflowing you

(*HADDATHA*, 229–30)

The song is an evocation of al-Hallaj's martyrdom: reportedly, he stood to trial for the heresy of stating "I am Truth!" (*anā al-ḥaqq*), making a blasphemous claim to the divine (al-Ḥaqq is one of the names of Allah). In the novel, the unidentified voice calls Abu Hurayra to submit to the "shores of eternity." Abu Hurayra responds with his own song of acceptance, "Truth, here I am!" and adds, "This is what I have been waiting for" (231). He then surges forward on his horse and disappears into the darkness. Abu al-Mada'in, the narrator of this incident, later recalls, "After a few moments, I heard rocks falling, a horse shrieking in pain, and a joyful cry that made me shiver" (234). When morning arrives, he discovers that he is on the top of a crag; below him, there are some bloodied rocks and a bottomless pit.

What are we to make of this ending and of its resonance of al-Hallaj's call? Before embarking on this last trip, Abu Hurayra invites Abu al-Mada'in to experience "a day out of time [*dahr*]," showing him an obscure sketch of "vertical lines, circles and black dots of various sizes, and in the middle of the page a striking blank," which he described as "time [*al-zamān*] decapitated" (222). Considering these temporal riddles, Mohamed-Salah Omri argues that "The Last Awakening" should not be read as a desperate suicide, but rather as a conclusion to Abu Hurayra's experience of a complete Sufi journey. Abu Hurayra reaches the "timelessness of the last station, being at one with the Absolute Being where eternity [*khulūd*] is attained. . . . The seeker reaches the highest stage of knowledge when Truth is revealed to him."[48] Omri claims that Abu Hurayra has succeeded in his spiritual quest for self-erasure, reaching a timeless way of being.

The notion of divinity as a timeless, absolute, and immobile realm entered Islamic philosophy in the ninth and tenth centuries, under the influence of Hellenistic philosophy, gradually replacing the concept of God's act as a form of continuous creative movement and renewal. Within this new ontology, Sufi writers described the mystical experience as an escape from the binds of time, passing through various stages of timelessness.[49] By viewing the novel as a completed Sufi journey, Omri's reading successfully argues for the coherent structure of a novel that too often has been called fragmentary or formless. Nevertheless, al-Mas'adi uses Sufism as a structure and an intertext, not as a system of meaning. Abu Hurayra's journey is not conceived within a theological mystical framework aiming for union with the divine, and even the nature of "truth" in this episode, the authenticity of the voice claiming it, is obliquely put into question, as I discuss at the end of the chapter. Rather than a theological space of unity, the timeless realm that Abu Hurayra leaps into so joyfully aligns with al-Masʿadi's definition of literature itself.

In 1957, the preeminent Egyptian writer Taha Hussein commented that al-Masʿadi's play *al-Sudd* (*The Dam*) is an obvious rewriting of Camus's narrative of Sisyphus, an existential search garbed in Islamic terms.[50] Al-Masʿadi denied the direct influence, claiming that *al-Sudd* was composed before Camus's *The Myth of Sisyphus*. Nevertheless, he admits that he and Camus were likely influenced by similar ideas and discussions, namely the emergence of existentialism in France in the 1930s. More interestingly, Hussein's comments inspire al-Masʿadi to articulate a theory of literature that he returned to often in later publications and engagements. Literature, al-Masʿadi claims, is a shared, humanist realm, and naturally those writing it return to the same themes and tropes: "It is clear that ancient and modern writers . . . have met in the same fields, shared the same concerns, and were brought together by the same tendency in feeling and thought. They strive to examine the reality of the human position, seek to understand human destiny and relate, describe, or contemplate the existential adventure."[51] Al-Masʿadi articulates a theory of literature as a realm of equivalence and timelessness, a space where ancient and modern, oriental and occidental, exist simultaneously. Abu Hurayra can be a Sufi mystic, a romantic hero sacrificing himself for beauty, or an existential seeker of meaning: the adventure is one, whatever textual form it assumes, "ancient" or "modern."

Identifying the specific relationship among temporality, literature, and literary form that is outlined in this model is made easier by comparing it to a more familiar theory of literary dynamism, as articulated by a contemporary Arabic writer, the Palestinian writer Jabra Ibrahim Jabra (1920–1994). An Oxford-educated and Baghdadi-based intellectual, Jabra was one of the most influential agents contributing to the spread of Euro-modernist poetic forms in the Arab world, not only in his creative writing but also in his capacity as an educator, a critic, and particularly a translator (of Faulkner, Wilde, and Beckett, as well as numerous works of literary criticism).[52] Like al-Masʿadi, he championed a vision bridging European and Arabic aesthetics that was widely influential. Members of the same generation, both authors criticized the formal and political rigidity of demands for committed literature (*iltizām*), which grew increasingly dominant in the 1950s (as discussed in the next chapter), and favored an approach to literature that was both more humanist and elitist.

In a 1968 lecture on the influence of Western literature on Arabic literary production, Jabra maintained that moments of political and historical upheaval necessarily translate to new aesthetics. "The change [in lifestyle] meant a change in form as well as content," he writes; "indeed content seemed intractable without doing violence to form."[53] In Jabra's account, historical political violence is transposed from bodies to text: form becomes the object of the violence of the modern encounter, and it is in literary form that this violence can later be read. Jabra's account of the development of modern Arabic literature outlines a model that has by now become familiar as Franco Moretti's "law of literary evolution": world literature as a planetary system, in which the modern novel rises as a "compromise between a western formal influence . . . and local materials."[54] Jabra contends that the encounter with Euromodernist formal devices (like stream of consciousness or flashback) allowed Arab writers to create literary works exceeding national significance as part of a global intellectual culture.[55] These devices were not merely neutral and readily applicable aesthetic tools, but helped Arab writers "come to closer grips with the problems that demanded expression," such as "man's alienation, his exile, his hope, [and] whether tragic confrontation is the determining factor in human existence."[56] Although Western forms uncovered (or perhaps dictated) new problems and concerns that "demanded" urgent expression, these problems were not merely Western or even modern, but problems of human existence. When adopting Euromodernist forms, Jabra concludes, Arab writers could produce texts that were "fundamentally Arab, but part of the human condition everywhere."

Jabra and al-Masʿadi share a notion of the literary as a realm of common human concern and expression: both writers would agree that literature is the "stage for the reconciliation," in Aamir Mufti's words, of all that is particularly "Muslim" or "Arab" with human and universal values.[57] However, their different literary techniques attest to their divergent ideas regarding literature's temporal dimension. Jabra conceives of world literature, or as he calls it, the "human civilization of today," as having a clear temporal dimension—despite its universal and existential appeal, it is time-marked, corresponding to its "historical" moment. In choosing Euromodernist forms as the focus of his talk, Jabra echoes one of modernism's principles of periodization, namely form's temporal value as emblem of the new. Modern problems demand modern forms.

Al-Masʿadi, on the other hand, contends that Arabic writing was always already engaged in a tragic exploration of human existence ("all literature is tragedy" is one of his most quoted phrases). Literature is always "of its time" precisely because it claims to be atemporal, not participating in the narrative of formal progress. For this reason, al-Masʿadi announces in *Haddatha*'s introduction that he has no interest in the new or original. He has no investment in passing phenomena (*al-ʿaraḍ al-ʿāriḍ*) but is rather concerned with the timeless essence that is literature's domain (*Haddatha*, 14). Literature emerges from this humanist definition as strangely nonhuman, sharing much more with the divine. Its realm might be secularized and humanized, yet it nevertheless exists in a timeless realm of simultaneity.

This contemporaneous plane of literature is the very setting of *Haddatha*, a literary, textual plane in which periodization and chronologies do not matter. *Haddatha*'s timeless deserts, in which Nietzsche and al-Maʿari, Ibn al-ʿArabi and Ibsen, can come together seamlessly, are the "fields" of literature on which the existential adventure plays out. This timeless present of literature's domain appears to radically contradict the literary program introduced at the beginning of the chapter, in which al-Masʿadi asserts his commitment to the human as shifting, changing, and always in flux. But a concession had to be made. For the modern Arabic text to be read as part of a global literary present rather than as an emblem of the past, al-Masʿadi has to argue that literature is, after all, static—it knows no time because its concerns are always timely. Abu Hurayra's jump into the abyss, his effort to step out of time and find a moment unblemished by the marks of history's flow, becomes equivalent to the work of the writer who enters the timeless fields of literature. *Haddatha* mimics this effort by staging the timeless space of a prehistoric Arabia. To wander its deserts is to read literarily: it is to visit an immutable site of origins through a mode of reading in which time does not exist or, rather, all of time exists at once.

MODES OF READING IN "'IDO VE-ʿENAM"

> In your writing we meet once again the ancient unity between literature and science, as antiquity knew it. . . . We honor in you a combination of tradition and prophecy, of saga and wisdom.
>
> —INGVAR ANDERSSON OF THE SWEDISH ACADEMY
> AT AGNON'S NOBEL PRIZE FOR LITERATURE RECEPTION

If literature is a particular practice of reading, then the Arabic or Hebrew text is always read doubly and suspiciously: as testimony to an ancient truth and as a literary artefact.[58] This tension is an implicit and structuring concern of Hebrew writer S. Y. Agnon's works and was made explicit at the Nobel Prize ceremony in 1966. When the host compared Agnon's writing to ancient texts in which one can find a holistic balance between literature and science, imagination and knowledge, he evoked the duality to which such texts are subject: on the one hand, celebrated for their scientific value as historical and philological sources, keys to comprehend the "wisdom" of an archaic culture; on the other, recognized for their genius as "literary" works. Agnon's Hebrew writing must signify dually.

Agnon's acceptance speech acknowledges this mode of reading with characteristic understated irony. Addressing the question of influences, he lists the canon of Jewish texts that shaped his work but refrains from mentioning any German authors who had influenced him. "Why, then, did I list the Jewish books?" he asks. "Because it is they that gave me my foundations. And my heart tells me that they are responsible for my being honored with the Nobel Prize."[59] Unlike other Nobel laureates, Agnon recognizes that he must share his prize with an archive and a birthright of foundational Jewish texts.

Throughout his literary career, Agnon undermined the influence of a non-Hebrew modern literary canon on his writing and was content to present himself as a traditionalist Jewish author.[60] Critics have long argued the effect of this feigned naïveté, and much of the early criticism dedicated to Agnon was concerned with his supposed adherence to, or departure from, a cohesive Jewish textual tradition.[61] Agnon himself was positioned between two modes of production, the writer and the archivist. Beyond his work as a celebrated author, he was also an anthologist of Jewish stories and commentaries and the secretary of Mekitsey Nirdamin (Awakening the Sleepers), a society dedicated to the preservation and publication of Hebrew manuscripts.[62] In Jerusalem, where he settled permanently in 1924, he was surrounded by a community of Orientalist and Judaic scholars, and a number of his literary works feature tireless (though usually hapless) researchers as protagonists.

Some of Agnon's stories employ techniques of formal anachronism and temporal disorientation similar to those used by al-Masʿadi. Agnon, too, largely abstains from using grammatical structures that emerged with

Hebrew's modern transformations, utilizing syntactic forms associated with earlier Jewish genres. In the short tale "Lefi ha-tzaʿar ha-sakhar" ("The Reward Is in Accordance with the Pain," 1962), the protagonist, Mar Ribi Zidkiyah, recites a liturgical hymn that, as the narrator comments, "was composed a few generations after [him]."[63] The narrator then provides an explanation: because the liturgies are first composed in heaven and reveal themselves to the poet as the case proves necessary, some righteous men can "sense" them before their actual manifestation in this world and can evoke them in their discourse with God. The timeless literary realm, where all of literature exists at once, is here identified directly with the divine—an association that was only implied in al-Masʿadi's analogous model. Nevertheless, rather than focusing on ahistorical stories like "Lefi ha-tzaʿar," I turn in what follows to "'Ido ve-'Enam," ("Edo and Enam") one of Agnon's "scholar" stories that thematically addresses the conjunctions of philological and religious readerships, as well as distinguishes them from a literary mode of reading that enacts its own timeless plane of equivalences. Weaving together countless references to Biblical and secondary Jewish sources, Greek myths, and German literary classics, "Edo and Enam" is a rich allegory of acts of reading and interpretation shifting among pious, scholarly, and literary modes.

"Edo" was published in 1950, a late period in Agnon's career when, as literary critic Baruch Kurzweil has grumbled, Agnon had developed "an entire system of complex and intricate disguises and riddles ... a kind of secret language that the author uses to converse with himself while speaking to an audience."[64] This observation is particularly pertinent to "Edo," which features a mysterious "secret language" as a central plot element. At the heart of the text is the private language that the young girl Gemulah shares with her father, Gevariah ben Geʿuel, and its relocation from their isolated mythical land to contemporary Jerusalem, together with the beautiful Gemulah. Three male characters shape this translation: Gabriel Gamzu, a one-eyed trader in rare Hebrew manuscripts who marries Gemulah and brings her to Jerusalem; Dr. Ginat, the young modern philologist who studies her language and translates her songs; and the unnamed narrator, "a common reader," as he defines himself, who is reminiscent of Agnon himself, as they share a number of well-known biographical details. Michal Arbel argues that the story's rebelliousness and its resistance to being reduced to a conclusive, allegorical reading emerges not only from the text's polyphonic nature but also from its intentional ambiguity regarding the stability of categories such as old and new, authenticity and fabrication, and reality and fiction, all of which circulate around the status of this secret tongue.[65] Taking heed of Arbel, the purpose of my reading here is not to provide a stable symbolic referent for all elements of the story, but rather to explore one of them: the Hebrew (or more generally the Jewish) text's transition from its status as either a religious object or as the Orientalist's object of study to its positioning as an object of literature and modern literary reading. The story stages the fraught position of the Jewish text surfacing from "timeless" origins, as it oscillates among traditional exegesis, philological scholarship, and literary consumption.

The tension between scholarly research and literary reading is introduced early in the story. The narrator, visiting his good friends Gerhardt and Gerda Greifenbach before their departure on a long trip abroad, is astounded to hear that Dr. Ginat, the famed reclusive scholar, is a tenant at their house:

> My heart beat fast as I heard this; not because of the Greifenbachs, but because they had spoken of Ginat as a "real" person. Since the time when the name of Ginat became world-famous, I had not come across anyone who could say he actually knew him.... I held down the turmoil within me and asked, "Is he here?" Even as I said this, I was amazed at my own question. Never had I been inside a house where Ginat had been seen. ("Edo," 102)

The young Dr. Ginat gained his fame among philologists with his radical new discoveries, first made public with the article "Ninety-Nine Words of the Edo Language," followed by the astounding study, *Grammar of Edo*. The narrator, however, is not drawn to Ginat for his findings in the field of philological linguistics, but rather for his discovery of the Enamite hymns, examples of "splendid and incisive poetry," which impressed even the most doubtful scholars. As a lay or common reader, the narrator's reading of these poems is markedly different from that of the philologists: "All these scholars affirmed that the gods of Enam and their priests were male; how was it that they did not catch in the hymns the cadence of a woman's song? On the other hand, I could be mistaken; for I am not, of course, a professional scholar, only a common reader who happens to enjoy anything beautiful that comes his way" ("Edo," 102).

The common yet sensitive reader's gendered intuition proves to be correct. The narrator, who stays at the Greifenbachs' house while they are away, discovers that the origin of Ginat's hymns and lexicons is none other than Gemulah, the beautiful young woman that Gamzu, a merchant of Jewish manuscripts, had brought from a remote Jewish community at the end of the Eastern deserts to be his wife. The story sets up a classic romantic triangle, to which the narrator is a reluctant witness. Gamzu, the one-eyed devoted husband, is enamored by Gemulah's songs and beauty, but she is in love with the studious scholar Ginat. Ginat, however, is only interested in Gemulah's exotic language and remains aloof to her romantic approaches. The story ends in a tragedy: Gemulah and Ginat both die under mysterious circumstances, having fallen off the roof on a night of a full moon.

Critical reception of the story has read Gemulah as an emblem of mystical, primordial, or unmanageable femininity,[66] but Ilana Pardes observes that the Orientalist scholar Ginat functions in the story as a mysterious object of desire who is just as arousing as the girl.[67] Both the narrator and Gemulah are drawn to the reclusive scholar. And although it appears that for Ginat, Gemulah is merely a linguistic source that requires careful recording and interpretation, after which she may return to her proper place alongside her husband, for Gemulah the encounter with Ginat is transformative. She longs to remain with the scholar who documents her language and promises to sing for him her most exquisite songs. Even Gamzu, the betrayed husband, expresses some interest in Ginat's books despite his contempt for modern linguistic scholarship. In stark contrast to the vivid and detailed descriptions of both Gemulah and Gamzu, be they mythically pastoral or grotesquely realist, Ginat is an unremarkable character, lacking in any distinguishing tropes. Yet the philologist is the driving catalyst of the plot, an empty locus for relations of desire, interest, or contempt. His nondescript figure highlights the promises and hopes invested in the philological study of ancient languages and cultures. The historian Maurice Olender comments that Orientalist philology views language as "a faithful witness to history that transcends the generations of humanity."[68] Echoing this observation, the narrator notes that Ginat's colleagues had discovered, in the language of Edo, "a new-found link in a chain that bound the beginnings of recorded history to the ages before" ("Edo," 102). The language of Edo is read as a fossil, a witness to an ancient site of origins.

On the other side of the romantic triangle is Gamzu, a traditional Jewish trader in religious manuscripts, who voices a strong rejection of such new scholarly practices of reading. "Those bible critics, who turn the words of living God upside down," he says. "In the depths of their hearts they know that no text of Scripture has any other meaning than that which has been passed to us by tradition" ("Edo," 124). He further complains about the scholarly separation between text and living culture: "People live out their lives according to the Torah, they lay down their lives for the heritage of their fathers; then along come the scholars, and make the Torah into 'research material' and the ways of our fathers into folklore" ("Edo," 142). Gamzu's criticism contrasts two modes of reading the biblical text, although when he associates Ginat with the scholarly model, he suggests that this critique applies to the academic study of Jewish ancient texts more broadly. As opposed to the scholars, Gamzu advocates for a reading practice that adopts the Bible as guide for praxis, a model that associates interpretation with living culture. While the scholars find the significance of the text in the ability to position it firmly in the past, secure in a chain of historical predecessors and successors, Gamzu views the text as living and intervening in the present.

The stark contrast between the two reading practices is blurred, however, when it comes to Gamzu's own approach to Gemulah and her songs. As a dealer in ancient Jewish manuscripts, Gamzu travels to remote destinations, purchasing neglected and unknown texts. In the most desolate places, he finds examples of unaltered religious practice: "If you wish to see Jews from the days of the Mishnah," he says, "go to the city of Amadia. Forty families of Israel live there, all God-fearing and true to the faith" ("Edo," 119). The Jewish communities Gamzu finds have been seemingly frozen in time, tracing their origins back to the mythical lost ten tribes of Israel or to the Babylonian exile. He views them as remote and impervious to change, timeless emblems untouched by history. This approach betrays the similarities between Ginat and himself. Both search for a genuine example of untouched authenticity, drawn to Gemulah's isolated community as a site where a primordial state of origins has been preserved. Commenting on the productive exchanges and parallels between the traditional manuscript hunter and the modern philologist, Pardes summarizes that "Ginat is far more indebted to traditional exegetical modes than meets the eye, while Gamzu rejects modern scholarship without realizing that there are unforeseen similarities between the interpretive practices he is accustomed to and the new scholarly trends."[69] More tellingly, both men's methods prove to be destructive for Gemulah, the textual object removed from its original setting. Gamzu tears her away from her native village and brings her to Jerusalem, where she grows depressed and ill. Ginat does not return her love, driving her to suicidal despair. Despite the temptation to position the two men as polar opposites, one representing a traditional form of Jewish scholarship and the other the new philological approaches, the relationship between them is one of reflection rather than opposition.

This feat of equalization, blurring any meaningful distinction between the two modes of reading, could only happen by means of the narrator, the common reader who models a literary practice of reading. The narrator is repeatedly positioned as a mediator between fields of knowledge and modes of interpretation. For example, when Greifenbach, "who had made a hobby of philology," begins to speak of the mysteries of language and the new discoveries in the field, the narrator is able to add "something of what [he] learned from the literature of the Kabbalah, which in this matter has anticipated academic scholarship" ("Edo," 106). The narrator is able to complement the philologist's views with a smidgen of Jewish mystical traditions. He brings the two realms into meaningful relationship, with the one not opposed to the other but rather "anticipating" and preceding it.

The narrator's presence also seems to be the condition for Gamzu and Ginat's encounter in the Greifenbachs' home. While the Greifenbachs are away, they ask the narrator to watch over their house, a task he largely neglects until one evening his legs lead him there almost unintentionally. That night, Gamzu, looking for his sleepwalking wife, also shows up at the house whose owners he is unacquainted with, not knowing how or why he came there. When he eventually finds Gemulah in Ginat's room, the narrator is present as a witness. Although Gamzu and Ginat may disagree about the proper way to "read" Gemulah, the literary narrator is the mediating occasion that allows for their encounter. It is also not incidental that the space in which the characters meet, a home that belongs to none of them and that they are all drawn to, inexplicably, on a night of a full moon, is the properly German home of the Greifenbachs: a couple who spend their evenings reading Goethe. Gerda Greifenbach even jokes that the recluse Ginat is writing the third volume of Faust. Their home becomes the literary space promised by Goethe, one of the early articulators of the idea of world literature as the humanist domain in which textual objects from different cultures and periods can meet. It is this notion of literature, as a worldly humanist plane of equivalence, that allows both philological study and liturgical exegesis to emerge as parallel and reflective forms of interpretation of the Jewish text.

LITERATURE AS TYPOLOGY

What, then, distinguishes a literary mode of reading, and how is it different from the two models of interpretation represented by Gamzu and Ginat? The narrator, a self-described "common reader," responds to the Enamite hymns viscerally, emotionally, and intuitively; their beauty stirs an echo in his depths. "Ever since the day I had first read the Enamite Hymns," he remarks, "that echo had resounded. It was the reverberation of a primeval song passed on from the first hour of history through endless generations" ("Edo," 103). Like the philologist, the narrator identifies in the hymns a link to a distant, primeval past—a point of imagined origins. But rather than a "faithful witness," he experiences them as an echo, a reverberation that strikes something familiar within him. His mode of reading, which positions the hymns within a literary framework, appreciates their echo of a "primeval song" without placing them in a prehistorical moment.

The intertextual engagements of "Edo" create the same experience of echoing familiarity, as they stage a performance of repetitions and variations. Goethe's appearance highlights other ways in which the story echoes the classics of German literature. Cynthia Ozick reads Gemulah as a variation on Heine's "Die Lorelei," which itself reverberates the Ovidian myth of Echo.[70] A particularly rich field of reverberations is created through variations on the story of the Golem/Pygmalion. When the Greifenbachs first hear Gemulah in Ginat's room, they joke that he must have invented a woman to amuse him. This reminds them of the legend of Rabbi Solomon Ibn Gabirol, who had created a woman to serve his needs. The narrator completes the story that they mention, adding that the king fell in love with this mechanical woman, forcing Ibn Gabirol to take her apart to prove that she was fabricated ("Edo," 106). This variation on the story of the Golem is quoted in an anthology collected by Gershom Scholem but with some significant differences.[71] When comparing the two versions, it appears that the king's passion for the mechanized woman is Agnon's own addition, tying the legend more explicitly to the myth of Pygmalion and its literary transmutations. One of them, E. T. A. Hoffmann's classic "The Sandman," seems to be especially pertinent: Gamzu obsessively fiddles with his empty eye socket, echoing Hoffmann's Nathanael, who is haunted by the fear of losing his eyes.[72] The chain of echoes continues: the eyeless Gamzu is apparently impotent, or at least unable to satisfy Gemulah, embodying the connection that Freud establishes between fear of losing one's eyes and fear of castration in the essay "The Uncanny," his classic analysis of "The Sandman."[73] This literary chain of reverberations and illusions illustrates a principle that "Edo" returns to repeatedly: the manner in which one story shadows another; one poem echoes all other poems. When the narrator recalls the night in which Gamzu found Gemulah in Ginat's room, he remarks,

> with my own eyes I had seen Gamzu snatch his wife away, and yet it seemed to me that it was only a story, like the one he himself had told me, of how on one occasion dances were held, and Gadi ben Ge'im was about to seize Gemulah, and Gamzu forestalled him. There is no event whose mark has not gone before it. Such is the parable of the bird: before it flies, it spreads its wings and they make a shadow; it looks at the shadow, raises its wings and flies away. (152)

The narrator witnesses the dramatic scene in which Gamzu grabs his wife, but he experiences it as a story, which is to say as an echo of an event that had already happened years earlier and in a faraway land. "There is no event whose mark has not gone before it": no event is truly new, the narrator concludes, but they all have their precedent as a model, like the bird observing its shadow before taking flight. In positing that all events are prefigured, Agnon adopts a typological model of reading, inherited from exegetic practices, and turns it into a practice of literary production: the bird views its own shadow, the two-dimensional image of a flying bird, in order to take its example and take flight. No creation is truly new but is rather a reverberation of an existing figure; neither novelty nor originality carries any currency in this literary model. "All the events of man are one event, and all times are equal, but their combinations are different," writes Agnon in "Hadom ve-kisse" ("Footstool and Chair"), a story composed a few years after "Edo."[74] Stories are reverberations, connected repetitions combined in new ways.

Al-Masʿadi, who declares his indifference to novelty in the introduction to *Haddatha*, develops a similar theory accounting for how new writing is nevertheless produced. In a chapter of *Haddatha* titled "Hadith al-tin" ("The Tale of Clay"), Abu Hurayra appears as a poet who seeks but is unable to find true novelty. In this choppy and nightmarish chapter, Abu Hurayra retreats to a remote valley, drawn by a fantasy of "the virgin land," untouched and still suspended in creative potential (*Haddatha*, 130). He composes an elegy for Adam and Eve, the only two people who have ever truly enjoyed the virgin moment of beginning that continues to elude him: "The two of them almost succeeded in teaching me how to be ignorant of the world and walk on a virgin path. And when I lost them, the beaten path guided me back to my old story and my old self. I wanted my path to be virgin and untouched by man, but it turns out it is already beaten like an old whore" (*Haddatha*, 131). Abu Hurayra's disappointment is illustrated in explicitly gendered and sexualized terms. He had sought a "virgin path," a space unmarked by other bodies, but everywhere he finds traces of past travelers and writers, even traces of his past self, and the path, he concludes, is violated and abused. A wind blows through the sand in the remote valley, revealing "ancient traces [*rusūm*] and a decayed skull.... No sooner does one seek solitude than one happens upon an effaced trace.... I had wanted to erase my story, but it is inside me even before Adam, and cannot be erased" (*Haddatha*, 132). Abu Hurayra encounters effaced traces of the same story wherever he goes. Even Adam was not the origin but merely an echo to a previously existing story. These traces are already present in the earliest preserved Arabic poetic tradition of *al-wuqūf ʿalā al-aṭlāl*, the figure that traditionally initiates the Arabic *qasīda*: standing over the traces of the beloved's ruined camp, which act as an incitement to poetic speech. Poetic creation, Abu Hurayra must painfully concede, is never an act of original creation but is always a revelation of effaced traces, an echo of a preexisting story.

Agnon and al-Masʿadi both translate the typological model—exemplified in Massignon's notion of history as an echoing chain of witnesses—from a method of theological reading to a theory of literary creation. In the plane of literature that they stage in their works, there is no purchase to originality. It is a realm of traces and reverberating echoes. Nevertheless, there is a significant distinction between the two models. Orientalist typologies are premised on a progressive telos, positing that the past is dead and the present alive. Agnon's and al-Mas'adi's returns to mythical sites of origin, however, allow the past and the present to exist simultaneously in the contemporaneous realm of literature, which knows no time.

SUCH IS THE PARABLE OF THE BIRD: OF SONGBIRDS AND PARROTS

Al-Mas'adi and Agnon both stage a return to origins that revokes the politics of literary periodization and challenges revival modernity's narrative of dynamic progress by delineating literature as a temporally static plane of contemporaneity, of echoes and reverberations. To the question of whether the Arabic or Hebrew text can truly be modern, they respond with a resounding no. "Modernity" is not a category that carries any purchase or meaning within the theory of literature that their writings perform. At the conclusion of both texts, their protagonists appear to be subsumed by this idealized literary domain. Abu Hurayra, as discussed earlier, is lured by a wondrous voice singing the song of truth from the darkness and gallops to his death at the bottom of a dark abyss (*Haddatha*, 230). In "Edo," it is also an "ultimate song," to use Ilana Pardes's term, that portends Gemulah's death.[75] Gemulah and Ginat fall off the roof on a moonlit night, an incident that appears to fulfill a threatening promise made earlier by Gemulah: when Gamzu carries her away, the heartbroken Gemulah tells Ginat, "I shall sing you the song of the bird Grofit, which she sings only once in her lifetime.... I shall sing the song of Grofit and then we shall die" ("Edo," 149–50). The narrator then explains that the Grofit sings when her time comes to leave this world. Her departing song reverberates all other songs of being:

> Songs are conjoined. They are linked up with one another, the songs of the springs with the songs of high mountains, and those of high mountains with the songs of the birds of the air. And among these birds there is one whose name is Grofit; when its hour comes to leave the world, it looks up to the clouds and raises its voice in song; and when the song is ended it departs from this world. All these songs are linked together in the language of Gemulah. ("Edo," 151)

In their deaths, both Abu Hurayra and Gemulah respond to the call of the absolute song, the song of creator and of creation, which reverberates through all times and all things.

And yet, once the two texts, with their strange echoes and similarities, are allowed to resonate against each other, the neat conclusion of these final scenes of transcendence grows somewhat murky. If we turn to what Gayatri Spivak calls "narrative framing" in these two texts, the cohesiveness of the timeless literary realm of echoes begins to fragment. In a reflection on echo as a model for feminist cultural critique (which she describes as a "parasitic" position), Spivak criticizes psychoanalytic theory's fixation on Narcissus gazing back at his own reflection as the primary scene of subject formation. Turning to the "framing" of Narcissus's story in Ovid, she unfolds the neglected narrativization of Echo, "the woman in Narcissus's story," finding a story of divine violence as sexual violence and "a punishment that is finally a dubious reward quite outside the borders of the self."[76] The story of Echo as a figure that is "obliged to echo everyone who speaks" becomes for Spivak an "ethical instantiation." Unlike the closed circuit of Narcissus, which always returns an exact reflection of the self, Echo has no identity proper but "is obliged to be imperfectly and interceptively responsive to another's desire."[77] She is a disembodied reverberation, an impossible voice that can only repeat with a difference. Spivak's attention to the story's framing discloses the gendered and sexual violence that "envelopes" both Narcissus's and Echo's tales.[78] Histories of rape and punishment condition Echo's ethical instantiation as an alternate, deconstructive mode of response.

An attention to the narrative framings of the final scenes of *Haddatha* and "Edo" reveals similar histories of gendered violence. As Abu Hurayra and his friend Abu al-Mada'in head out to the desert, Abu Hurayra tells two troubling and seemingly unrelated anecdotes from his youth. In the first, he confesses to killing a prostitute with whom Abu al-Mada'in had a close relationship (*Haddatha*, 224). The dead woman enables the intimate connection between the two men; it is hinted, if not stated explicitly, that she was killed for the sake of their friendship. The second is an account of a practical joke: Abu Hurayra was hosting a group of friends and presented them with special entertainment concealed behind a screen: a new slave girl with a wonderful singing voice. The guests, enchanted, quarreled for the right to spend the night with the singer, and Abu Hurayra eventually promised to circulate her among them fairly. Finally, after the men were sufficiently worked up and made exuberant promises, he drew back the screen, only to reveal a large, multicolored parrot that proceeded to mimic the men's enraged outcries (*Haddatha*, 226–27).

Abu al-Madaʾin is perplexed by these two stories and doesn't understand why Abu Hurayra brings them up, but the obvious connection between them is the figure of the woman circulated among men, an exchange underlined by violence. Casually mentioned at the conclusion of the novel, the murdered prostitute is also a reminder of Abu Hurayra's wife, whose accidental/wished for death at the book's opening allowed for his adventure to begin. Abu Hurayra's story suddenly appears to be bookended and enabled by the violent deaths of women. Similar tropes are found in "Edo," a story of a woman circulated among men that begins and ends with violence. Gemulah's recurrent "snatching" is a narrative engine, and the various men's attempts to read her lead to her demise. The fate of women in both texts insinuates that although the contemporaneous realm of literature may offer a space for the male writer-hero, its universality is based on continued exclusions, if not on explicitly sexual and obliterating violence.

Meanwhile, Abu Hurayra's anecdote of the singing girl who proved to be a parrot directly destabilizes the scene of poetic transcendence that follows. The enticing song in the anecdote was eventually revealed to be a bird's mindless and misleading mimicry. Who can tell if the voice calling out to Abu Hurayra from the abyss is not just another mockingbird, an existential prankster? The ultimate song of truth coming from the timeless literary realm might indeed be a fraud, this framing seems to caution. In "Edo," too, the authenticity of Gemulah's song and of the Enamic hymns appears doubtful when considering an offhand remark made by Gamzu. Gemulah and her father, he says, had invented a secret language for the two of them to converse in. Might the historical tongue of Edo, immortalized through Ginat's scholarship as the philological key to ancient wisdom, be a private childhood game invented between the two of them? "Edo"'s echoing stories of mechanized dolls and female golems insinuate that every song might be a beautiful forgery and an enchanting delusion.

What are we to make of the fact that the protagonists' scenes of poetic transcendence are ironically undermined? This framing establishes a critical distance that casts the two texts' staging of literature as a universal and timeless realm of reverberation as a mode of "strategic anachronism," doubtful of its constructions even as it stages them in the text. "Strategic anachronism" is used here with a nod to Spivak's discussion of "strategic essentialism" as a rhetorical-political practice. In the 1987 essay "Subaltern Studies: Deconstructing Historiography," Spivak acknowledges the need to accept a temporary essentialist approach to a shared identity for the sake of politically motivated interpretation. She identified the practice of "strategic essentialism" in the work of the Subaltern Studies Group as "a strategic use of positivist essentialism in a scrupulously visible political interest."[79] The significance of strategic essentialism depends on its performative awareness of both the functions and the dangers of assuming an essentialist position. Strategic essentialism, Sangeeta Ray notes, outlines a transactional mode of reading, one that recognizes and makes explicit the political gains and compromises of its premises.[80] A transactional reading of al-Masʿadi and Agnon highlights how they both make the shortcomings and compromises of the static literary model they establish scrupulously visible by underscoring its inherent gendered oversights.

Agnon's and al-Masʿadi's returns to origins stage a theory of literature as a static realm of timeless reverberations, of one song echoing though all times. But this song is always accompanied by static in the second sense: static as a parasitic intruder, a grating against the ear. This is the repeated insinuation that the perfect song is a fake, a manipulated fraud, and that its appearance is conditioned on a series of violent, gendered exclusions. This ambivalence is at the core of Agnon's and al-Masʿadi's works—as mock-classicist texts, they are clear fabrications, soliciting the readers' desire for authenticity while revealing this desire's mechanisms and cogwheels. Both writers recognize the political space that literary-universal reading practices provide for modern writers, especially for writers of Arabic and Hebrew texts whose proper presentness is always put to question. They participated in its construction, envisioning a literary space of timeless echoes, a mode of reading that is based on repetition, recognition, and commonality and that disregards the unequal political realities of the present. Simultaneously, their returns to origins are laid bare as inventive fabrications, mimicking and mocking the historicist search for the true origins of man or nation in textual archives.

Chapter Two

SCRATCH

The Present Out of Work

Toward the end of Francophone Egyptian writer Albert Cossery's novel *Les Fainéants dans la vallée fertile* (*Laziness in the Fertile Valley*, 1948), the protagonist, Serag, sneaks out of his house to an appointment at the "statue of the Renaissance" by the Cairo train station.[1] As readers familiar with Cairo would be quick to recognize, Serag is on his way to *Nahḍat Maṣr*, *The Awakening of Egypt*, the famous statue by the sculptor Mahmoud Mukhtar. Designed in celebration of the 1919 anticolonial uprising, the monumental sculpture features a peasant woman lifting her veil with one hand while awaking a rising sphinx with the other. It became an instant icon of the Egyptian national liberation movement upon its unveiling in 1928.[2] The statue mobilizes both the pharaonic sphinx and the figure of the peasant as emblems of an optimistic Egyptian national project, establishing a link between the mythical past, the present struggle, and a proud future.

The Awakening of Egypt is a fitting destination for Serag, who is escaping his family of chronic sleepers, a clan that has made laziness and idle lounging into an ideology and a way of life. Serag, the youngest son, is tormented by an inexplicable desire to work (an activity he has only heard rumors about), which horrifies his father and siblings. He closely follows the construction of a nearby factory, convinced that there he would be able to find "real work"—not the idle, absurd existence of the drowsy shopkeepers and sleepy clerks that he sees around him. When Serag realizes that the factory will never be completed, he decides to go to the city and sets up a meeting at *The Awakening of Egypt*. Alas, Serag never makes it to Egypt's awakening and to the city's promise of redeeming labor. On the way, he is overcome by exhaustion and falls asleep by the roadside.

Laziness in the Fertile Valley captures the contours of a revivalist national culture harnessed to an ideology of productivity: the narrative of awakening from existential slumber is joined by a demand for physical, strenuous, and redeeming labor, ultimately striving toward an organic vision of a healthy, productive national body. This ideology was present in both Arabic and Hebrew revivalist cultures, and literature was not spared from the demand to labor for a national future. For early twentieth-century Hebrew writers committed to the Zionist cause, the relationship between the nation and literature was symbiotic: the health of Hebrew literature was a reflection of the health of the Hebrew nation.[3] In the writing of this period, Dina Berdichevksi notes, the writer's task is often described as a heroic striving to expose reality's material core and is "attributed with a sense of *physical labor*."[4] In Arabic, similar debates crystalized a couple of decades later under the broad label of *iltizām* (commitment), and more specifically the vitalist vision of "art for the sake of life" (*al-fann fī sabīl al-ḥayā*), in which literature was attributed with the role of producing a utopian future.[5] Under the auspices of the developmentalist state, literature was harnessed to an ideology of labor and cast as a productive endeavor, measured by its positive contribution to the national project. In both these contexts, literature was put to work.

Cossery (1913–2008) occupies a marginal position in Egyptian literary history, a writer whose reputation for indolence and depravity has overtaken critical engagement with his work.[6] In the 1940s, he was associated with the anarcho-surrealist Jamāʿat al-Fann wa-l-Ḥurriyya (Art and Liberty Group, 1938–1948), and his stories were translated into Arabic and published in their journal.[7] Many of the members of this group had left Egypt after the 1952 revolution, their cosmopolitan identities and identifications being largely at odds with the period's dominant national-modernist demands. Cossery himself had already left in 1945, settling in Paris and writing exclusively in French. Nevertheless, Egypt remained the primary setting and subject of his work (apart from one novel). It is not merely that Cossery was, as Zainab Halabi states, "uninterested in the doxa that reigned over the Egyptian literary field," by which she means the archetype of the socially conscious writer who mobilizes his work for national liberation and social progress through a social-realist style.[8] Cossery's novels, steeped in Egyptian national figures, idioms, and landmarks, are a direct mocking attack on this archetype and its associated ideals, caricaturing Egyptian nationalism's fetishization of productive labor, industrial progress, and social enlightenment. Cossery's writing is no less committed than the literature of *iltizām*—but its commitment is to a purposefully contrarian ethos, which favors the "annihilating sweetness" of sleep and renounces all ambitions that fool individuals into crowning labor a value and productivity a desired good.[9] Cossery's protagonists may try to awaken, but they eventually embrace the warm cocoon of sleep and its nest of familiar and pungent body odors. The greatest threat to their way of life is the specter of a woman who might penetrate their sanctum, wash their sheets, and sweep away the layers of dust and dirt accumulating in their chambers.

The three texts analyzed in this chapter—the Arabic novel *al-Jabal* (*The Mountain*, 1957) by Egyptian writer Fathi Ghanem (1924–1999) and the Hebrew novella "'Atsabim" ("Nerves," 1910) and the novel *Shkhol ve-khishalon* (*Breakdown and Bereavement*, 1920), both by writer Yosef Haim Brenner (1881–1921)—fictionalize debates on productive settlement in a modern national context to ask about the work of literature itself. Is writing valuable only when it is productive? What is it that the fiction writer ultimately produces? Like Serag, these texts embark resolutely on the path to (the monument for) national awakening, only to abandon themselves to the lure of idleness, futile loitering, and a literature that produces nothing. Alongside the productivist national ethos, they outline an alternative stance of futility, embodied in the static figure of scratching (*gerud* in Hebrew) and scraping (*kaḥt* in Arabic). This static form is both a bodily gesture and a literary mode, a parasitic and excessive position that does not produce anything. If national ideologies of awakening insist that the present should be dedicated to working and producing a vigorous, wholesome, national future, the present of scratching, while somewhat filthy or disgusting, is self-content and removed from visions of redemptive labor.

The Mountain takes place in 1947 in a village in Upper Egypt and is based on a true incident, a failed project of resettlement and social reform of the peasants living among the archeological digs of the Valley of the Kings.

Both "Nerves" and *Breakdown and Bereavement* concern Jewish settlement in Palestine in the years before the First World War, the former focusing on the Zionist agricultural colonies and the latter on the "old *yeshuv*," the Jewish community in Jerusalem, which at this point was still somewhat removed from the Zionist colonial project, although the novel charts their increasing entanglements. These two distinct historical settings, an impoverished village in Upper Egypt and Jewish Zionist settlement in Palestine, are linked through their parallel engagements with an ideology of modern productive settlement, which aims to solve the problem of the inefficient, unruly, and abject movement (or stuckness) of the Arab or Jewish subject. If the previous chapter explored how Arabic and Hebrew authors mobilize a realm of literary timelessness in order to negotiate a position for themselves in *time*, or in the present historical moment, this chapter turns to the problem of inhabiting space—of how Arabic and Hebrew literatures imagine and legitimize modes of residing and settling. These novels of settlement explore whether unruly individual bodies, which are always both too mobile and too still—too itchy—to be properly settled, are formed into settled, rooted, national bodies, which belong in their place. The plight of the indigenous Egyptian peasants initially appears to be directly opposite to that of the Eastern European Jewish settlers: the former are too rooted in their mountain, the latter are not rooted enough anywhere. And yet, in its essence, their problem is the same: neither group is sufficiently productive within a modern national framework to justify its mode of habitation. They are scratching subjects, plagued by idleness, nonproductivity, and lack of any hygienic standards. This is enough to deem them improperly settled and potentially moveable. Settlement is legitimized when it is engaged in productive labor within a national context that posits "the people" as a resource for national wealth.

Although both writers were clearly invested in this ideological model, Ghanem's and Brenner's texts emerge as staging grounds for conflicting ideologies of settlement that manifest in inconsistencies of both plot and literary form. To trace these countercurrents, my reading focuses on the itchy, unwashed bodies that feature in these texts and on the networks of illicit desires that they provoke, coded between fascination and disgust. Reading for disgust, a minor or "politically inadequate" affect, as Sianne Ngai has called it, means shifting the gaze away from dynamic, major narratives of national, productive becomings to static textual moments in which movement is reduced to repetitive, futile scraping at surfaces.[10] Scratching, in frenzy or in lazy stupor, appears in these texts as the opposite of a future-oriented productive ethos, a Brownian, vectorless movement that leads nowhere. It becomes an emblem of nonproductive existence: just loafing around or scraping to get by. Steven Connor notes that "itching and scratching involve a rising to the surface of ourselves, a centering of ourselves at our edges."[11] And indeed, reading for the static figure of scratching involves turning away from an obsession with depth, of the psyche and the text, toward a careful exploration of the texture of surfaces.[12] Such a reading illuminates a basic conflict between two political models of settlement— and of writing—that underlie these texts: an emphatic, dynamic model, based on a metaphor of depths and on a symbiotic connection between the subject and the land, and a static, impassive model, located at the surface: at the level of dirt, skin, and written language.

Ghanem's and Brenner's works, despite their marked difference of setting and style, illuminate one another, and reading them together reveals their shared ideological and aesthetic conflicts. This chapter moves between them: it begins by establishing a link between the indigenous "squatters" and the diasporic Jews as both subject to ideologies that judge them and their economic basis as parasitic, and hence as always mis-settled; continues with distinguishing between productive and non-productive labor in Ghanem's *The Mountain*; and then returns to Brenner's "Nerves" and *Breakdown and Bereavement* to argue that these conflicting models of labor and settlement are also about the productive ends of writing. When the idle, non-productive ethos of scratching, in which the present aims to produce nothing beyond itself, threatens to overwhelm the productive ethos of the present as a site of labor that produces the future, literature too writes itself out of work.

UNSETTLED FILTHY BEGGARS

The novella "Nerves" was written in 1910, shortly after Brenner's own immigration to Palestine in 1909. At the time, Brenner was already a well-known figure in the small realm of Hebrew letters, a fiery polemicist and influential editor. His immigration is often marked as the end of the European sphere of Hebrew writing and the beginning of a new Hebrew cultural center in Palestine.[13] "Nerves" is an *'aliya* story, a narrative of "ascendance" or immigration to Erets Yisra'el, and as the first literary text that Brenner wrote in Palestine, it incarnates the symbolic immigration of literary centers that it narrates. Nevertheless, it is a strangely nonconclusive text, employing, as Boaz Arpaly notes, the familiar heroic narrative genre of a journey from Eastern Europe to Palestine in the least heroic fashion.[14] The hectic, torturous journey does not conclude with a cathartic reunion with a long-abandoned homeland, but rather with festering disappointment. "So this is what our promised land is like!" the protagonist proclaims with bitterness.[15]

The formal structure of "Nerves" dramatizes this disillusioning encounter. The narrative takes place as the narrator and his unnamed companion (to whom I refer as the protagonist from here on), a sickly and self-diagnosed neurotic newcomer to Palestine, take an evening stroll around the newly established Hebrew colony.[16] The two are day laborers, yet there is little labor for them. As they wander, the protagonist is stirred to recount the story of his journey to Palestine, while the narrator interjects with scenic descriptions of their surroundings. Two time frames continually contrast and interact: the first is the narrative time of the dramatic journey to Palestine, and the second is the present moment of narration. The end of the journey is therefore known in advance: Erets Yisra'el, the object of desire in the mythic ʿaliya story, is structurally juxtaposed to the real, existing, Palestinian landscape.

The structure of "Nerves" neatly lends itself to the dialectic model that Fredric Jameson outlines in *Antinomies of Realism*, which reads the modern novel as a collision between a narrative impulse, or *récit*, and a static or scenic impulse, which Jameson calls affect.[17] The framed tale of migration is exemplary of the narrative impulse: It ties character to a unique destiny (the migrant Jew to the Land of Israel), linking the past to the future according to the demands of both genre and history. The frame story, in contrast, is the registry of the present, consisting primarily of descriptions of the characters' surrounding, their perceptions and reactions. According to Jameson, writing this present implies a reduction to the body "inasmuch as the body is all that remains in any tendential reduction of experience to the present."[18] The present of the two companions in the frame story is marked through the material encounter of their bodies with the weather and the land: they sweat, shiver, or sit on the thorns of a prickly pear. Jameson argues that unlike *récit* or narrative, affect is genre-less, but I would contend that it is a mode of writing whose genre is precisely the illusion of immediacy, the staging of seemingly unmediated access to the physical, prelinguistic body. This immediacy is a genre with its own politics and ideologies of relation between self and space. The protagonist continuously yearns for a different form of interaction with the land, one that is deeper, rooted, more established. He bemoans the newness and transience of the Hebrew colony, condemns the members of the second generation for leaving in search of a more luxurious life abroad, and likens the colony to "trees that have grown wings rather than roots."[19]

The precarity of the colony is apparent, the protagonist says, when compared to the surrounding Palestinian villages:

> The villages! The old ones, I mean, not ours. Those that blend in, the sun is their sun and the rain is their rain, that aren't merely a quarter of a century old.... Well, [the Arabs] may be filthy beggars themselves... oh I'm sure of it: they are! But at least they are not the filthy outcasts of the earth.[20]

The protagonist is struck by the way the Palestinian villages are rooted in the landscape. The have a relation of *ownership* to the natural elements—the sun is their sun and the rain is their rain. In fact, they are so embedded that at first they are invisible to the narrator, as if they were a part of nature.[21] The Jewish colony, however, viewed against this example of indigenous belonging, is blatant and foreign and might disappear just as quickly as it was established. It is only superficially settled, lacking deep roots.

The Palestinian connection to the land is a matter of envy and desire, but in the same breath, it is also undermined: the Arabs are seen as "filthy beggars" rather than farmers or peasants. Failing to be properly productive, they lack the means to properly inhabit and cultivate the land, and as such, they are depicted as not so different from those Zionist settlers who begged their way to Palestine. Hillel Halkin's translational flourish, which replaces the first iteration of the word "filthy" (*mezohamim*) with "filthy beggars," highlights the parallel. The protagonist's observation establishes that there is more similarity than difference between the Palestinian natives and the Jewish settlers, those "filthy outcasts of the earth" (*mezohamey 'olam*). The Zionist settler, as the war of 1948 will decisively demonstrate only a few decades later, views the Palestinian natives as improperly settled and therefore potentially moveable. But at this moment, the beggarly filth of the Jewish settler and the Palestinian native deem both parasitic and potentially transient because they fail to engage in productive labor.

Fathi Ghanem's novel *The Mountain* (*al-Jabal*, 1957) also narrates a journey and a precarious settlement. Its protagonist is an urban government investigator, a far cry from the impoverished Jewish refugee of Brenner's text, but his gaze at the small village community that he is sent to is similar: a combination of disgust and envy, contempt and desire.[22] The government had decided that the impoverished residents of the village, currently occupying caves and hovels located over the ancient pharaonic tombs across the Nile from Luxor, must be evacuated for the benefit of both archeologists and tourists. The villagers, however, refuse to leave the mountain and relocate to the modern model town that has been built for them on the plain. The investigator, named, like the author, Fathi Ghanem, is charged with inspecting acts of vandalism in the new town. Like earlier canonical Egyptian novels, such as Taha Hussein's *The Days* (*al-Ayam*, 1926) or Tawfiq al-Hakim's *Diary of a Country Prosecutor* (*Yawmiyat na'ib fi al-aryaf*, 1937), *The Mountain* dramatizes the rift between the urban administration and the native inhabitants of the countryside: the investigator's allegiances, it is implicitly and explicitly stated, should be with the forces of reform rather than with the unruly, unbathed villagers. But as can be expected, the investigator has a change of heart and by the end of the novel he is won over to the villagers' cause and resigns from his position.

The novel is based on Ghanem's personal experience. After graduating from law school in 1944, he spent a number of years working, as does *The Mountain*'s protagonist, for the Investigation Bureau in the Ministry of Education, where he met fellow progressive writers Ahmad Baha' al-Din and 'Abd al-Rahman al-Sharqawi. And like the novel's protagonist, he was sent on a mission to Upper Egypt. The novel is based on a famous historical episode in which several of the period's central social concerns intersected and coalesced: from debates on population management, rural reform, and criminality; to statist engineering of a productive national labor force; through conflicting claims of patrimony over Egyptian antiquities and their associated profits.[23] In 1945, the world-renowned Egyptian architect Hassan Fathy was commissioned by the Egyptian Department of Antiquities to design a model village in order to house some seven thousand residents of Gurna (al-Qurna), a cluster of villages located among the tombs and archeological digs of the Theban Hills on the western bank of the Nile, opposite Luxor.[24] Fathy's model village, New Gurna, boasted modern facilities, community institutions, and a sustainable building style based in Nubian vernacular traditions, which Fathy envisioned as the birth of an Egyptian "national style." Marketed as a project of modernization and improvement, it aimed to remove the villagers from their so-called parasitic economic subsistence—an illicit economy that relied on the archeological and tourist industries—and integrate them into a productive national labor force.

The project, however, was never completed and the model village remained empty, primarily because the residents of Gurna refused to move. Writing his account of the events some twenty years later, Fathy denounced the villagers as tomb robbers who "had no intention of giving up their nice, profitable squalid houses in the cemetery with treasure waiting to be mined under their floors, to move to a new, hygienic, beautiful village away from the tombs."[25] Timothy Mitchell notes the irony of Fathy's project: it aimed to uproot villagers from their longstanding ways of life even as it was billed precisely as celebrating peasant traditions as emblems of Egyptian nationalism. It was the villagers' lawlessness and hygienic habits, Mitchell writes, that gave pretext to building the new village: "It was only by addressing the problems of the ignorance of the peasant and the absence of civilization that an architect interested in a program to create a modern, peasant vernacular could find an opportunity to work."[26]

New Gurna was only one among a series of state-sponsored civilizing projects that displaced villagers to new habitats in order to make them model national subjects, often justified by the perceived failure on the part of the villagers to labor and produce efficiently. This rationale points to a continuity between the extractive colonial regime and the reformist state project under Gamal Abdel Nasser.[27] Both are grounded in a dichotomous ideology of civilization, which Edward Said has associated with colonial practices of displacement:

> Among the supposed juridical distinctions between civilized and non-civilized peoples was an attitude toward land, almost a doxology about land, which non-civilized people supposedly lacked. A civilized man, it was believed, could cultivate the land because it meant something to him; on it, accordingly, he bred useful arts and crafts, he created, he accomplished, he built. For an uncivilized people, land was either farmed badly (i.e., inefficiently by Western standards) or it was left to rot. From this string of ideas, by which whole native societies who lived on American, African, and Asian territories for centuries were suddenly denied their right to live on that land, came the great dispossessing movements of modern European colonialism, and with them all the schemes for redeeming the land, resettling the natives, civilizing them, taming their savage customs, turning them into useful beings.[28]

Said outlines a capitalist-colonial ideology of settlement bound to ideals of productivity, underlying global histories of expansion, displacement, and extraction. A civilized and proper mode of settlement implies putting the land to productive use—inhabiting it in a *meaningfully productive* way. Uncivilized natives, in contrast, are improper inhabitants of the land and can always be moved to make room for more useful subjects or be resettled where they can finally be put to work. In Gurna, the misuse of the land's potential was specifically associated with the pharaonic artifacts buried under the villagers' homes. As Elliott Colla notes, Egyptian peasants were seen as the chief threat to ancient monuments, interfering with the modernist goals of preservation and acquisition, in both the British colonial narrative and Egypt's national enlightenment narrative.[29] Numerous studies of the ongoing efforts to resettle Gurna have underlined how claims of patrimony over Egyptian antiquities served as a vehicle for state-sponsored violence, in which "preservation of ancient monuments has taken precedence over the needs of the living," in the words of archaeologist Lynn Meskell.[30] Gurna's modest economic basis, relying on the industry that developed around the archeological sites, was deemed illicit and destructive profit rather than a productive use of the land and its resources.

The agent of this ideological apparatus in *The Mountain* is the urban, sophisticated government inspector. He is strikingly mobile, going from the city to the village, from the new Qurna to the old one, with little obstacle. Paradoxically, civilized settlement also civilizes movement: the political subject who is most mobile, who enjoys the most "freedom of movement," is the civilized (Westernized) urban citizen—a subject position that is most often tied to stability and sedentarism.[31] Because he is properly settled, the civilized subject is also the most legitimate and proper traveler—as tourist, scholar, businessman, humanitarian, or colonizer. Forms of movement *and* forms of settlement that do not emerge from the settled base of the civilized subject, such as the movement of colonized populations and refugees, their modern descendants, are vilified and proscribed.[32] This double structure, which conditions proper movement on proper settlement, illuminates the link between the non-European native and the European Jew, always improperly settled and displaceable within a structure of modern nation-states.[33] Lacking a meaningful relation to the land, the native and the Jews appear to live merely on its surface. Either too stagnant or too mobile, they are never sufficiently rooted to be able to properly move elsewhere. Their moves will always be an aberration or a threat, while their settlement is never fully legitimate.

LABOR WITHOUT PRODUCT

Narrated in the first person, *The Mountain* initially resembles a detective thriller, a heroic tale of dangers and adventures in the Upper Nile region. The narrator arrives at the village boasting the demeanor of a modern administrative official, repeatedly stating that he is entering a world "far from reality," familiar to him only from novels or the cinema.[34] His allegiances are initially with the agents of reform rather than with the unruly villagers, who are associated with danger and nihilist violence. Upon his arrival, however, nothing proceeds as planned, and the generic framework quickly crumbles in a process of self-reckoning and defeat. After seeing the village and meeting its people, all his ideas on social reform projects dissipate "like water evaporating from a pot over the flames."[35] If, as Samah Selim suggests, the literary framework of "an investigation" is a means to write an authoritative, conclusive narrative, *The Mountain* stages the metropolitan writer's loss of authorial voice: the narrator, Ghanem's double, eventually concedes his authority to the villagers' stories and accepts his painful marginality, submitting an empty dossier to his boss.[36]

Selim positions *The Mountain* within a tradition of Egyptian village novels and in the context of Egyptian committed realism of the 1950s, a progressive literary project engaged with interrogating the junctures of power and ideology in Egyptian society. Critical of elitist politics, progressive writers of the 1950s, such as Ghanem, ʿAbd al-Rahman al-Sharqawi, and Yusuf Idris, placed the oppressed Egyptian peasant as the historical subject at the center of an anticolonial Egyptian nationalism.[37] *The Mountain*, however, is an outlier among progressive village novels. It can hardly be read as a celebration or reclamation of the true productive forces of Egyptian society, as al-Sharqawi's *al-Ard* (*The Land*, 1953), the most iconic of the period's village novels, clearly is. The "people of the mountain," as they are known, explicitly differentiate themselves from agriculturalists, the dwellers of the plain. The Gurnawis are not *fallāḥīn* (farmers), and the productive value of their labor is questionable.[38] According to the government officials, it is parasitic: the Gurnawis subsist on the margins of the tourist industry around the archeological digs, making counterfeit pharaonic figurines and selling them to gullible tourists. And as the narrator eventually learns, their true pursuit is a futile and excruciating search for treasure in the mountain's depth. The prospect of waged labor in the construction of New Qurna looms as a threat of exploitation and loss of autonomy, but whereas in al-Sharqawi's *al-Ard*, the transition to wage labor means precarity and the loss of agricultural productivity, in *The Mountain*, it entails abandoning a mode of life that is explicitly nonproductive.

Unexpectedly, this nonproductivity fascinates the narrator and ushers his transformation. Initially fearful of visiting a village rumored to be full of saboteurs and bandits, soon after his arrival he begins to covet and idealize the villagers' life among the burial caves. His conversion to the villagers' cause is occasioned through a series of encounters that transform his trepidation into desire and identification. The first is with a young girl who wears her hair in the pharaonic style. This encounter echoes a famous scene in the opening chapter of *al-Ard*, in which a village girl mocks the romantic literary tropes that litter the speech of a city-educated boy who is trying to woo her.[39] Here, however, it is the narrator himself who rejects literary platitudes in favor of localized, naturalized similes when trying to describe the girl: "I cannot describe this girl by saying she was beautiful like the moon or gentle like a spring breeze." More truly, he continues, she was "compassionate [ḥanūna] like the green earth, flaring [fāʾira] like the summer sun, noble like a pharaonic queen."[40] This encounter evokes a common trope of the village novel, a class- and origin-traversing heterosexual love story, which Selim argues is the central allegorical vehicle for the consolidation of an idealized male national subject and the symbolic unification between the male intellectual and the rural woman as "the national feminine."[41] Here, however, this narrative trope is evoked only to be immediately rejected. The romantic option is abandoned as the narrator recognizes that he and the girl come from worlds too different for any real connection to form between them. What could he, an urbanite, understand of her needs and desires, and what could she understand of his? An insurmountable gap between them is acknowledged.

Nevertheless, this lack of common ground is overcome when the narrator finds a new object of desire that functions through a logic of gender identification rather than gender difference: Husayn ʿAli, a young man from the village. Husayn ʿAli tracks the narrator down as he is about to leave the village and invites him to spend the night there while he explains the villagers' position. Initially fearful of the powerful young man, the narrator quickly becomes fascinated by him. His interest in Husayn ʿAli, although not consciously sexual, is articulated in explicitly erotic terms: "A desire to challenge Husayn ʿAli possessed me. . . . His pride provoked me and his masculinity excited me [*kānat tastafizzni*] in spite of myself and demanded that I test him. . . . I wanted to test his masculinity because I wanted to touch it [*almushā*], to see it clear and exposed in front of me."[42] The desire to touch, witness, and experience Husayn ʿAli's masculinity quickly evolves into a desire to be, or be *like*, Husayn ʿAli. The erotic appeal is also an invitation to emulate this same masculine stance, a masculinity long lost to city dwellers, as the narrator laments (*al-Jabal*, 92). Whereas the heterosexual desire for the girl amplifies the differences between the village and the city and remains a fantasy, this homoerotic desire allows for identification and national unification. Husayn ʿAli provides a bridge by means of which the investigator can overcome the distance between these two social sites through a gendered code of homoerotic desire, concealing differences of class and status behind masculine identification.

The narrator's attraction to Husayn ʿAli inspires a humanized concept of the villagers, organized around a metaphor of depths. "These [mountain] people have such stores of humanity sedimented in their depths," he thinks, whereas the people of the city "have no deep feelings about anything. . . . How do we transport the mountain people's humanity to the city people without ruining it, and how do we convey the city's development and advancement without creating a void in the villager's depths, making them into empty, hollow souls?" (*al-Jabal*, 95). Sedimented, multilayered depth, as opposed to the superficiality of the aesthetic depictions or to the hollowness of the city, becomes a metonymy for humanity. It is also a reflection of the Gurnawis' mode of habitation, living and burrowing into the mountain. As darkness falls, Husayn ʿAli finally shares with the narrator the story of the villagers' persistent attachment to the mountain. The Gurnawis are immersed in an all-consuming search for an elusive pharaonic treasure hidden in the mountain's depth. This pursuit, passing from one generation to another, is dubbed with an idiosyncratic name among the villagers: not digging or burrowing, but *kaḥt*, a gerund meaning to scratch or scrape. The term highlights the absurdly strenuous futility of this gesture, a Sisyphean labor that produces nothing. Unlike digging (*ḥafr*), which denotes an excavation of depth, scraping is a slow process that focuses on surfaces, stripping them layer by layer in recursive repetition. More dramatically, the term *kaḥt* also denotes curettage, the scraping of the uterus to induce an abortion, a gesture that negates the production of life and of value. The villagers view *kaḥt* as an inevitability—more efficient methods of digging for the treasure are not even considered. It is a dangerous and almost always futile practice, claiming the lives and limbs of many villagers but rarely, if ever, yielding any finds. When the scrapers reach a dead end or a bottomless abyss, they simply start scraping at a new location. "A new *kaḥt*, a new tunnel, new victims, new spilled blood," the inspector thinks (*al-Jabal*, 133). *Kaḥt* is an exercise in futility to which the villagers are fatally committed. It is labor that is the opposite of both productive and reproductive futurity, a practice that is directed toward the past of buried ancestors rather than toward the future.[43]

Nevertheless, once he hears about *kaḥt* from Husayn ʿAli, the narrator realizes that "scraping is the only option, the only hope, for those that live on the mountain."[44] This claim has a materialist basis, since there are no clear sources of income in New Gurna, only exploitation. But the story of *kaḥt* also inspires a new profound transformation in the narrator—a new understanding of Husayn ʿAli, of the villagers, and of their labor that exceeds this economic analysis. In the narrator's eyes, Husayn ʿAli becomes an awe-inspiring force of nature; he "is actually the mountain itself . . . these natural views that surround me, the mountain and its caves, the desert and its sands, the sky and its stars, all these have no value [*lā qīma lahā*] without Husayn" (*al-Jabal*, 134).[45] The depth of the mountain and the depth of its people merge together. Husayn attributes the mountain with value and worth, but this is not the same extractive or productive value as the one established in the "doxology about land" that Said identifies. The value of the mountain is no longer found in the potential value of the hidden pharaonic gold, to be realized once it is unearthed, but rather in the fruitless, strenuous labor of *kaḥt*, which is bound to produce nothing, in the ongoing metonymic interaction with the people that live on it. Everything else, particularly the systems of value that uphold the narrator's life in Cairo, suddenly appears petty and pointless.

Learning of the Gurnawis' intimate communion with the mountain makes the narrator question the very law that he is supposed to represent. The law seeks to establish an extractive, productive relation between the villagers and their mountain, or between workers and profit-yielding commodities. The law views the villagers as thieves of antiquities, removable subjects that can be put to more productive ends, and sees *kaḥt* as a fanatic, ritualistic commitment to death. But for the Gurnawis, it is New Gurna, with its domed domiciles reminiscent of tombs, that is associated with a graveyard (*al-Jabal*, 67). The narrator's transformation establishes *kaḥt* as an alternate life practice removed from the prospect of productivity. The futile physical exertion of scraping becomes an end in and of itself, and its product-less drudgery becomes a parody of ideologies of productive labor.

After coming down from the mountain, shaken and transformed by the vision of a life governed by futile scraping, the narrator dreams a solution to the Gurnawis' predicament. In his dream, the villagers would stay on the mountain and allow the authorities access to extract the pharaonic treasures. Archeologists and tourists would then flock to the mountain, looking to spend money, and the villagers would be there to comply:

> The local women weave their beautiful mats, and the men sell their figurines. This is the true treasure [*al-kanz al-ḥaqīqī*] discovered by the people of the mountain. Their handiwork is the true treasure. These crafts are the true relics, they are not forgeries, because they are the fruit of their labor, the product of their work. . . .
>
> Labor [*al-'amal*] is the true treasure.
>
> I was carried away by my dream: The government would realize the need to build factories for figurines and textiles, in which the men and women of the mountain would work. New factories would be built . . . factories, which are the true treasure that they have been searching for all along. (*al-Jabal*, 156)

The villagers would be redeemed through work, a regime of industrial, unalienated labor replacing a deceptive treasure with a real one. This involves a significant conceptual shift in the status of the villagers' handcrafts: from counterfeits posing as degraded versions of original pharaonic artifacts to works of artistry and products of labor. Relying on traditional handcrafts is supposed to guarantee that the villagers' labor would remain authentic, nonalienated, and nonexploitative. The irony, however, is that the expansion of such practices to an economic basis entails the commodification of the villagers' output, industrially producing authentic handcrafts to satisfy the tourists' appetites.

The narrator soon dismisses his dream as an impossible fantasy for the simple reason that the government would never support such a plan.

This part of the novel takes place in 1947, and the critique is directed at the soon-to-be-toppled monarchy, a regime depicted as disconnected and decadent, embodied in the figure of an arrogant, ignorant, and debased princess who happens to visit Luxor at the same time as the narrator. *The Mountain*, published in 1957 at the height of Nasserism, eventually pays its tribute to the new revolutionary regime. On the novel's final page, the narration skips several years forward, and Nasser makes a brief cameo, featured in a news snippet detailing his visit to the archeological sites accompanied by the Indonesian president Sukarno, a gesture toward the utopian, developmentalist promises of Afro-Asian solidarities in the years following the Bandung Conference.[46] In drastic contrast to the villagers' humiliating encounter with the princess, Nasser sits down with the ʿ*umda*, the village chief, to eat oranges—a meeting of equals, which suggests that the villagers might see better days, perhaps even a factory, if the Nasserist regime lives up to its rhetoric.

Contemporary reviewers of the novel latched onto Ghanem's industrial vision as the novel's "deep message" ("*al-dars al-ʿamīq*"), a genuine solution to the problems of the peasantry, in line with the developmentalist state ideology of the period.[47] Yet, as Emily Drumsta remarks, even Ghanem himself, in later years, regretted the stark didacticism and explicitness of some parts of the novel.[48] The narrator's dream appears as a blunt concession to the productivist ethos of the developmentalist state, and is at odds with the narrative and formal logic that guided the novel up to this point. The dream—a fantasy solution that solves nothing—divulges that the fundamental tension of the novel is not the much-commented-upon conflict between the city and the country or between the alienated urban writer and the authentic peasants. Instead, at the core of the novel's formal instability is the discord between the narrator's erotic fascination with the villagers' utterly futile exertions—the ethos of *kaḥt*—and the supposed solution to the villagers' predicament, a redemptive vision of productive labor. To an extent, this tension is emblematic of what Omnia El Shakry calls the "central contradiction of national identity within Egyptian colonial society—at the same time that [the peasants] were localized by the nationalist elite as the repository of cultural authenticity, they were also demarcated as a locus of backwardness to be reformed and reconstituted as modern moral subjects of the nation-state."[49] The villagers are romanticized and idealized only to be marked as the object of reform that will fundamentally change them. Within this paradoxical structure, the villagers' *kaḥt* operates as a kind of a "vanishing mediator,"[50] an ideological object of identification that enables the narrator's transition from affiliation with the government to affiliation with the villagers, eventually leading him to the Nasserist vision of productive industrialization.

This fundamental tension reflects an unsolved anxiety in the novel regarding literature's productive capacities. If *The Mountain* is a Künstlerroman, or a novel about how Fathi Ghanem (the author and the character) left his government inspector job and became a writer, then its narrative negotiations of labor and its ends are also a means to consider the work of the writer: What kind of work does the writer do and where does he fit in the national productivist ethos? What does he produce, if he is productive at all? After hearing about *kaḥt* from Husayn ʿAli, the narrator realizes that he is no longer an investigator: "I forgot my role as an investigator and I forgot the meaning of my job, and I no longer understood its significance in this place."[51] He submits an empty dossier to his boss and eventually quits his job. Presumably, instead of writing an investigative report about the mountain, he wrote a novel—the novel *The Mountain* that the reader is now holding in their hand. In the novel, the writer finds himself mesmerized by labor's other—by exertion without product and, by extension, by a vision of literature that is not valued according to its productive ends but instead is parasitic, subsisting on the productive economy's margins. Within the affective economy of this novel, *kaḥt* never truly vanishes. It persists as the catalyst that leads the narrator to his new writing career, as a specter of an alternate model of nonproductive labor, and as a metaphor for writing itself.

The novelist's work is different from that of the investigator. The investigator discovers that the mountain cannot be investigated, recorded, or solved; it overwhelms the very categories and distinctions upon which the investigator relies in order to create a coherent narrative of criminals and innocents, the uncultivated and the civilized, depravity and reform. The writer, however, approaches the mountain differently, through the practice of *kaḥt*: scraping slowly and blindly until hitting an empty pyre, then retreating and starting again at a new point. This nonproductive, self-contained scraping becomes the task of the writer: unlike the investigator, who is bound to a narrative of improvement, of solving crimes and reinstating order, the writer embraces the ongoing, laborious act of scraping, which is an end in itself and not integrated into the pursuit of the social good. Against the demand to integrate literature into a productive national economy, *The Mountain* manifests a not-very-hidden desire for writing to meander and produce nothing, to futilely scrape at the tomes of the past rather than excavate them, to labor yet not be put to work.

DEPTHS AND SURFACES

In *The Mountain*, a productive model of writing for social reform is nearly overwhelmed by the specter of an alternative model of writing as scraping and of nonproductive labor. Brenner's prose similarly stages a struggle between two modes of settlement and of writing: one committed to the productive ethos of Zionism and the other overwhelmed by the attractions of futility. Read in terms of Said's doxology of land, Zionism is a self-civilizing mission aimed to solve the problem of improper Jewish mobility by establishing a proper mode of national settlement in Palestine. Settlement "in one's own land," as the Zionist slogan goes, was supposed to solve the problem of Jewish movement. Early twentieth century psychopathology and medical race studies intersected in the figure of the Jew, who was allegedly brimming with neurotic symptoms.[52] Zionism was supposed to solve both problems, the Jew's unproductive migration in space and the impulsive, compulsive, unproductive gestures of his body, finally creating a healthy, modern "New Jew" who is both properly settled and can properly move.[53] "Nerves" explicitly stages the connection between involuntary corporeal nervous movements and the unsettled body, what Dana Olmert has called the "geographic nervousness" of Brenner's protagonists.[54]

The title of the novella encapsulates a prevalent mode of relating to the body in Brenner's prose as well as in the scholarship dedicated to him. Nerves are those cable-like fibers that make up our body's communication system, but colloquially, the term refers to a range of manifest symptoms of a person's mental state: the expression "it's just nerves" is never just nerves, but points to the existence of "deeper," more complex problems. This association goes back to the early days of modern medicine, when neuroses were defined as "disorders of sense and motion" that could not be attributed to physiological causes and, instead, were associated with the mysterious work of the nervous system.[55] With the development of psychoneurotic and psychoanalytic theory, the origins of neurosis underwent a process of abstraction, from the movement of organs throughout the body and the flow of various fluids, to the obstructed flow of energy and eventually psychic dynamic drives. Impulsive movements, such as scratching or twitching, were reconfigured as physical and involuntary *symptoms* of a malfunctioning psychic system that could be "tuned back" into ordered control.

As a rich critical tradition eloquently attests, Brenner's nervous protagonists and rhetoric invite psychological and psychoanalytical readings.[56] Attending to "the talking body," this tradition reads the expressions and gestures of Brenner's characters as clues to conflicting psychological dynamics or as hysterical symptoms revealing the truth of the psyche. These dynamics are often then traced back to Brenner himself, a famously charismatic, tortured, and sexually conflicted character in Zionism's self-narrated origin story.[57] It is important not to overlook, however, that Brenner's protagonists tend to talk just as explicitly and knowingly of the meaning of their symptoms as the critics do. His characters track their own psychologies, providing their own relentless self-analysis and leaving no dark corner of their psyche undocumented or accounted for. The unnamed protagonist of "Nerves" repeatedly identifies his actions or gestures with psychological symptoms: "These too are nerves!" he comments on his own speech.[58] Hefetz, the protagonist of *Breakdown and Bereavement*, identifies his physical symptoms with sexual and gendered anxieties that have to do with masculine models of virility and productivity. The characters' confessional speech brilliantly corroborates and consciously acknowledges the hysterical pleasure of self-torment and the painful symptoms of a repressed sexuality. In the meta-poetic article "The Erets Israeli Genre and Its Accouterments" ("ha-Janer ha-erets yisra'eli ve-avizarehu"), Brenner claims that his belletristic writing aims to record the "psychological depths of characters" and that literature should be the "revelation of an inner life."[59] It should come as no surprise that psychoanalytic readings "fit" with Brenner so well—his texts already stage their own symptoms *as well as* their interpretations. If Brenner's texts have an "unconscious," or a realm that should be mined for nonmanifest meaning, it is not lurking at that deep abyss of the psyche, which is, after all, unfailingly disclosed by the characters and exposed for all to see, but is rather on the surface of the text, at that porous boundary where the fictional body rubs against language and against the world. As tempting as it is to follow Brenner's characters on their tormented self-explorations, there is some truth to the poet Hayim Nahman Bialik's 1909 critique of Brenner:

> The tragic—I don't give much credit to the tragic when it declares and celebrates itself as such. Regarding most of our Prometheuses, who, like cranes, shriek that the vultures are pecking at their hearts, one must suspect that they are being bitten by fleas: Those sorrows of the world, burdening them like an ugly hump . . . their origins do not lie in the deep abyss [*omka detehoma raba*] of the world's decline, or with Adam's original sin, but can be found somewhere much closer.[60]

The psychological torments of Brenner's characters, Bialik reminds us, are not a symptom but a literary trope, an authorial and authoritative effect. Rather than focus on this excavation of depths, it is worthwhile to notice the fleabites—the itchiness and irritation, the filth and disgust—that pervade Brenner's texts. Brenner's disgusting is not the deep, disturbing abject that Julia Kristeva defines, the preoedipal basis that the symbolic order must disavow.[61] The disgusting does not arouse existential terror but irritation. Reading Brenner can amount to a mild sense of not-unpleasant disgust, which Bialik compared to eating "smoked herring with honey."[62] Staying "much closer" to the skin, as Bialik recommends, means turning attention away from the tormented Brennerian psyche and staying with the body's surface interactions and sensations as a record of experience, without reading them as symptoms of psychic anguish. It means focusing on the Brennerian affect of nervous irritation, evoked in the readers by the excessive, chatty verbosity of his prose. Finally, it means shifting the focus away from the framed story in "Nerves" to the frame, from a dynamic, major narrative of journeys and destinies to static narrative moments of minor description and embodiment.

The Zionist solution to the Jew's nervous predicament is repeatedly expressed in Brenner's texts through a double appeal to depths—both the depths of the soul and the depths of the earth. The protagonist of "Nerves," for example, tries to explain what drew him to Palestine in characteristically self-questioning terms, which mock the pathos of the words as they are being uttered. "Perhaps what quivered in my 'depths' was yearning for a shadow of a *homeland*, which as a Jew I had never known," he suggests. "What do you think? Maybe a trace of the hope to find a grasp, some hold, maybe to suckle, *there*, in that picturesque corner of Asia."[63] The depths of the soul yearn for the depths of the earth: for a deep-reaching network of roots that grasp at the land, suckling (*linok*, a verb used for a nursing baby) and absorbing its nutrients. This symbiotic relationship is based on a doubled evocation of depths—of the psyche and of the land. A similar image is evoked in Brenner's longer novel *Breakdown and Bereavement*, composed a decade later. Rambling in feverish madness, the novel's protagonist Hefetz, a young man very similar to the unmoored protagonist of "Nerves," tells a shaggy-dog story of a "poor Italian [who] loved life, and even more than he loved it, he felt rooted in it, rooted just like an onion. The only problem was that here, in Palestine, he hadn't seen a single onion. Not one farm grew them."[64] The many-layered onion is an analogy for the "deeply structured" settled subject, rooted deep in the earth. In both examples, a deep psyche corresponds to an access to and a rooting in the very depths of the land.

This "depths to depths" model remains an unattainable fantasy for the Zionist settler—as he notes, he finds no onions growing in Palestine. At its core, this is a fantasy of nativeness, a natural rootedness in a particular place. Ghanem's investigator thought he found it in the people of the mountain, although there was no symbiotic or nourishing suckling there, only *kaḥt*—futile labor that produces nothing and a hollow, empty mountain. In "Nerves," deep settlement—a form of native belonging—is written as an unattained desire evoked and denied through a carefully constructed series of landscape descriptions rich with biblical allusions and linguistic ambiguities. The bible was supposed to be the Zionist settler's guidebook to native belonging, a textual medium for navigating the landscape of Erets Yisra'el. Unlike other colonial settlers, for whom the encounter with the colonial landscape always posed a crisis of representation in its strangeness, the Hebrew writer had the biblical text as a unique frame of reference for comprehending and approaching the Palestinian landscape.[65] The bible promised the means for settlers to be returning natives. The protagonist echoes this logic when he tries to explain the vision of Palestine that attracted him: "*There*, in that picturesque corner of Asia in which Bedouin, the great grandchildren of Abraham the Hebrew, pitch their tent to this day and bring to the well real camels as once did his bondsman Eliezer.... *There* ... I mean: *here* ... ah, let me cross over and see that goodly land, its fair mountains and the Lebanon."[66] The tone is self-consciously ironic, as the speaker both confesses his desire and retreats from it. The biblical narrative was supposed to forge an undisturbed continuity between the Jewish presence in Canaan, in preexilic times, and the "returning" settlers. To this end, the Bedouins (the local Palestinians) are cast as biblical figures suspended in time: not threatening and foreign natives, but emblems of one's "own" Jewish past. This biblical structure is quickly acknowledged as a fantasy ("more to the point, where third-and fourth-generation children of Jewish moneylenders to Poles are learning to follow the plow," the protagonist cynically acknowledges), but this passage admits to further failures of the project to "arrive" at the homeland. The homeland is always located *there* rather than *here*, in an absent site of yearning, and the speaker must repeatedly remind himself that this distance had actually been traversed. The quote concluding the passage, from Deuteronomy 3:25, is borrowed from Moses, who never crossed the Jordan River. Like him, the settler is still waiting to cross over and arrive.

The bible could be used as a Zionist guide not only by virtue of its recognizable narratives, sites, and characters but also by means of its Hebrew language: the revival of Hebrew as a spoken tongue was an inextricable part of the Zionist settlement project and its vision of a new native Jew. Before Brenner decided to leave Europe, he received a letter from his friend Yaakov Rabinovitch recommending that he go to Palestine because "there is only one corner where a Hebrew world is constructed—Erets Yisra'el . . . the place whose language is spoken by children."[67] It is not only that Erets Yisra'el is the site of a unique social experience—a purely Hebrew community—but that Hebrew *is* the language of the place, as if there was some intrinsic relation, an immediate link, between the land and the Hebrew language.

Ariel Hirschfeld has demonstrated how "Nerves" is "a journey in language," a metapoetic treatise on language and the failed correspondence between "words and things."[68] Already in the novella's first sentence, the aspiration for a native and natural correlation among settler, land, and language is disappointed: "A smell of *parfum* rose around us—from the low *shitot* bushes, or 'mimosa' as others call it, at the slope of the Hebrew colony in the Land of Judea."[69] This is first and foremost a verbal landscape, drawing awareness, by its own reservations, to the fact that it is landscape mediated through words and names. The excess of foreign words, such as perfume and mimosa, immediately undermine the phrase "Hebrew colony." Two different names are offered for the surrounding bushes—the first is the Hebrew-biblical one, recently revived in a project of classification of biblical flora and fauna, and the second is the Latin term, the one commonly used. The link between signifier and signified is revealed not as natural and unified but as random and multiple, like the artificial smell of perfume. The land does not speak Hebrew and neither do the characters. "A bird, whose Hebrew name neither of us knew, flew brilliantly by, its multicolored wings green against the sky-blue," notes the narrator, underscoring their linguistic alienation ("Nerves," 37).

Arrival is not simply impossible, it is forbidden and dangerous. One of the sources of the protagonist's torment of during his journey is his overwhelming desire toward one of his travel companions, a girl of about eleven. Consuming this desire is inconceivable. The figure of "the shore" (*ḥof*) becomes another symbol of the danger of arrival or consummation of desire. The shore is first mentioned in the context of a collateral event that had left a lasting mark on the protagonist. One of his fellow immigrants at a Jewish boarding house in London, who has been separated from his family, commits suicide in his room one night without any prior indication. In the morning, he is found in "perfect tranquility" (*mirgaʿa*), having crossed to a "different shore" ("Nerves," 42). From here on, the shore, perfect tranquility, and death are bound together, each bearing the other's traces. "From shore to shore . . . he came to the shore . . . and when would I?" wonders the protagonist. And when the protagonist finally arrives at the shore of Haifa, he cries emotionally, "I felt whisperings of glory in my heart. Tranquility! Good!" Rather than marking a triumphal arrival, the unusual word *mirgaʿa* evokes the desperate suicide in London. Arrival at the shore is not the beginning of a new life but rather life's end. The end goal of the journey and the promise of settlement are synonymous with death. This structure readily lends itself to a Freudian reading: the settler's arrival at the shore is imagined as an ecstatic, erotically charged encounter, where pleasure comes dangerously close to death. Similarly, Freud identifies the death drive—the desire to return to a static state—at the very climax of sexual passion: the culmination of erotic desire is deathlike stasis.[70] Arrival is synonymous with stasis and with death and is therefore inconceivable, necessitating a compulsive departure only in order to return again (as Hefetz departs and returns in *Breakdown and Bereavement*).

In his critical essays and in his political career, Brenner insisted that agricultural settlement and the creation of a new, healthy, civilized Hebrew subject are the only hope for the Jewish diaspora.[71] Why, then, does the literary text evoke the desired possibility of Jewish settlement and then depicts its failure? Hannan Hever addresses this question in his reading of "The Erets Israeli Genre and Its Accouterments," Brenner's programmatic essay referenced earlier in this chapter. Reflecting on Brenner's "prohibition" on generic or holistic depiction of life in the Zionist colonies in Palestine, as if they were established villages that had been there for decades, Hever argues that Brenner posits literature as a site of utopian tension: to recruit the fictional text to the Zionist project, the project should not be depicted as realized. Instead, it should be portrayed as a reality that does not *yet* exist: the literary text must sustain the dynamic desire for its realization precisely by depicting the utopian ideal as lacking.[72] In other words, literary texts must continue to illustrate the ongoing necessity of the political project of Hebrew settlement because an aesthetic "arrival" at this desired ideal is equivalent to its conclusion—to stasis or death. Hever thus provides a tidy solution that reconciles Brenner's fragmentary and defeatist aesthetics with his activist and optimist political opinions, resolving the seeming contrast between the characters' tormented psychology and the utopian political project in which Brenner is involved.[73]

Nevertheless, this solution leaves much of the text unaccounted for. What emerges if the scenic descriptions of the colony and its surroundings are read for what they are rather than what they are not? For the present relationship with the land that they depict rather than the projected relationship that they fail to depict? Framing the dramatic and torturous journey narrative, these scenes comprise a surplus that escapes the neat economy that joins the aesthetics of tormented psychic conflict to the ideology of settlement as a deep symbiotic relationship. The descriptions of the settlers' and the colony's present are not merely descriptions of a failure, but they gesture towards an alternative mode of habitation in lieu of the deep, symbiotic embeddedness of the roots and the onion. These static scenes of presentness chart sensorial input, registering embodied relations between the characters and their surroundings that remain only skin deep: picking up a blade of grass and mulling it between the fingers, getting too close to a prickly pear. This mode of inhabiting the colony and its landscape can be called a "settlement on the surface." It replaces the desire for depths with a dispersed network of erotic relations and intensities.

This aesthetic emerges in the descriptions of the Hebrew colony itself, to which the two companions eventually return. Instead of the detailed visual account of the landscape and the changing colors of the sky that dominated the opening sections of the novella, this section is a soundscape inhabited by shadows and silhouettes, a record of detached voices and bodies. I quote at length to capture the web of both erotic and antagonistic relations mapped here:

> A bareheaded adolescent girl stepped out of one of the colony's houses and crossed the narrow street, humming the words of the poet's "folk song" to a pleasant Arab melody
>
>> Pretty golden bird, fly far away
>> Find me a husband for my wedding day.
>
> From a courtyard opposite a voice that could have been either a man's or a woman's rose through the night air: "*Rukh, rukh min hun! S'tezikh tsugetsheppet?*"—the voices collided. The little colony's dark synagogue looked down on us with its broad but dark windows. Beneath them some local citizens stood discussing their affairs as proprietors. "It's time I fired Ahmed," one of them said. "I've never seen such a thief in my life." This sentence rolled on until it came to a dark ditch by the side of the street, from which suddenly appeared the silhouettes of two young workers, one in a costume of dark cloth, the other in torn linen pants, a shirt and completely barefoot. From somewhere came the words, "Innkeeper, here's seven piasters," and the lamenting song on two Zionists who would not sit together. The notes quivered until interrupted by a soft Polish-Jewish voice that said: "Tomorrow it will be exactly four months since I arrived in this country." "And how many months will it be since you've been out of work?" laughed the second one, Russian by his accent and anarchic in his demeanor, thoroughly enjoying himself.
> The evening endured.[74]

The Hebrew colony emerges here in a multiplicity of languages and hierarchies, caught up in a daily routine. A sentence rolls until it hits two shadowy silhouettes: the passage's immediate political concern is "*kibush ha-'avoda*" (the conquest of labor), the demand made by members of the second *aliya* that the landowners in the Zionist colonies hire only Jewish laborers. At its center is a contrast between "Ahmed," the specter of cheap and supposedly unreliable Arab labor preferred by the landowners, and the unemployed Zionist newcomers. At the same time, the passage provides a window to the "Hebrew colony's" culture in the form of a mini playlist. Both songs mentioned in this passage were very recently composed. The young girl hums "Between the Tigris and the Euphrates" ("Beyn nehar prat u-nehar hidekel"), a poem composed by H. N. Bialik and published in 1906 in a cycle of four poems titled "Folk Songs."[75] Brenner puts the word "folk song" between quotes, highlighting the irony: Do folk songs have a poet? Should they not originate from the timeless origins of the "folk"? Bialik drew on Yiddish folk songs for this cycle, and in "Between the Tigris and the Euphrates," he dresses the Eastern European setting in the garb of an Oriental-biblical fantasy of palm trees and golden birds. This faux-folkish poem was paired, in Palestine, to an Arab melody and quickly became popular.[76] What is the folk from which this amalgam originates? The "lament" is also an ironic evocation: the song "Ten Zionists," composed by the satirist Kadish Yehuda Leib Silman after a popular Yiddish song, is a comic elegy about diminishing Zionist numbers.

This scene also constructs a set of hybrid uncertain forms and figures that evoke a discrete sensuality grounded in the gestures of routine. Against the bareheaded girl's song rises a voice of uncertain gender, speaking in two languages: "Go away! [in Arabic], why are you touching this [in Yiddish]?" The ambivalent gender of the speaker is directly related to their ambivalent linguistic identity, positioned between Yiddish and Arabic. Yiddish in this period was imagined as endowed with feminine qualities—weakness, impurity, or unproductively—especially against the masculine Hebrew.[77] Arabic, on the other hand, was associated with a native masculinity desired by many of the settlers. Intermingling, however, is not positioned only as a threat but is neutralized by an understated and queered erotic undercurrent, opening with a bare head and ending with a bare foot. The acoustic scene is located at the point where language is no longer measured against national accomplishments. And if the story of the journey was structured as an erotic quest of the male settler toward a forbidden feminized land—to penetrate its shore and then die—here the erotic objects are scattered, charting a diversity of desires and unregulated pleasures. Finally, instead of complete tranquility (*mirga'a*), the colony is a continuous formal movement of bodies merging and breaking up again: Hebrew poem and Arab melody, man and woman, voice into shadows, shadows into silhouettes. This is an ongoing, vectorless movement that has no utopian vision beyond itself.

This mode of writing aligns with what Dina Berdichevsky has called Brenner's essayistic style: reflective, impressionistic writing that she associates both with a Jewish migratory and unsettled position and with a parasitic relation to established genres.[78] The novella concludes with such a nonemphatic sketch: the two companions return to their inn and join the host family as they set up the table for dinner, discussing various illnesses and errands. "All was as before. They smoked, they yawned, drank coffee, and ate pickled herring."[79] This passage could be read as another instance of Brenner's negative aesthetics, postponing the utopian-romantic realization of productive becoming of native and homeland. Yet such an interpretation forces tension into a scene of daily calm. The passive movements of routine, which are perhaps slightly repulsive but all too familiar, hint at a mode of settlement that is not caught up in the psychological drama of forbidden arrival or realization. Although this idle static mode only briefly appears in "Nerves," it is further developed in *Breakdown and Bereavement*.

THE SCRATCHING SUBJECT

Breakdown and Bereavement (*Shkhol ve-khishalon*), published in 1920, can be read as a sequel to "Nerves."[80] Like the protagonist of "Nerves," *Breakdown and Bereavement*'s Hefetz is a young Zionist settler suffering from a nervous condition, which in his case develops into periods of psychosis that require hospitalization. In the opening scene of the novel, he collapses while working in the fields and seeks medical attention in Jerusalem. Hefetz does not return to the colony after his mental and physical health improves but stays with his relatives in Jerusalem: his uncle Reb Yosef and his two daughters, the young and beautiful Miryam and the older, sour Esther, with whom Hefetz develops a painful relationship anchored in repulsion and self-contempt. *Breakdown* is concerned with the possibility of Jewish settlement and habitation both existentially and politically, moving from the Zionist agricultural colony to the midst of what is called "*ha-yeshuv ha-yashan*," the "old" Jewish population of Palestine, which has little investment in the Zionist project. It is a novel about homes and houses in the most mundane sense of the word, obsessively tracking the real estate market of old Jerusalem: who moved where and with whom, which building was purchased by what estate, and who remained homeless in this process. The protagonist Hefetz, always unsettled, reliant on the support of others, and full of self-derision, contrasts himself directly with the "homeowners," imagining their scorn of a person such as himself:

> If some respectable homeowner or poet of beauty and high ideals (the two were not as far apart as seemed at first glance) were to know what I was thinking at this moment, he would surely look the other way. He would sniff categorically and say in a single breath, "How cynical!" "How ugly!" "How disgusting!" and he would be right. Homeownership and beauty are always on the right. He, Hefetz, the dross of the human race, was in no position to argue.[81]

Homeownership, or a proper mode of habitation and settlement, is also the basis for proper aesthetics: *baʿaley ha-bayit* (the homeowners) have not only a grasp in the world but also a mandate on the concepts of beauty and truth. Hefetz's own suffering, however, cannot enjoy the poetic veil of melancholy because of his existential homelessness. Instead, he must accept his place as "the dross of the human race," relegated to the realm of the disgusting.

Breakdown is probably the most disgusting of Brenner's texts, or the text that makes the most use of the aesthetics of disgust. While composing the first draft of *Breakdown* in 1913, Brenner was also writing his large critical essay on the writer Sholem Y. Abramovich (known as Mendele Mocher Sforim, Mendele the Book Peddler), "Self-Assessment in the Three Volumes," and Mendele's grotesque depiction of peddlers and beggars in the Jewish Eastern European towns of the previous century seems to have penetrated Brenner's own prose. *Breakdown* is the most "mendelesque" of Brenner's works, full of "old-style" Jews. The residents of Jerusalem are vividly and excessively described as badly dressed, unwashed, petty, narrow-minded, and particularly idle and unproductive. The disgusting figures prominently in the relationship between Hefetz and Esther, whose moments of physical intimacy are replete with belches, foul smells, and evocations of rotting corpses. Finally, the disgusting is present in Hefetz's own repeated gestures of self-loathing and flagellation.

How are we to read the disgusting in this text? Brenner himself assigned a particular historical role to the disgusting in Mendele's literature, which he read as truthfully mimetic, a stance that more than anything else reveals Brenner's acceptance of anti-Semite physical and moral stereotypes of East European Jewry. Mendele, Brenner maintains, portrays the condition of the diaspora Jew as it is: morally and aesthetically repulsive, the two categories inseparable: "We are ridiculous and lowly because we are weak, and thus not beautiful, and thus immoral!"[82] The historical role of Mendele's literature, he explains, is to provide brutally honest self-assessment. Only by recognizing and reflecting the depraved condition of the Jew can the Jew aspire to overcome this condition. The literary disgusting, Brenner maintains, is a denouncement of the historical conditions of the present, ushering the utopian desire for "different Jews" that must come in the future.[83] But does this verdict hold true in Brenner's novel (let alone in Mendele's)?[84] As in "Nerves," the surplus of disgust and irritation in *Breakdown and Bereavement* exceeds the economy of negative utopianism, establishing a parallel static model of nonproductive and nervous movement that is about inhabiting the present rather than subjecting it to the demand to labor for the future.[85]

One of the most agitated scenes of the novel takes place in the courtyard of the Jerusalem hospital, which is "filled to overflow with the sighs and groans of the ill and the afflicted, the indigent and in need, invalids on crutches and in bandages."[86] The suffering of the ill is reduced to its auditory secretions, narrated through the disturbance it causes to those that must encounter it. Hefetz listens to the invalids' conversations, taking in the suffering that surrounds him, but remains indifferent—he feels nothing. The narration weaves in and out of his thoughts, as both he and the world about him become petrified: "Nothing. The breeze blew through the yard of the hospital, the stones lay idly about. The world was turned to stone. *Stone.* It was all one" (*Breakdown*, 32). It is in this ossified setting, among individuals floundering in petty gossip and schadenfreude, sharing tales of bureaucratic incompetence, slobbering and beating their chest—it is here among the most repulsive of human specimen—that Hefetz declares, "I have become a Jerusalemite." And he goes on to explain: "Now I'll stand around and do nothing [*holekh batel*]. Or rather, I'll sit [*yoshev batel*]" (*Breakdown*, 32). Hefetz's new condition mimics the petrified Jerusalem around him, as he transitions from active to passive participle. The name Hefetz itself means "a thing" or "an object," a passive dumb entity. From a *poʻel*, or a worker, a word that also means an active subject in the grammatical sense, Hefetz becomes a passive object (*ḥefets*).[87] This transition marks the difference from the active worker's form of settlement—*hityashvut*, a reflexive active verb that denotes a continuing action—to the passive sitting (*yoshev batel*) of the Jews of Jerusalem. From a settler (*mityashev*) he becomes a sitter (*yoshev*).

However, the embrace of idle sitting does not imply an end of movement. Instead, Hefetz's movement becomes compulsive and nonproductive:

> What an ugly way to suffer... in the book of Job the Leper it is written: "And he took a potsherd to scrape himself with." ... Only I am not Job: I have no complaints against God. In fact, I have no God. I have nothing to do with God. And even if I could complain—I'm not complaining and I don't wish to protest. I'm not Job. And I don't sit in the ashes either, but in refuse, in the garbage of my own ugly suffering. Only I don't let go of the potsherd. I can't stop scratching. Yes, a potsherd is probably the one thing I can't do without.[88]

Hefetz, always ready to pity himself, quotes from the Book of Job (2:8), comparing himself to its protagonist. But despite his compulsive inclination toward suffering, he recognizes that the analogy to Job must fail. Hefetz is removed from the drama of faith because his faith is long gone, and he has no one with whom to plead his case. Even Job's mound of ashes, which evokes a ritual of repentance and mourning (Job 2:2), is replaced by a pile of garbage, a symbol of suffering that is repulsive and refused. The only attribute of the original Job that remains is the gesture of scratching, which Hefetz fully appropriates as a futile and repulsive compulsion.

Because it is associated with succumbing to a desire, scratching is often accompanied by a sense of failure or shame, and is considered a lazy and superficial mode of attending to a symptom rather than searching for deep cause. It is a form of immediate attention to the way the skin is irritated and aroused by the encounter with the world. The skin is a "locus of some of the worst forms of the disgusting"—a bearer of disease, deformities, and old age.[89] Hefetz begins to scratch when he accepts passivity, immobility, and idleness—when he accedes to the inertia of Jerusalem life and abandons the productive life of agricultural and nationalist labor.

There are, as in the above examples, two ways of reading this scene. The first would be to read it in line with the negative aesthetic theory that Brenner developed to read Mendele. This reading would deem it to be a condemnation of Jewish life in Jerusalem, unproductive and parasitic, attending only to the most basic and visceral demands of the body, and illustrating, by virtue of its excessive disgusting and negative elements, the urgent need for a Zionist revival. This could have been a satisfying reading were this scene not repeated, with some variation, at the very conclusion of the novel, thereby offering a markedly different interpretation to the abject gesture of scratching.

The protagonist of the repeated scene is Haim, Hefetz's older relative. The entire bereaved family, who had just lost several of its members as well as its Jerusalem home, had come to Tiberias in the hope of improving Reb Yosef's failing health. Haim goes in the morning to sit at the shore of the Sea of Galilee when the image of water and ships suddenly transforms, behind his closed eyes, to a landscape of stone: "Out on the water the mast of the single boat that sailed from Tiberias to the station, where one set out for Jerusalem, flashed with like gravel stones. The craft rode evenly on the surface like the Jerusalemite guesthouse on its chapel of rocks."[90] Jerusalem, once again here depicted as a petrified "stony" city, seems to appear, magically floating, on the water of the Sea of Galilee. The gravel and stones evoke the scene at the hospital, where Hefetz saw the world turn to stone before his eyes. But while Hefetz was jeering at the passivity of the Jerusalemites, the scene at the shore of the Sea of Galilee develops as an ode to passivity and static reflection. Haim, lying in a ditch dug out by Arab merchants, lets his thoughts wander, reflecting that "clothes wore out quickly in Palestine because of the sweat, so it was best to lie quietly and not tear them" (*Breakdown and Bereavement*, 309). Following this thought, he lies back and watches as the Arab merchants return, take off their cloaks, and jump into the water. Haim watches the "strong, swarthy, muscular bodies of the swimmers in the distance" with delighted fascination, but then a "queer inexplicable notion" comes to his mind:

> In the mikveh, he thinks, they couldn't swim either, not even in the summer. An odd smile spread over his cheeks as the queer inexplicable notion flashed through his aging mind. In his eyes there appeared what might have been a vision of mild retribution at the thought that somewhere there were waters, un-grand waters, the waters of the mikveh, in which even the Bedouin would have no advantage over his brother or himself. . . . One didn't drown if one was frightened of the water. . . . People like them never drowned. People like them kept alive. (*Breakdown*, 309)

The absurdity of the idea of swimming in the mikveh, the Jewish ritual bath, makes Haim smile, though he still finds comfort knowing that the strong, native Bedouin swimmers, who appear to be the embodiment of virility, can have no advantage over the Jews in this confided Jewish space. Furthermore, he reasons, those who do not swim also do not drown; they stay alive—a notion that his name, *ḥayim* (life), underlines. With this pleasant realization and feeling of well-being seeping through him, Haim picks up a pebble and, putting it under his shirt, begins scratching and scratching with great gusto (*Breakdown*, 310).

This scene reenacts the incident in the hospital courtyard but redeems it. It evokes the same obsessive scratching that Hefetz succumbed to earlier, but in this instance, scratching is a gratifying gesture, a pleasurable abandonment to the sensations of the skin that accompanies Haim's surprising espousal of his and his brother's passivity and weakness. Scratching his back with great pleasure, Haim embodies the figure of the old Jew, the one who suffices with the water of the mikveh and has no need to jump into the great oceans of the world. And with this comes a realization that concludes a book full of meaningless and unnecessary deaths: those who are frightened of the water, who stay away from the great seas, do not drown; they are the ones who stay alive. And what could one wish for in life beyond the undeniable pleasure of scratching one's back with a pebble?

This scene is also strikingly similar to the quiet settlement scene concluding "Nerves," which I have called a "surface settlement" because of its focus on bare skin and surface interactions between sounds and bodies. Both scenes conclude turbulent and resoundingly conflictual texts with open-ended calmness and a moment of idleness. In both, such calm is intertwined with the subdued presence of illicit and dispersed eroticism, as it is in the case of *The Mountain*'s inspector's homoerotic desire for the masculinity of Husayn ʻAli. Haim's gaze at the bare-chested Arab swimmers parallels the song of the bareheaded girl, and in both cases, the erotic dimension of the encounter is present and a network of desires is recognized, but neither generates any action. Finally, the repetitive, obsessive gesture of scratching is a form that remains on the surface. Rather than striving for a symbiotic, constitutive relation at the depths, like the suckling roots or the multilayered onion, contact with the earth takes place at the surface, at the pleasurable but utterly nonproductive encounter of the scratching pebble with the skin. And rather than approaching *land*, as a fertile resource to be owned, cultivated, or sanctified, scratching is eventually about *dirt*: dirt that gathers under the fingernails and on the skin and can easily be carried away or dusted off.

IDLENESS AND INDECISION

Can those various voices and models of settlement be reconciled? *The Mountain*, "Nerves," and *Breakdown and Bereavement* all respond to the problem of the stuck, idle, and filthy native/Jew with two models of settlement. The first model corresponds to the symbolic, productive economy of the nation. In Ghanem's *The Mountain*, it takes the form of an industrial utopia, in which the "true treasure" is the people's labor power and their ability to extract profit from their native mountain. In Brenner's work, this national model implies that the Jew would become a Hebrew native, a proper landowner and homeowner using the land productively, renouncing the filth and dirt that bind the Jew and the Arab together. This model is based in a metaphor of depths and in a symbiotic productive relationship between the land and the national laboring subject. The second model of settlement found in these texts is the idle, nonproductive mode of habitation embodied in the futile gesture of scraping or scratching and in the abject materiality of dirt. It undoes the symbolism of depths, either by exposing the mountain as sterile, hollow, and empty (in *The Mountain*) or illustrating a mode of "settlement on the surface"—settlement that is transitory and only skin deep (in Brenner's writing).

These two models of settlement map onto two understandings of immobility or "settling" that are already present in the concept of *stasis* itself. Reflecting on the etymological and political possibilities of the concept of *stasis*, Dimitris Vardoulakis retrieves a line of poetry by Alcaeus of Mytilene, a seventh-century Greek poet, that captures the paradoxical nature of the term. The poem describes a ship caught in stasis, rendered immobile by the clash of winds blowing in contradictory directions so that they cancel each other out. The result is a "restless repose," a tense space of immobility that is sustained by continuous movement. There are two ways to read this space, Vardoulakis writes: "The space where the counter-directional winds cancel each other out can be viewed either as a dialectical overcoming, a station toward the anticipated result that legitimates it in advance, or as the sidestepping of any dialectical progression, a reversal of the dialectic or a 'dialectic at a standstill' that eschews all attempts at legitimacy."[91] To paraphrase, Vardoulakis maintains that there are two ways to think of *stasis*: as a step within a teleological dialectic or as a stepping out from the dialectic and from the idea of destiny. Whereas Vardoulakis reads these two options as possibilities for thinking the limits of political theology, I borrow his image to illustrate the two aesthetic ideologies shaping Ghanem's and Brenner's writing.

Ghanem's investigator accepts that the villagers should stay on the mountain rather than be moved to the "modern" town to become modern citizen-subjects, but this respite is only temporary. Eventually, they should abandon their futile project of *kaḥt* or compulsive scraping, which had been such a source of illicit and motivating desire for him, making him a writer, and they should become producers, part of the nation's progressive economy. The static form is a step in the dialectic that eventually leads to the model of national productivity, though *kaḥt* provides a glimpse of an alternative model of writing and inhabiting the present. Brenner approaches the native model negatively, as a utopian ideal that should not be represented, only conceived through its marked absence. The text sets up a suspended, static site of utopian tension between desired ideal and compromised present. However, this tension too is a temporary respite: the static aesthetics should eventually be overcome, as it charts a desire for progressive movement toward the ideal of native, national belonging. The depth model represents the end goal of the dialectic, which is a symbiotic relationship between the depth of the soul and the depths of the earth, and it creates the conditions for this tension through psychological effects.

The aesthetics of scraping and scratching, in contrast, registers ongoing, constant movement that is caught within stasis, going nowhere, overstepping the dialectic. It is a continuous movement that does not lead to change or progress. Scratching is a static form full of nervous movement without trajectory or goal and sustained by inertia. And if we turn to that most common metaphor of writing, that of the scribe scratching letters on a white page, the aesthetics of scratching presents a mode of writing that is ultimately content with itself and engaged with the present, with creating a record of bodily presence and affect, rather than with a prophetic and progressive narrative of historical destinies. It is a model of literature out of work, a space of idleness and contemplation rather than production.

Both of these aesthetic models are present in Ghanem and Brenner's prose and are by no means reconciled. As Jameson writes of the narrative impulse and the scenic impulse, they are engaged in struggle and no reconciliation between them is possible: one will ultimately overcome and vanquish the other. In Ghanem's text, the productive socialist work ethic crudely steps in to close the alternative vistas opened to the narrator by the futile life of *kaḥt*, but in Brenner's writing, the conclusion is not clear cut. This is, perhaps, why *Breakdown and Bereavement* is subtitled "The Book of Indecision": it has not yet decided what kind of book it wants to be, and what kind of settler it should become—*poʻel* or *yoshev*, a worker or a sitter, active or sitting idle?

Chapter Three

ROUTINE

The Present of Reproductive Labor

> The daily fight in which the human body is engaged to keep the world clean and prevent its decay bears little resemblance to heroic deeds; the endurance it needs to repair every day anew the waste of yesterday is not courage, and what makes the effort painful is not danger but its relentless repetition.
>
> —HANNAH ARENDT, THE HUMAN CONDITION

The two novels at the center of this chapter, *Tilk al-raʾiha* (*That Smell*, 1966) by the Egyptian writer Sonallah Ibrahim and *Levaya ba-tsohorayim* (*Funeral at Noon*, composed 1966; published 1973) by the Israeli Yeshayahu Koren, are classics of modern Middle Eastern literature. I've had the occasion to teach both of these books a number of times in undergraduate classrooms, an exercise that usually begins with frustration. "Nothing happens in this book," the students half-observe, half-complain about both texts. This observation is manifestly false and easily refutable, as demonstrated by relating some plot lines. In *That Smell*, a released political prisoner recounts to a friend's wife how her husband was tortured to death in front of his eyes. He contends with the loss of a home, a job, a community, and a political vision, not to mention the death of his mother. In *Funeral at Noon*, a young housewife seduces a soldier, while the boy she looks after runs away and dies after falling into an abandoned well. Something indeed happens. Moreover, there is no lack of explicit, dramatic episodes in these novels. *That Smell* has some horrifically graphic scenes of torture, execution, and sexual abuse. *Funeral at Noon* confronts its protagonist, and the reader, with the boy's marred body and with his grieving mother. Nevertheless, the students are not convinced. "Nothing happens" is a *feeling*, not an objective description of the text. How is this feeling evoked? And why is it that only the static moments are remembered and that these too are remembered as "nothing"?

I suspect that the primary reason for the feeling that "nothing happens" is that, for many paragraphs, these novels detail practices of maintenance and waste management, charting sustaining yet nonproductive cycles of cooking-eating-washing, wash-rinse-repeat. "I slept," the narrator of Sonallah Ibrahim's *That Smell* recounts. "I got up and washed. I put some powdered soap in a basin of water and stirred it until the foam rose, then put my dirty clothes in."[1] And in Koren's *Funeral at Noon*: "She began washing the dishes and put the kettle on the gas. The water hit the saucepans and dishes in the sink, spraying clear drops on her dress. . . . She dried the dishes and put them away in the cupboard. Then she went to the bedroom and took a clean pair of socks, a white shirt, and pressed trousers out of the wardrobe."[2] This cataloguing of daily routines goes on. These are novels of the daily management of the body and its needs, succinctly and methodically chronicling the administrative and repetitive rituals of the home and the self. Their orderly, clipped sentences are committed to the documentation of these tasks, undeterred by dramatic happenings. Not precisely housewife novels (a term I return to later), they are nevertheless texts that take up the repetitive and necessary routines of housework as both a theme and a formal principle.

The shared detailed and isolated gestures of housework should not obscure the fact that their performers are so different: one is a man, the other a woman; one is narrated in the first person and the other in the third; one has only to clean after himself, the other is tasked with caring for a husband and a child, albeit not her own. Their settings, too, differ significantly: *Funeral at Noon*, by the Israeli writer Yeshayahu Koren (b. 1940), takes place in a small and drowsy Israeli colony in the late 1950s and narrates a local tragedy unfolding around a young housewife in an unhappy marriage. *That Smell*, by the Egyptian writer Sonallah Ibrahim (b. 1937), trails a political prisoner confined to house arrest, trying to find his bearings in the alienated urban environment of Cairo in the aftermath of Gamal Abdel Nasser's repression and cooptation of communist activists. Conjoining them is a formal conceit: the seemingly objective detailing of the precise gestures of life's maintenance and reproduction; the repetitive, incremental, and relentless static form of routine. Both writers have attributed their writing style to an electrifying encounter with the work of Ernest Hemingway, an origin story testifying to the global networks by way of which literary forms and techniques travel from the metropole to the periphery.³ Nevertheless, the routes of world literature do little to explain why both Ibrahim and Koren took Hemingway's terse style and used it to carefully document kitchen routines (Is there any sphere less Hemingwayesque?). More pertinent than simply pointing out Hemingway's influence on Middle Eastern modernism is to ask why his style appealed to both these writers as a formal solution at this moment of the mid-1960s in Egypt and in Israel and why they both claim to adopt it while displaying such profound interest in routines of reproductive labor.

Both *That Smell* and *Funeral at Noon* were composed in 1966, but it is practically impossible now not to read them in relation to the June 1967 Arab–Israeli War, an event pinpointed as a watershed moment in both Egyptian and Israeli historiographies. *That Smell* has been canonized as emblematic of leftist disenchantment in the aftermath of the Arab military defeat of 1967 because of its departure from the social realist committed idiom discussed in chapter 2.⁴ Meanwhile, every review of *Funeral* explicates that the border, which plays such a decisive and ominous role in the text, is one that has been effectively dissipated in the aftermath of Israel's occupation of the West Bank. Yet the fact that both novels, so invested in dailyness, routine, and repetition, were written *before* the war and the epistemic breaks it is said to herald is central to my argument in this chapter, in which I analyze literary forms that dissipate and undermine such decisive narrative "breaks." I identify the mid-1960s with a temporality I call "state time," a postindependence or postrevolutionary period in which the state consolidates and affirms its sovereignty. If the liberation struggle is a heroic time of productivity, busily producing the nation, "state time" is a time of cyclical reproduction and maintenance. Whereas the lawmaking violence of revolution, conquest, or civil war is spectacular, the law-preserving violence of the state, embodied in actions such as policing, boundary surveillance, population management, and censorship, is concealed through its embeddedness in the routines of everydayness, the sense that "nothing happens."⁵ Like housework, state-maintaining violence is self-effacing, little seen and little noticed while performed in plain sight.

The 1960s is when housewives and housework became increasingly visible as public figures, not only in Israeli and Egyptian fictions but also globally, through globalized patterns of consumption. The "housewife novel," charting the housewife's liberation from the monstrous routine of the everyday, became an identifiable genre.[6] The interest of this chapter is not in housewife novels per se, but in how *That Smell* and *Funeral*, novels of housework written by men, use the affordances of the housewife novel to other ends, namely to reflect on the effaced, ongoing violence of the state. Thus, although the conventional climax of the housewife novel as a genre is the redemptive event of liberation from the routines of the home, these two novels are anti-eventual in the manner defined by Michael Sayeau: they are novels in which the eventual structures of plot are maintained in place but at the same time are ironically undercut, eroded, or exposed as reflexive tropes.[7] Both novels adopt the repetitive, circular, self-effacing temporality of routine as a literary form. This aesthetic form generates a unique affective economy of reading, experienced as mild revulsion or irritated boredom, and so despite the ongoing encounter with violence and its obvious devastating effects, the reader is left with the feeling that nothing has happens. In both novels, the routines of housework are a means to write the affective present of the state—a present of maintenance and social reproduction. Their critical stance is minor and static, embodied in the figures of a glitch in the machine and the asymptotic graph rather than the slammed-door departure.

NOTHING HAPPENS

In chapter 2, I explored how the demands for national productivity and productive labor are coded and undermined in literary form. Against a model of symbiotic, productive settlement, Brenner's and Ghanem's texts mobilize an ethos of busy idleness, embodied in the gesture of scratching and scraping, surface level engagements with dirt. In this chapter, I turn to the realm of reproductive labor, or the activities and behaviors involved in maintaining life, both daily and intergenerationally. The distinction between productive labor (of commodities) and reproductive labor (of the labor force itself), originally made by Marx, has been developed significantly since the mid-1960s by feminist theorists who highlight how the routine tasks of cooking, cleaning, and raising children has been ignored as an essential component of the economy.[8] As gendered, devalued labor, housework is simply not counted among the noteworthy or significant activities of social and individual life.[9] Even when housework *is* represented and made explicit in modernist literature or film, be it openly feminist or not (and both *Funeral* and *That Smell*, despite their domestic concerns, are by no means feminist texts), it simply disappears, subsumed under the all-pervasive categories of "the routine" or "the everyday." Rather than content or labor, the gestures of housework are regularly read as a shorthand for the superficiality, tediousness, or even oppression of routine, and housework itself becomes merely a symbol of insignificance, of time in which "nothing happens."[10]

Consider, for example, the case of Domietta Torlasco's brilliant video essay, "Philosophy in the Kitchen," which curates, edits together, and makes visible countless scenes of housework from the European art cinema repertoire.[11] A characteristic reading of this piece begins by crediting Torlasco with unveiling the invisible labor of housework, only to assert, a few pages later, that what we see on the screen is "the nothingness that is housework," reaching the confusing conclusion that "women are exhausted by nothing."[12] In Marxist-inspired criticism, housework appears briefly only to disappear again behind labels such as "pure duration," "empty time," "busywork without doing," or simply "the banality of the everyday." The post–World War II field of everyday studies routinely recognizes housework as a burden precisely because it is *not* labor, because it cannot boast of a finished product. A moment in Henri Lefebvre's *Critique of Everyday Life* encapsulates this move when it cites a report sent by Christiane Peyre to his research group in 1960:

> Every day, thousands upon thousands of women sweep up the dust which has gathered imperceptibly since the previous day. After every meal, too numerous to count, they wash the dishes and saucepans. For times too numerous to count, by hand or in the machine, they remove the dirt which has built up bit by bit on sheets and clothes; they stop up the holes the gentle rubbing of heels inevitably makes; they fill emptied cupboards and refrigerators with packets of pasta and kilos of fruit and vegetables.[13]

Based on this account, Peyre suggests a definition of everyday life that highlights reproductive labor: "The ensemble of activities which of necessity result from the general processes of development: evolution, growth and aging, of biological or social protection or change." Lefebvre, however, concludes that the everyday is "the reverse side of all praxis," once again defining the everyday and its routine reproductive activities as a time in which nothing is done.[14] Such staggering disappearing acts are enabled by housework's ephemeral, self-consuming materiality (what is cooked is eaten, what is cleaned becomes soiled) and its "relentless repetition." This widespread nullification of housework is where a collective cultural attachment to a concept of value defined through production and progress becomes most apparent.

Against prevalent readings of housework as a symbol or a symptom of an inadequate life, "the reverse of all praxis," I attend to it in these two novels as a thing in itself, a practice of daily reproduction. By this, I do not intend a reclamation or celebration of reproductive labor and its dailyness as an alternative—feminine—sphere of value and contentment. Such feminist reversals of the existing gendered hierarchy of labor, more often than not, naturalize the division between production and reproduction and fail to address the structures of inequality sustaining it.[15] Housework is hardly glorified in these novels, nor is it celebrated for its nourishing, nurturing aspects. Both novels do not shy away from the fact that housework is terribly boring; that it can be disgusting, as it forces us to come in close contact with the decomposing matter of life; and that it often appears to be exhaustingly futile. But they also do not engage in fantasies of a sphere outside of housework's repetitive labor, outside housework as form, in the manner in which many housewife liberation novels do. As such, they remind us that housework's affects (boredom, futility, disgust) are typical of most forms of (usually low-paid) labor that generate profit (though not necessarily for the worker). Housework is significant not because it is a particularly monstrous, demeaning, or meaningless kind of labor, as second-wave feminism has strategically presented it to be, but because it is gendered and devalued: naturalized to be the instinctive occupation of certain bodies, housework could remain unwaged in a wage economy and invisible even when seen. The gendered and devalued everyday work of reproductive labor is a site where "the unevenness of lives endlessly reproduced," in the words of Harry Harootunian, can become visible against capitalist modernity's promises of an even, eventless, frictionless future.[16]

Reading housework departs from a critical tradition that views the novels' everyday temporality as merely a symptom of alienation or crisis, a tradition that draws, implicitly or explicitly, on a Marxist trajectory that finds the everyday to be interesting only in its capacity as a catalyst for what must transcend it: namely, a robust sense of historicity.[17] According to this critical tradition, women and men who are the subjects of the everyday, oblivious as they are to the complex forces of capitalism that shape their lived present, are doomed to an "ahistorical" existence: superficial, phantasmatic, inauthentic, and complicitous with the workings of capitalist modernization.[18] I am wary of this mode of critique, which assumes that a genealogical historical understanding of the past in the present is the basis for any action that really counts (at times even subscribing a pedagogical program of historical consciousness-raising to literary characters). This chapter demonstrates that such critique not only is gendered and often strangely patronizing but also assumes a limited and melodramatic idea of what it means to "live in history" or to be "ahistorical." Rather than assert that affects associated with the repetitive narrative structures of housework, such as boredom, exhaustion, or disgust, are symptoms of ahistoricism, I follow Lauren Berlant in maintaining a reading for affect "as the very material of historical embeddedness," the means by which a period's "historical atmosphere" can be gauged.[19]

Novels that adopt housework as a literary form capture the affectivity of a historical present in which transformative events seem impossible and political life is invested in reproduction of the same. Of course, novels of routine, noneventfulness, and the everyday have been central to the development of modernist literature, as several scholars have demonstrated in recent years, providing a necessary corrective to modernist studies' customary focus on velocity and change.[20] The novels of the mid-1960s examined here, however, are contextually different from fin de siècle novels contending with new standards of speed and change or from the late modernism of the interwar years. If in earlier literary experiments the everyday and the ordinary were a means of integrating novelty or shock into familiar rhythms and thus domesticating them, the Middle Eastern novels of the 1960s emerge from the lived experience of a reality conceived as circular and repetitive. Their temporality is also distinct from the static temporality of the *aftermath*, or "the ruins of postsocialist and postcolonial futures-past," which David Scott identifies with the late 1980s.[21] Rather than registering the disillusionment of living on after collapse, they inhabit the static temporality of an expanding consumerist middle class and of a state engaged in the relentless business of self-maintenance. Through the circularity of routine, they chart the gradual grating away of future aspirations.

STATE TIME

As chapter 2 pointed out, Zionism and Egyptian nationalism share some ideological formations, despite the vastly different material contexts of their emergence and especially their relation to Western imperial powers and interests. In a comparative study of the rise and decline of Marxist politics in the two states, Joel Beinin argues that "despite the lack of symmetry between Egypt and Israel, the processes by which nationalist ideologies became the hegemonic political discourse in the two countries were both similar and dialectically related."[22] By the mid-1960s, the two states appeared to be on two divergent trajectories in their international and ideological alignments, exemplified most clearly in the fallout of the Suez crisis. In Egypt, Gamal Abdel Nasser promoted a pan-Arabist and anti-imperialist nationalism that was socialist leaning and associated with the nonaligned movement. Israel, in contrast, in its second decade of statehood, became increasingly dependent on American financial and military aid. Nevertheless, social dynamics in the two states were to some degree interrelated and bounded by the same ideological, economic, and political forces, which in turn gave rise to somewhat parallel temporal forms and affective structures. The institution of the nation-state, as an overarching political structure, generated a temporality I call "state time," a narrative of the present that emerges after the "successful" culmination of the struggle for liberation or independence and is occupied with the circular rhythms of state maintenance and management.

In the early 1960s, Nasser's regime was intent on organizing all political activism under the auspice of the state, taking increasingly repressive measures. The young Sonallah Ibrahim's initial involvement with party politics, leading to his arrest, is illustrative of the changing political contours in Egypt in the mid-1960s. Ibrahim joined the Egyptian Communist Party in 1959, when he was about twenty years old. Almost immediately, he was arrested in a sweep that targeted the majority of the Egyptian Communist Party members, accused of broad political conspiracy, and sentenced to seven years in prison, of which he served five. Despite their arrest and documented torture in prison, many of Ibrahim's fellow party members continued to support Nasser and his policies even while imprisoned, and in 1965, the two major Marxist organizations were dissolved and integrated into the state's political apparatus.[23] "In the sixties," Egyptian political activist Arwa Salih wrote, "the intellectual's role was scripted by the Nasser regime: a reasonable prison sentence, discharge, then a job in one of the regime's bustling bureaucracies."[24] Nasser's socialist-inspired statism pulled the carpet from under the feet of Egyptian progressive intellectuals, who found themselves to be "both the children of the [1952] revolution and its strategic enemies," in Samah Selim's apt phrase.[25] Commenting on the political atmosphere that Ibrahim encountered when he was released from prison in 1965, *That Smell*'s English translator Robyn Creswell suggests that the novel captures "the feeling of life *after* politics. It registers the cooling temperatures and lowered expectations of a moment when Nasser's 'holy march' towards Arab unity has stalled in the sands of economic reality and popular disaffection."[26]

What can we make of the phrase "life after politics"? Politics was by no means over, of course, but the phrase gestures toward a social structure of feeling, a "lived experience of the quality of life at a particular time and place."[27] "Life after politics" is a narrative structure: politics requires a narrative form in order to be legible and to organize its horizon of expectations, and "life after politics" marks the notion that although the political battles are fought and over, their conclusion remains undecipherable and unscripted. It is the feeling that new struggles are lacking a form or genre to fall back on, what Alberto Moreiras calls "a historical moment of denarrativization."[28] Events no longer organize themselves into an affectively coherent genre but remain untethered in a moment marked, on the one hand, by liberatory anticolonial rhetoric and, on the other, by repressive political violence aimed at consolidating and maintaining political hegemony.

Among much of the Jewish Israeli public, the mid-1960s were also a period of "cooling temperatures," new economic stability, and the consolidation of a middle class. Beinin states that after the Israeli state withdrawal from Sinai and Gaza in the aftermath of the Suez Crisis in 1957, "Zionist élan declined, and most Jewish Israelis sought 'normalcy.'"[29] The mid-1960s might have been a period of suspense and preparation among the military echelons, but for the majority of the Jewish public, this was unstructured time. Looking at letters and diaries from this period, the historian Tom Segev identifies a widespread sense of despair caused by "the burden of boredom," what the poet Haim Gouri called the "second-day crisis" of the revolution. Now that there was no immediate object of struggle in sight, what was to come next? "The time of dull routine seemed to have come too soon," Segev concludes.[30] The time of large-scale mobilization for independence has nominally ended, and in both countries, the making of history seemed to be overtaken by consumption. *That Smell* registers Egypt's entrance into a global consumerist economy as the supersession of political or historical progress by a vision of progress as consumption in the domestic sphere.[31] Its characters are predominantly occupied with the prospect of buying a bigger refrigerator, a cheaper soap dish, or a faster washing machine. A similar process was unfolding in Israel. Having emerged from almost a decade of austerity (1949–1959), the Israeli economy was rapidly improving with the assistance of German reparation funds. Segev's samples of letters written by middle-class Israelis to their relatives abroad in 1965–1966 seem to be taken straight out of the pages of *That Smell*, with their detailed accounts of the purchase of new furniture, wood paneling, and telephones.[32] The feelings of "life after politics" in Egypt and "the day after the revolution" in Israel are similarly characterized by the replacement of a linear collective narrative with a commodified domestic routine. This repetitive, administered temporality of consumption and administration, devoid of events or narrative, is what I refer to as "state time."

As the English term *state* insinuates (as do the terms used in both Romance and Germanic languages, such as *état* or *Staat*), a political philosophy of static spatiality is at the heart of modern Western state theory.[33] The Hebrew and Arabic terms for the state have etymological histories related to earlier or alternative political models. In Hebrew, the word *medina* (state), which first appeared in the period of the second temple, comes from the root *d-y-n*, associated with jurisprudence and law. *Medina* is simply a region or area bound by a legal system, and over the years, the term was associated with a variety of geographical/administrative units, including a city, a region, or a country.[34] The origin of its modern use passes through its Arabic cognate: the Arabic word *madīna* means a city, and in medieval Arab philosophy it was used to translate the Greek term *polis*, or city-state. It is probably through Judeo-Arabic philosophical texts that the Hebrew word *medina* came to be associated with the modern-day political institution of the state. The Arabic term for the modern state, *dawla*, derives from the root *d-w-l*, which means to turn, alternate, or cycle. Early dictionaries define the term as periodic change and, by implication, a period of rule, reign, or dynasty.[35] It is a nonterritorial term, referring primarily to the ruling elite and to the cyclical nature of power, as famously discussed by the fourteenth-century historian Ibn Khaldun. The word became associated with the modern state during the Ottoman period, as the Turkish variant of *dawla*—*devlet*—was the term used by the Ottoman empire (*Devlet-i ʿĀliye-yi ʿOsmāniyye*).

The Hebrew and Arabic terms ground political sovereignty in juridical authority or the cyclical nature of rule, respectively. But these etymologies serve mostly as a reminder that the political institution of the modern nation-state is the product of only one among many philosophies on the nature of sovereignty and its relation to institutional bodies. Despite the historical "baggage" that the Hebrew or Arabic words carry, the states of the modern Middle East are largely modeled after the modern European nation-state, whose assumed idealized temporality is stasis.[36]

In the early 1970s, Lefebvre turned to Hegel's view of the state as the end of history and of the dialectic process to argue that the state is a spatialized static form, cut off from the history that constituted it: "The Hegelian end of history does not imply the disappearance of the product of historicity [i.e., the state]. . . . [Rather] it persists in being through its own strength. What disappears is history, which is transformed from action to memory, from production to contemplation. As for time, dominated by repetition and circularity . . . it loses all meaning."[37] The struggle for political sovereignty culminates with the constitution of the state; a temporal form characterized by repetition and circularity replaces dialectical progress. David Lloyd echoes Lefebvre when he writes that the state "puts an end to the epic of [the nation's] historical destiny in a performative act that abolishes history at the same time it allows the epic to be fulfilled."[38] History has reached its zenith and is displaced into cultural education: "Culture becomes a sphere of reproduction—or recreation—rather than production, repetitively mediating the interpolation of individual subjects into citizens."[39] National holidays, commemorations, and ceremonies ensure the reproduction of the state by reinvoking its foundation and the terror of its constitutive violence. These two forms of time, epic national struggle time and reproductive state time, are clearly gendered. The linear time of struggle bears a masculine ethos associated with productivity, historical dynamism, and sacrifice. The repetitive time of the state, in contrast, is a feminized sphere of *re*-production, consumption, and commemoration. State time is the time of border management, bureaucracy, and maintenance; the time of reproducing a labor force and particular social relations in "relentless repetition"; and a time in which events seem suspect if not impossible, effaced by the invisible violence of the repetition of the same. To put it explicitly, state time is the time of housework, and its allegorical figure is the housewife.

HOUSEWORK AND THE FETTERS OF THE EVERYDAY

The February 1959 issue of the Egyptian, socialist-leaning cultural journal *al-Ghad* (*The Morrow*) featured a bookish cartoon: a bespectacled man presents a chained young woman to the broadcasting editor at the radio station, declaring: "Editor, I have the best serialized story here!" (*al-muḥarrir, di aḥsan qiṣṣa musalsala*). The joke is based in a couple of double entendres: the word *musalsala* means "serialized" but can also mean "fettered"; the word *muḥarrir* means "editor" but also "liberator." The best serialized story (the most common means of publishing novels at the time) is a story about a fettered woman set free, liberated through the means of publicity itself. Women liberation stories, the cartoon implies, are a commodity in high demand, a setup in which the woman remains a desirable commodity.

The concern with women's liberation is of course not new to the 1950s. In the late nineteenth century and the first decades of the twentieth century, housewives were at the center of vast modernization projects framed as projects of liberation in Egypt as well as in the Zionist settlements: the argument for women's education was often framed by the need to educate women to be better wives and mothers for the sake of the nation's next generation.[40] Countless new journals and publications focused on scientific, modern approaches to hygiene and childrearing in order to produce "children worthy of modernity," in Afsaneh Najmabadi's apt phrase pertaining to parallel processes in Iran.[41] The late 1950s, however, witnessed a fundamental shift in the image of the modern woman, from the ideal educated housewife to the working woman: a woman who actively contributes to the state project by working outside the family home. Both the Egyptian and Israeli state apparatuses were instrumental in this shift. In Israel, it was in the 1960s that the state actively started encouraging Jewish women to join the workforce though new judicial initiatives, with clear implications for the number of women integrated into waged labor.[42] In Egypt, Nasserist state feminism vigorously encouraged women to join the labor market and invest in time-saving modern household appliances. Although the number of actual working women remained low, the symbolic figure of the modern woman liberated from domestic labor dominated the public sphere, performing an important ideological role in the postrevolutionary state and its declared commitment to "progress."[43]

Women frustrated with their domestic duties began to appear as an increasingly recognizable literary trope. The growing interest in the rhythms of women's domestic labor in Egypt is evident, for example, in Naguib Mahfouz's *Cairo Trilogy* (1956–1957), in which the most memorable female character is Amina, the obedient and patient housewife. Novels by women writers, such as *al-Bab al-maftuh* (*The Open Door*, 1960) by political activist Latifa al-Zayyat or *Yawm baʿda yawm* (*Day After Day*, serialized 1964–1965, published 1969) by Zaynab Sadiq, narrated the feminine routine of the household as a space of oppression. Their heroines sought liberation outside the home, in work, in illicit love, and in political activity. Hebrew novels of the 1960s also began featuring housewives burdened and limited by the routines of the home, a trend led by women writers gaining recognition in a literary sphere previously dominated by debates among male authors and protagonists: books such as Yehudit Handel's *Rehov ha-madregot* (*Street of the Stairs*, 1955), Amalya Kahana Carmon's *Be-kfifa ahat* (*Under One Roof*, 1966), and a bit later, Rachel Eitan's *Shida ve-shidot* (*Pleasures of Men*, 1974) introduced female subjects and routines previously unexplored in Hebrew modern texts (Eitan was presented as "an anonymous housewife" who had reached literary fame after the publication of her debut novel).[44] The most famous Hebrew housewife of the late 1960s, however, was written by a man. Hannah Gonen, the protagonist of Amos Oz's celebrated novel *Mikhaʾel sheli* (*My Michael*, 1968), compensates for the dissatisfactions of her daily routine as a housewife through violent erotic fantasies about her childhood friends, the Palestinian brothers Aziz and Halil. Parallel concerns can be found in films of the same period, from screwball comedies such as the Egyptian *My Wife the General Manager* to modernist dramas such as the Israeli film *Siege*. In all of these works national anxieties remain close to the surface: the housewife—rather than, for example, a desired young woman as in the village novels discussed in chapter 2—became a locus for a national allegory of oppression and liberation.

The identification of housework as a *uniquely* oppressive form of lived experience was part of an emergent global discourse to which both feminists and Marxist cultural critics contributed. In the 1950s and 1960s, housework and housewifery began to be explicitly associated with a certain modern type of monstrous temporality: the everyday. Earlier writing on the everyday from the pre–World War II period, by social theorists such as Georg Simmel, Georg Lukács, Siegfried Kracauer, or Walter Benjamin, identified the everyday in modern experiences of urbanity, industrialization, and mass-produced culture.[45] Its representative subject was the implicitly male clerk or industrial laborer in the anonymous and overwhelming city, although everybody in capitalist society was understood to be experiencing the everyday's alienated repetitive rhythms.

By the late 1940s, however, a new conviction seemed to emerge according to which women experience the everyday *more*. "Everyday life weighs heaviest on women," wrote Henri Lefebvre in 1968. "Some [women] are bogged down by its peculiar cloying substance; others escape into make-believe. . . . They are the subject of everyday life and its victims."[46] There is an established cultural genealogy for this association: studies of the everyday as a modern temporal structure often begin with Gustave Flaubert's *Madame Bovary*, a novel whose allure can be attributed to its attitude of simultaneous pity and contempt for its housewife protagonist, bound to the tedious rhythms of the home.[47] Mikhail Bakhtin chose *Madame Bovary* to illustrate the chronotope of a provincial town, characterized by circular everyday life: "Here there are no events, only 'doings' that constantly repeat themselves. Time here has no advancing historical movement; it moves rather in narrow circles."[48] As Rita Felski demonstrates, the feminization of the everyday aligns with older distinctions between the masculine figure of "time's arrow" and the feminine figure of "time's cycle." Because modernity has been associated with linear progress and development, she writes, the time of the everyday has been conceived as "belated," antiquated, even a relic of "the conventions of pre-industrial society."[49] Associating the everyday directly with housework, everyday studies could configure housewives and their habitual home-centered routines as "modern subjects in waiting."[50]

The everyday, often touted in post–World War II critical theory as that which is impossible to pin down, appears from this angle to have quite specific and concrete content: rituals of maintenance and sustenance; the upkeep of the body; reproduction, rather than production; and private, unsocialized labor. Both liberal and Marxist strands of feminist theory have contributed to the depiction of domestic labor as repetitive, meaningless, and futile, opposed to and defined against the supposedly meaningful and productive labor carried on in the masculine sphere outside the home.[51] To save herself from a life of repetition, the housewife must leave the sphere of the home and join the linear, progressive temporality of the productive workforce.[52] In relatively young and developmentalist states, such as Egypt and Israel in the 1960s, the feminist demand to abandon the repetitive and "belated" temporality of housework aligned with other political and economic discourses. Narrating stories of women's liberation—freed *from* the oppressive drudgery of the static time of the household, *to* the linear time of the labor market—allowed the story of time's progress to linger a bit longer, as more and more groups were incorporated into the labor market in the postrevolutionary or postindependence moment.[53] Eventually, two developmentalist discourses on housewives—an early one on liberating women *through* (modernized) housework and a later one on liberating women *from* it—positioned women as a scale by which to measure the nation's modernity. Whereas the former treated housework as an object of modernization, the latter presented it as oppressive and inauthentic. In this new discourse, the housewife becomes a new subject in the story of liberation—she must be released from her premodern, cyclical temporality and join the march of progress. She therefore fulfills a double role: the housewife is an allegorical figure for the temporal crisis of state time, engaged in repetitive projects of maintenance, sustenance, and consumption, and she is the solution to this crisis, her liberation from domestic drudgery allowing a reignition of the nation's narrative of progress.

WRITING ROUTINES OF MAINTENANCE

The first edition of *That Smell* was famously confiscated upon its publication, and the pirated versions that began circulating subsequently had numerous scenes cut out. Only in 1986 was the novel published in Cairo in full. At this point, Ibrahim's reputation as a writer and the radical influence of *That Smell* as a pioneering work of Egypt's "Sixties Generation" (*jīl al-sittīnāt*) were already widely acknowledged.[54] The novel is regularly celebrated as a watershed moment, a text that supposedly transitioned Egyptian literature from social realism to bleak modernist style and foreshadowed the cultural and intellectual crisis following Egypt's military defeat in the 1967 war. Remarkably, this view is not just retroactive but was established with the publication of the novel itself, before it had a chance to circulate and prove its impact. In the original introduction, the eminent writer Yusuf Idris declared the novel to be "a revolution and a new beginning."[55] Ibrahim's friends thought so too: the cover of the first edition of *That Smell* featured a typical modernist manifesto signed by three of Ibrahim's companions, declaring that "to shatter this climate of artistic stagnation [*tajammada*, literally: that has frozen], we must turn to the kind of sincere and sometimes agonized writing you find here."[56] The metaphor that the manifesto relies on is familiar: *shattering and breaking* things that have become *solid and fixed* is often considered the basic gesture of modernity, a trope so worn that it hardly merits attention. Critique itself has often been defined as and tasked with breaking that which has congealed, "reliquifying thought," and allowing it to assume its natural flow again.[57] That which has frozen must be set in motion because flow and liquidity are presumed to be the natural state that has been obstructed.

And yet, the expectation that *That Smell* should liberate frozen forms appears discordant with the book's paratactic, de-emotional style, which makes any happening so hard to discern and obscures any kind of breaking event behind the repetitive veneer of routine. Ibrahim has called it an "iceberg style," a term he borrows from Hemingway but makes his own. For Hemingway, the iceberg principle was an art of omission and precise economy, which means that, just like the iceberg's mass, seven-eighths of the story should lie beneath its manifest surface.[58] For Ibrahim, Hemingway's minimalist technique had a "particular luster set against the conventional flabby eloquence of Arabic literature."[59] It is not only the art of omission that appealed to him, but also the sleek, level, and featureless façade of the iceberg, devoid of ornamentations and texture, evenly smooth. Like an iceberg, the novel's nameless protagonist seems to move by inertia or external compulsion rather than by any internal or agential conviction. If indeed Ibrahim's static form of routine is a means of critique, it is a critique that operates according to a logic different from that of a break, mobilizing a separate set of organizing images: not a revolutionary shattering of that which has solidified, but a mimetic habitation of congealed forms, residing within their limits, adopting the shape of their contours. *That Smell* takes up the repetitive, cyclical gestures of housework as its guiding form.

As such, *That Smell* differs from what readers would rightfully identify as Ibrahim's quintessential housewife novel, the award-winning *Dhat* (*Zaat*, 1992).[60] *Zaat* intersperses the story of the eponymous heroine, trapped in a petit bourgeois life of marriage, children, and the race for modern consumer goods and electrical appliances, with documents and newspaper clips chronicling Egyptian political and economic events from the early 1970s to the late 1980s. The montage technique of *Zaat* outlines parallels between Zaat's household and Egypt's period of infitāḥ, or "opening" to neoliberal markets starting in the early 1970s, showing how neoliberal economic policies and widespread corruption bear direct effects on gendered labor in both the domestic and public spheres.[61] Readers of the novel often comment that its housewife protagonist is not merely an exemplary subject but also an allegorical figure for the Egyptian state as a whole. In contrast, Yoav Di-Capua suggests that the relationship between Zaat's everyday narrative and the documentary archive is one of disconnect. Zaat and her family, Di-Capua argues, exemplify a mode of "living ahistorically," displaying an inability to process the events documented in the newspaper clips into a historical narrative that is the only basis for critical and ethical action.[62] As often happens when critical theory confronts the practices of reproductive labor, this reading views the habitual routines of the everyday as impoverished, lacking historical consciousness and hence incapable of transcendence. Di-Capua argue for the necessity of historical consciousness to save the "moral landscape bulldozed by the everyday."[63] Zaat's epistemic discontinuity, he comments, is an effect of trauma. But it is precisely this insightful observation that points to the relation between the news snippets and Zaat's story. Rather than attributing Zaat's traumatized subjectivity to her childhood clitoridectomy, the 1967 war, or the barred access to historical archives in Egypt, among the causes that Di-Capua suggests, we can look for its source in the sociopolitical context documented in the news excerpts: political and corporate corruption, unchecked capitalist expansion, and commodity fetishism, which themselves are based on a logic of concealment and unknowability. Commodity capitalism both embodies and conceals vast, complex processes by causing "definite social relation between men" to assume "the fantastic form of a relation between things."[64] The traumatic state of alienation, of a disconnect between knowledge and experience, is "built in" to consumer capitalism. Rather than being ahistorical, Zaat's everyday narrative is precisely the way in which history, as documented in the newspaper archive, is embedded in lived experience.

Critical readings that psychoanalyze Zaat or read her narrative as a sociological record of the changes undergone by the late twentieth-century Egyptian housewife tend to ignore the novel's narrative voice, which mediates between Zaat's story and the reader. This is a third-person omniscient narrator, omniscient also of all the ironies and injustices of history that Zaat fails to recognize. The novel is premised on a condition of asymmetry. The reader knows much more about Zaat than Zaat herself, not only because the reader can access the newspaper snippets that intersperse Zaat's story but also because this story is mediated through the narrator's patronizing commentary. Consider a typical passage concerning the courtship of Zaat and her future husband:

> It was a period of great hopes, bold aspirations, and dreams: night dreams and day dreams in all their varieties (the dry and the wet). By the duck pond in the Merryland Gardens, [Zaat] said to [Abdel Maguid, her husband to be]: "Washing clothes is no longer a chore thanks to Omo. Just a little in a bowl of water and a quick swish to make lots of foam, then you throw in a shirt or a blouse and go off to make the tea or do some cooking."[65]

Bold aspirations and dreams are contrasted with a slogan for the wondrous qualities of laundry detergent (which *is* a truly wondrous development for women responsible for the laundry cycle). This scene eerily reenacts Henri Lefebvre's anecdote about his "discovery" of the concept of everyday life, when his wife walked into the apartment holding a box of laundry soap and said, quite seriously, "This is an excellent product."[66] That his wife could be serious about such frivolity obviously gave Lefebre pause. In these texts, laundry soap is the epitome of everyday life's mystique, a symbol of the feminine capitulation to its deceptions. Throughout the novel, Zaat and Abdel Maguid remain animated cartoon characters viewed from the external perspective of the narrator, evoking little empathy even when they are trapped in an imposing cycle of impoverishment. This is not to claim that the narrator of *Zaat* resents his docile petit bourgeois characters, but he does seem to judge that their wrong life under consumer capitalism cannot be lived rightly.[67] The narrator of *Zaat* can occupy a heightened perspective from which to view this life wrongly lived, which if not escaped can at least be disdained.

This is not the case in *That Smell*, in which the routine rhythm of housework takes over the narrative voice itself, immanently relating the minor gestures and repetitive rhythms of maintenance:

> I went back to my room and turned the light off and lay down on the bed and went to sleep. I woke up startled by the sound of the bell. When I opened the door no one was there. I went back to my room and left its door open and went back to sleep. I got up early in the morning and shaved and dressed and took a clean shirt to the clothes presser and went back and changed, then went downstairs and looked for a place to get my shoes shined. I bought the papers and finally got on the metro.[68]

The main technique of *Zaat* is the montage: a method of parataxis that gestures toward the inability to integrate the broad view accumulating in the news snippets—their labyrinthine accounts of scandal, corruption, and tragedy—with the individual rhythm of daily life, as if the only way to include them both in one narrative is through the disjointed, awkward, and abrupt shifts between the two scales and genres of writing.[69] In *That Smell*, parataxis, the practice of placing phrases or parts of speech next to each other without coordinating or subordinating conjunctions, operates on the sentence level. The first-person account often leaves the causal or logical connections between individual sentence units unspecified, creating the effect of an objective enumeration of facts that is largely responsible for what Paul Starkey has called Ibrahim's "de-emotionalized" style.[70] Idwar Kharrat has similarly identified Ibrahim's writing with an "objectifying current" (*tayyār al-tashyīʾ*), in which language seems "as if it doesn't care."[71] Parataxis creates the impression of a narration formed at random, without a guiding subjectivity.

In the introduction he wrote for the 1986 edition of *That Smell*, Ibrahim provides an etiology for this style, going back to the months following his release from prison while he was still under nightly house arrest and keeping a diary:

> One night I won't forget I glanced over the diary, composed in a telegraphic style, which I wrote in every night after the policeman's departure. . . . I read

the whole thing, then shivered with excitement. There was a buried current running through that telegraphic style, a style that never stopped for self-examination, didn't bother to search for *le mot juste*, not to make sure that the language was neat and tidy, nor that all ugliness [*qabḥ*] such as might shock delicate sensibilities had been scrubbed away.... I felt that here was the raw material for a work of art. It only needed some arranging and polishing. I felt that I'd finally found my own voice.[72]

This origin story relies on imagery of dirt, cleanliness, and maintenance to describe the labor of writing. Writing is equated with the practice of scrubbing (or not), of tidying up, and of generally managing "ugliness" or dirt. Yasmine Ramadan calls the novel's investment in various bodily fluids and odors an "aesthetic of excremental fiction," reminding us that "that smell" of the title is the waft of raw sewage that overruns Cairo's streets.[73] Yet the routines of managing, flushing, disposing, and continuously erasing traces of unpleasant odors is just as much part of the "ugliness" that Ibrahim's newly discovered style doggedly documents. It is present not only in the content—an odorous fart in a bourgeoise living room is the one Ibrahim mentions—but also in the novel's form, which takes up housework's reproductive labor as a model.

That Smell is not far removed from these diary entries: it is a first-person account of a released political prisoner, a writer confined to nightly house arrest. Every evening a policeman knocks on his door, checking that he is in for the night. The novel maintains the non-eventual structure of a diary, bound to a repetitive routine of daily life, and refrains from elaborate, descriptive, or figurative language. As in *Funeral at Noon*, this static narrative of everyday routine is interspersed with other modes of writing, visually differentiated by their font: intimate memories and stark flashbacks to torture scenes in the prison. These sections, despite their explicit violence, emotional cadence, and poetic richness, are eclipsed by the account of the narrator's routine and the paratactic barrenness. The style of the diary is functional, but it is a style, nonetheless, and an effective one. Its reproductive routines appeared to Ibrahim as an apt solution for the problem of "how to write" of political violence and its normalization within the historical moment of denarrativization, in the self-sustaining present of state time.

Tracing what Ibrahim himself was reading in this period can illuminate the process that made this style appealing. During his time in prison, Ibrahim kept a different kind of journal: fragmented notes of his ideas, writing exercises, and reflections on what he read—the few books and magazines that made their way into the prison. These notes were smuggled out of the prison on cigarette paper and eventually published in 2005 under the title *Yawmiyat al-wahat* (*The Wahat Diaries*), named after the prison complex in which Ibrahim was held.[74] Ibrahim's prison journals allow tracing a clear shift in his views of the methods and ends of literary writing. The first entries, from 1962, are lists of potential writing projects, all centered on dramatic reversals or moments of disillusionment: "Cairo commits suicide. The fire of '52. The city that rose up and fell destructively on itself. Story of freedom in the streets, among the people."[75] In June 1962, he writes: "The following statement on the art of writing is attributed to Chekhov: 'When you sit down to write, you must be cold as ice.' No . . . No! The writer's blood should boil as he writes, his face should pale with hatred, he should laugh and he should cry."[76] By the following year, however, Ibrahim's interests change significantly: he writes of Virginia Woolf and Italian neorealist cinema (which he has not viewed but read of in the newspapers), praising their focus on the ordinary, the quotidian, and the mundane.[77] He struggles to form an understanding of T. S. Eliot's "objective correlative" as a mode of combining personal content with an objective form. He cites and underlines a quote from Hemingway: "*All bad writers are in love with the epic.*"[78] These shifting interests, from emphatic drama to the quotidian modernism that eventually characterizes *That Smell*, are not simply a matter of changing tastes or "borrowed forms" migrating from English literature to Arabic. They reflect Ibrahim's search for a literary form that can respond to the form of political life in postrevolutionary Egypt.

That Smell's overarching plot structure is circular and rhythmically constrained, undermining any event that threatens to be transformative or decisive. This structure is apparent in the novel's very first scene: the narrator is released from prison, but because he has no address, he is sent back to jail for another agonizing night. On the next day, settled in his sister's apartment, he begins a daily routine: leaving his room in the morning, he wanders the streets of Cairo during the day and hurries back to his room every night by sunset, when the policeman in charge of enforcing the house arrest knocks at his door. Mahmud Amin al-'Alim notes that both temporal and spatial movements of the novel are restricted, circular, and repetitive, and hence sterile, aiming for nothing and achieving nothing.[79] Constrained by the terms of the house arrest, the narrative itself takes on a nonproductive circular form.

This circularity is an anti-evental mechanism, a means to efface or erode the effect of any event that appears in the text. By "event" I mean a particular narrative structure that has tangible effects, "*a change of the very frame through which we perceive the world and engage in it,*" in Slavoj Žižek's terse definition.[80] Not merely an occurrence that can be smoothly integrated into daily routine (like a glass breaking in the sink or a cake that came out well), the event is a rupture that changes the very terms by which the world is understood. Defined as such, the event is perhaps the earliest narrative structure to be codified and theorized. In the *Poetics*, Aristotle posits a formula for tragedy based on a two-tiered breakdown of the event: *anagnorisis*, recognition or a change from ignorance to knowledge, and *peripeteia*, a reversal in fortune or turning point. "*Anagnorisis* combined with *peripeteia* will produce either pity or fear; and actions producing these effects are those which, by our definition, Tragedy represents,"[81] Aristotle wrote, succinctly capturing the way in which genre operates as a normative narrative structure that is associated with particular affects and thus tied to a set of expectations. We expect *recognition* to be followed by *reversal*. Otherwise, the affects associated with the genre—pity and fear—would not take hold and the tragedy would no longer be a tragedy. By actively making use of the conventions of recognized genres, texts activate and interfere in the affective structures associated with them.[82] *That Smell* alludes to Aristotle's foundational generic structure only to frustrate and subvert it: recognition, or new knowledge, repeatedly fails to constitute an event that would disrupt the routine of maintenance.

This mechanism appears most clearly in the final pages of the novel. The narrator arrives, seemingly accidentally, at his mother's old house, where he finds three old female relatives who had not seen him since he was a child. Any emotions generated by this unexpected reunion do not prevent his grandmother from turning on the radio for the women's daily ceremony of listening to the serialized romantic thriller: "A somber voice on the radio announced another episode of 'The Shadow.' The episode began with a young man's voice saying tearfully: How can I live when I know my father is a murderer? I sat and listened in silence. All the women gazed at the radio."[83] The radio drama evokes the most basic tragic narrative structure: discovery (*anagnorisis*) followed by reversal (*peripeteia*). The weeping young man has gained new knowledge: his father is a murderer. This means that nothing will be as it was; life cannot continue as it did. The primary purpose of evoking this generic structure in the radio drama is to highlight *That Smell*'s departure from it. Shortly after the radio show ends, the narrator learns from the elderly women that his mother, who was mentally unstable, had died merely a week earlier, unbeknown to him. And yet, the question of "How do I live when I know my mother is dead?" is never posed. Instead, the narrator looks at his watch, realizes that sunset is near and that the policeman will soon check on him, and leaves for the metro. The potentially shattering event is effaced, and discovery is overcome by the circular constraints of routine.

The narrator's routine is dominated by the daily visit of the policeman, the representative of the state's surveillance apparatus, but also by the labor of self-maintenance and the sustaining yet nonproductive cycle of shopping-cooking-eating-washing: "I went in and took my clothes off and put my trousers on a hanger and hung them from the wall. Then I showered" (*That Smell*, 39). "In the morning I bought a magazine and a small glass of milk and some bread. I went home and boiled the milk and put some sugar in it, then dunked the bread in the milk while reading the magazine" (*That Smell*, 40). "I took off my clothes, washed my face, then prepared a cup of coffee and tidied up my desk, wiping away the dust that had gathered on it" (*That Smell*, 44). These tasks are the business of maintaining the present. The future, in the form of intergenerational reproduction, is repeatedly deflected. The narrator of *That Smell* encounters young children and talk of marriage everywhere, but he categorically removes himself from reproductive sociality. And although women, both strangers and acquaintances, are the constant object of both gaze and fantasy, the narrator is incapable of emotional or physical intimacy with any of them. When a former lover comes to visit, she refuses his approaches. He asks a friend to hire a prostitute but is unable to have sex with her. Instead, sexual gratification becomes an enclosed economy, a self-administered task:

> I put my hand between my legs. I began playing with myself and at last I sighed. Then I threw myself back in the chair, exhausted, staring at the page with a blank look. A little while later I got up and stepped carefully over the traces I'd left on the floor under the chair and went into the bathroom to wash my socks and shirt and hang them by the window. (*That Smell*, 44)

Masturbation, so often spurned as "wasted" labor, does not merely replace heterosexual intimacy in this scene, but also the labor of literary production: writing. The narrator's blank look reflects the still blank page, and instead of words, he leaves his mark in remnants of sperm on the floor. Moreover, after leaving the empty page on the desk, the narrator immediately resumes the housework routine, turning his attention to the laundry. The masculine/productive labor of writing is replaced by the feminized/sustaining labor of cleaning.

This masturbation scene is frequently cited as an example of what Hoda al-Sadda identifies as the "emasculation/desexualization of the national hero" in the late 1960s, a symptom of disillusionment with the role of the committed intellectual.[84] The novel's impotent, nonvirile, and feminized hero, according to this reading, is an expression of a general crisis of masculinity. Yet such prognosis of a masculinity in crisis, as tempting as it is, serves to affirm rather than challenge established gender norms—the normative association of domestic labor with women's bodies, for example. Focusing on housework as a form (of labor, of narrative) reveals something other than a broken masculine ethos that seeks recovery. After all, there *is* a product to masturbation, in the form of semen on the floor. As meticulous as the narrator is about his laundry, he nevertheless allows those remnants of sperm to settle under his chair throughout the following days as he carefully observes them: an alternative writing project, composed in traces of ejaculate.

What is the meaning of such a writing project? When *That Smell* initially appeared, the eminent critic Yahya Haqqi, to whom Ibrahim had personally handed a copy, published a scathing review in his weekly column in *al-Masa'*, singling out this scene in particular:

> Not content to show us his hero masturbating (if the matter had ended there it would have been of little importance), he also describes the hero's return a day later to where the traces of his sperm lie on the ground. This physiological description absolutely nauseated me, and it prevented me from enjoying the story despite its skillful telling. I am not condemning its morality, but its lack of sensibility, its lowness, its vulgarity.[85]

Haqqi makes a claim about the proper and improper objects of revulsion, separating between moral aversion (the wasted self-gratification that is masturbation) and a visceral-aesthetic aversion (those physiological traces that remain on the floor). Although moral condemnation should not be a factor in literary appraisal (it is "of little importance"), he considers the viscerally disgusting an improper intruder into the literary space. In his

1986 introduction to the reissued novel, Ibrahim responded to Haqqi, creating an analogy between political violence and the ugliness that his writing practice fails to clean away: "Wasn't a bit of ugliness necessary to expose an equivalent ugliness in 'physiological' acts like beating an unarmed man to death, or shoving a tire pump up his anus, or electric cords into his penis?"[86] Ibrahim's comment seems to suggest a mode of analogy between state violence and the ugly literary work written in semen. If the state has torture devices at its disposal, creative beyond anything a writer could make up, the writer has his own semen, farts, and hygienic failures to document. The disfigurement or debasement of the artwork, wrenching it from the realm of the beautiful to the realm of the disgusting, reflects a similar debasement that has taken place in political life.

If anything, however, this analogy confesses the shortcomings of literature as a meaningful response to state violence. The disgusting, Sianne Ngai observes, is the affective idiom of art that wants to make itself intolerable while recognizing its own political irrelevance and social powerlessness.[87] Discarded semen is hardly an adequate or revelatory response to a disgusting or ugly political reality. Nevertheless, this scene evidently draws a far more visceral response than the episodes explicitly documenting torture. The violence of the torture scenes in *That Smell* is effectively effaced by reproductive routines, the everyday's relentless repetition. The moment in the text that is viscerally felt is when maintenance momentarily breaks down, producing a writing project in sperm and allowing it to endure. Leaving the semen on the floor is a curated oversight, a minor disruption in an otherwise well-kept routine of cleaning and maintenance. It is a glitch, a momentary breakdown that interrupts the functioning routine, "revealing the wiring beneath the technology."[88] Such a minor slipping draws attention to the workings of the system far more effectively than the exposure or documentation of its all-too-smooth functioning in the torture cell.

In a piece titled "Manifesto for the Broken Machine," media theorist Sarah Sharma suggests a feminist politics that operates from the position of "being understood as a technology that does not work properly" within patriarchy.[89] Rather than searching for a fix or an update, Sharma calls to "co-opt the already attributed status of Broken Machine and continue this work of not working well" as the basis for a resistant practice.[90] Sharma refers to feminist bodies that are viewed as failing to properly perform the roles assigned to them in patriarchy. The body of the narrator of *That*

Smell is clearly not that body—as a male body, it is supposed to perform a different set of roles, such as sexual virility or heroic productivity, and its association with the routines of reproduction is already a disorienting gesture. Nevertheless, its meaningful political moments are not in this substitution itself, read simply as a metaphor of failed masculinity. The narrator's body becomes visible when it occupies the position of a glitching, broken machine, missing a beat in its otherwise smooth operation of the tasks of routine maintenance. Being a broken machine is not at all like breaking the machine. It is an alternative model of critique, which recognizes and inhabits the mechanistic cyclical temporality of routine. Writing-as-sperm-traces does not break or shatter anything; it does not reliquify a stagnated sphere or usher in a new era. Instead, it reveals the workings of a violent order in minor moments of breakdown or disruption.

AN EVER-RECEDING BORDER

That Smell adopts the self-effacing form of reproductive labor to narrate the effects and affects of the state's law-preserving violence. Yeshayahu Koren's *Funeral at Noon* similarly employs the static form of maintenance routine, but it is more explicitly concerned with the domestic space of the marital home and its gendered dynamics. The protagonist of *Funeral*, Hagar Erlich, is a young housewife living with her husband, Tuvia, in an unnamed Israeli colony in the late 1950s, a few kilometers from the Jordanian border. It is a small place, and everyone keeps a close watch on their neighbors. Hagar's days are filled with the repetitive, administrative tasks of the everyday: shopping, cooking, eating, cleaning, washing, sleeping. She and Tuvia have no children, as several of the other characters critically note, and their relationship is distant, nearly wordless. The townspeople generally disapprove of Hagar, who too often is seen wandering outside the home. "She is always out there, seeking," one of the neighbors notes.[91] In the ruins of a neighboring Arab village, Hagar meets a soldier and sleeps with him, unaware that Yiftach—a neighbor's ten-year-old son, left under Hagar's care—followed her and saw them. That evening, Yiftach does not come home. His body is found in an old well in the fields several weeks later, and Hagar is blamed for the tragedy. By the novel's end, she packs her bags to leave. This quick sketch of a plot makes *Funeral* appear like a classic housewife novel: a dissatisfied housewife, exasperated by the futile routine of domestic and reproductive labor, goes out to seek illicit adventure. Her stepping out of order leads to catastrophe, but it is a tragic sacrifice necessary for her liberation: finally, she is able to leave the home and its cyclical rhythms and join the linear flow of time.[92] The narrative scaffolding of a novel of housewife liberation is evident, but the circular, repetitive rhythms of housework once again efface all events and pivotal transformations, making the genre inoperative.

Funeral establishes a clear connection between the routine of the housewife and the young state by zealously mapping geographical landmarks, paths, and borders. The space surrounding the colony is a detailed textured landscape, its markers fixed repeatedly into place: the olive trees next to the Arab village, the village in front of the stone fence, the fence leading to the old orchard, the old orchard giving way to the new orange grove, the grove concealing the military base, and so on. The repeated iteration of this geography almost urges the reader to take out a pencil and sketch the layout of the colony's few streets and the agricultural lands around it, to draw a map for the characters' wanderings. This fetishized and static space of the state is the outcome and residue of historical time.[93] There are two distinct time frames in *Funeral*, marked by two narrative styles. The novel's present, the time of statehood, is narrated in a paratactic, slowed-down mode: every action is broken down to its minute gestures until it becomes a series of states, all equally unexceptional. This narrative of the present is occasionally interspersed with historical "background," interludes that give a partial backstory to some of the characters and to the colony's growth. These "historical" sections are composed in a more conventional narrative mode: longer sentences clearly aligning cause with effect and discerning the noteworthy from the marginal. The time of the past is linear and progressive; its characters have clear trajectories. The time of the present, which is state time, is suspended in the circular, reproductive temporality of the everyday.

At the center of *Funeral*'s geography, and dividing these two temporal modes, is the site where the novel's most dramatic and significant events take place: "the abandoned Arab village" neighboring the colony. The colony's residents still remember how in prestate times, merely ten years earlier, they used to buy milk and eggs from the villagers. How the village was destroyed and what happened to the villagers are never mentioned. As the critic Ayman Siksek notes, these stories are "expelled from the text."[94] Early commentators on *Funeral* had also overlooked the specificity of the village, treating it as if it were an ahistorical and natural part of the local landscape, as the novel's characters tend to do.[95] But since the early 2000s, critical scholarship began addressing the village's present-absent role in the text as indicative of the way knowledge of the hundreds of villages violently emptied and destroyed in 1948—the Palestinian Nakba—operates in the Israeli public psyche. Gil Hochberg argues that the village's ruins are "a ghostly presence": like a phantom, the village exerts powerful influence on the characters and the plot even though, or rather because, there is no real reckoning or acknowledgement of the constitutive violence that destroyed it.[96] The empty village is a constant reminder of the moment of the state's founding and the violence that enabled it, the expulsion of the Palestinian population.

Continuously evoking the unnamed village, the novel is caught in the cyclical temporality of state time that the village's destruction initiated and enabled. This repetitive cycle appears in *Funeral*'s very first lines: "Hagar Erlich was sitting on the veranda overlooking the deserted Arab village. An open magazine was lying on the floor next to the round, wooden legs of her chair. She sat looking around her. Among the houses of the ruined village she suddenly noticed a platoon of soldiers. There were packs on their backs. They were walking in a long line."[97] What Hagar observes, in this first scene from which the novel sets out, is a reenactment of the village's conquest in 1948. The soldiers use the village as a training site, returning daily to stage its conquest and occupation. Hagar becomes fascinated with the soldiers' moves through the village, looking out for them in the following days: "On Friday afternoon she again sat on the veranda and watched the Arab village. And on Saturday too, when they got back from the beach. But it was only on Sunday, after lunch, that she saw them again. Appearing and disappearing between the ruined houses. A platoon of soldiers. Wearing packs and steel helmets" (*Funeral*, 9). The word "only" betrays, in this objective, functional narration, that Hagar was not just looking at the village but looking out for the soldiers as they reenact the moment of the village's conquest.

The soldiers' presence eerily resuscitates the village—when Hagar visits it in their wake, "the smell of the *tabun* [outdoor ovens] still lingered. . . . The troughs were full of water. An old pail, tied to a rope, lay on its side on the paving stones bordering the well. There was smoke rising from one of the courtyards" (*Funeral*, 4). The village is brought back to life, prepared once again for the following day's conquest. These repeated reenactments embody the circular, self-effacing temporality of state time in a macabre parody of ceremonies of commemoration. Hagar's fascination with them marks an affinity between the circular time of the state and the circular temporality of the housewife. Like Hagar's labor, practices of border policing and sovereignty maintenance are productless and self-effacing, invested in the reproduction of the present. The everyday temporality conceals such acts of routine, law-preserving violence.

As in *That Smell*, the dramatic events of *Funeral* are effaced and rendered ineffectual. Rather than the Aristotelian model of discovery that leads to reversal, the novel is full of open secrets—knowledge that does not lead to a palpable difference in the world.[98] Characters continue to fulfill the duties of routine rather than voice their knowledge and integrate it into their actions. Tovia knows of Hagar's lies and sexual encounter with the soldier, and Hagar knows he knows, yet they silently continue their life together. Their silence parallels the epistemological place of the Arab village and its known-yet-unmentioned history in the text, which Hochberg calls a "visible invisibility."[99] *Funeral* employs two kinds of techniques to evade the eventual logic of plot and subsume it under the static form of routine: the first is to bar access to the characters' interiority, which I discuss later in this chapter, and the second is to deter attention from the event to its material residues and minor gestures. As Idan Landau notes, in many of Koren's stories the plot disappears behind its numerous traces, forcing the reader to toil on its extraction from among countless details and suspensions.[100] Although the groundworks for a dramatically decisive plot are in place—marital infidelity, the death of a child, Hagar's eventual departure—none of these are narrated directly but rather through their residues and minute effects. Time is not divided to before and after a decisive turning point but is broken down to tiny traces and shifts.

Hagar's transgression of the conventions of marriage is anticipated early in the novel, in the first of the two funerals that bookend it. The deceased is a local schoolteacher, a model of feminized reproductive care ("a good woman," the mourners comment repeatedly) that Hagar is supposed to emulate—she later half-heartedly attempts to take up the deceased teacher's position at the school. During the funeral, Hagar "does not mingle with the mourners" and remains "behind the fence" of the cemetery, removed from the crowds.[101] The expression "behind the fence" (*me'aḥorey ha-gader*), mentioned twice in this scene, is conspicuous. It is the title of a famous 1909 novella by H. N. Bialik, which narrates an illicit erotic affair between a Jewish boy and a Russian peasant girl. The term is borrowed from Talmudic disputes associated with eavesdropping or sexual deviance.[102] These disputes all concern *pritsut*—a term most immediately translated as "harlotry" but that etymologically connotes a breaching and transgression of borders. The desire for such illicit transgression is said to characterize a post-Temple world, fallen from grace. *Prutsa*, the term used for a harlot, a prostitute, or a woman associated with sexual deviancy, is a woman whose borders have been penetrated and left open. It is the same term used for a fence that has been breached.

This intertextual moment prefigures Hagar's own transgression of the marital codes, setting up an expectation for a dramatic breaching of borders. Yet such clear spatial transgression is noticeably absent from the account of Hagar's meeting with the soldier: the two of them meet in the ruins of the Palestinian village and walk east, in the direction of the mountains visible across the state border. They cross a field, a canal, another abandoned settlement, more fields, a row of pine trees, and an orchard: a series of endless spatial deferrals.

> Beyond the orchard was an old tarred road. Next to the road there was a sign: "Stop! Border ahead!"
>
> "We already crossed the railway tracks," she said. "Where are you leading me?" She took a step towards him and put her hand on the knitting bag in his hand.
>
> "Don't be frightened," he said, "it's only a warning. It's another four hundred meters to the border." The sign was yellow, and someone scribbled on it in white chalk. The letters were red.[103]

The border is never crossed but remains a warning (or a promise). Like a mirage, it is continually postponed and pushed back, its authoritative stance blurred by chalk marks. Hagar and the soldier never actually cross the border, never transgress it, but follow an asymptotic curve, getting infinitely closer to it. The reader, expecting a transgressive event, keeps bumping at knitting bags, stumbling over loose gravel, getting pebbles in their shoes—the event is persistently postponed by the material of routine. One never crosses the border to its other side.

Against the two dominant narrative forms of the event and the everyday, *Funeral* suggests the form of the asymptotic curve, a model that eats away at both the event's claim of singularity and at the everyday's promise of repetition in favor of infinitesimally minor and gradual change. Likewise, the end of Hagar's marriage is not a slammed-door departure but an accumulation of details that conceals it:

> "Will you help me take the suitcases to the bus station?" she had asked Tuvia in the morning. She was standing on the ladder and climbing up to the storage loft over the bathroom. There was a Band-Aid stuck to her forehead, and white powder falling into her hair. He took the dusty cases from her and put them down on the floor. Out of the corner of her eye she saw him brushing off the dust. "Yes," he said. After that he said nothing. With a sharp knife Hagar tried to scrape the calcium deposits from the kettle.[104]

The event of Hagar's departure never decisively takes place, neither as a transgression nor as liberation, but rather accumulates and hardens like the calcium residues at the bottom of the kettle, residues that cannot be simply cut off but demand protracted physical labor of scraping at the hardened calcium with a knife. Notably, it is the stuff of housework—dust, the Band-Aid covering the previous night's scratch, the water kettle—that are the means of narrating this departure. Hagar's departure cannot be narrated as a decisive entry into a new temporality because the border, the moment of "crossing over," is continuously postponed and dissipated.

CONCRETE BODIES

Proceeding through minor accumulation and amplification, the novel appears to be a snapshot of regular, daily, "Israeli life," as put in one of its early reviews, turning away from tales of heroes and historical events.[105] The novel's attention to the body, to its physical needs and to its encounter with its material surrounding, has been associated with what critics call Koren's "tangible" or "concrete" (*muḥashi*) rhetoric. This concreteness has been the basis for widely divergent interpretations. Whereas Landau comments on the "sensorial ecstasy" of the haptic encounter with the concrete world, which always exceeds cognitive processing, Kfir Cohen-Lustig associates Koren's concreteness with Alain Robbe-Grillet's aesthetics of the Nouveau Roman and with a desire "to block the symbolic and allegorical levels of the text," eventually arguing that this concreteness is a mark of Hagar's "impoverished body's" lack of "political spirit."[106] Both approaches frame Koren's engagement with the concrete and material as a shift away from a literary style whose political allegories are explicit to a writing aesthetic that captures life "as it is." Their focus on the same textual feature—Koren's meticulous attention to detailed material and sensory input—has nevertheless inspired two seemingly opposing interpretations: the former finds that the concrete is throbbing with ecstatic secular immanence, while the latter argues that the concrete is the signature of a world bereft of spirit. Against both, I suggest withholding the assumption that the concrete is an attempt to touch life or experience "in its bareness" (and so get dragged into an ontological discussion of what that bare experience is), and instead focusing on concreteness as a textual form and on the affective experience of reading that it generates.

Despite its apparent concreteness and mundaneness, *Funeral at Noon* remains, for lack of a better word, mysterious. The reader feels as if they are hovering at the periphery of a great discovery, left perplexed if not frustrated that "at the end of the novel we still know nothing."[107] Every element in the material descriptions of the dusty colony emanates potential symbolism. The supposedly singular concrete reality is rife with repeating details and fetish objects—most perplexing among them is a military canteen that continuously changes hands between Hagar, the soldier, and Yiftach. This is partially explained by Maurice Blanchot's fundamental paradox of the elusiveness of the everyday: if the everyday is that which is insignificant, its inclusion in the formal framework of the text or the novel inevitably singles it out and attributes it with significance.[108] But *Funeral* continuously makes promises for allegorical and intertextual significance and never quite delivers. Just beyond the plot of the small border colony hovers a biblical allegory whose characters and tropes have been scrambled: Hagar and Sara (Yiftach's mother); procreation, banishment, and sacrifice; bushes, thickets, wells, and thirst—all key words from the verses relating the biblical Hagar's banishment (Genesis 21), the binding of Isaac (Genesis 22), and the sacrifice of Jephthah's daughter (*bat Yiftach*, Judges 11). These circulate like a riddle begging to be solved, intimating that alongside the overt narrative level, a moral and historical allegory is at work.[109]

Erich Auerbach memorably argued that the biblical text, which "remains mysterious and 'fraught with background' . . . is permeated with the most unrelieved suspense."[110] *Funeral* shares many attributes with the biblical style, as Auerbach diagnoses it. Here, too, speech does not serve to manifest or to externalize thoughts, but "on the contrary, it serves to indicate thoughts which remain unexpressed." In fact, "everything remains unexpressed," creating a text "greatly in need of interpretation."[111] There is an evident difference, too, between Koren's text and the biblical one, for whereas in the biblical narrative, "the decisive points alone are emphasized, what lies between is nonexistent,"[112] in *Funeral*, the "space between" the decisive points is filled with sensorial input, so that it is nearly impossible, as discussed earlier, to recognize such evental, decisive points when they do occur.

If the affective correlate of the biblical text is unrelieved suspense, *Funeral*'s affect is more akin to irritated, fraught boredom. The promise of allegorical interpretation grates against the detailed, seemingly mundane and secular concreteness, creating a particular mode of embodied reading, at once suspenseful and uninterested, both irritated and wearied. Despite its appearance as or association with emptiness, boredom is often *experienced* as a fidgety intensity, "a desire for desire," in Tolstoy's known phrase.[113] Boredom is a state of suspended anticipation for an unspecified, unarticulated object, a restless yearning for *something* different. As Elizabeth S. Goodstein argues, the inability to find meaning in experience is the particular mark of boredom as a modern affect.[114] This observation illuminates how *Funeral*'s shuffling between the concrete and that which demands (and fails) interpretation becomes a vessel for a reading experience that is simultaneously suspenseful and bored.

Is Hagar simply a bored housewife?[115] This question is difficult to answer. The narrative voice provides no access to Hagar's feelings or thoughts, only to her embodied gestures and sensations, delivering a minute record of seemingly objective sensorial input. Such restricted character construction creates a structural difficulty within the conventions of the housewife genre, which is premised upon access to a female character's interior dramas—the narration of her dissatisfaction or desires. Numerous scholars have argued that the psychological novel has developed as a necessary correlate to heroine-centered fiction because in earlier storytelling genres feminine action often "distinguishes itself from inaction only minimally."[116] Forgoing the narration of psychological, "interior" narrative, *Funeral* resurfaces the structural difficulty of female-centered fiction by positioning Hagar as a passive body whose meanings cannot be satisfactorily and conclusively read. The concrete narration creates a sense of a body driven by inertia rather than agentive will. Internal conflict and deliberation are displaced onto geography: "To her left the road continued to the shops and the square. To her right—to the ruined Arab village. In the middle of the open field in front of her was a narrow path. A solitary donkey, tethered to the stump of a tree, was grazing on the grass. She stepped onto the path and walked towards the village."[117] The seemingly concrete landscape description conceals a drama of choice, a hesitation regarding whether to walk toward the colony's social and commercial center or toward the unsanctioned space of the emptied Arab village. The donkey diverts the reader's attention from the decision that in fact has been made. Internal conflict has been externalized and depersonalized in a manner that makes the body itself appear mechanistic. The third-person narrative voice stays close to Hagar's body, documenting physical, embodied affects, such as thirst, fatigue, or skin-surface irritation, as well as her minute sensorial experience of her surroundings:

> [Hagar] opened her eyes, looked at the wall opposite, at the open window and the closed shutter. Then she spread her hands on the table. Her arms were bare, and a breath of cold air from the window brushed them. Her fingers touched a dry piece of paper. It was the theatre ticket which Tuvia had left on the table before going to bed. The stub was still attached to the ticket. (*Funeral*, 138)

The narration consists of sensorial input: first visual (seeing the window), then haptic (the cold air, the dry piece of paper), and only finally factually cognitive (the identification of the paper as a theatre ticket and the associated, barely mentioned drama of Hagar missing the show). Hagar's thoughts, feelings, and decisions are secreted and concealed behind this mode of narration.

Skin-level contact is the primary means of the text to communicate affective states. Hagar is constantly rubbing and running against the dry, itchy, irritating bits of the material world: "a dry leaf got into one of her flat shoes" (*Funeral*, 3); "there was a grain of salt sticking to Hagar's hand" (6); "she placed the white ribbon on her throat. The ribbon irritated her skin slightly" (213); "a mosquito hit her forehead and got entangled in the lock of hair falling over the scratch. The mosquito whined and buzzed in her ear" (248). Hagar's unease and fatigued irritation is made apparent through descriptions of grating textures rubbing against her skin. Her boredom, if it is indeed boredom, is an irritated, stuffy, ear-buzzing and skin-scratching kind of boredom: a boredom underlined by a low-level drone, physically experienced as aggravated restlessness.

This embodied restlessness risks overtaking the reader as well. Cognitive images introduced by text can have unpleasant visceral effects: "The fingernails scratched at the wall. The soft fingers were misshapen"(*Funeral*, 16). The transmission of irritation, however, is not limited to such mimetic moments. As action is slowed down, suspended, and dismantled into innumerable details, language too departs from its transparent function of mimetic description, allowing for increased awareness of its material texture. The deceleration of action reduces information to texture, just like when zooming in on a photograph, the image eventually becomes simply noise or static, unreadable visual marks. The reader's encounter with the blown-up text, like Hagar's encounter with the concrete world, is noisy, grating, and scratchy, putting the reader in the same state of irritated suspension that is characteristic of Hagar's boredom. Language is concrete, not merely because it refers to a concrete "real" world but because its material texture becomes evident. Reading slowly, against the tangible resistances of language and matter, becomes "a kind of special work" to use Karl Schoonover's term, a practice of reading that yields no tangible product beyond irritated sensation.[118]

HOUSEWORK AS GROUND ZERO

The routine of housework, as dull and sordid as it is, cannot simply be refused. Silvia Federici writes in her later work that the complexity of any political stance centered on reproductive labor has to do with its "double character:" On the one hand, reproductive labor "reproduces us for capital" and for the market as labor power; on the other hand, it produces and sustains our lives and potentially the resistance to capitalism as well. The inherent contradictions of the sustaining labor of housework make it the "*ground zero* of revolutionary practice."[119] "It is impossible to draw a line between the two corresponding aspects of reproductive work," Federici writes, "but maintaining the concept brings out the tension, the potential separation, it suggests a world of conflicts, resistances, contradictions that have political significance."[120] The static form of routine that structures both *Funeral* and *That Smell* gestures toward the need to maintain the tension between housework's repressive and liberationist aspects. These novels do so not through melodramatic fantasies of escape to a sphere where the daily labor of maintenance is no longer pertinent or by glorifying the cyclicality of unacknowledged care work, but instead by doubling down and adopting housework and its circularity as a literary limit. It is within the logic of this circular, repetitive labor that their practice of critique of state time, and of the violence inherent to it, takes place. Both of these novels are strict exercises in form, inhabiting its circular, repetitive, and mundane boundaries in order to explore what can be achieved within them. Repetition is not only their structure, but their mimetic technique, as they interrogate the affective textures of the labor of reproduction: boredom and revulsion. Within the formal logic of state time, they suggest alternative models for critical practice, departing from the imagery of the slammed-door departure or the revolutionary rupture in favor of forms of minor adjustment: the asymptotic graph, the glitch in the machine. By adopting the temporality of state time as a form, they uncover its ongoing and hence unnoticed violence, and yet they remain within its confines, committed to the ground zero of housework.

The temporality of routine as it is narrated in the two novels allows for a reconsideration of the "event" against which they are so often read: the 1967 war and its popular historiography in both Egypt and Israel. The extent that 1967 is cast as a transformative break in models of statehood, citizenship, and culture, in both Egypt and Israel, cannot be underestimated. Known in Arabic as *al-naksa* (the setback or relapse), which positions it within a particular historical narrative of ascendance and regression, or *al-hazima* (the defeat), 1967 is commemorated as a moment in which Arab nationalism was revealed as bankrupt. The impact of the defeat was intensely debated by writers and critics at the time: Was it a decisive rupture, a natural progression of the events of the decade, or a defeat that had all but been clearly predicted by the artists of the age?[121] Intellectual histories of the Arab Middle East still tend to be organized around the rupture point of 1967, making it difficult to escape the lasting legacy of this historiographical narrative on concepts of the present.[122] In Israel, meanwhile, the Six-Day War, as it is known, established the ongoing occupation of the West Bank and Gaza and the factual evacuation of any of the state's claims to a democratic regime. The quick and unequivocal victory marked the emergence of a period of political euphoria and messianic aspirations. Military chauvinism and national pride came together in a newly established assurance in the future survival of a state.

The novels of routine read in this chapter challenge the temptations of an event-based historiography that posits 1967 as a singular transformative event. Ibrahim's *That Smell*, although it was published in 1966, already gives full articulation to the intellectual crisis associated with the 1967 defeat: distrust of language, loss of faith in intellectual life, and political impasse. Rather than granting the book prophetic powers, it is more accurate to see it as expressing currents, tensions, and modes of experience already present several years before the military defeat itself. A novel that Ibrahim composed in 1968 in Beirut under the title *67* appears to corroborate this view.[123] *67*, which was stowed away for years and eventually published in 2015, covers the entire year, depicting a disintegrating social sphere. The six days of war, in the middle of the novel, bring about little change and merit little attention—if anything, the war exacerbates trends that were present earlier.

Similarly, the games of attraction and trepidation that *Funeral at Noon* stages around the border have been read as an antidote or corrective to Israel's triumphant expansionism of 1967, even though the novel was composed almost a year before the war.[124] Such chronologies tend to forget that Israel's drive to enlarge its borders was not born in 1967 but was ongoing, as evident in the 1956 occupation of the Gaza Strip, which lasted only a few months as a result of international pressure. *Funeral at Noon*'s static form highlights the ongoing violence of routine state maintenance as well as the expansionist phantasm underlying settler colonial statehood, rather than condemning the moment in which the state "exceeds its bounds."

The contours and limits of this kind of critique are manifest in a short obituary for the writer, editor, and translator Aharon Amir, published by Koren in the daily newspaper *Ha'aretz* in 2018. After a complimentary tribute to Amir's role in encouraging Koren as a young writer, the true topic of the essay emerges: Amir's Canaanite vision of a vast "land of the Hebrews," extending far beyond the Jordan River.[125] A few months before the 1967 war, Koren relates, Amir told him that Israel is about to become a regional empire in a few short years, and he subsequently saw the war as the first step toward the realization of that vision. Amir, Koren relates, "loved the flap of the great wings of History and wanted to become part of it through the dream of the Great Hebrew Nation."[126] The title of the obituary, "It Rained Weakly," refers to Koren's account of a meeting in a Paris café in which Amir laid out his vision. "My own opinion was very different," writes Koren, but he doesn't elaborate. Instead, he continues: "Outside, it rained weakly. We sat alone at a small café. When we were about to leave, even the waiter had disappeared. We left a few old francs on the table and went out. The rain hadn't stopped, but Aharon was still quietly weaving his great dream. Only when I returned to my room I realized I had left my umbrella at the café." Nothing is said, and nearly nothing happens. Koren contrasts Amir's dreams of imperial mastery merely with "weak rain." Transcendental history dissipates in the minor gestures of everyday life, overwhelmed by a forgotten umbrella. The dream of empire is marginalized, forever postponed by the necessary routines and minor objects of daily life.

Chapter Four

THRESHOLD

The Limit of Correspondence

Up to this point, this book has followed a comparative structure. Modern Arabic and Hebrew writers, the previous chapters argued, often wrote within and against the context of parallel institutions and ideologies, mediating similar structures of feelings. The comparative reading enabled the Hebrew and Arabic texts' extraction from a national and monolingual lineage, placing them instead in the context of regional and global dynamics and modes of literary production. The following final chapter, however, which turns to Palestinian literature from the first two decades of the twenty-first century, departs from the bilingual framework that has structured the book thus far. There are a number of reasons for this shift. First, without overburdening the paradigm of the historical break that was discussed in the previous chapter, the war of 1967 and its regional and localized aftermaths mark the disintegration of the usefulness of the comparative framework that has structured this study so far. *Static Forms* began with the shared problem of "revival modernity" and proceeded to examine discourses of modernization of time, settlement, and labor. As of the mid 1970s, the underlying material conditions, political institutions, and ideological formations of Hebrew culture increasingly diverge from those of its Arab contemporaries, and the developmental discourse of modernization no longer supports a framework for a parallel reading. Israel's "adoption" by the United States and its growing alignment with neoliberal market policies set it on a different trajectory than its neighbors—no longer in the global economic periphery but at its center. The limbo-like political status of the occupied Palestinian territories in the West Bank, Gaza, and East Jerusalem, nominally temporary but de facto always headed toward annexation, made the Israeli state a sovereign structure that denies its own borders, governs millions of noncitizen subjects, and relies on a labor force of noncitizens, both Palestinians and migrant laborers. There is of course a framework for a productive reading of Hebrew and Arabic cultural production under neoliberalism, which would likely focus on works from Israel alongside those from the United Arab Emirates or Saudi Arabia, other sites rapidly integrated into the core of a globalized financial economy and relying on similar structures of labor and population management. It would exceed, however, the scope of this study, which focuses on literary temporalities in relation to modernizing discourses.

The second reason pertains specifically to chapter 5's focus on Palestinian literature. In an article that concludes with a reading of Adania Shibli's *Minor Detail* as a worldly text, Ella Elbaz offers a thorough analysis of the affordances and shortcomings of the scholarly tendency to read Hebrew and Palestinian literature together and comparatively, arguing that this coupling often puts "one side of the equation to work for the other."[1] Reading Palestinian literature with, against, or through Hebrew literature often delimits the scope of questions, themes, and tropes that the text is made to speak to. The previous chapters of *Static Forms* "coupled" Arabic and Hebrew texts not through their encounter in the geopolitical space of Palestine and Israel, but because of their formal affinities—the parallel solutions they came up with to narrate their present. But the "Israeli present" and the "Palestinian present"—which here means the present as narrated by Israeli Jews and the present as narrated by Palestinians in the geographic space of Palestine/Israel—simply do not align.[2] Their genres of the present are different.

This is not to say that they are not subject to some of the same dynamics. Both Jewish Israeli and Palestinian writers are part of a global present shaped by broader economic trends, namely globalization and the shift to neoliberal economic rationales, structures of governance, and models of subject formation. Kfir Cohen identifies this "common global *condition*— i.e. a form of private life for whom politics has become a problem, and social life has turned into a text to be read rather than an object to be made," as the shared historical and aesthetic basis for a global comparative study, which is the framework in which he reads Israeli and Palestinian texts together.³ The temporality of a prolonged, expanded, and chronic present, which Mathias Nilges sums up as "the collapse of the future into the long now," emerges everywhere in relation to this global condition.⁴ This sense of a stubbornly and claustrophobically prolonged present is evident in both Jewish-Israeli and Palestinian cultural production since the late 1990s and can certainly be traced back to the global trends usually associated with the present's stagnation: the end of the Cold War, the speed of changes in technology and consumption that paradoxically produces the feeling that "nothing can change anymore,"⁵ and most prominently, capitalist logics of accumulation's seizure of most spheres of social life and the individualized subjects they produce. Nevertheless, this stagnated temporality translates into distinctly localized narratives in Palestinian culture and Jewish Israeli culture, shaped by the radically unequal modes of access to political sovereignty for Palestinians and Jewish Israelis. My argument is not that the "national" in this case is still taking precedence over the "global" or the "economic," but rather that to speak of them separately makes little sense: it is global economic logics that shape national-political dynamics and narratives, within which Israeli and Palestinian literatures still very explicitly place themselves, attempting to define, often quite explicitly, a "Palestinian condition" or an "Israeli condition."⁶

In both Palestinian and Hebrew literatures, the post-Oslo period is often described as a time of stagnation and stasis. The Oslo Process, which culminated in the signing of the Oslo Accords in Washington, DC (1993), and Egypt (1995), was supposed to lead to the conclusion of the Israeli-Palestinian conflict through the establishment of an independent Palestinian state alongside Israel. It created the Palestinian National Authority (PA) as an interim self-government with restricted power in some areas of the West Bank and the Gaza Strip.⁷ Both the vision of Oslo and its aftermath were aligned with global economic open-market initiatives, what Kareem Rabie calls "ideological practices centered around markets as political solutions."⁸ In explicit contradiction of Oslo's stated aims, Israel continued and accelerated the West Bank settlement project. Oslo's failure of establishing Palestinian political autonomy led to the second intifada in 2000, to which Israel responded with the implementation of an extensive and repressive regime of surveillance, curtailed mobility, and fragmentation of Palestinian space. The Israeli state's nominal political commitment to "conflict resolution" shifted to a policy of "conflict management," a set of practices for violent administration of people and space "yoked to a forever deferred future solution."[9]

The sense of the suspended present in Palestine, as I elaborate in the following chapter, was inevitably bound with these new developments: a vision of decolonial struggle was replaced with a horizon of neoliberal accumulation, increasingly normalized violence, bantustanization of space, and governance practices producing pervasive uncertainty about the future, which all led to the sense of a "future impossible," as Hoda El-Shakry calls it.[10] These changes pertain primarily to Gaza, which has become a prison and a war zone, and to the West Bank, and to a lesser extent to Palestinian citizens of Israel, even though they have been subject to similar surveillance mechanisms as well as practices of displacement, especially in the Negev. Explicitly countering the geographic and political fragmentation of Palestinian society and space in Oslo's aftermath, a new term emerged in this period to define the Palestinian present as pertaining to the entire geographical area of Palestine and its inhabitants, subject to any modality of Israeli rule: *al-nakba al-mustamirra*, the Ongoing Nakba. I historicize the use of this term in chapter 5, but here I will note that the Ongoing Nakba is a genre of the present: it is a historiographical paradigm that highlights the Nakba as an ongoing and present settler colonial condition rather than a singular paradigmatic event that had lasting cataclysmic consequences. At stake in the term the "Ongoing Nakba" is not the revelation of new "facts" about Palestinians and the Israeli state, but rather a new temporal framework into which these facts fit. The Ongoing Nakba is a structure of feeling, an experience of the present as an ongoing catastrophe, "a barren temporality of suspended yet enduring life."[11]

Hebrew culture of the early 2000s was also marked by a sense of a suspended, continuous present, a modality encapsulated in the term *ha-matsav* ("the situation"). Evoking *ha-matsav* was a mode of speaking about the occupation and Palestinian resistance, epitomized in those years in the threatening figure of the suicide bomber, as an ongoing, static state of being, fluctuating but never coming to an end.[12] As several scholars have argued, this condition has permeated the temporality of Hebrew literature. Already in 1999, Anat Weitzman diagnosed the pervasiveness and absolutism of the Israeli present, which she associated with a rejection of the past and with literature's explicit desire to diagnose the "Israeli condition" as a result of a lack of confidence in its stable existence.[13] Elana Gomel and Vered Karti Shemtov define a new literary genre of the "continuous present," which they call limbotopia and associate with a "sense of being stuck in an historical quicksand that enables neither radical change nor escape into a different reality." Although limbotopia is a global condition, they argue, in Israel, it became "the dominant modality of the historical imagination" since the late 1990s, when "the quasi-messianic hopes of the Israeli left for a decisive resolution of the Israeli-Palestinian conflict were dashed by the assassination of Yitzhak Rabin, the collapse of the Oslo treaties, and the intifada."[14] Developing an analysis of a crisis of historicity in Hebrew literature, Oded Nir borrows Eric Cazdyn's term "Chronic Time" to characterize the time of continued violence in Israel, "time from which not only the possibility of cure, but also that of death, is removed."[15]

Al-nakba al-mustamirra and *ha-matzav* are two genres of the "continuous present" shaped by neoliberal horizons of expectation, but their logics are distinct. *Al-nakba al-mustamirra* looks back to the past and sees the present as still caught within it, subject to the same logics and processes. The stagnant present extends from a stagnant past. *Ha-matzav* is a present removed from any past or context, as if history, or rather time, has just began and is a stillborn, unable to proceed. It gives "complete autonomy to the present at the expense of the past," in Raef Zreik's words.[16] These differences, which are enabled by completely different modes of access to individual and political sovereignty, not only imply different modes of "reading" or interpreting history but also have vastly divergent ethical implications. Because reading them together serves primarily to highlight their divergences, the final chapter focuses on static forms in the Palestinian present in the post-Oslo period, and leaves aside the exploration of the literary forms of the suspended present of *ha-matzav*.[17]

Chapter Five

TOUCH

The Present of Crisis Ordinariness

In 2004, four years into the Second Intifada, the novelist and essayist Ahdaf Soueif traveled to Ramallah where she met with several women Palestinian writers. One of them was Adania Shibli, "the most talked about young writer in the West Bank."[1] Soueif asked her about how the occupation affects her writing. In those years, Israeli forces would regularly attack and invade Palestinian towns in the West Bank and Gaza to pursue arrests; the Israel Defense Forces (IDF) were operating nearly fifty permanently staffed checkpoints in the West Bank and had placed hundreds of roadblocks preventing access to and from Palestinian towns and villages.[2] Shibli's response is stark: she "retreats into a kind of autism (*tawaḥḥud*)," she says. She goes on to describe a mode of focused dissociation, sitting in front of a man "who's talking about how a missile hit his car and killed his wife and his three children and I am taking in the details of how much grey he's got in his hair."[3] Shibli's use of the term "autism" in this instance is generic rather than specific, evoking its colloquial associations: emotional opacity, a withdrawal from sociality to the self, and immersion in supposedly minor or neutral tangible details, such as the grieving man's gray hairs.[4] The autistic position figures here as a defensive move, an instinctive reaction to ongoing, normalized, and relentless violence. It is a move that allows for self-preservation against the threat of complete emotional annihilation. In Shibli's next sentence, however, this position also becomes the basis for literature and writing: "That's fiction [*al-qaṣṣ*]," Shibli comments on the scene. "Reality now is too frightening, impossible to grasp. Yet you could say that fiction becomes a kind of digression or deviation [*inḥirāf*]."[5]

Shibli returns to this paradoxical stance again in a 2017 interview with José García, in response to his question on how she avoids becoming desensitized and "used" to violence. (It is worthwhile pointing out the assumptions embedded in this question: first, that desensitization, or emotional vacuity, is the response to ongoing violence; second, that becoming desensitized is equivalent to getting used to violence; and third, that this is an undesirable mode of reaction overall.) Shibli first expresses skepticism that habituation is something one can fight against. But she continues by reflecting on how a writing practice fits into the emotional economy of ongoing crisis. "In real life, you need to neutralize all your emotions and become numb," she states, "but then writing neutralizes that neutralization. Other people don't have words for their rescue. But something else, a walk, a pavement, a tree, a stone, endless minor objects that turn into the place where they practice their humanity, a place where oppression cannot reach or destroy."[6]

What does it mean to say that writing *neutralizes the neutralization*? Putting down words, in this account, is an investment in a "minor object," something insignificant and mundane in and of itself, like the asphalt or a tree or a stone. Such objects can, through a mode of attentive contemplation, become a site for "practicing humanity," maintaining a sense of a self not completely engulfed by violence and surveillance. Writing is no different from these other mute, inanimate objects, which are nevertheless so crucial for self-preservation. If routine violence demands that one neutralizes and numbs their emotions, then minor practices, like watching a tree or writing, can "neutralize" this numbness and turn it into what Shibli calls a "martial arts move."[7] This doubled neutralization is evocative of the way the term is used in surveillance theory, as a mode of undoing the effectiveness of surveillance technologies.[8] Tactics such as face paint, for example, "neutralize" facial recognition software, concealing or undoing the fluctuating registers and differences tracked by surveilling machines by creating a smooth, undifferentiated, and uninterpretable surface. A tactic of self-defense, neutralization can swiftly become a tactic of passive resistance when it is adopted intentionally as a writing practice—a seemingly neutral, indirect resistance, yet effective nonetheless.

These anecdotes reflect on writing as a practice rather than on its eventual product. What does the neutralized/neutralizing text look like? What is its form, and how does this form relate to neutralization as the emotional practice or structure of feeling that emerges in response to prolonged, normalized violence? This chapter examines how neutralization translates into an aesthetic practice whose formal principle is *touch* or hapticity. "Neutrality" in this context has little to do with political neutrality, but rather with a practiced impassivity and emotional vacuity, the scandalous position that Roland Barthes has identified with "the neutral."[9] While I focus on Shibli's writing, tracing persistent concerns as well as developments in a body of work that now spans more than twenty years, I also periodically allude to the work of Palestinian filmmaker Elia Suleiman, whose films pioneered a distinctive "neutral" style, embodied in the silent and blank-faced character E. S.[10] Suleiman has been an influential interlocutor in Shibli's own work, and the discussion of his films *Chronicle of a Disappearance* (*Sajl ikhtifaʾ*, 1996) and *Divine Intervention* (*Yad Ilahiyya*, 2002) allows this chapter to reflect more broadly on Palestinian cultural production since the 1990s, a time that is often referred to as the post-Oslo period: a period of political stagnation, the deepening entrenchment of the occupation, and the normalization of routine violence in the West Bank and Gaza. I position these works, however, against a historiographical concept that refers to a much longer timeline and diffused geography: *al-nakba al-mustamirra* or the Ongoing Nakba, the ongoing process of dispossession and ethnic cleansing of Palestine that has been consolidated with the establishment of the State of Israel in 1948 and is still enduring.

Within this present of ongoing, normalized violence and its attendant structures of feelings—emotional neutralization and numbness among them—writing takes on a haptic form. Hapticity is a literary aesthetics documenting sensory input, anchored in the minimal dramas of embodied perception rather than in psychic geographies of interiority or emotional narrativity. It registers both "minor" and "major" encounters equally, marking no differentiation between the mundane and the exceptional. This egalitarianism of attention means that haptic forms register, for the reader, as static: white noise that drowns out extremities and fluctuation into one neutralized sound. Thus, hapticity as form necessitates a haptic reading practice—a practice that traces and unfolds static noise into narrative.

When I evoke autistic forms of perception or response in this chapter, I have no intention of extending a diagnosis to fictional characters. Instead, this chapter inquires about the political affordances of the depiction of certain patterns of behavior and perception, such as social aloofness, impassivity, rigidity, or preoccupation with supposedly minor details. These are all means to question and challenge common notions of agency and bodily autonomy in a political situation in which agency is severely curtailed. My use of the term "autism" is indebted to numerous writers and activists, both autist and neurotypical, whose work recasts autism as a particular mode of experience and attentiveness rather than as a deficit or a pathology. Unlike mainstream medical debates on autism, which define autism spectrum disorder (ASD) as a disorder of social communications and of restricted/repetitive behaviors—that is, through its external, interpersonal effects—the scholars and writers I learn from strive to identify forms of perception and expression that characterize autistic modes of experience. An early theory of autistic experience can be found in the work of psychoanalyst Thomas Ogden, who departs from the much-berated psychoanalytic tradition that associated autism with "refrigerator mothers" and early infancy deprivation and instead adopts a phenomenologically inspired approach.[11] Ogden, following Melanie Klein, identifies three basic psychological modes whose interplay structures human experience: the depressive mode, the paranoid-schizoid mode, and the "autistic-contiguous position."[12] The autistic-contiguous position is a psychic organization that is presymbolic and sensory dominated, in which the haptic experience of surface touch is the principal medium through which connections are made and organization achieved. "Sequences, symmetries, periodicity, skin-to-skin 'molding,' are all examples of contiguities that are the ingredients out of which the beginnings of rudimentary self-experience arise," Ogden writes. "The experience of 'self' at this point is simply that of a nonreflective state of sensory 'going on being.' "[13] The autistic-contiguous position embodies a seeming contradiction that will recur in this chapter: while the term "autistic" etymologically connotes isolation or disconnectedness from other subjects, the term "contiguous" denotes the predominant mode of perception in this mode, as a continuous and uninterrupted input of textured surfaces and interacting forms. Meaning in this mode is created through haptic touch, a perceptual experience that, as Eve Kosofsky Sedgwick notes, "makes nonsense out of any dualistic understanding of agency and passivity."[14]

Ogden relies on studies of autistic children to characterize the autistic-contingent position, but he emphasizes that this mode is neither pathological nor an early developmental stage one would outgrow (as the Kleinian approach would have it). Instead, it is a psychological structure that dynamically and dialectically interacts with others in forming human experience. Similarly, the philosopher Erin Manning relies on a growing corpus of interviews and texts by autistic writers to identify a mode of "autistic perception," an unparsed sensory field undifferentiated into categories and hierarchies, "alive with tendings that create ecologies before they coalesce into form."[15] Manning defines autistic perception as sensory input that is not yet parsed into existing configurations and hierarchical differentiations between color, sound, and light and between human and nonhuman and emphasizes that autistic perception is not limited to, inherent to, or definitive of autism but "is a necessary factor in all human experience . . . lived in different ways to different degrees."[16] For neurotypicals, the distribution and division of perception into preestablished categories of self and world, matter and light, and color and movement might happen rapidly and automatically, but these processes can be suspended through practicing alternate modes of attention.

Hapticity is a mode of writing that practices autistic experience—a literary genre composed of unparsed sensorial and embodied input, particularly attentive to texture, rhythm, and form. Hapticity stages a contiguous textual/textural terrain in which the haptic takes precedent over emotional and intersubjective content. To this extent, my appeal to autistic experience differs from other textual-literary studies, such as the identification of autistic rhetoric in output by autist writers, which M. Remi Yergeau pursues in *Authoring Autism*, or the unearthing of similarities between autistic patterns of speech and culturally sanctioned literary works, as in Julia Miele Rodas's *Autistic Disturbances*.[17] Haptic poetics, as practiced in Shibli's writing, adopt autistic perception as an aesthetic principle, privileging the autistic contiguous position over other aspects of experience.

Touch, as noted earlier, upsets common divisions of agency and intentionality. Yergeau observes that "involuntarity dominates much of the discourse on autism, underlying clinical understandings of affect, intention, and socially appropriate response."[18] Rather than accepting a binary of volition/determination, Yergeau demonstrates how autism can queer and challenge normative notions of intent. Shibli's employment of hapticity similarly straddles the line between volition and involuntariness, complicating their opposition. A model of this present-absent intentionality can be found throughout Shibli's body of works. A blueprint for it appears in her very first published piece, a faux-ingenuous review of Elia Suleiman's film *Chronicle of a Disappearance* (*Sajl ikhtifaʾ*, 1996)—a film that, with its long static scenes and famously mute and unaffected protagonist E. S., pioneers the appearance of emotional neutralization in Palestinian cinema.[19] Shibli was a young student living in Jerusalem when she wrote this piece, and she readily admits her lack of experience as a film critic: writing a film review, she remarks, is like entering a dark room and imagining all that it may or may not contain. She then takes full advantage of her "ignorance" of the rules of the genre and composes an idiosyncratic, associative, and personal essay titled "A Dialog with/about the Cinema of the Orient After Watching *Chronicle of a Disappearance*." Despite that, or perhaps because, she is a dabbler in film criticism, Shibli crowns Suleiman's work with the exorbitant "birth of an Oriental cinema [*sīnimā sharqiyya*]," identifying it as an authentic model for the production of a local—Eastern—image. Suleiman doesn't beautify anything, she writes, nor does he ridicule his objects. He creates "non-banal images of the banal."[20]

Nevertheless, the model of the gaze that Shibli associates with Suleiman's work is anything but "authentic," but rather excessively contrived. As an illustration, she begins her review recounting a minor predicament. The previous evening, she had dropped a piece of tomato and stained the same shirt she had planned to wear to the film screening. This accident was not the result of simple clumsiness but rather of an ill-fated experiment: she attempted to eat her salad using her left hand instead of the usual right. Despite the upsetting outcome, she notes the eerie pleasure of using the wrong hand, the hand one cannot so easily control, for such a simple task. Luckily, the name of the film she is scheduled to watch and review, *Chronicle of a Disappearance*, reminds her of a product in the supply cabinet designed to "make oil stains disappear," and so the evening is saved.[21] Shibli returns to this anecdote at the very end of the review to characterize Suleiman's cinematic technique, which she identifies with the salad experiment. The stakes of the experiment become clearer once we realize that the Arabic word *salaṭa*, or "salad," is spelled identically to the word *sulṭa*, or "authority" (inspiring many popular jokes about the Israeli government) and that the shared spelling makes it effectively impossible to establish whether Shibli's experiment is "eating a salad" or "handling/managing control," or more precisely, relinquishing self-control. Watching Suleiman's banality onscreen reveals something hitherto unknown, she writes, akin to "the joy of not being able to control one's left hand."[22]

What Shibli relishes here, and what she recreates in her future literary works, is the experience of looking at one's own body as if from the outside, from the vantage point of a detached stranger, challenging the assumption of a body inhabited and controlled by intention. Shibli has little interest in the model of a Cartesian subject divided into a willful mind and obedient body or, alternately, an autonomous interiority that conceals itself in a body that manifests its desires or wants. The salad experiment casts the autistic "withdrawal into the self" as something new, revealing it to be also a disembodiment or dishabituation of the self, a willing disavowal of the fantasy of intentional control. Yergeau argues that in the medical discourse, "involuntarity is a project of dehumanization," and they are certainly correct.[23] Yet Shibli claims the withdrawal from intention, or the aesthetic practice of autistic perception, precisely as that which allows one to continue practicing their humanity. The simultaneity of being both self-focused and without self, which is so often the paradoxical diagnosis leveled at autism, becomes a site to investigate the many instances in which the distinction between voluntary and involuntary action is meaningless—instances constitutive of action and experience as such. As a formal practice, hapticity dislocate subjectivity from its embodied performance.

The salad experiment also manifests static forms' concern with dirt as a site for negotiating agency and complicity. In chapter 2, Brenner's and Ghanem's protagonists took pleasure in the body's surface contact with dirt and dust, giving in to the temptation to scratch at the skin's and the land's abrasions. In chapter 3, ceremonies of cleaning marked the reproductive circularity of political time. Shibli's work shows most clearly how attention to filth and the ceremonies of its elimination are a means of investigating the workings of power and the boundaries of the self. Dirt, dust, body fluids, and smells appear throughout her oeuvre in moments of disintegration and loss of boundaries, whereas obsessive rituals of hygiene are a means of exerting control on a menacing environment.

Hapticity, as I have defined it thus far, involves an unparsed, haptic mode of perception, a withdrawal from assumptions of willful intentionality or agentive control, and a disinvestment in emotionality or interiority in favor of tracking physical embodied sensation. All these features contribute to a frustrating reading practice, continuously blocking the circulation of sentiment between text, character, and reader. My primary concern, however, is not to argue for the disruptive, queering potential of autistic perception (the writers I have cited earlier already do so forcefully) but rather to examine why it becomes a meaningful, useful form in Palestine in the first two decades of the twenty-first century. What does this form "afford," to borrow Caroline Levine's term, to the writers and cinematographers that employ it?[24] Why does it appear to be the proper vessel for the Palestinian present?

THE PRESENT AS ORDINARY CRISIS

Since the early 2000s, the IDF checkpoint has become the primary site from which to theorize and diagnose "Palestinian time" as a time of suspended waiting.[25] "Undeniably, waiting has become a mode of Palestinian life," Helga Tawil-Souri wrote in 2017, "Palestinians are collectively in-waiting.... This stuckness in waiting has been experienced since at least 1948."[26] This retroactive reading of more than sixty years as a time of suspended waiting is shaped by an affective present of stuckness and deferral, evoked by a number of material and political developments. Prominent among them is the failure of the 1993 Oslo Accords to establish an independent Palestinian state even on a small segment of historic Palestine. In the wake of the Oslo Accords, Palestinian space was fragmented into tightly controlled enclaves and Palestinians themselves were spatially and politically divided, some within the boundaries of 1948 Israel, others subject to direct Israeli military occupation, and yet others governed under the severely curtailed sovereignty of the Palestinian Authority (PA). The separation between Palestinians living inside the 1948 borders and those living in the West Bank was physically buttressed by permanent barriers such as the Separation Wall, and the siege on Gaza enforced its people's severance from both. In the wake of the 2000 Intifada, Israeli policy officially shifted from "conflict resolution" to "conflict management" as a constant rather than temporary political strategy, a shift that entailed the normalization of military violence inflicted on Palestinians in the West Bank and Gaza and the further entrenchment of settler colonialism in the West Bank.[27] These developments were accompanied by Israel's deployment of an extensive surveillance apparatus, monitoring and limiting mobility. Meanwhile, the liberationist politics of the PA were largely succeeded by what Raja Khalidi and Sobhi Samour call "neoliberal liberation," enabling the PA to work toward globalized neoliberal development without directly opposing the occupation.[28] These geopolitical shifts all contributed to a sense of a suspended present—a loss of historical narrativity and a clear future vision.

It is in this period that the term *al-nakba al-mustamirra*, or "the Ongoing Nakba," gradually begins to be used to refer to the Palestinian present. The *Nakba*, literally meaning catastrophe, has become since 1948 the predominant term referring to the Palestinian expulsion with the establishment of the Israeli state.[29] The new terminology, however, reconfigures the meaning of the Nakba: no longer referring to a consequential yet singular event, the Nakba came to mean an ongoing process of settler colonial dispossession and elimination of Palestinians. The first recorded use of the term *al-nakba al-mustamirra* is in a speech delivered in 2001 by Palestinian politician Hannan Ashrawi at the United Nations World Conference Against Racism, Racial Discrimination, Xenophobia, and Related Intolerances.[30] Over the next several years, the term appeared sporadically in Arabic and English publications, but by 2008, it had become ubiquitous. Joseph Massad gave the concept one of its first coherent articulations in a 2008 article in *al-Ahram Weekly*, defining the Nakba as an ongoing process rather than a past event dating to 1948.[31] Massad argues that Palestinians are not living in a post-Nakba world, but are rather living through and resisting the Nakba, an ongoing historical epoch, on a daily basis. Elias Khoury reiterated this point in a 2012 article, published simultaneously in Arabic and English, positioning the "continuous Nakba" against debates in new Zionist historiography.[32] Khoury emphasizes that the Nakba is not only a regime of material violence but also an ongoing battle of interpretation, a system aimed at silencing and erasing the Palestinian story by relegating it to the past.

The change in terminology is significant because it recasts the Nakba from a historical disjuncture driving Palestinians "out of place, out of time," as Elias Sanbar characterizes it, to an ongoing process, and from a focal object of memory that provides a "nagging counter-story of the myth of the birth of Israel," in Lila Abu-Lughod and Ahmed H. Sa'di's words, to a present event that is actively experienced and resisted.[33] In the post-Oslo period, it became apparent that the Nakba is not merely a pivotal point that led to the following displacements, massacres, and repressions of Palestinians within the state of Israel and in the *shatāt* (the Palestinian diasporas), but rather is "a regime," a "present continuous," and "an ongoing and unrelenting ordeal," as Rabea Eghbariah insists.[34] If, at the beginning of the twenty-first century, Abu-Lughod and Sa'di emphasized the importance of memory as a buttress of Palestinian claims, endangered by the "Nakba generation's" aging, nowadays memory seems less significant than the perpetual experience of exclusion, dispossession, and genocidal ethnic cleansing.

The concept of the Ongoing Nakba therefore replaces previously prominent narrative structures of Palestinian dispossession and struggle, such as the narrative of "Nakba and Naksa" ("setback," referring to the 1967 displacement), which is based on the concept of a ruptured national history, or the narrative of a regional and global anti-imperialist liberation struggle. Esmail Nashif identifies a parallel shift in narrative frameworks in Palestinian literature written within the 1948 borders, tracking how previously dominant forms for narrating the Palestinian tragedy—victimization / sacrifice (*ḍaḥiyya*) and resistance (*muqāwama*)—were replaced by a narrative model that he calls "*al-fuqdān al-mutakarrir*" (recurrent loss), which first emerged in the late 1990s.[35] There is no doubt that the burgeoning of settler colonial studies as a comparative paradigm has contributed significantly to recasting the Nakba as a governing structure rather than as a one-time, cataclysmic, and shattering event.[36] But it is not incidental that it emerged in the aftermath of the perceived failures of both armed struggle and diplomatic negotiations, as Israeli violence and dispossession in the curtailed semisovereign spaces of the West Bank and Gaza became both intensified and routine.

The Ongoing Nakba is a historiographical paradigm, but it is also a structure of feeling, a means of making sense of the Palestinian historical present no less than a model for interpreting the Palestinian past. As the term reconfigures the scope of the 1948 expulsion, it also recasts the present as part of an ongoing situation, replacing both the psychoanalytic temporality of traumatic aftermath and the Marxist concept of the present as the "historical sedimentation" of past events. As Nora Parr points out, the concept of "trauma," which suggests a momentous scene of exception that throws an otherwise ordinary existence off course, no longer seems adequate to the Palestinian situation when the Nakba is viewed as an ongoing process or condition.[37] Parr's questioning of the applicability of "trauma" to the Palestinian past-present echoes the work of other scholars who aim to dislodge the discourse of trauma from its prominent position as the defining psychosocial structure of the twentieth century. Trauma, as Lauren Berlant argues, is a particular narrative form or genre that has become ubiquitous in the past eighty years, but its prevalence has overshadowed and concealed other structures of experiences and narratives forms of encountering and making sense of violence and instability. Turning away from the event-based model of trauma in order to speak of entrenched, structural violence, Berlant suggests the term "crisis ordinariness": a crisis that is "not exceptional to history or consciousness but a process embedded in the ordinary, that unfolds in stories about navigating what's overwhelming."[38] The lived quality of crisis ordinariness is the experience of "treading water" rather than drowning—the continuous ordinary adjustments and adaptations that Lori Allen identifies as means of "getting by" and "getting used to" the occupation.[39]

What are the structures of feeling that arise within the prolonged temporality of the ongoing Nakba as a normalized, everyday crisis? What affective forms emerge in a condition of increasingly restricted mobility, both in time and in space? Shibli's early short story "al-Talaʿub bi-l-ʿadid min dharrat al-ghubar" ("Playing with Innumerable Specks of Dust"), published in the Palestinian cultural journal *al-Karmel* in 2002, outlines two possible emotional trajectories: overwhelm or withdrawal.[40] A choppy, fragmented text, it maps the affective landscape of the Palestinian "crisis ordinary" as a pendulum, swinging between the two extremes of feeling too much and feeling too little. Through its careful charting of emotional management and disintegration in the context of daily routines under occupation—its narrator crosses the Qalandia checkpoint between Jerusalem and Ramallah, goes to the market, or sends a package at the post office—it offers an early experiment with some of the characteristics of the haptic form that emerge in Shibli's later work. The story opens with the construction of the checkpoint, a sudden intervention interrupting a fraught routine:

> We were sitting around a kitchen table in Ramallah, making holiday cookies. Only one kilogram of dates for whatever was left of hope, of which we'd already grown tired. A magically nimble hand, like the one making the cookies, would play with daily life, making changes gradually, but never radically.

> But suddenly, as I was returning from Ramallah to Jerusalem that night, giant slabs of cement formed in the air, filling the heart with awe as if they were tablets of law brought down by the angels themselves.
> "Stop. Checkpoint ahead." The first and last commandment.
> For hours, I witnessed the steady construction of a new checkpoint, to be called Qalandia.[41]

Two temporalities of violence contrast in this account. The first is routine: everyday apparatuses of surveillance and control are likened to a "magically nimble hand" whose work proceeds gradually, barely noticed until life has been significantly altered. The second is radically transformative. Into the routine enters an extreme, awe-inspiring intervention, mimicking the hand of the divine power delivering the Ten Commandments, and establishes a new order: a checkpoint. The checkpoint dominates the road between Ramallah and Jerusalem and so dominates the mobility of the narrator who lives between the two cities.

The Qalandia checkpoint was built in 2001, intensifying and solidifying the permit regime that, since 1991, had subjected the circulation of West Bank people, goods, and services to Israeli control.[42] Qalandia is one of the few entryways through the Separation Wall that cuts across what was once a continuous urban fabric, separating some East Jerusalem neighborhoods from others and from the city's urban center. Its construction marked a radical change in the geography of the city and in the choreography of people's movement across it. Qalandiya is not isolated: during this same period, the Israeli military set up a tight network of roadblocks, both permanent and temporary, on the roads between Israeli and Palestinian territories as well as within the West Bank itself, severely hampering movement between the villages and cities. The checkpoint emerged in the early 2000s as a metonymy for the occupation as a whole. It became a common cinematic setting, leading critics to identify an emergent genre of roadblock movies.[43] In Elia Suleiman's 2002 film *Divine Intervention* (*Yad ilahiyya*), for example, checkpoints are unusual nodes of emotional intensity and cinematic fantasy, providing some of the most memorable and spectacular images in a film whose images are otherwise mundane, slow, and emotionally impassive. As a clear, physical manifestation of obstructed agency, the checkpoint came to be associated with a defined set of affects, from frustration to defiance and rage.

In "Dust," the checkpoint is a setting and an impetus for emotional and social disintegration, occasioning a personal and interpersonal collapse. If in the opening paragraph the Israeli military sovereign is characterized as a detached hand, meddling with the life of the occupied population through gradual and minor changes that lead to the gradual attrition of hope, the construction of Qalandia appears with the force of a biblical commandment, a radical upheaval threatening to sever the minimally functional domestic and social routine that opens the story. "Nobody crosses Qalandia check point without a nervous breakdown [*inhiyār*], at least a minor one," the narrator remarks.[44] Temporality at the new checkpoint is characterized by enduring, senseless waiting and random and humiliating acts of routine violence, but its effects colonize time and space far beyond this site. In brief journal-like and essayistic fragments, the story delineates how the breakdown occasioned by the checkpoint spreads to all aspects of the narrator's life. All her interactions become underscored by aggression, suspicion, or hostility: she nearly slaps a clumsy child, is maddened by hatred for fellow passengers in a taxi, and is increasingly convinced that those around her treat her with similar contempt, suspecting her of being a collaborator and a traitor. "Living, it seems, asks nothing more of me than self-destruction," she concludes.[45] Aggression toward others is the impetus for aggression toward the self. The narrator invites the reader not to empathize but to join her in self-flagellation and contempt.

What the narrator finds most distressing are not dramatic moments of violence or suffering, such as soldiers shooting at the checkpoint or stories of families torn apart, which remain in the background, but rather the daily attrition of routine interactions. The way violence and crisis become embedded in the ordinary is through the seemingly minor but potent element of *dust* [*ghubār*]. "Dust. This is how the tragedy [*ma'sa*] is able to engulf all. Even those who walk in the most neutral [*ḥiyādiyyatan*] manner. My hair my face my hands my clothes, all heavy with dust and despair."[46] As Liron Mor writes, dust in this story is neither an allegory nor a symbol, but "is an indexical sign that physically participates in and is directly affected by the phenomenon it represents."[47] Dust materializes the workings of power: it clings, penetrates the body, pollutes it. Crossing the Qalandia checkpoint on foot and walking through the soft layers of dust on the roadside means that the narrator carries a material residue of the checkpoint with her wherever she goes.

Even the determination to remain neutral, uncaring, or uninvolved cannot save her from the contaminating touch of dust, nor can her sporadic cleaning sprees overcome it. In an attempt to come to terms with it, she reasons that it is filth she must bear, proof that she crossed the checkpoint like everyone else, yet there is nothing heroic about being marked with the filth of the checkpoint and of the surveillance regime. To the contrary, dust leaves no unoccupied plot, infiltrating and polluting every supposedly independent stance of defiance, and with the dust, the regime of surveillance and control establishes itself within the self. "What can I defy if these checkpoints are now set up inside me?," the narrator asks.[48] Her anxiety about cleanliness is manifestly political, becoming an anxiety about agency and collaboration. Every small act is a potential collaboration with power, marred with dust; no position can be free of incrimination. Dust is the link between the abstract apparatus of power and the individual body: its filth sinks in, making the skin's surface inconsequential. The narrator eventually turns to a dermatologist for help. She has become porous, lacking a skin to separate between herself as an autonomous agent and the workings of power.

Dust's contamination is a means of narrating the impossible position of hampered agency created by Israel's regime of surveillance, as becomes apparent by the penultimate scene. The narrator is stopped by a soldier who asks why she is carrying a passport rather than an ID card.

> I say because I am free. He repeats his question, so I answer: Because I'm free, because I'm free, because I'm free, because I'm free, because I'm free. Just like that. Because I'm free.
>
> He asks me to step aside. I scream and scream and scream. Just like that. I do nothing but scream. I scream like a mad woman. I scream because I am not a collaborator. The officer comes and hands me my passport as he finds no reason to detain me. But I am still screaming and he asks me politely to leave. And I do not know why he is speaking to me politely. What if someone passed by and saw the officer speaking to me politely, and what if this officer returned and spoke to me politely next time, and what if he memorized my name and called me by it while I am crossing with hundreds of others, to ask me how I was doing that day! What will I say to the passersby! I will scream again, and instead of saying I am a collaborator, they will say I am mad. ("Dust," 103–4)

What is the freedom the narrator can lay claim to? If any polite and smooth interaction with the soldier can be read as an incriminating collaboration, the only recourse is a performance of madness—screaming and screaming as a means of proving one's own freedom by submitting to madness's frenzy. Screaming is another instance of "managing control" (*tanāwul al-sulṭa*) in a situation where any mode of independent agency or self-sovereignty is an illusion. It is preferable to be seen as mad—in other words, not in control of one's own actions and reactions—rather than continue in the routine dictated by the checkpoint's power.

Alongside the haptic tracing of dust accumulating on skin and penetrating the body, "Dust" provides a chronicle in the first person of emotional management. The narrator crosses the checkpoints in order to visit her friends, but that no longer becomes a source of pleasure but a self-imposed duty, a provocation against the checkpoints rather than a joyful social engagement. "I no longer even know whether my friends desire these visits, or if they still love me," she says. "I can no longer feel" ("Dust," 96). But although one effect of the checkpoint is to null one's emotions of intimacy and sociality, it also triggers hostility toward others and subsequently the self, which necessitates conscious management. "I say from inside my pain, 'I don't feel'" (100); the narrator tries to convince herself that the pain is not hers. She tries to learn proper emotional comportment from a friend who cannot visit her family in Nablus because of the checkpoints and has therefore decided "not to miss them too much." Her own problem, the narrator concludes, is that "I think more than necessary, I feel more than necessary, much more than necessary" (101). But not feeling has its own dangers and fears—its own attendant and persistent feelings: "I crossed the checkpoint casually," she notes. "And to accomplish it, all I had to do was freeze all my feelings, deny them for just a short time. But then I became frightened. I was afraid that after I crossed the checkpoint and walked a few meters, I would not be able to regain my capacity to feel. What if I lost the few feelings that still remained to me!" (101). By the end of the story, the narrator is paralyzed; she tries to find a motivation to leave her house, but all she can find is "a trace of neutrality" (103). Feeling too much and feeling too little become hardly distinguishable—both are paralyzing and self-destructive.

Although most of "Dust" is a record of the narrator's interior monologue and of her emotional adjustments, there are sections in which the neutralized, haptic mode of narration begins to emerge. In these moments, embodiment takes precedent over interiorized subjectivity. Standing in line at the post office, the narrator notices two little girls; they "look at me and

I don't know why, I don't want to smile at them. They continue to look at me, especially the one in front of me. I look back at her, until I think I notice a glimpse of fear in her eyes, and my eyes fill with tears. I lower my eyes, and a teardrop falls from my nose to the floor between my feet. The little girl continues to look at me" ("Dust," 97). The emotional drama of this moment, culminating in tears, remains detached from the measured, clipped, and documentary narration—a discrepancy between the narrating consciousness and the emotional apparatus it describes. Both the narrator and the reader examine the responses of this reacting body from outside, despite the use of the intimate first person; the narrating voice does not identify with the body that produces these embodied affects (aggression, tears), nor does it explain them, but it reports them neutrally. Such moments of neutralized yet intimate narration are the kernel of the haptic mode of Shibli's later prose.

"Dust" is a literary experiment in emotional disintegration, swinging violently between feeling too much and feeling too little until it is no longer possible to tell the two apart. Both options come down to a crisis of not feeling "as necessary" (*al-lāzm*) and properly, as if there could be a proper way of responding to the crisis ordinary of the occupation. The story embodies this crisis formally; its choppy form, composed of sections only a few lines long, allows Shibli to include both of these extremes in one tempestuous text. This narrative schizophrenia appears to be unsustainable, and Shibli's first two books divide these emotional peaks (feeling everything; feeling nothing) among them. *Misas* (*Touch*, 2001) develops a neutralized, unaffected mode of narration, pursuing the literary possibilities of haptic form. *Kulluna baʿid bi-dhat al-miqdar ʿan al-hubb* (*We Are All Equally Far from Love*, 2004) features a loosely related series of nameless protagonists tortured by the overwhelming, violent, and desperate pain of the end of love, their uncalibrated aggression (toward self and others) spreading through the novel like a contagion. In both of these short novels, Palestine and the Ongoing Nakba remain in a murky, nonexplicit background. As Shibli notes in an interview with José García, she is not writing about Palestine, but from within its structure of experience.[49] "Dust" functions as a key text to these two novels, linking between their investments in emotional neutralization and emotional unraveling, respectively, and the Ongoing Nakba's structures of experience.

HAPTIC READING

In the review of Suleiman's *Chronicle of a Disappearance* discussed earlier, Shibli makes a dizzying historical detour through discussions of religious iconoclasm, Islamic conventions of modesty, and the "origins" of Arab visuals in the thirteenth century, all to make the point that early Eastern cinema forwent a local visual tradition and instead relied on a Western visual vocabulary as a model. Shibli argues that Western cinema emerged from a long visual tradition grounded in mimesis—the visual imitation of reality—which had no real equivalent in Eastern art traditions. Western cinema's guiding values, such as purity or immortality, hail back to an imagined Greek ancestry and remain the dominant terms in the writing of film theorists like Gilles Deleuze and Roland Barthes.[50] Suleiman's film, she claims, departs from this tradition and succeeds in some mysterious way to tap into Shibli's intimate dream images and project them on the screen. It is a spectacularly audacious reading that saddles Suleiman's film with a historical-civilizational significance, and Shibli herself treats her theorizing with characteristic flippancy (though her constant need to resort to English concepts, written in Latin script, such as "visuals," "imitating," "images," or "framing," illustrates better than any historical anecdote the claim that Arabic lacks a local vocabulary for cinematic analysis). Nevertheless, it proves productive to follow the intuition that modes of vision and visuality in the premodern Arab-Islamic tradition might be pertinent to how both Suleiman and Shibli approach their own method of image making: a tradition that is ornamental rather than mimetic, haptic rather than optic. Laura Marks, in developing the term "haptic vision," argues that abstract, ornamental works of Islamic art "invite a haptic look—one that moves along their surface and discovers momentary ways to make sense of them."[51] This process of sensemaking through visual-sensual touch occurs along the image's surface or skin: the surface is not a window into depth, as in a Renaissance painting, but opaque. It does not invite a penetrating gaze into an assumed interiority, but rather a caress from "a seeing hand, a fingering eye."[52] Simon O'Meara follows Marks, noting that much of premodern Islamic material culture makes a virtue of superficiality, "hiding nothing and rendering interiority as folded exteriority."[53] Examining textual treaties on vision and the spatial geography of the Islamic city, he argues that in premodern Arab-Islamic culture, vision is normatively habituated to look superficially rather than penetratively. The penetrating, discerning, and possessive gaze remains the prerogative of the king or of God.

Whether Marks and O'Meara's generalizing theory is actually applicable to the vast archives of Islamic material culture is beyond the point. What is significant here is that "haptic vision," as they conceive of it, offers an entry point to the mode of image making that Shibli identifies in Suleiman's cinema and subsequently adopts in her own writing. In the novel *Touch*, hapticity rather than interiority becomes the mean of constructing textual images, as well as the method of reading them, through slow sensory input. "Touching. Not mastering," writes Marks.[54] The title of *Touch*, *Misās*, is a word of instruction on how to read its episodes.[55]

Touch traces the perceptions of a young girl, the youngest in a family of nine sisters and a brother. Narrated in the third person, the book organizes the girl's experience into four chapters—"Colors," "Silence," "Movement," and "Language"—as well as a final episode titled "The Wall." Each of the chapters is divided into eight short episodes related to its theme. There are a number of key events these episodes return to, as if the linear narrative has been cut up and rearranged thematically according to the focus on a particular sense. Dramatic events, be they within the personal family sphere, such as the death of a brother, or historical, such as the 1982 Sabra and Shatila Massacre, are never narrated directly but rather obliquely, through their minor material traces and sensorial elements. Not quite vignettes or mere situations, the aesthetic genre of these segments most closely resembles the snapshot, a semirandom, nonorchestrated genre that captures everything in front of the camera, significant or minor, intentional or accidental. By extension, the genre of *Touch* appears to be the family photo album, fragmentary evidence to a narrative. However, unlike a family album, *Touch*'s snapshots of experience resist familiarity. They are images constructed haptically, and therefore, they need to be unfolded before they become articulate:

> The girl stretched her hand up toward the soft sky above her, but she could not feel it; it was too soft. Her feet though, were crisscrossed with dry white lines that the coarse stubs had drawn on them as they touched. The softness of the sky was above the softness of the sun, which was above the softness of the big shepherd boy's nose, and beneath him the hay stubs bent. A piece of hay almost entered his ear; it would if he turned towards her.[56]

Unlike "Dust," which documented the narrator's feelings and unspoken thoughts directly, *Touch*'s narration is limited to the girl's sensorial impressions: the expected soft tactility of the sky and the rough texture of the hay stubs. The haptic image, chronicling relations between textures and shapes rather than between discrete agents and objects, requires translation in order to be put into narrative form: a nose and an ear appearing against the soft texture of the sky for a boy; the spatial blueprint of the hay stubs for location; and the tension of the one stub on the threshold of an ear concentrating into it the entirety of the girl's want and anticipation. Only then can a story be put together—of a girl lying next to an older boy on a haystack, under the summer sky, hoping for him to turn his face toward her. The narration is limited to sensorial perception of minor gestures, contiguous surfaces, blots of color, and patterns of movements, and somewhere through them, there exists a story. To read such snapshots, the reader must trace their lines and contours haptically, unfolding rather than excavating meaning.

Whose voice narrates this sequence? The precise, seemingly objective third-person narrator is uneasily positioned, following the girl closely yet still maintaining a disorienting distance. The narrative voice is both internally focalized on the girl and barred from any interior monologue.[57] This mode of narration is a kind of somatic variation on free indirect discourse. If free indirect discourse (FID) allows the third-person voice to be occupied by a character's narrated emotions, desires, or thoughts, in free indirect *somatic* discourse (FISD), the third-person narration reports the character's somatic or bodily awareness. It traces the girl's most minor perceptions (the straw just outside the ear), sensory input (the softness of the sun), and gestures. The final sentence of the above quote, "A piece of hay almost entered his ear; it would if he turned towards her," is a rare instance in which the objective description can be read as an echo of the girl's wish. This mode of narration allows for some of FID's narrative accessibility but does away with its effect of intimacy and familiarity, instead producing estrangement. FISD stages the disorienting effect created by purposefully using one's weak hand, removing sensory input from a willfully intentional agency. It registers how parts of the girl's body merge into an undifferentiated sensorial texture: sweat on her palm glistens just like the rusted metal on an old water tank, her shadow mixes with the moving shadows of other children, and sounds pile up inside her ears. Several of the novel's episodic snapshots are concerned with repeating rhythmic patterns and movements rather than with the emotionally fraught actions and decisions of human actors: the sight of the wind blowing through the green wheat fields, softly flattening the blades of grass, is then repeated in the traces left by the mother's ten fingers on the green prayer rug, "ten velvety lines push[ing] the rug's soft hair backward, where the green was less green than in front."[58] An episode that starts with the girl's swaying, unsteady steps continues with the same swaying movement as the daughter of a visiting laborer tosses her long hair and ends with the swaying body of the laborer who had hanged himself in the shed.[59] The story connecting between these different movements needs to be traced and unfolded by the reader. The narration is textural rather than agential, replacing actor- and action-based plotline and narrating events through the interactions of form, color, movement, and sensation:

> She stood there looking towards the ambulance, which had no white left, after the black drape of women wrapped it. But above, on top of the ambulance, the red light kept spinning inside itself, not veiled by anything, switching regularly from dark red to light red. She waited for its regular return to dark red, so that it would look like the red label on the empty [Coke] bottle in her hand.[60]

Only several episodes later do readers understand that this scene takes place at the funeral of the girl's older brother. This human tragedy is narrated through seemingly minor and material details—the little girl's search for dark clothes, her attempt to conceal a hole in her pants—as well as through the interplay of colors as the girl perceives them: white (of the ambulance) veiled by black (of the women's robes) topped by vacillating dark and light red (of the revolving warning lights). The death of the brother unfolds only through a haptic decipherment of visual perception—the rhythm of reds echoing the red label on a Coca-Cola bottle in the girl's hand and the reappearance of the black liquid, which had already spilled, in the black-draped figures.

As a record of experience, composed in high resolution and overwhelming in its attention to minor details, *Touch* registers information not according to preestablished hierarchies or concepts, but preconceptually, according to patterns of color, movement, and temperature. This is a haptic mode of narration that recreates what Manning identifies as "autistic perception," a mode of experience in which "there is yet no hierarchical differentiation . . . between color, sound, light, between human and non-human and what connects to the world."[61] What is at stake in identifying *Touch*'s narrative mode with a performance of autistic perception is not a diagnosis of its protagonist. There might be aspects of her behavior that align with recognized autistic behavior patterns, but she is, after all, a collection of textual cues.[62] My claim, rather, is that *Touch* is a literary experiment that *practices* autistic perception by elaborating a poetics of hapticity. Its choreography of nonvolitional movement, in which bodies, objects, sounds, colors, and lights interact, articulates experience in the autistic-contiguous mode. *Touch*'s somatic narrative is not only a means for conveying the subjectivity of a small child encountering an incomprehensible world for the first time but also an aesthetic strategy, demanding a haptic, texture-oriented practice of reading.[63]

THE PRESENT IS THE PAST

"Dust" and *Touch* are narratives claustrophobically bound to the suspended present. The geopolitical spaciotemporal constraints in Palestine are reflected in these texts in the restriction to the somatic body—its limited sensations and perceptions—what Ogden calls a state of sensory "going on being."[64] *Tafsil thanawi* (*Minor Detail*, 2017), Shibli's third novel, marks the first time that her prose exceeds the claustrophobic Palestinian present and forays into the past, integrating elements from various literary genres: detective fiction, historical novel, ghost story, and road trip narrative.[65] Despite all these dramatic genres snaking through it, it reiterates the themes of Shibli's earlier work: there is no escape from the present and from the body. History in this novel becomes haptic, narrated through material and mundane minor details. The suspended present cannibalizes the past and the archive's "assumed role as the past guardian is replaced" as Gil Hochberg writes, "with an understanding of the archive as the guardian of the present as we know it."[66]

J. M. Coetzee, on the back cover of the American issue of *Minor Detail*'s English translation, calls its protagonist a "Palestinian amateur sleuth high on the autism scale," but at no point in the novel is the protagonist identified as being autistic, and the possibility and function of such a diagnosis are questionable. It is not clear, for example, if being autistic would make for a better or worse sleuth. Rather than dubious character diagnosis, my interest is why this novel, Shibli's first foray into the subject of the Nakba as a historical event and especially into the relationship of the present to the past, makes use of autistic perception. More specifically, I ask what happens to the historical archive and to its ability to generate both a history and a community when it is accessed haptically, through minor details and objects, rather than emotionally, through assumed affective ties.

Minor Detail recounts a true event: in August 1949, shortly after the end of the 1948 war, a unit of Israeli soldiers positioned in the Nirim outpost just outside the newly drawn border with Egypt captured a Bedouin girl and raped and murdered her. The incident was investigated at the time, and twenty soldiers who were involved, including the platoon commander, were court-martialed, but the trial proceedings and documents all remained confidential. Only in 2003, after a historian of law at Tel Aviv University stumbled upon some of the trial documents among papers relating to the Kafr Qasim Massacre, was "the Nirim outpost incident" exposed in the Israeli newspaper *Ha'aretz*.[67] The long article, by Aviv Lavie and Moshe Gorali, was based on court documents found in the Israeli archives and on interviews with many of the people who were involved or might have been aware of the murder at the time—soldiers, military prosecutors, and politicians—and still remains the only investigation of this case. It provides a reconstructed timeline of the events but is primarily concerned with the military climate in which such acts were perpetrated: Who were the perpetrators and where are they today? How did this story of rape and murder square with the IDF's self-image as the world's "most moral army"? The question of the girl's identity is acknowledged briefly at the end of the piece. Nothing is known about her, not even her age.

Minor Detail is a fictionalized investigation of the real murder in two acts. The first part, narrated in the past tense and third person, takes place in 1949 and narrates the girl's capture, rape, and death from the vexing perspective of the platoon commander who orchestrated them. This first section makes extensive use of indirect somatic discourse: it remains close to the commander's skin, tracking every minor irritation and perception, but bars the readers from his thoughts, emotions, or reflections. The second part of the novel, in present tense and first person, takes place around 2008 and is narrated by a nameless Palestinian woman from Ramallah who reads about the Nirim outpost incident in the newspaper. Haunted by the realization that the girl was murdered on the same date as her birthday—by all accounts a minor, insignificant detail—she decides to pursue the "complete truth" of the girl's story.[68] Despite acknowledging that she is utterly inadequate to the task, she steals through the checkpoint in a rented car and embarks on an investigation through Israeli archives and erased Palestinian landscapes. The voice in this section is similarly descriptive and factual, documenting the narrator's minor perceptions and thought process, but refrains from emotional narrativization.

Structurally, the novel's two acts contrast two historical moments, about sixty years apart, and posit a set of questions on the epistemological and ethical relations between them. What kind of claim does the past have on the present, when it intrudes in the form of a minor detail in the newspaper? What kind of responsibility does the present have for redeeming, or even knowing, the past? These are the same questions that Saidiya Hartman poses in "Venus in Two Acts," the companion essay to her monumental *Lose Your Mother*, which shares some striking similarities with *Minor Detail*.[69] Hartman reflects in this essay on her efforts to recover the story of a girl, Venus, who survives in the archives of the Atlantic slave trade only through the brief mention of her violent death. "The necessity of recounting Venus's death is overshadowed by the inevitable failure of any attempt to represent her," writes Hartman, acknowledging the archive's intractable limits. Nevertheless, she adds, "wrestling with the girl's claim on the present is a way of naming our time, thinking our present, and envisioning the past which has created it."[70] Hartman's emphasis in this archival excavation is on the present: while she recognizes the ethical impetus to uncover the horrors of the past and to appease its ghosts, coming to terms with history, *knowing* its terms, is eventually a means of thinking our present—of giving the present a name and a form.

Minor Detail is a similar exercise in diagnosing the present of the Ongoing Nakba by staging an effort to answer the faint, indeterminate claim of a dead girl lost to history. Like *Lose Your Mother*, Hartman's personal account of her encounter with the material traces of the Atlantic slave trade, it is a travelogue staging a return to the geographical site of violence. The narrator of *Minor Detail*, like Hartman, believes that she might learn something new by returning to the scene of the crime, but all she finds are the archives and monuments set up by the Israeli state. Underlining both texts is an anticipated and missed encounter with history. And although they are structured as a forensic search, their sustaining mystery is not the murder:

the perpetrators are known to be the victors whose records make up history; the girl's identity remains unrecoverable. What these historian and amateur detective protagonists need to discover is the relationship between the past and the present.

Despite the similarity of their search, Hartman and Shibli come up with two different answers to the question of the past's presentness. Their two answers allow us to consider the variances between the Black experience in the afterlife of slavery, as Hartman calls it, and the Palestinian reality of ongoing settler colonial violence, a distinction that is important to make given the proliferating interest in Black and Palestinian transnational solidarities, grounded in a shared analysis of white supremacy and imperialism.[71] This distinction also demonstrates what is at stake in Shibli's haptic poetics and the way it marks the limits and possibilities of writing the suspended Palestinian present.

The presence of the past is taken for granted by both writers. "I, too, live in the time of slavery," Hartman writes, "by which I mean I am living in the future created by it."[72] There are of course material and structural connections between the past and the present, relations of consequence and accumulation, but what interests Hartman is the affective and emotional ties that bind them. Having reached the historical archive's epistemological limits, she develops an affective method of doing history, intimating that the link between the present and the past should pass through the historian's body and its emotional capacities. Stephen Best notes that this archival practice is, in its structure, melancholic, driven by the premise that the historian as well as their reader should come to *feel* the loss of the past in the present moment.[73] This is to say that the form in which the past materializes in the present is *personal* and *emotional*. The past is present because we can feel it—or at least "we" should feel it. As Best adds, melancholy historicism assumes and is directed toward the recovery of a "we" at the point of violent origin, a Black sociality grounded in the scene of horror.[74]

A similar melancholy mode can be found in a number of important novels that return to the silent archives of the Nakba, material as well as oral—for example, Radwa Ashour's *The Woman from Tantoura* (*al-Tanturiya*, 2010) and Elias Khoury's *Children of the Ghetto* trilogy (*Awlad al-ghitu*, 2016). Both of these expansive novels write the violence of 1948 while grappling with the absence and destruction of archives, and in both, history is eclipsed by silence, felt rather than known. The belated temporality of trauma seems to be the governing structure of these novels, which inquire into what cannot be narrated and represented. They aim for affective intimacy using personal and subjective narrative devices, such as oral testimonies and found diaries. In *Minor Detail*, however, the link between the present and the past is always potentially random, impersonal, and inanimate. Instead of affective links, the connection between the past of the first section of *Minor Detail* to the present of the second section is a coincidence: the chance correspondence of the date of the murder and the narrator's birthdate. Is there any significance to this minor detail? (Is this the way the past makes its claim on the present?) Or is the narrator simply an obsessive eccentric? Is this minor, mundane detail simply static noise, or is it in fact meaningful, a real portal to the past? Considering this question, the narrator notes that "there are some who consider this way of seeing, which is to say, focusing intently on the most minor details, like dust on the desk or flyshit on a painting, as the only way to arrive at the truth and definitive proof of its existence."[75] The oblique reference here is to historian Carlo Ginzburg, famous for developing the field of microhistory: a historical narrative of a small-scale and minor object that nevertheless addresses monumental questions. The narrator goes on to cite, unattributed, one of the "fables" that Ginzburg tells in order to illustrate the principle of his historic-forensic method:

> Three brothers meet a man who has lost his camel, and immediately they describe the lost beast to him: it is a white camel, blind in one eye, carrying two skins on its saddle, one full of oil and the other of wine. You must have seen it, shouts the man. No, we have not seen it, they reply. But he does not believe them and accuses them of stealing his camel. So the four men are brought before the court, where the three brothers prove their innocence by revealing to the judge how they were able to describe an animal they had never seen before, by noticing the smallest and simplest details, such as the camel's uneven tracks across the sand, a few drops of oil and wine that spilled from its load as it limped away, and a tuft of its shedding hair.[76]

Shibli seems to provide a bibliography for her interest in minor and material details: Ginsburg teaches us that these seemingly nonimportant details, unnoticed by most historians, can allow us to tell unknown stories, and even solve historical mysteries. But Ginzburg's method relies on careful and skillful reading: the ability to discern which random details are significant, what they mean, and how they fit in a linear trajectory of cause and effect, affliction and symptom. Ginzburg associates this skill with hunters, bearers of knowledge "characterized by the ability to construct from apparently insignificant experimental data a complex reality that could not be experienced directly . . . arranged by the observer in such a way as to produce a narrative sequence."[77] Shibli's narrator, however, is a bad reader, unable to properly decipher and assess the world around her and its codes. Her reading is haptic, sensorial, and immediate rather than narrative, symptomatic, or based in emotional identification.

In his commentary on Shibli's *Touch*, Kfir Cohen Lustig argues that new divisions of private and public lives under globalized capitalism create "a new aesthetico-epistemological relation, one turning Palestinian life into a text and the writer/character into a reader."[78] He stresses that this is not a consequence of the Israeli occupation per se, but of changes brought about by neoliberal global processes.[79] The identification of *Minor Detail*'s narrator as a reader of signs rather than a "maker" of social worlds is precise, but the novel also makes it clear that the basic position of deciphering the world is complicated, doomed to failure in fact, by the ongoing occupation. The narrator's "ordinary" encounters with soldiers on her way to work or on the bus underscore that both neoliberal regimes and a "normalized" military occupation make a similar demand of their individual subjects: that they be proficient, resilient readers, prepared for crisis and flexible in their response. The narrator, however, admits her complete failure in this regard. Reflecting on scenes that echo the embodied porousness of the early story "Dust," she describes her failure to assess dangerous situations as an "inability to identify borders, even very rational borders, which makes me overreact sometimes or underreact at other times, unlike most people."[80] This is a compulsive tendency to misread and hence transgress borders, a tendency neither conscious nor willed but rather the result of "sheer stupidity."[81] The borders she encounters are not only the shape-shifting yet ever present borders of apartheid in Palestine but also everyday codes of behavior, such as shopping for vegetables or drinking coffee. Yet it is in the encounter with the crisis ordinary of military subjection that the narrator displays the most jarring inability to "evaluate things rationally," unable to differentiate what is just "ordinary" violence and what is an exceptional situation that requires adjustment. This is a problem of reading: the narrator cannot read the world around her proficiently and hence cannot respond—cannot emote—as deemed proper either.

This incapacity proves tragic, if only because the narrator's present is riddled with remnants of the past that she cannot properly decipher. There are countless minor details that link the novel's two parts, holding up its careful architecture: the continuous barking of dogs, the lingering smell of gasoline, spiders in the corner of the ceiling. As readers, we recognize these details, having read the first part of the book, but the narrator-detective remains oblivious to the clues and traces of the past that are present all around her. She wanders through a haunted landscape, but she cannot sense any of the ghosts; it is a parody of the melancholy ghost story, an emptied-out form.

This hollowed out ghost story reverses the book's temporality. In the stagnating temporality of the ongoing Nakba, who is to say that the past came first? The second part of the book, the futile search through the partial archive, highlights the fabulated, authored nature of the first part, which narrated the murder from the commander's perspective. It is not the details of the past that are reappearing in the narrator's present, but rather the minor details of her present appearing in the fabulated history of the past. *Minor Detail* constructs a perverse, nonintuitive temporality in which it is the present that persists into the past, not the other way around.

When Hartman reaches an archival dead end in her search for Venus, she outsteps her role as a historian and resorts to what she calls "critical fabulation": narrative in the subjunctive mood, trying "to imagine what might have happened or might have been said or might have been done."[82] In *Lose Your Mother*, she imagines for a few brief pages the state of mind of a young girl beyond the trace she had left in the accounts of her tormentors: the girl's increasing and then disappearing hunger, the gulls squawking above the deck, her fierce dedication to dying. "If the story ended there," Hartman writes, "I could feel a small measure of comfort."[83] Hartman recognizes that she is inventing a romance, a comforting tale that is very much at odds with the fragments found in the archive itself. The subjunctive offers an unhappy but needed balance between what she looks for in the archive and what is actually found there. More importantly, the deliberately impossible narrative, in which we as readers also partake, solidifies the emotive circulation among Venus, the historian, and her reader.

As a fiction writer, Shibli is supposedly not restricted by what Hartman calls "the boundaries of the archive,"[84] and yet her permissible basis for historical fabulation seems even more constrained. The landscape of *Minor*

Detail's past is made solely by the present's materials; the present is all pervasive, imperialist. Hartman finds respite in the subjunctive mood, but Shibli's grammar for history's scene of subjection is the future perfect, or the prior future. The form of this static tense, first discussed in the introduction, is the "will have been," a future happening that does not open new horizons but is concluded and decided, a future already foreclosed by its past. In *Minor Detail*, the past is a history whose future horizon has been decreed and defined by the present moment, the stagnation of an ongoing apartheid. In other words, the problem with the past—the reason we cannot know it—is not its foreignness but its familiarity, its utter identity to the present from which it is impossible to escape. In Shibli's writing, the present is not populated by ghosts (those beings that are felt, that inhabit the self, and that try to communicate) but by dumb, inanimate objects, and its link to the past is always potentially random or askew.

The emotional evacuation of haptic poetics structures the novel's final scene: the narrator, who lost her way in the desert, encounters a group of Israeli soldiers. They yell at her and raise their guns. Panicking, she nevertheless tries to properly respond, neither over- nor underreact:

> I have to calm down. I must be overreacting. Yes, just like the usual. My chewing gum. Where is it? I have to calm down. I reach my hand toward my pocket, for the pack of chewing gum.
>
> And suddenly, something like a sharp flame pierces my hand, then my chest, followed by the distant sound of gunshots.[85]

She puts her hand in her pocket in order to reach for a piece of gum, and this move triggers the gunshot that strikes her, possibly at the same spot where the Bedouin girl was killed sixty years earlier.[86] The past happens to her again—not as a feeling, not as a haunting presence, but as a stupid, abrupt incident, triggered by an object as minor and tactile as chewing gum. "If you go there and stand in the place where it was, it will happen again," the formerly enslaved Sethe warns her daughter, referring to Sweet Home, the plantation from which she had escaped, in Tony Morrison's *Beloved*.[87] Stephen Best identifies this warning as the literary model of melancholic historicism. In *Minor Detail*, Morrison's warning materializes in its most literal, nonfigurative form: the narrator presumably dies right where the girl she is looking for was killed. But this repetitive structure is an empty formal gesture, almost parodic, lacking the emotional content that establishes identification and makes melancholic historicism coherent. Its carefully staged moves reiterate Shibli's early experiment with salad/control: observing a body that both is and isn't one's own, that is sensing but not feeling.

HAPTICS AND RESISTANCE TO READING

In conclusion, let us return to Shibli's statement that writing can "neutralize the neutralization" occasioned by ongoing violence. What is the political significance of the haptic form? What can a practiced autism achieve? In the psychoanalytic therapeutic context, behavior patterns associated with autism have often been viewed as recalcitrance, a fierce resistance to analysis or, in other words, a resistance to reading. In *The Interpretation of Dreams*, Freud defines resistance as "whatever interrupts the progress of analytic work" (although this concept becomes increasingly unmappable in his later writing.)[88] In other words, the psychoanalyst should be suspicious of anything the analysand says or does that obstructs the "work." The work of analysis is configured here as a continuous labor of meaning-making: it is an ongoing procession, a flow that resistance aims to impede. Defined simply as the obstruction of process, resistance can refer to pretty much anything: to silence, to jokes, to attempts to preempt your analyst or overwhelm them with insignificants.[89] But as Rebecca Comay points out, resistance is necessary for the work of analysis to proceed; if there was no resistance, the work of analysis would be over before it started because everything would already be known—there would be nothing to uncover.[90] Resistance generates *more* analysis. It is an impasse, an obstruction, that generates the movement of interpretation around it. Wendy Anne Lee describes this as the "propulsive nature of narrative, which turns anything to motion, to story. What might appear to shut down circulation (of affect, language) becomes a blank canvas for more."[91] In other words, resistance becomes in itself a symptom, a symbol to be interpreted. Silence, originally a means of staying out of the game of meaningful speech, eventually congeals into a sign, as in the family dynamics of *Touch*: "The girl did not choose sides. To the rest of the world, which chose the first option, this meant she had chosen the second."[92] Commenting on this bind, Roland Barthes concludes that for the neutral to maintain its neutral stance, it cannot equate simple inaction but must fashion itself as "an ardent, burning activity," alongside the contours of power.[93]

Hapticity, therefore, is more akin to neutralization as defined in surveillance theory: the kind of tactics employed by a subject in order to resist, or resist cooperation with, systems of surveillance. Unlike methods that directly challenge the legitimacy and deployment of surveillance apparatuses, either through legal and political channels or through symbolic expressions of rebellion, neutralization is a mode of undoing the effectiveness of surveillance technologies and includes behaviors such as face painting to confuse facial recognition software or putting a thumbtack in one's shoe to distort the physiological reactions tracked by a polygraph.[94] Neutralization conceals or undoes the fluctuating registers and differences tracked by surveilling machines by creating a smooth, undifferentiated, and uninterpretable surface. In a memorable scene in Suleiman's *Chronicle of a Disappearance*, two Israeli soldiers burst into the East Jerusalem apartment of E. S., the film's silent, deadpan protagonist. E. S. shuffles before the soldiers from room to room, presenting himself to them in his pajamas. But despite his readiness to be seen, the soldiers pay him no attention, repeatedly passing him by. E. S.'s neutral demeanor makes him invisible to the determined soldiers.[95] In the following scene, E. S. calmly eats a bowl of spaghetti while in the background, through a military radio transmitter, the soldiers report a list of everything they have encountered in the house: "two doors, four windows, a fan . . . a painting of a chicken, four wicker chairs . . . a Japanese book, Sonallah Ibrahim, Carver, nylon curtains, a man in pajamas." E. S. becomes an object listed among other objects, noted but not worthy of investigation. His neutralized impassivity renders him untrackable and so unexceptional that the mechanisms of surveillance pass him over.

Haptic poetics functions as a neutralization tactic of this kind. As contemporary surveillance technologies increasingly focus on turning the body and its gestures into strings of data, "interiority"—defined as the "unmarked aspects of the subject," unavailable to the surveilling machine—has come to be seen as a site of authenticity and, by extension, a reservoir of secret freedom, subversion, or resistance that cannot be tracked or completely controlled.[96] Literature and art are often staged as sites of exposure of these affective, interior reservoirs. Yet touch, as a haptic literary form, has no interest in and no use for interiority. Its neutralizing tactic adopts the surveilling gaze: it records everything that is "markable," without hierarchy or discrimination, featuring a subject that is at once exposed yet opaque—a subject unfolding at the surface of the text and the body, a scandalous subject that appears to have no interiority at all.[97] Opacity here does not assume a secret cache of oppositional individuality or interiority. To the contrary, the efficacy of Suleiman's and Shibli's works emerges from their scandalous suggestion that there may be no hidden interior at all, no secretly defiant core, behind the neutralization. Instead, they position the neutralized, impassive subject at the heart of their works, witnessing how it throws existing political structures and systems of meaning into disarray.

CONCLUSION
Civil War

In *How to Read a Moment: The American Novel and the Crisis of the Present*, Mathias Nilges argues that in "our" contemporary moment, meaning the early twenty-first century in the United States, when the future appears to have collapsed into the long now and the present is experienced as extended, expanded, and inescapable, the contemporary novel offers a way out: the novel theorizes "time in history" and elaborates a historical sense of the present by "engaging with time itself as form."[1] As I hope this book has demonstrated, the close relation between literary form and the temporality of the present is not merely definitive of the contemporary American novel but, rather, is constitutive of modernist aesthetics more broadly. The novel, I argue, has been belabored with articulating a form for the present since it first became an object of theorization and contemplation in Arabic and Hebrew literary debates of the early twentieth century. *Static Form*'s inquiry began by highlighting how Arabic and Hebrew writers were concerned with translating an existential problem—What is the present and how does one live in it?—into an aesthetic one: How can this questionable present be articulated in a literary form? Whereas Nilges differentiates between the novel's attention to the phenomenological, subjective experience of time and its engagement with "time itself" at the level of literary form, thus positing a supposedly firm opposition between experience and form, between phenomenology and knowledge, my method in this book

CONCLUSION

has been to show that the two are not so easily distinguishable. The experience of the present cannot be separated from the form of the narrative in which it is embedded; concurrently, the notion of "time itself" depends on material, social, and political conditions. What is at stake in forging a link between the experienced present and the literary text is not simply the characters' experience of time, as Nilges sometimes implies, but the structures of experience that underlie modes of knowing and telling time—that is, the temporalities of the present—and the way they find their way into writing at the level of form.

My contention has been that the present's literary forms are *static forms*; it is static that mediates the present. The literary texts studied here were composed at historical moments and within sociopolitical structures that made the present acutely felt as a lived problem as well as a literary one, producing an archive of static forms: the simultaneity of *reverb*; the self-gratifying, incessant *scratch*; the nonproductive, gendered circularity of *routine*; and the contiguous texture of *touch*. This list is not meant to be definitive or exhaustive. To the contrary, I hope that the social-affective-literary model developed here can be used in other sites and modernist archives to further open up the question of the relationship between prose forms, felt sociohistorical experience, and the way literature theorizes itself as a praxis, a medium, and a product. Nevertheless, this conclusion offers an opportunity to reflect on some of the shared characteristics of the static forms that populate this book, which I would suggest are not just incidental but definitive.

When I originally started collecting *Static Form*'s archive of stagnant and stuck literary temporalities, I did not expect so much of it to be about cleaning. And yet, there it was. An inquiry that began with *stasis* as fixedness and immobility kept hitting against static as unwanted interference, grime, and ongoing hygienic maintenance. Literature of temporal and spatial suspension seemed to be obsessed with dirt and the methods of managing it. Why is the problem of the present so urgently a problem of cleanliness? Perhaps this was inevitable because of the starting point of this archive: the civilizational discourse on a properly modern literature, which is the same discourse that made the filthy mis-settled Orientals the target of a mass hygienic project, as Ghanem and Brenner both illustrate. A straight line can be drawn between the Zionist settlers' view of the long-established Palestinian village as full of "filthy beggars" in Brenner's 1910 novella "Nerves" (at this point, a site of pained identification for the unrooted settlers) and the Israeli commander in the first part of Adania Shibli's 2017 novel *Minor Detail*: a character whose methodological ceremonies of personal hygiene and campaigns of insect extermination mirror his military mission, the ethnic cleansing of the newly conquered territories of the Naqab. The unnamed commander publicly washes his young Palestinian prisoner and has her hair shaved and her clothes burnt before he rapes her. This public ceremony of cleansing is one of the only concrete details documented in contemporary accounts of her murder. If in "Nerves" and in *The Mountain* dirt is reclaimed as an emblem of an alternative, nonproductive mode of settlement, in *Minor Detail*, cleanliness is associated with a monstrous obsession of an eliminationist settler colonial order.

And yet, there is more to dirt and cleaning beyond the ideological binary of modern, genocidal sanitation and uncivilized neglect. Residual dirt, noise, or unwanted material debris is inevitable to any system of transmission—which is to say, as Michel Serres shows in *The Parasite*, to the fact of being in relation.[2] Part of the ongoing problem of inhabiting the present is what to do with these parasitic interlopers. Cleaning *is* the present's maintenance. On the one hand, it manifests a desire to do away with the markers of time: getting rid of accumulated dust and of signs of decay is, as Roland Barthes notes, "a practice of immobilizing time,"[3] sustaining that fantasy of a lasting virginal "moment of dawn" that al-Masʿadi's Abu Huraira so forcefully desired. This is the fantasy of the smooth and frictionless simultaneity of capitalist modernity, concealing the very unevenness upon which modern capitalism depends. On the other hand, this supposedly eternal uneventful present requires constant, ongoing, and unequally distributed labor that boasts of nothing but the reproduction of the same: the labor of the present.

As formal mediators of the present, static forms waver in the tension between three definitions of what the present *is*: the abstracted fantasy of a static, timeless present; static as aural dirt, as a parasitic interruption, or as an interloper on the proper flow of narrative, which defines the lived, experienced present of the individual within an anticipated linear history; and static as ceremonies of cleaning and waste management and, more broadly, as a regime of labor, which is the counterpart to the ongoing present of social reproduction of collectivities. As the present remains an unstable

CONCLUSION

category functioning at different scales (the abstracted present, the individually experienced present, and the social-collective present), so will the static forms that articulate it.

In addition to static's investment in dirt and its attendant ceremonies, the previous chapters also mapped a departure from mental or emotional "interiorities" in favor of the documentation of embodied habits and sensorial reception and the depiction of character as composed of surfaces, contiguities, and textures. Writing the present, perhaps surprisingly, departs from a "stream of consciousness"-style confessional documentation, with its commitment to the figure of unstoppable flowing waters. Body surfaces, in these novels, are not simply sites of a symptomatic eruption of hidden depths, but a textured plane to be traced and unfolded. The characters' impassivity—both in the sense of their withdrawal from intentionality and agency in favor of inertia and in the sense of their opacity, their position as impasse—appears as a challenge to the novel's mechanism of sympathy or identification. Writing the present relishes in the body and in its minute, continuous adjustments to its environment, positing an impasse to narrative desires. It is suspended in sense perception before its translation to a narrative of the self. Static forms detach character and sensorial input, staging bodies as opaque sensing machines.

Across the various case studies in this book, opaque characters and the static forms they inhabit offer a series of figures for political action that depart from the much-heralded modernist gesture of the break. Nothing is shattered or ruptured in these books, and rarely are conclusive realizations or recognitions reached. Abandoning fantasies of escape or strategies of exit, the texts are instead invested in behaviors of minor adjustment, renunciation, divestment, and restraint, embodied in figures such as the asymptotic curve drawing incrementally closer to a boundary but never crossing it, the dry accumulation of dust, the futile but gratifying act of scratching, or the unheroic daily labor of cleaning, which cannot be simply refused or abandoned. Opaque, impassive narratives perform the basic operation of immanent critique: by taking on these forms of alienated labor rather than discarding them, static forms perform political critique as "a possibility immanent to the existent society," grounded in the nature of its social context.[4] Static literary forms turn away from the foreclosed future and double down on the present at the site for political investment.

CONCLUSION

If the literary development of conventions of interiority, what Katherine Gallagher called characters' "unreal knowability and their apparent depth," fostered the kind of affective investments in literature that accompany the development of liberal sociality, what do we make of the abandonment of interiority as a convention?[5] What are opacity's aesthetic-political affordances? What is at stake in these works is not quite the same as the "right to opacity," which Édouard Glissant claims for colonized subjects. "If we examine the process of 'understanding' people and ideas from the perspective of Western thought," Glissant writes in *Poetics of Relation*, "we discover that its basis is [a] requirement for transparency."[6] For Glissant, opacity and illegibility become techniques of resistance when confronting a project of colonial domination based on Enlightenment ideals of transparency and knowability. Opacity is a refusal to be known on the terms of the colonizer, the state, patriarchy, etc. But viewing opacity merely as a reactive, oppositional strategy is reductive, keeps "opacity" an unanalyzed, purely negative domain, and risks romanticizing an interior realm of alterity. What we find in these static narratives is not a protected cache of privatized interiority, but rather an insistence on the materiality of the body and on its exteriority. Their scandalous suggestion is that there might not be any hidden site of resistant interiority, only narrative gestures and effects.

What are the stakes of opacity as a mode of narration? In conclusion, I turn to a final text in which exteriority operates as an aesthetic principle. In the novel *Abwab al-madina* (*City Gates*, 1981), by Lebanese writer Elias Khoury, the body is made impersonal and its affects are dispersed and anonymized. Against the present of the Lebanese civil war, Khoury develops a poetics of *ashla'*, dismembered body parts.[7] Writing literature as *ashla'* is an attempt to write beyond the defining parameters of Arabic literary modernity, at a moment when its revivalist project appears to collapse. There is a way in which civil war undoes the political course that *Static Forms* traces: if the trajectory of social forms outlined in the book began with revival modernity and led to the nation-state and to the limbo of statelessness, civil war is the place where this trajectory is cut off. Civil war is the state's other: it is conceived both as the condition of primordial violence that the sovereign state suppresses and contains and as the state's ultimate self-implosion, its undoing from within.[8] In Greek thought, *stasis* is the factional "war of positions," a conflict that suspends the proper flow of politics.[9] According to Giorgio Agamben, *stasis* undoes the very condition of the political.

CONCLUSION

A strife among those bound by ties of kinship, civil war dissolves the constitutive boundary between the domestic and the political.[10] The Arabic term *ḥarb ahliyya*—which literally translates as a domestic or family war—alludes not just to the way the national community is imagined as a family unit but also to the war's penetration of a domestic sphere that is often conceived as external to public political life. Likewise, the Hebrew term *milḥemet aḥim*, fraternal war, illustrates that this kind of strife exceeds the domain of political and civic relations and enters the realm of the family, of those bound by a relation of kin.

In the introduction to the book, I introduced the term "revival modernity," which Elias Khoury coined in the 1979 article "al-Dhakira al-mafquda" ("The Lost Memory").[11] This article, occasioned by a special journal issue on Arab modernity/modernism, was written in the midst of the protracted series of conflicts known as the Lebanese Civil War (al-ḥarb al-ahliyya, 1975–1990) and is surprisingly the only article in the issue that reflects on the war directly.[12] In hindsight, this article emerges as part of an extensive aesthetic-theoretical project that includes essays published in various Beirut-based journals as well as several experimental literary works. All of them diagnose the crisis for Arabic expression occasioned by the war by reflecting on how "language is touched upon in advance by unmournable losses," in Jeffrey Sacks's words, and demand previously unimagined and radically new literary and cultural forms to write the present.[13] Khoury's call for a language of complete novelty in his wartime essays seems to put him at odds with the impassive politics of static surveyed so far, aligning him with far more emphatic and declarative modernist modes. Nevertheless, the aesthetics that he developed in this period, in *City Gates* and in other novels, converse directly with the static forms explored in the preceding chapters.

City Gates, which Khoury described as a response to his experience of the war, is the most abstracted of the multiple novels he published in those years.[14] At the center of the text is the figure of a nameless stranger who arrives at a nameless city. The boundaries of this character are fraught: at times, he seems to merge with the narrator or with another figure called "the storyteller." The city is a labyrinthian nightmare, where distances and figures shift and melt. Stories slip into stories, and characters merge and diverge, momentarily materializing and then disappearing into the

CONCLUSION

textured mesh of language. The stranger himself becomes a listener, a witness to others' stories of loss. The text is an incantation: repetitive, rhythmic, and tactile, it has an oratory quality enhanced by the simple register and straightforward syntax, which belie the surrealist unfolding of the world it describes. The relationship between *City Gates* and the war is clearly not mimetic, nor does it lend itself to a simple allegorical or symbolic interpretation. Readers of the novel have argued that its fragmentary form stages the undoing of subjectivity in trauma, forging "an allegory of the traumatic demarcations of the war," in Nouri Gana's words.[15] Yet putting this novel in conversation with Khoury's historical-aesthetic analysis in "al-Dhakira al-mafquda" reveals something other than a literary staging of the individual's and the community's disintegration in trauma. As a record of the present experience of civil war, *City Gates* stages a theory of literature as a site of static and impersonal modes of address. Trying to write itself out of the trappings of revival modernity, it anonymizes experience and documents the affective present without attaching it to a sensing subjectivity.

The civil war, Khoury writes, has stripped naked the nahḍawi project of Arab modernity, which had produced the institution of the modern state, and made its logics and texts illegible. The state was "modernity's goal, modernity's horizon, modernity's crisis," but the civil war toppled the state as if it were "a child's game."[16] Realities veiled by statist institutions, such as sectarianism, kinship, or substantial social contradictions, were now exposed, having lost their ideological cover. The war is not a "regression" emerging against other more "advanced" Arab societies, Khoury emphasizes, responding to the view of civil war as a primitive state that enlightened modernity has overcome.[17] Rather, the opposite might be true, as the war exposes the illusions of revival modernity and the unstable present it has produced. This collapse means that the present moment is a terrifying one of absolute beginnings, lacking any guidelines or models:

[This moment] recalls, to some extent, the chaos [*fawḍā*] of the beginnings of the period of the *nahḍa*. But the difference is that the new chaos is precisely the internal chaos that the first chaos had concealed. In the chaos of the *nahḍa*, the conflict of cultural alternatives found its realistic solution, dictating incorporation into the margins of Western capitalism. . . . But the new chaos takes place on all levels and standards. It is the chaos of a beginning that does not begin.[18]

CONCLUSION

The revival project's mission was to salvage the Arabic language, but in the current chaos, Khoury writes, "words splinter as the sectarian groups splinter, social forces come loose as the details of the text come loose; [chaos] destroys the text's readymade form, offering it as a permanent question."[19] Both the social text and the literary text lose all anchoring legibility. And yet, the rubble (*rukām*) of civil war is also a site of endless and terrifying potential, the place where radically new forms can emerge.

What can literature look like, in this present that is no longer the present produced by revival modernity? What are its guiding forms? Not unlike the *nahḍawis* that he criticizes, Khoury seeks to answer the crisis of the present through an imaginary appeal to the past. Sensing that the principles of the *nahḍa* were losing their explanatory power, he takes an interest in the textual heritage that the *nahḍawis* turned away from, the literary traditions of *inḥiṭāṭ* or "Ottoman decadence," which were abandoned in the nationalist revivalist moment.[20] Whereas the *nahḍawis* appealed to the "golden age" of Arabic poetry as a site of authenticity and a source of national pride and sovereignty, Khoury turns to the prose of *Alf layla wa-layla* (*A Thousand and One Nights*), describing it as a book that "gives form to historical experience."[21] In an essay titled "Death of the Author" ("Mawt al-mu'allif"), published in October 1980 in *al-Safir*, Khoury recuperates the *Nights* as a memory or oblique inspiration for the new literature that is yet to emerge in the chaotic present. In the *Nights*, he finds an accessible "prose poetics," which gives expression to common experience rather than serving as a mouthpiece for ideological or political power.

City Gates clearly resonates with Khoury's interest in the *Nights*: it echoes their imaginary geographies, especially the narrative known as the "City of Brass."[22] Although Khoury's essayistic writing from this period insists on attending to reality as it has been revealed by the war and on bearing witness to the present, *City Gates* takes place in an ahistorical time of myth, cyclicality, and repetition. The nameless city of *City Gates* is surrounded by high walls, and its gates are guarded by beautiful and deceptive temptresses. In the center of the city lies a sleeping king, guarded by seven weeping women. The city is subject to disastrous calamities: fire, deluge, plague, and small locust-like swarming animals. Such mythical-mystical references and allusions position *City Gates* alongside the mock-classist, timeless texts discussed in chapter 1: as in those faux-mythic texts, *City Gates*'s allegorical geographies of cities, deserts, and seas are the setting for a male protagonist

CONCLUSION

passing through mythologized female bodies, both seductive and threatening, tragically victimized and vengeful. But whereas Agnon and al-Masʿadi are invested in expanding and eventually reasserting a humanist canon, Khoury is committed to the value of storytelling as a communal, restorative oral practice that escapes canonization.[23]

Accordingly, the reason that Khoury finds *A Thousand and One Nights* to be so influential for a new prose-poetics is that it is a collection of stories, an authorless text. A text with no author has no focalized center of authority; it is a voice coming from, as he writes, "a place with no boundaries, from the accrual of historical experience that gushes through daily life."[24] This idea was central to Khoury's wartime writing. Emily Drumsta shows how in Khoury's novel *White Masks* (*al-Wujuh al-bayda*ʾ), published in the same year as *City Gates*, the author is transformed from "a puppet master into a mere 'medium' through whom others, particularly disenfranchised or 'victimized' others, might speak."[25] At times, *City Gates* adopts such a collective voice, gathering stories and testimonies narrated by figures that are hardly distinguishable. More often, however, the narrative voice is completely disembodied by the instability of pronouns, sometimes shifting in midsentence. The impersonal third-person narrator slips into the intimate first person, merging into the character of the stranger or splitting into the enigmatic figure of the storyteller (*al-rāwī*).

The overall effect is that the author in *City Gates* is not simply pluralized or crowded out by other characters, but rather disappears into space and texture, in an experiment of writing a record of experience without a subject. In "Death of the Author," Khoury calls for writing that seizes on the extremes of subjectivity as it "disintegrates into scattered body parts [*ashlāʾ manthūra*] in the poetics of reality."[26] The word *ashlāʾ*, body parts or severed limbs, is a sudden, shocking intrusion of enfleshed materiality into the otherwise abstracted literary essay, a glimpse of the reality caused by planted bombs and shelling, but it simultaneously functions as a formalist term: *manthūra* means scattered as well as prosaic or pertaining to prose (*nathr*). The material *ashlāʾ*, scattered limbs and dismembered flesh, are also the basis for a new prose-poetics.

When the individual is nothing but anonymized *ashlāʾ*, body parts provisionally and haphazardly held together, from whence comes the narrative voice? *City Gates* is attentive to vision, smell, and texture, but displaces these inputs to scattered and anonymized organs. Characters merge and diverge, momentarily materializing and then disappearing into the textured mesh of language; their stories slip one into the other, losing all specificity. Affective reactions take on an independent existence, as in the simple sentence "and there was weeping" (*wa-kāna al-bukāʾ*), doing away with a specific body or subjectivity to perform it. Speech emerges from women's stomachs and falls to the ground; colors become presences (*al-azhar*, *al-aṣfar*), isolated from matter or object; and the entire square becomes an eye and then "one vast ear."[27] Rather than personification of the landscape, this is the impersonification of sensation, divorcing it from a sensing subjectivity. Even when affects and sensorial input are nominally attached to the stranger, they are misplaced: he can taste with his fingers or "feels tears coming out of his shoulders."[28] *City Gates* spreads out the affective experience of the present to anonymous *ashlāʾ*. It is an affective account of dismembered body parts and organs.

In *City Gates*, bodies are no longer simply opaque. As a form, *ashlāʾ* writes the present's affective experience, turning affects into objects and actions in the world. They are not expressive of the emotions of the subject, not an external production of an internal state; instead, they are an insistent exteriority, forms to be read on their own terms. *City Gates* models a prose poetics for civil war, a time in which "affect has shed the subject" and the body has morphed purely into form, and so the stranger is "like a point turning into angles and like an angle turning into circles and like a circle shrinking into a distant point."[29] Writing with the prose of *ashlāʾ* removes the present of civil war from narratives of historical and political subjects, allowing *City Gates* to emerge as a singular experiment, a laboratory space for writing a present in which the contours of Arabic literary modernity seem to momentarily falter. *Ashlāʾ* is the static form for writing a modern present in which modernity is not merely obstructed but lays in ruins.

ACKNOWLEDGMENTS

This book has been in the making for a long time, and its key terms—stasis, stuckness, settlement, domestic routine—have changed their meaning and timbre repeatedly over these years. I'd like to extend gratitude to the many people and institutions that were part of these transitions and who taught me to think and write through them.

Some of the sentences in this book were written when I was still an undergraduate student, and I extend thanks to Uri S. Cohen and Taoufik Ben Amor for diverging me from abstract mathematics and setting me back on the path of literature. At UCLA, I entered a lively, passionate, and ruthlessly critical environment. At its origins, this project was an attempt to bring together all that I learned from Ali Behdad, Arne de Boever, Ra'anan Boustan, Michael Cooperson, Nouri Gana, Eleanor Kaufman, Aamir Mufti, David Myers, and Sarah Abrevaya Stein, among many others. Gil Hochberg's sharpness, humor, and clarity kept me focused, but it is her friendship that I value most.

I have been incredibly lucky to find an academic home at the Department of Asian and Middle Eastern Studies at the University of Minnesota (UMN). I am exceedingly grateful to my colleagues Palita Chunsaengchan, Joseph Farag, Alia Goehr, Christine Marran, Jason McGrath, Martha Mockus, Baryon Posadas, Nida Sajid, Suvadip Sinha, Katrien Vanpee, and Travis Workman for sustaining a one-of-its-kind department: the supportive, cordial, and generous space that academia should be but rarely is. My gratitude extends to Susannah L. Smith and Bianet Castellanos for a productive collaborative environment during my fellowship at UMN's Institute for Advanced Studies.

The book was informed and improved by conversations held at numerous conferences and workshops. I would like to thank Tarek El-Ariss, Sadia Agsous-Bienstein, Maya Barzilai, Orit Bashkin, Eyal Bassan, Reut Ben Yaakov, Jeffrey Clapp, Ahmad Diab, Maurice Ebileeni, Yuval Evri, Shai Ginsburg, Rachel Green, Roni Henig, Hannan Hever, Lital Levy, Muhsin al-Musawi, and Anna Ziajka Stanton for organizing and participating in these forums, and for engaging generously with my work. Michael Allan, Rebecca C. Johnson, Nasrin Rahimieh, and Jeffrey Sacks have read earlier versions of the manuscript and provided much-appreciated feedback, saving me from some embarrassing oversights. Kali Handelman read every word and assured me they indeed came together as a book. My deepest gratitude goes to Philip Leventhal and Emily Elizabeth Simon at Columbia University Press, as well as the entire editorial team, for bringing this book to fruition.

Sections of chapter 2 appeared previously in the *Journal of Arabic Literature*, and parts of chapter 5 were published in modified form in *Arab Studies Journal* and in *The Los Angeles Review of Books*. I would like to thank Anna Ziajka Stanton (again!) and Sherene Seikali for their careful editing, as well as the anonymous reviewers of the two journals.

I owe the most to my interlocutor-friends, whose brilliance, generosity, and camaraderie make this profession worthwhile. Woven among these pages are strands of ongoing and priceless conversations with Nasia Anam, Leeam Azoulay-Yagev, Ainsley Boe, Fatima Burney, Roanne Cantor, Will Clark, Jennifer Croft, Arash Davari, Zen Dochterman, Boris Dralyuk, Danielle Drori, Emily Drumsta, Ella Elbaz, Elik Elhanan, Oded Erez, Robert Farley, Sheer Ganor, Carol Hakim, Aaron Hall, Suleiman Hodali, Noga Malkin, Roni Masel, Melissa Melpignano (partner in everything), Liron Mor, Dipali Mukhopadhyay, Ethan Pack, Zozan Pehlivan, James Robertson, Yael Segalovitch, Omar Sharifi, Levi Thompson, Duncan Yoon, and many others.

To my parents Tal and Yizhar, my grandparents Shula and Oded, and my siblings, Tamar, Ayelet, and Omri—I always miss you and now more than ever. Many, many thanks to Debbie and Kamran Jabbari, who welcomed me into all of their homes.

A very special thanks goes to Alexander, copyeditor and partner extraordinaire—even though it's been barely two months, I can't imagine going through any of it without you. And to Asef, who every day becomes more wonderful, disproving all the premises of this book.

NOTES

INTRODUCTION

1. Mahmoud Darwish, *La ta'atadhir 'amma fa'alta* [Don't be sorry for what you have done] (Riad el-rayyes, 2004), 93. Joudah's English translation appears in Mahmoud Darwish, *The Butterfly's Burden*, trans. Fady Joudah (Copper Canyon, 2007), 255.
2. Huda J. Fakhreddine, *The Arabic Prose Poem: Poetic Theory and Practice* (Edinburgh University Press, 2022), 142.
3. Darwish, *The Butterfly's Burden*, 255, translation slightly modified.
4. In classical Arabic grammars, sentences that begin with a noun are divided into two parts, *mubtadā* (beginning) and *khabar* (information). While the *mubtadā* is "bereft of pronounced influences" such as verbs, the *khabar* can be a semisentence containing a verb. See *al-Ajurrumiyya* and its explication in Muhammad Muhyi al-Din 'Abd al-Hamid, *al-Tuhfa al-saniyya bi-sharh al-muqaddima al-ajurrumiyya* (Dar ibn kathir, 2018), 70. For modern analysis of the noun sentence, see Karin C. Ryding, *A Reference Grammar of Modern Standard Arabic* (Cambridge University Press, 2005), 58–59.
5. Darwish, *The Butterfly's Burden*, 255.
6. "Targilim be-'ivrit shimushit" first appeared in the journal *Siman kri'a* 9 (1979) and was subsequently published in Dan Pagis, *Milim nirdafot: shirim* (ha-Kibbuts ha-me'uhad, 1982). The translations in the book are mine unless otherwise noted.
7. My method of reading form as a means of assessing the present's affective structure is based on the work of Lauren Berlant, who argues that "affect's saturation of form can communicate the conditions under which a historical moment appears as a visceral moment, assessing the way a thing that is happening finds its genre, which is the same as finding its event. . . . I am claiming that the aesthetic or formal rendition of affective experience provides evidence of historical processes." Lauren Gail Berlant, *Cruel Optimism* (Duke University Press, 2011), 16.

INTRODUCTION

8. See Caroline Levine, *Forms: Whole, Rhythm, Hierarchy, Network* (Princeton University Press, 2015). See also the argument in favor of form's definition being "inquiry specific" in Jonathan Kramnick and Anahid Nersessian, "Form and Explanation," *Critical Inquiry* 43, no. 3 (2017): 650–69.
9. Catherine Gallager comments on narratologists' fondness for graphs and charts, noting that "formalist analyses seem bent on showing that, although a novel represents temporal sequence by means of temporal sequence, it nevertheless has, or should have, a form that can be made apprehensible all at once, in a picture or a fractal." Catherine Gallagher, "Formalism and Time," in *Reading for Form*, ed. Susan J. Wolfson and Marshall Brown (University of Washington Press, 2006), 306.
10. Elliott Colla concludes that "Zaynab was not recognized as particularly unique in either form or theme at the moment of its first publication." Its fame and claim to singularity as the first "authentic" Egyptian novel was established retroactively in a process that began fifteen years after its original publication, when Haykal rebranded himself as a populist aspiring politician. Elliott Colla, "How Zaynab Became the First Arabic Novel," *History Compass* 7, no. 1 (2009): 217. The recuperation process peaked when *Zaynab* was crowned the first "artistic" novel in Egypt in Abd al-Muhsin Taha Badr's monumental *Tatawwur al-riwaya al-ʿarabiyya al-haditha fi misr: 1870–1938* [The evolution of the modern Arabic novel in Egypt, 1870–1938] (Dar al-maʿarif, 1963). See also Samah Selim's two superb critical studies of the Egyptian literary landscape in which Zaynab appeared, *The Novel and the Rural Imaginary in Egypt, 1880–1985* (Routledge, 2004); and *Popular Fiction, Translation and the Nahda in Egypt* (Palgrave Macmillan, 2019).
11. The Egyptian journal *al-Bayan* was founded by ʿAbd al-Rahman al-Barquqi in 1911 and over the following decade became one of the most influential venues for the development of a new Egyptian literary scene. See Elisabeth Kendall, *Literature, Journalism and the Avant-garde: Intersection in Egypt* (Routledge, 2006), 34.
12. "Matbuʿat jadida" [New publications], *al-Bayan*, October 13, 2013.
13. See Selim, *Popular Fiction*, 21–46; Ali Shalash, *Nashʾat al-naqd al-riwaʾi fi al-adab al-ʿarabi al-hadith* [The origins of novel criticism in modern Arabic literature] (Maktabat gharib, 1992), 38; Ahmad Ibrahim Hawwari, *Naqd al-riwaya fi al-adab al-ʿarabi al-hadith fi misr* [Novel criticism in modern Arabic literature in Egypt] (Dar al-maʿarif, 1978).
14. "Ha-sofrim ha-ʿaravim" [The Arab writers] by Yitzhak Shami, appeared in *ha-Poʿel ha-tsaʿir* in two segments on October 22 and November 7, 1911, and was republished in the collection *Tahanat ha-hayim* [Life's mill], ed. Joseph Zernik (Kinneret zmora bitan, 2015). *Ha-Poʿel ha-tsaʿir* was the official journal of ha-Poʿel ha-Tsaʿir party, a Zionist-Socialist workers party focusing on agricultural colonization and the promotion of Hebrew culture.
15. Shami, a gifted fiction writer, was often viewed as a "native informant" in the small Hebrew literary sphere. The past couple of decades have seen efforts to position Shami as an emblem of a pre-Zionist, nonpartitioned, Arab-Jewish identity. However, as Keren Dotan demonstrates, this theoretical framework fails to account for the broader contexts of secularization and modernization in the Ottoman empire in which Shami was operating. Shami was a dedicated Zionist, and as Dotan notes, Arabic was a language he mastered but not an identity he would claim for himself. See Keren Dotan, "Likhtov moderniyut mi-mizrah" [Writing modernity from

INTRODUCTION

the East: secularism, traditionalism, and modernism in Yitzhak Shami] *mi-Kan 17* (2017): 78–81. For readings of Shami as an Arab-Jew, see Hannan Hever, "Yitzhak Shami: Ethnicity as an Unresolved Conflict," *Shofar* 24, no. 2 (2006): 124–39; Salim Tamari, "Ishaq al-Shami and the Predicament of the Arab Jew in Palestine," *Jerusalem Quarterly*, no. 21 (August 2004): 10–26; Adina Hoffman, "In Search of Yitzhaq Shami," *Raritan* 28, no. 3 (Winter 2009): 1–8. For a biography of Shami, see Yigal Schwartz and Joseph Zernik, "Yad ʿanakim zdona u-botahat," in *Yitzhaq Shami, Tahanat ha-hayim* (Kinneret zmora bitan, 2015).
16. Shami, "Ha-sofrim ha-ʿaravim," 286.
17. Shami, "Ha-sofrim ha-ʿaravim," 286.
18. Shami, "Ha-sofrim ha-ʿaravim," 289.
19. Yoseph Haim Brenner, "Ha-janer ha-erets yisraʾeli ve-avizarehu," in *Kol kitve Y. H. Brenner* (Shtible, 1927). Erets Yisrael, or the Land of Israel, was the common term for Palestine used by the settlers and is still used to differentiate the State of Israel from the geographical territory. When I use it in this book, it is to convey the worldview of the discussed group or persons by employing their own terminology.
20. For sources on this polemic, see Nurit Govrin, *Meʾora Brenner: ha-maʾavak ʿal hofesh ha-bituy* [The Brenner affair] (Yad yitshak ben-tsvi, 1985). For a detailed (and sometimes hagiographic) biography of Brenner, see Anita Shapira, *Yosef Haim Brenner: A Life*, trans. Anthony Berris (Stanford University Press, 2015).
21. Nurit Govrin, *Brenner: oved ʾetsot u-more derekh* [Brenner: drifter and leader] (Misrad ha-bitahon; Tel-Aviv University, 1991).
22. Brenner, "ha-Janer," 268.
23. Brenner, "ha-Janer," 270.
24. Brenner, "ha-Janer," 269.
25. For a contemporary text concerned with the urban present (not called a novel at the time because it was composed in the episodic genre of the Arabic *maqāma*) see Muhammad al-Muwaylihi, *Hadith ʿIsa ibn Hisham aw fitra min al-zaman* (Muhammad al-kutubi, 1923). On the politics of the representation of peasants in Egypt, see Michael Ezekiel Gasper, *The Power of Representation: Publics, Peasants, and Islam in Egypt* (Stanford University Press, 2009); Selim, *The Novel and the Rural Imaginary*.
26. It is very likely that Shami, who considered Brenner a literary mentor, had read Brenner's article, especially since Shami is one of Brenner's many targets in the essay. Brenner mocks the literary trend of writing seemingly objective stories on "The Life of the Łódź Jews," "the Life of the Galicians," or "the Life of the Sephardim" ("ha-Janer," 268). "From the Life of the Sephardim" was the title of Shami's first published story. Even if Shami was simply adapting Brenner's aesthetic theory, its application in the parallel context of Arabic literature highlights the apparent comparability of these two literary cultures in that moment.
27. Walter Benjamin, "On Some Motifs in Baudelaire," in *Illuminations*, ed. Hannah Arendt (Schocken, 1968), 163. Important examples of this paradigm's omnipresence in studies of Arabic and Hebrew literatures include Tarek El-Ariss, *Trials of Arab Modernity: Literary Affects and the New Political* (Fordham University Press, 2013); and Shachar Pinsker, *Literary Passports: The Making of Modernist Hebrew Fiction in Europe* (Stanford University Press, 2010).
28. Abdallah Laroui, *L'ideologie arabe contemporaine: essai critique* (François Maspero, 1977), 66.

INTRODUCTION

29. The temporality that Laroui associates with the future anterior is markedly different from the one evoked that very same year by a more famous North African Francophone writer, Jacques Derrida, in an oft-quoted passage opening *On Grammatology*. The future anterior in Derrida's model is an absolute unknown, a potential of total alterity, "that which breaks absolutely with constituted normality and can only be proclaimed, *presented*, as a sort of monstrosity." Jacques Derrida, *Of Grammatology*, trans. Gayatri Chakravorty Spivak (Johns Hopkins University Press, 1976), 5. Although for Laroui the future anterior is an expression of the limitations imposed on both the future and the past, always doomed to be read through the European future, for Derrida, the future anterior is adjacent to the messianic, a performative statement capable of changing or creating its past. It is tempting to trace these divergent readings to the different intellectual trajectories of Derrida and Laroui. Born to a Sephardic Jewish Algerian family who received French citizenship already in 1870, Derrida was able to insert himself into a trajectory of European philosophy as a participant and shape its future. (And what is the power of deconstruction if not its ability to radically refashion the past?) Meanwhile, the Moroccan Muslim Laroui, despite his French education and his Marxist analytic methodology, would always be seen as *responding* to this philosophical trajectory, an interloper commenting and reflecting on it from the outside.

30. Elias Khoury, "al-Dhakira al-mafquda," *Mawaqif* 35 (April 1979): 68. Reprinted in *al-Dhakira al-mafquda: dirasat naqdiyya* [Lost memory: critical essays] (Dar al-adab, 1990), 25–43.

31. Muhammad ʿAbid al-Jabiri, *al-Khitab al-ʿarabi al-muʿasir: dirasa tahliliyya naqdiyya* [Contemporary Arab discourse: a critical and analytic study] (Dar al-taliʿa, 1982), 18.

32. I return to Khoury, to the Lebanese Civil War as the context for his intervention, and to his vision of an escape from revival modernity's missing present in the conclusion.

33. The Arabic word *ḥāḍir* went through a semantic shift in the early nineteenth century. Originally an adjective describing "that which exists/is present," only in the early nineteenth century does it begin to be used as a noun to translate the word "the present" from European languages—to depict both the period of time and the name of the grammatical tense. Classical Arabic grammar has three tenses: past perfect to denote a completed past (*al-māḍī*); imperfect for the nonpast (*al-muḍāriʿ*), which is generally equivalent to the present tense; and imperative (*al-amr*). In Hebrew premodern grammars, the present tense is called *"leshon hove"* (present tongue), using the word used for the present as period (*hove*). The modern grammatical term, however, is *beynoni* (middle, middling) because the verb in the present tense can be either a verb or a noun and is considered "between" them.

34. Michael North, *What Is the Present?* (Princeton University Press, 2018), 8. Scholarship on neuroscience, physics, and the perception of time is vast. See, for example, Valtteri Arstila and Dan Lloyd, eds., *Subjective Time: The Philosophy, Psychology, and Neuroscience of Temporality* (MIT Press, 2014).

35. Theodore Martin, *Contemporary Drift: Genre, Historicism, and the Problem of the Present* (Columbia University Press, 2017), 5. See also Reinhart Koselleck, *Futures Past: On the Semantics of Historical Time*, trans. Keith Tribe (MIT Press, 1985);

INTRODUCTION

Chris Lorenz and Berber Bevernage, eds., *Breaking Up Time: Negotiating the Borders Between Present, Past and Future* (Vandenhoeck & Ruprecht, 2013).
36. Lauren Berlant, "Critical Inquiry, Affirmative Culture," *Critical Inquiry* 30, no. 2 (2004): 446.
37. Armen Avanessian and Anke Henning have recently developed a convincing countermodel to these assumptions, arguing that literature and writing do not refer to existing temporal orders, but rather create an understanding of fictional time in the present moment of reading. Armen Avanessian and Anke Henning, *Present Tense: A Poetics*, trans. Nils F. Schott and Daniel Hendrickson (Bloomsbury, 2015), 2–3.
38. Paul De Man, "Literary History and Literary Modernity," *Daedalus* 99, no. 2 (1970): 398.
39. Although there have been a number of studies in the past few years arguing that the present emerged as a site of crisis in the context of accelerated capitalism and globalization in the early twenty-first century, some of which are discussed and mentioned in this book, I would contend that these are simply the latest manifestations of a problematic that emerged much earlier. For an example that locates the beginning of modernity's changed attitude to the present in the French Revolution, see Peter Fritzsche, *Stranded in the Present: Modern Time and the Melancholy of History* (Harvard University Press, 2004).
40. Harry Harootunian, "Remembering the Historical Present," *Critical Inquiry* 33, no. 3 (2007): 481.
41. See Lorenz and Bevernage, *Breaking Up Time*, 17.
42. North, *What Is the Present?*, 67.
43. Benedict Anderson, *Imagined Communities: Reflections on the Origin and Spread of Nationalism* (Verso, 1983), 30. The phrase "homogenous, empty time" originally comes from Walter Benjamin's "Theses on the Philosophy of History," in *Illuminations*, trans. Harry Zohn (Schocken, 2007), 261.
44. See a useful overview of relevant literature in Amanda Lagji, *Postcolonial Fiction and Colonial Time: Waiting for Now* (Edinburgh University Press, 2022), 10–16.
45. North demonstrates how the majority of modern and contemporary discussions about the present are normative, assuming there is a proper way of living the present from which we have strayed rather than recognizing that the present is a socially created object. North, *What Is the Present?*, 73.
46. Edward W. Said, "Arabic Prose and Fiction After 1948," in *Reflections on Exile* (Harvard University Press, 2000), 47. The essay was written as an introduction to the 1974 English translation of Halim Barakat's novel *Days of Dust* ['Awdat al-ta'ir ila al-bahr] (Three Continents, 1969).
47. Said, "Arabic Prose," 47.
48. Said, "Arabic Prose," 49.
49. Said, "Arabic Prose," 53.
50. Tarek El-Ariss explores the literary performance of embodiment in Arab modernity, extending from the *nahḍa* to the twenty-first century, in *Trials of Arab Modernity*.
51. Raymond Williams, *Marxism and Literature* (Oxford University Press, 1977), 132. Williams goes on to write that the term is "difficult" and in a way misleading and suggests "structures of experience" as an equally unsatisfying alternative.
52. Kathleen Stewart, *Ordinary Affects* (Duke University Press, 2007), 1; Lauren Gail Berlant, "Thinking About Feeling Historical," *Emotion, Space and Society* 1 (2008): 5;

Erin Manning, *Always More Than One: Individuation's Dance* (Duke University Press, 2013), 30.
53. Fredric Jameson, *The Antinomies of Realism* (Verso, 2013), 34.
54. Jameson, *Antinomies*, 184. It is here that Jameson's argument comes close to György Lukács in Lukács's most reactionary moments.
55. Stewart, *Ordinary Affects*, 4.
56. The term of course refers to the crucial critique in Eve Kosofsky Sedgwick, "Paranoid Reading and Reparative Reading; or, You're So Paranoid, You Probably Think This Essay Is About You," in *Touching Feeling: Affect, Pedagogy, Performativity* (Duke University Press, 2003), 123–51.
57. On surface reading as an anti-interpretive mode, see Stephen Best and Sharon Marcus, "Surface Reading: An Introduction," *Representations* 108 (2009): 1–21. I benefit here from Carolyne Lesjak's Marxist critique of surface reading in "Reading Dialectically," *Criticism* 55, no. 2 (2013): 233–77.
58. The French word *parasite* means both a parasite as used in English and static noise. Michel Serres makes full use of this semantic ambiguity as the basis of a philosophical ontology that posits the parasite as a unidirectional formal relation, a disturbance that is nevertheless "the most common thing in the world. . . . Mistakes, wavy lines, confusion, obscurity are part of knowledge; noise is part of communication, part of the house. But is it the house itself?" Michel Serres, *The Parasite*, trans. Lawrence R. Schehr (Johns Hopkins University Press, 1982), 11–12.
59. On noise as part of any communication system, see Claude Elwood Shannon and Warren Weaver, *The Mathematical Theory of Communication* (University of Illinois Press, 1949), 95.
60. Greg Hainge, *Noise Matters: Towards an Ontology of Noise* (Bloomsbury Academic, 2013), 5.
61. Julie Beth Napolin, *The Fact of Resonance: Modernist Acoustics and Narrative Form* (Fordham University Press, 2020), 8. Napolin relies in this distinction on F. V. Hunt: "*acoustic* is used when the term being qualified designates something that has the properties, dimensions, or physical characteristics associated with sound waves; *acoustical* is used when the term being qualified does not designate explicitly something which has such properties, dimensions, or characteristics." F. V. Hunt, "Acoustic vs Acoustical," *The Journal of the Acoustical Society of America* 27, no. 5 (1955): 975.
62. Franco Moretti, *The Bourgeois: Between History and Literature* (Verso, 2013), 72–81.
63. Dimitris Vardoulakis, "Stasis: Beyond Political Theology?," *Cultural Critique* 73 (Fall 2009): 127.
64. Classical Arab linguists have grouped such words under the title *aḍdād*, words that have contradictory or seemingly opposite meanings. The comparative philologist Carl Abel "unveiled" this phenomenon in 1884, claiming that "contradictory words" were a universal phenomenon purported to abound in the "oldest" languages, Arabic in particular. These claims have been refuted by later philologists who work to demystify the lasting predispositions toward the nature of Arabic. However, Abel's claims enjoyed some traction in psychoanalytic theory, particularly in Freud's work on negation and the unconscious and later in Derrida's writing on deconstruction. See Sigmund Freud, "The Antithetical Meaning of Primal Words" in *The Standard Edition of the Psychological Works of Sigmund Freud*, ed.

INTRODUCTION

and trans. James Strachey (Hogarth, 1995), 154–61; and Jacques Derrida, *Dissemination*, trans. Barbara Johnson (University of Chicago Press, 1981), 220.
65. Nicole Loraux, *The Divided City: On Memory and Forgetting in Ancient Athens* (Zone, 2002), 24.
66. Loraux, *The Divided City*, 105; Vardoulakis, "Stasis," 125. See also the debate on *stasis* as the threshold between the nonpolitical domestic space and the political city and as the condition for politicization itself in Giorgio Agamben, *Stasis: Civil War as a Political Paradigm*, trans. Nicholas Heron (Stanford University Press, 2015), 16.
67. This interpretation is informed by my reading of Anne-Lise François, *Open Secrets: The Literature of Uncounted Experience* (Stanford University Press, 2008); Eleanor Kaufman's discussion of "Bartleby the Scrivener" in *Deleuze, the Dark Precursor: Dialectic, Structure, Being* (Johns Hopkins University Press, 2012), 137; and Anahid Nersessian, *Utopia, Limited: Romanticism and Adjustment* (Harvard University Press, 2015).
68. Douglas Mao and Rebecca L. Walkowitz, "The New Modernist Studies," *PMLA* 123, no. 3 (2008): 737–48. The problem of modernism and periodization is discussed in more detail in chapter 1. Key surveys and anthologies of global modernism, sometimes called transnational modernism or world modernism and arguing for the study of modernist aesthetics as a *world* phenomenon, include Mark A. Wollaeger and Matt Eatough, *The Oxford Handbook of Global Modernisms* (Oxford University Press, 2012); Susan Stanford Friedman, "Planetarity: Musing Modernist Studies," *Modernism/Modernity* 17, no. 3 (2010); Eric Hayot and Rebecca L. Walkowitz, *A New Vocabulary for Global Modernism* (Columbia University Press, 2016); and the essays collected in a special issue on "Modernism and Transnationalisms" in *Modernism/Modernity* 13, no. 3 (2006). For a discussion of how Middle Eastern modernisms fit into new modernist studies, see the introduction to Levi Thompson, *Reorienting Modernism in Arabic and Persian Poetry* (Cambridge University Press, 2022).
69. Jahan Ramazani, "Modernist Bricolage, Postcolonial Hybridity," *Modernism/modernity* 13, no. 3 (2006): 445–63.
70. Even though I do not follow his method of categorization, I rely here on some of the arguments in Eric Hayot, *On Literary Worlds* (Oxford University Press, 2012), 10.
71. Khaled Furani pursues a similar question in relation to poetry, albeit from an anthropological angle, arguing for a connection between "poetic forms" and "forms of life," in *Silencing the Sea: Secular Rhythms in Palestinian Poetry* (Stanford University Press, 2012).
72. Fredric Jameson, *A Singular Modernity: Essay on the Ontology of the Present* (Verso, 2002), 34; 40.
73. Michael Geyer and Charles Bright, "World History in a Global Age," *The American Historical Review* 100, no. 4 (1995): 1052.
74. Alberto Moreiras, *The Exhaustion of Difference: The Politics of Latin American Cultural Studies* (Duke University Press, 2001), 50.
75. Judith Butler, *Parting Ways: Jewishness and the Critique of Zionism* (Columbia University Press, 2012), 4.
76. Ella Elbaz, "Factoring Asymmetry Into the Equation: On Juxtaposing Palestinian and Israeli Literatures," *Journal of Arabic Literature* 55, no. 1 (2024): 127. Commenting primarily on historiographies of Jews in the modern Middle East,

INTRODUCTION

Moshe Behar observes that many of the scholars engaging in such work were pursuing their graduate studies during the years of the Oslo Peace Process and its fatal disintegration. Both the liberal hopes and the immense disappointments following Oslo's failures drove young scholars, unwilling to accept the view of the Israeli-Palestinian conflict as a zero-sum game, to search for its origins as well as for the "paths not taken" in the recent historical past. Moshe Behar, "Fusing Arab Nahda, European Haskalah and Euro-Zionism: Eastern Jewish Thought in Late-Ottoman and Post-Ottoman Palestine," *Journal of Modern Jewish Studies* 16, no. 2 (2017): 271.

77. The forerunner of this avenue of research is Amiel Alcalay, *After Jews and Arabs: Remaking Levantine Culture* (University of Minnesota Press, 1993). Notable examples include Gil Anidjar, *The Jew, the Arab: A History of the Enemy* (Stanford University Press, 2003); Gil Anidjar, *Semites: Race, Religion, Literature* (Stanford University Press, 2008); Gil Z. Hochberg, *In Spite of Partition: Jews, Arabs, and the Limits of Separatist Imagination* (Princeton University Press, 2010); Lital Levy, *Poetic Trespass: Writing Between Hebrew and Arabic in Israel/Palestine* (Princeton University Press, 2014); Nancy E. Berg, *Exile from Exile: Israeli Writers from Iraq* (State University of New York Press, 2012); Anna Bernard, *Rhetorics of Belonging: Nation, Narration, and Israel/Palestine* (Liverpool University Press, 2013); Hella Bloom Cohen, *The Literary Imagination in Israel-Palestine: Orientalism, Poetry, and Biopolitics* (Palgrave, 2016). These studies are all in conversation with new histories of the relationships between Jews and Arabs beyond the framework of Zionism, too many to recount here. Orit Bashkin provides a valuable overview of this body of work in "The Middle Eastern Shift and Provincializing Zionism," *International Journal of Middle East Studies* 46, no. 3 (2014): 577–80.

78. Liron Mor, *Conflicts: The Poetics and Politics of Palestine-Israel* (Fordham University Press, 2024); Kfir Cohen Lustig, *Makers of Worlds, Readers of Signs: Israeli and Palestinian Literature of the Global Contemporary* (Verso, 2019).

79. On language revival and its literary ambiguities, see Roni Henig, *On Revival: Hebrew Literature Between Life and Death*, University of Pennsylvania Press, 2024

80. Stephen Sheehi, *Foundations of Modern Arab Identity* (University Press of Florida, 2004). Recent years witnessed a flourishing of historiographic and critical interest in the *nahḍa* in English language scholarship. In addition to studies cited previously and below, see also Jens Hanssen and Max Weiss, eds., *Arabic Thought Beyond the Liberal Age: Towards an Intellectual History of the Nahḍa* (Cambridge University Press, 2016); Jeffrey Sacks, *Iterations of Loss: Mutilation and Aesthetic Form, Al-Shidyaq to Darwish* (Fordham University Press, 2015); Tarek El-Ariss, *Trials of Arab Modernity: Literary Affects and the New Political* (Fordham University Press, 2013); Tarek El-Ariss, *The Arab Renaissance: A Bilingual Anthology of the Nahda* (Modern Language Association of America, 2018); Elizabeth M. Holt, *Fictitious Capital: Silk, Cotton, and the Rise of the Arabic Novel* (Fordham University Press, 2017); Marilyn Booth, *Classes of Ladies of Cloistered Spaces: Writing Feminist History Through Biography in Fin-de-Siècle Egypt* (Edinburgh University Press, 2015).

81. Amnon Raz-Krakotzkin, "Exile, History and the Nationalization of Jewish Memory: Some Reflections on the Zionist Notion of History and Return," *Journal of Levantine Studies* 3, no. 2 (2013): 56.

INTRODUCTION

82. Shaden M. Tageldin, *Disarming Words: Empire and the Seductions of Translation in Egypt* (University of California Press, 2011), 67–72.
83. Lital Levy, "The Nahḍa and the Haskala: A Comparative Reading of 'Revival' and 'Reform,'" *Middle Eastern Literatures* 16, no. 3 (2013): 302.
84. For Hebrew linguistic projects, see Robert Alter, *The Invention of Hebrew Prose: Modern Fiction and the Language of Realism* (University of Washington Press, 1988); Olga Litvak, *Haskalah: The Romantic Movement in Judaism* (Rutgers University Press, 2012). For Arabic, see Nadia Bou Ali, "Collecting the Nation: Lexicography and National Pedagogy in *al-nahda al-ʿarabiyya*," in *Archives, Museums and Collecting Practices in the Modern Arab World*, ed. Sonja Mejcher-Atassi and John Pedro Schwartz (Routledge, 2012), 33–56.
85. The writer Yehuda Burla (1886–1969) was a Jerusalemite born to an established Sephardi family and, like Shami, had aligned himself with the Zionist movement. He wrote this essay while working as a teacher in Damascus. A second promised installment, on modern Arabic poetry, was apparently never published. For more on Burla's writing between Arabic and Hebrew and Jews and Arabs, see Yochai Oppenheimer, "ha-ʿAravim be-ʿeynayim mizrahiyot" [The Arabs from a Mizrahi perspective] *Mikan* 9 (2008); Almog Behar, "mi-Yehuda Halevi le-Yehuda Burla" [From Yehuda Halevi to Yehuda Burla], in *ha-Piyut ke-tsohar tarbuti*, ed. Haviva Pedaya (ha-Kibbuts ha-meʾuhad, 2013).
86. Yehuda Burla, "Ha-sifrut ha-ʿaravit" [Arabic literature], *ha-Tkufa* 18 and 19 (1922): 462.
87. Burla, "Ha-sifrut ha-ʿaravit," 461.
88. Dipesh Chakrabarty, *Provincializing Europe: Postcolonial Thought and Historical Difference* (Princeton University Press, 2000), 8, 30–34.
89. Amnon Raz-Krakotzkin, "The Zionist Return to the West and the Mizrachi Jewish Perspective," in *Orientalism and the Jews*, ed. Ivan Davidson Kalmar and Derek J. Penslar (Brandeis University Press, 2005), 167.
90. See Samir Amin, *Accumulation on a World Scale: A Critique of the Theory of Underdevelopment* (Monthly Review Press, 1974), originaly published in Arabic in 1958. In relation to literary production, see the Warwick Research Collective WRec, *Combined and Uneven Development: Towards a New Theory of World-Literature* (Liverpool University Press, 2016), 10–15. Cf. Peter Hill, *Utopia and Civilisation in the Arab Nahda* (Cambridge University Press, 2020), 248–51; Oded Nir, *Signatures of Struggle: The Figuration of Collectivity in Israeli Fiction* (SUNY Press, 2018), 11–13.
91. On Barak, *On Time: Technology and Temporality in Modern Egypt* (University of California Press, 2013), 5.
92. See Shmuel Almog, "ha-Bsora ha-ruhanit shel avodat ha-tarbut," [The spiritual message of cultural labor] in *Tsiyonut ve-historya* (Magnes, 1982); Hannan Hever, "Guru lakhem min ha-galitsaʾim: safrut galitsya ve-ha-maʾavak ʿal ha kanon ba siporet ha-ʿivrit" [Beware of the Galicians: Galician literature and the struggle over the Hebrew literary canon], *Teʾorya u-vikoret* 5 (1994). I thank Roni Masel for the final point.
93. R. Radhakrishnan, "Why Compare," *New Literary History* 40, no. 3 (Summer 2009): 454.
94. Mor, *Conflicts*, 24.
95. Cf. with Kfir Cohen Lustig's proposal to shift the subject of analysis from nation to social form, *Makers of Worlds*, 10–11.

INTRODUCTION

96. Nadera Shalhoub-Kevorkian, "Ashlaa' and the Genocide in Gaza: Livability Against Fragmented Flesh," Hot Spots, *Fieldsights*, October 31, 2024, https://culanth.org/fieldsights/ashlaa-and-the-genocide-in-gaza.
97. Hito Steyerl, "In Defense of the Poor Image," *e-flux Journal* 10, no. 11 (2009), https://www.e-flux.com/journal/10/61362/in-defense-of-the-poor-image/.

1. REVERB: LITERATURE'S ABSENT PRESENT

1. Goldberg began writing *Avedot* in 1936 and published sections of it in various literary journals in Palestine before abandoning the manuscript in 1939. Giddon Ticotsky published an edited version of the manuscript in 2010 as Leah Goldberg, *Avedot (mukdash le-antonya)* [Losses (dedicated to Antonia)], ed. Giddon Ticotsky (Sifriyat ha-poalim, 2010).
2. Kron's travails in the department of Orientalist studies are no doubt shaped by Goldberg's experience as a scholar of semitic philology in Berlin and then in Bonn, where she completed her PhD in 1933. On Goldberg's years as a student, especially in relation to the German Orientalist tradition to which she was initiated, see Yfaat Weiss, *Nesi'a u-nesi'a meduma: Le'a Goldberg be-germanya, 1930–1933* [A journey and an imaginary journey: Leah Golberg in Germany 1930–1933] (Merkaz zalman shazar, 2014); Yfaat Weiss, "A Small Town in Germany: Leah Goldberg and German Orientalism in 1932," *The Jewish Quarterly Review* 99, no. 2 (2009). After her immigration to Palestine, Goldberg, who according to Weiss was always ambivalent about the discipline, quickly established herself as one of Hebrew's foremost poets and literary commentators, and when she did return to the university, it was to teach comparative literature.
3. Allison Schachter, "Orientalism, Secularism, and the Crisis of Hebrew Modernism: Reading Leah Goldberg's *Avedot*," *Comparative LIterature* 65, no. 3 (2013): 345.
4. Goldberg, *Avedot*, 309.
5. I rely here on Michael Allan's work on the emergence of literature as a modern practice of reading, in Michael Allan, *In the Shadow of World Literature: Sites of Reading in Colonial Egypt* (Princeton University Press, 2016).
6. Arjun Appadurai mobilized the term the "hegemony of Eurochronology" to address the politics of cultural flow in what he calls "the global cultural economy," in Arjun Appadurai, "Disjuncture and Difference in the Global Cultural Economy," *Theory, Culture & Society* 7, no. 2–3 (1990): 3. Emily Apter adopted the term to address the historiographic biases of literary criticism in a global context, in Emily Apter, *Against World Literature: On the Politics of Untranslatability* (Verso, 2013), 6. For a similar discussion of "the problem of Eurochronology," see Christopher Prendergast, ed., *Debating World Literature* (Verso, 2004), 6.
7. El Shakry uses the term "extratemporal" to describe al-Mas'adi's 1940 novella *Mawlid al-nisyan* [The birth of forgetting] in Hoda El Shakry, *The Literary Qur'an: Narrative Ethics in the Maghreb* (Fordham University Press, 2020), 16.
8. Mohamed-Salah Omri claims that al-Mas'adi's work is studied in Tunisia more than any other living local writer, meriting its own field: *madrasat al-Mas'adi* (the al-Mas'adi school). In Mohamed-Salah Omri, *Nationalism, Islam and World Literature: Sites of Confluence in the Writings of Mahmud al-Mas'adi* (Routledge, 2006), 3. Agnon might be the only Hebrew writer who had an entire academic journal,

1. REVERB

'Ayin-gimel, dedicated to him, though it survived for only two issues (see https://www.biu.ac.il/js/li/aj/index.html).

9. For a fantastic analysis of Agnon's use of irony, see "Motivim be-yetsirato" [Some motifs in his work, 1948], in Leah Goldberg, *ha-Ometz le-hulin* [Mundane bravery], ed. A. B. Jaffe (Sifriyat ha-poalim, 1976), 104. On the role of irony in al-Mas'adi, see Omri, *Nationalism, Islam and World Literature*, 96.
10. Mahmud al-Mas'adi, *Haddatha Abu Hurayra qal* (al-Dar al-tunisiyya li-l-nashr, 1973). All translations from this text are my own unless otherwise noted. Shmuel Yosef Agnon, "'Ido ve-'enam," in *'Ad hena* (Schocken, 1966). I quote Walter Lever's translation, "Edo and Enam," from Shmuel Yosef Agnon, *Two Tales by S.Y. Agnon: Bethrothed and Edo and Enam*, trans. Walter Lever, ed. Jeffrey Saks (Toby, 2014), with modifications when noted.
11. Susan Stanford Friedman, "Periodizing Modernism: Postcolonial Modernities and the Space/Time Borders of Modernist Studies," *Modernism/Modernity* 13, no. 3 (2006): 433.
12. Adonis, *al-Thabit wa-l-mutahawwil: bahth fi al-ittiba' wa-l-ibda' 'inda al-'Arab* [The mutable and the immutable: a study of creativity and adheration among the Arabs] (Dar al-'awda, 1974). Huda J. Fakhreddine has further developed this insight, identifying parallel techniques and positions in the modernist poetry of the ninth and the twentieth centuries, in Huda J. Fakhreddine, *Metapoesis in the Arabic Tradition: From Modernists to Muḥdathūn* (Brill, 2015).
13. Eric Hayot, *On Literary Worlds* (Oxford University Press, 2012), 113.
14. Allan, *In the Shadow of World Literature*, 174.
15. This statement summarizes numerous insights from Gauri Viswanathan, *Masks of Conquest: Literary Study and British Rule in India* (Columbia University Press, 1989); Sheldon I. Pollock, *The Language of the Gods in the World of Men: Sanskrit, Culture, and Power in Premodern India* (University of California Press, 2006); Gil Anidjar, *Semites: Race, Religion, Literature* (Stanford University Press, 2008); Aamir Mufti, *Forget English! Orientalisms and World Literatures* (Harvard University Press, 2016); Shaden M. Tageldin, *Disarming Words: Empire and the Seductions of Translation in Egypt* (University of California Press, 2011).
16. Jeffrey Sacks, "The Philological Present: Reading the Arabic Nineteenth Century," *Journal of Arabic Literature* 47, no. 1–2 (2016): 171.
17. Marc Nichanian, *Mourning Philology: Art and Religion at the Margins of the Ottoman Empire*, trans. G. M. Goshgarian and Jeff Fort (Fordham University Press, 2014), 3.
18. Edward W. Said, *Orientalism* (Pantheon, 1978), 72.
19. On this history, see Auerbach's classical essay on the *figura* as an organizing model of relations between Christians and Jews. Erich Auerbach, *Scenes from the Drama of European Literature* (University of Minnesota Press, 1984), 11–76.
20. On typological models in the work of French Orientalists, see chapter 1 in Aziz al-Azmeh, *The Times of History: Universal Topics in Islamic Historiography* (Central European University Press, 2007). For typological readings of the figure of the Jew in the German tradition, see Jeffrey S. Librett, *Orientalism and the Figure of the Jew* (Fordham University Press, 2014).
21. Al-Mas'adi, *Haddatha Abu Hurayra qal*, 45. Henceforth cited in text as *Haddatha*.
22. Abu al-'Atahiyya was canonized as a poet of asceticism (*juhd*), known for his pessimistic and moralistic ruminations on the fleeting nature of time.

1. REVERB

23. Omri, *Nationalism, Islam and World Literature*, 5.
24. See also Abu Hurayra's and Rayhana's discussion of erotic pleasure as the overcoming of age and time on page 102.
25. Omri, *Nationalism, Islam and World Literature*, 6.
26. Mahmud al-Masʿadi, *al-Aʿmal al-kamila* [Complete works], 4 vols. (Dar al-janub, 2012), 3:111.
27. Al-Masʿadi, *al-Aʿmal al-kamila*, 3:109.
28. Much of the premodern Arabic literature of Islamic jurisprudence is concerned precisely with the problem of how to reconcile a fixed and revealed scripture with human reality and custom, which is constantly changing and evolving. The different responses to this problem determine much of the divergences of the various *madhāhib*, or schools of jurisprudence. This is not to say that colonial modernity did not introduce new modes of historicity to Islamic and Arab thought, but perhaps their most prominent characteristic was their declared "newness" and detachment from the past. For a discussion on historicism in early modern Arabic writing, see for example Dana Sajdi, *The Barber of Damascus: Nouveau Literacy in the Eighteenth-Century Ottoman Levant* (Stanford University Press, 2013), and Jeffrey Sacks's discussion of it in "The Philological Present."
29. Kathleen Davis, *Periodization and Sovereignty: How Ideas of Feudalism and Secularization Govern the Politics of Time* (University of Pennsylvania Press, 2008), 8–9.
30. Generally stated, this is the project of postcolonial theory and its influences on other fields of knowledge. The term "the imaginary waiting room of history" is Dipesh Chakrabarty's succinct image of the place that historicism assigns to colonized nations, in Dipesh Chakrabarty, *Provincializing Europe: Postcolonial Thought and Historical Difference* (Princeton University Press, 2000), 8.
31. James E. Montgomery, "The Empty Ḥijāz," in *Arabic Theology, Arabic Philosophy: From the Many to the One, Essays in Honor of Richard M. Frank*, ed. James E. Montgomery (Peeters, 2006), 203.
32. Al-Azmeh, *The Times of History*, 54.
33. Aamir Mufti, "Orientalism and the Institution of World Literatures," *Critical Inquiry* 36, no. 3 (Spr 2010): 462–64; Abdallah Laroui, *L'ideologie arabe contemporaine: essai critique* (François Maspero, 1977). Much has been written on the colonial writer's turn to an archive of "tradition" in order to establish an authentic postcolonial national identity and culture. The most effective reading of the fetishizing of cultural roots in order to maintain national continuity remains "On National Culture" in Frantz Fanon, *The Wretched of the Earth*, trans. Richard Philcox (Grove, 2004).
34. Maurice Olender, *The Languages of Paradise: Race, Religion, and Philology in the Nineteenth Century* (Harvard University Press, 1992), 12.
35. Some *ḥadīth* scholars distinguish between *khabar* as any transmitted knowledge, *ḥadīth* as a report about the prophet, and *athar* as a report about the companions and successors, whereas other scholars treat the three terms as synonymous.
36. Ziad Elmarsafy suggests the translation "Thus Spoke Abu Hurayra" because it echoes the novel's Nietzschean affinities, in Ziad Elmarsafy, *Sufism in the Contemporary Arabic Novel* (Edinburgh University Press, 2012), 67.
37. Khalid al-Gharibi, *Jadaliyat al-asala wa-l-muʿasara fi adab al-Masʿadi* [The dialectics between authenticity and contemporaneity in al-Masʿadi's writings] (Samid

1. REVERB

li-l-nashr wa-l-tawziʿ, 1994), 151–55; Omri, *Nationalism, Islam and World Literature*, 105–35; Elmarsafy, *Sufism*, 66–77.
38. In an interview, al-Masʿadi tells of the disappointment, if not rage, expressed by readers in a Saudi book fair who confused between the two Abu Hurayras. Mahmud al-Masʿadi, "Interview with Mahmud al-Masʿadi," interview by Mohamed-Salah Omri, *Comparative Critical Studies* 4, no. 3 (2007): 438.
39. Omri, *Nationalism, Islam and World Literature*, 54.
40. See Georgine Ayoub, "Un idiome clair et pur: Le trésor enseveli," in *Cent titres 3: Poésie de langue Arabe* (Centre Internationale de Poésie, 2002).
41. Jacques Waardenburg asserts that despite his influence on a number of theological and scholarly factions, Massignon's nonsystematized, often unsupported or uncited, and highly personalized scholarship had limited academic impact. Jacques Waardenburg, "Louis Massignon (1883–1962) as a Student of Islam," *Die Welt des Islams* 45, no. 3 (2005): 336.
42. Said, *Orientalism*, 267.
43. For more on the Eranos circle, see Steven M. Wasserstrom, *Religion After Religion: Gershom Scholem, Mircea Eliade, and Henry Corbin at Eranos* (Princeton University Press, 1999).
44. al-Masʿadi, *al-Aʿmal al-kamila*, 3:392.
45. Massignon gave numerous accounts of this experience, for example in "Visitation of a Stranger," in *Testimonies and Reflections: Essays of Louis Massignon*, ed. and trans. Herbert Mason (University of Notre Dame Press, 1989), 39–42.
46. Louis Massignon, *Essay on the Origins of the Technical Language of Islamic Mysticism*, trans. Benjamin Clark (University of Notre Dame Press, 1997), xxvii. Massignon was not alone in "redeeming" Sufism as a laudatory form of Islam. Tomoko Masuzawa explores how scholars of religion configured Sufism as a late Persian Islamic tendency, unrelated to its Semite origins. This Aryan form of religiosity was therefore much more compatible with "religion as such," regardless of doctrine and ordinance, and later more similar to the universal religion of Christianity. See Tomoko Masuzawa, *The Invention of World Religions, or, How European Universalism was Preserved in the Language of Pluralism* (University of Chicago Press, 2005), 203. Massignon, it should be mentioned, argued for the Qurʾanic origins of Sufi thought and viewed its Persian evolutions as excessively sensualist. He associated Persian with the other idolatrous Indo-European languages prone to the vanity of the aesthetes, such as French.
47. For an overview of Massignon's relationship with Iraqi Orientalists, see ʿAli Husayn Jabiri, *Maʾsat al-Hallaj bayna Masinyun wa-l-bahithin al-baghdadiyyin, 1908–1998* [The passion of al-Hallaj, between Massignon and the Baghdadi scholars] (Dar ninawa, 2008).
48. Omri, *Nationalism, Islam and World Literature*, 130.
49. Massignon gives an overview of this development in the essay "Time in Islamic Thought" in *Testimonies and Reflections*, 48.
50. Hussein's article appeared in the Egyptian newspaper *al-Jumhuriyya* on February 27, 1957, reprinted in Nur al-Din Sammud, *Mahmud al-Masʿadi wa-kitabuhu al-Sudd* [Mahmud al-Masʿadi and his book The Dam] (al-Dar al-tunisiyya li-l-nashr, 1973), 73. Hoda El Shakry argues that Hussein misread al-Masʿadi and that his response "renders legible the critical biases that codify false binaries of the secular/sacred,

public/private, political/personal, and social/individual." In El Shakry, *The Literary Qur'an*, 162–65.
51. Reprinted in Sammud, *Mahmud al-Mas'adi wa-kitabuhu al-Sudd*. I borrow this translation from Omri, *Nationalism, Islam and World Literature*, 46.
52. I borrow the useful term "Euromodernist forms" from Jahan Ramazani, "Modernist Bricolage, Postcolonial Hybridity," *Modernism/Modernity* 13, no. 3 (2006): 445–63.
53. Jabra Ibrahim Jabra, "Modern Arabic Literature and the West," *Journal of Arabic Literature* 2, no. 1 (1971): 78.
54. Franco Moretti, "Conjectures on World Literature," *New Left Review* 1 (2000): 58.
55. It is telling that the three examples Jabra lists, *Men in the Sun* by Ghassan Kanafani, *Season of Migration to the North* by Tayyib Salih, and *Chattering on the Nile* by Najib Mahfuz, are probably still the most likely Arabic-language texts to appear on a world literature syllabus.
56. Jabra, "Modern Arabic," 86.
57. Mufti, "Orientalism and the Institution of World Literatures," 468.
58. Marc Nichanian usefully summarizes this model, noting that "philology is an ideological-conceptual apparatus that has two operational phases: it transforms what is usually defined as literature into a witness; but, historically, what is defined as literature is so defined only in reaction to philology's inauguration of its own comprehensive, contextual, and secularized project [i.e., to define everything as literature or philology's object]." Nichanian, *Mourning Philology*, 70.
59. Shmuel Yosef Agnon, "Banquet Speech," Nobel Prize in Literature 1966, Stockholm, Sweden, December 10, 1966, https://www.nobelprize.org/prizes/literature/1966/agnon/speech/.
60. For instance, his famous denial of the unquestionable influence of Freud and Kafka on his work in, among other places, Shmuel Yosef Agnon, *Me-'atsmi el 'atsmi* [From myself to myself] (Schocken, 1976), 256.
61. Dalia Hoshen provides a comprehensive overview of how Agnon's critical reception constructed an opposition between "believer" and "sceptic." Consequently, she offers a reading that nulls this binary, identifying Agnon as the successor of a Mishnaic tradition that already embodies the ruptures associated with modernity. Dalia Hoshen, *'Agnon: sipur (ena) sugiya ba-gemara* [Agnon: a story is (not) a talmudic question] (Reuven mas, 2006).
62. Alan L. Mintz and Anne Golomb Hoffman, "Introduction," in S. Y. Agnon, *A Book That Was Lost: Thirty-Five Stories*, ed. Alan L. Mintz and Anne Golomb Hoffman (Toby, 1995), 18.
63. Shmuel Yosef Agnon, *ha-Esh ve-ha-'etsim* [The fire and the wood] (Schocken, 1998), 14.
64. Baruch Kurzweil, *Masot 'al sipure Shai 'Agnon* (Schocken, 1962), 142–43.
65. Michal Arbel, *Katuv 'al 'oro shel ha-kelev: 'al tfisat ha-yetsira etsel Shai 'Agnon* [Written on the dog's skin: creation in S. Y. Agnon] (Merkaz heksherim at Ben Guryon University, 2006), 110.
66. The linguistic and allegorical links between Gemulah and the Kabbalistic feminine figure of the Shekinah have been pointed out by numerous scholars, See, for example, Michal Oron, "Smalim u-motivim kabaliyim ba-sipur 'ido ve-'enam le-Shai 'Agnon" [Kabbalistic symbols and motifs in Agnon's Edo and Enam], *Ba-Seminar* (1977); Tzahi Weiss, "Lada'at mibli lada'at" [Knowing without knowing], *Reshit* 1 (2009).

67. Pardes claims that Ginat's character is based on Agnon's close friend, the ethnologist and orientalist Shelomo Dov Goitein, in Ilana Pardes, *Agnon's Moonstruck Lovers: The Song of Songs in Israeli Culture* (University of Washington Press, 2013), 103.
68. Olender, *The Languages of Paradise*, 5.
69. Pardes, *Agnon's Moonstruck Lovers*, 107.
70. Cynthia Ozick, "Agnon's Antagonisms," *Commentary* 86, no. 6 (1988): 43.
71. Gershom Scholem, *Pirke yesod be-havanat ha-kabala u-smaleha* [Fundamentals of the kabbalah and its symbols] (Mosad bialik, 1980), 419.
72. E. T. A. Hoffmann, "The Sandman," trans. R. J. Hollingdale, in *Tales of Hoffmann* (Penguin, 2004).
73. Sigmund Freud, "The Uncanny," in *The Standard Edition of the Complete Psychological Works of Sigmund Freud*, ed. James Strachey (Hogarth, 1995).
74. Shmuel Yosef Agnon, "Hadom ve-kisse" [Footstool and throne], in *Lifnim min ha-homa* (Schocken, 1975), 139.
75. Pardes, *Agnon's Moonstruck Lovers*, 96. Pardes ties the song of the inscrutable bird Grofit to the Song of Songs, which in *Zohar Shemot* is identified with the "totality of the whole Torah, totality of the whole work of Creation, totality of mystery of the patriarchs.... Whatever was, whatever is, and whatever will eventually be." Pardes, 119.
76. Gayatri Chakravorty Spivak, "Echo," *New Literary History* 24, no. 1 (1993): 17; 23.
77. Spivak, "Echo," 27.
78. Spivak, "Echo," 22.
79. Gayatri Chakravorty Spivak, "Subaltern Studies: Deconstructing Historiography," in *The Spivak Reader: Selected Works of Gayatri Chakravorty Spivak*, ed. Donna Landry and Gerald MacLean (Routledge, 1996), 205.
80. Sangeeta Ray, *Gayatri Chakravorty Spivak: In Other Words* (Wiley-Blackwell, 2009), 109.

2. SCRATCH: THE PRESENT OUT OF WORK

1. Albert Cossery, *Laziness in the Fertile Valley*, trans. William Goyen (New Directions, 2013), 164. Like all of Cossery's works, this novel was originally composed in French. The English translation first appeared as *The Lazy Ones* in 1949. An Arabic translation, by Mahmud Qasim, appeared only in 1996.
2. See Elliott Colla, *Conflicted Antiquities: Egyptology, Egyptomania, Egyptian Modernity* (Duke University Press, 2008), 228. Originally located across from the Cairo train station, the statue was moved to Giza in 1955.
3. Menahem Brinker, *'Ad ha-simta ha-tveryanit* [To the Tiberian alley] (Am oved, 1990), 197.
4. Dina Berdichevsky, "Yehudim, masa'im ve-sh'ar hasrei ha-janer: ha-mikre shel Brenner ve-tkufato," *mi-Kan* 20 (2020): 29. Highlighted in the original.
5. The debates on literary *iltizām* were sparked in Egypt with Taha Husayn's discussion of Jean-Paul Sartre's *Qu'est-ce que la littérature?* in the journal *al-Katib al-masri* in 1947 and quickly spread all over the Arab world. For an overview, see Verena Klemm, "Different Notions of Commitment (Iltizam) and Committed Literature (al-adab al-multazim) in the Literary Circles of the Mashriq," *Arabic and Middle Eastern Literatures* 3, no. 1 (2000): 51–62. On the theoretical fuzziness

of the concept and its efficacy, see Qussay Al-Attabi, "The Polemics of Iltizām: Al-Ādāb's Early Arguments for Commitment," *Journal of Arabic Literature* 52, no. 1–2 (2021): 124–46. On the slogan "literature for the sake of life," see Shir Alon, "The Writer Sweating at His Desk: Labor and Literature in Fatḥī Ghānim's *al-Jabal*," *Journal of Arabic Literature* 55, no. 2-3 (2024): 322–48.

6. On Cossery's reception in Egypt, see Richard Jacquemond, *Conscience of the Nation: Writers, State, and Society in Modern Egypt*, trans. David Tresilian (American University in Cairo Press, 2008), 116–17. On the international networks of anarchist fiction that circulated and translated Cossery's and Georges Henein's works, see James Gifford, *Personal Modernisms: Anarchist Networks and the Later Avant-Gardes* (University of Alberta Press, 2014), 101–5.

7. See Sam Bardaouil, *Surrealism in Egypt: Modernism and the Art and Liberty Group* (I. B. Tauris, 2016).

8. Zeina G. Halabi, "The Literary Lives of Umm Kulthūm: Cossery, Ghali, Negm, and the Critique of Nasserism," *Middle Eastern Literatures* 19, no. 1 (2016): 85.

9. Cossery, *Laziness in the Fertile Valley*, 46.

10. Sianne Ngai, *Ugly Feelings* (Harvard University Press, 2004), 183.

11. Steven Connor, *The Book of Skin* (Cornell University Press, 2004), 230.

12. Eve Kosofsky Sedgwick, *Touching Feeling: Affect, Pedagogy, Performativity* (Duke University Press, 2003), 14. I am indebted in this chapter to Sedgwick's work on reading for surface textures and learned much from the polemics about "surface reading" that it inspired, for example in Stephen Best and Sharon Marcus, "Surface Reading: An Introduction," *Representations*, no. 108 (2009). Nevertheless, I am far more interested in the political work that figures of depth and surface do in the texts themselves than in a program of reading that equates literary interpretation with a depth model. See the introduction to this book for more on this question.

13. Barukh Kimmerling, *Mehagrim, mityashvim, yelidim* [Immigrants, settlers, natives] (Am oved, 2004), 80.

14. Boaz Arpaly, *ha-'Ikar ha-shlili* [The negative principle] (ha-Kibbuts ha-me'uhad, 1992), 83.

15. Yoseph Haim Brenner, "'Atsabim," in *Kol Kitve Y. H. Brenner* [The complete works of Y. H. Brenner], 4 vols. (ha-Kibbuts ha-me'uhad, Dvir, 1960), 2:1229–61. I cite Hillel Halkin's English translation throughout, with modifications when noted; Yoseph Haim Brenner, "Nerves," trans. Hillel Halkin, in *Eight Great Hebrew Short Novels*, ed. Alan Lelchuk and Gershon Shaked (New American Library, 1983), 38.

16. The "Hebrew colony" is unnamed in the story, but it is identifiable as one of the *moshavot*, agricultural settlements based on private land ownership established by immigrants of the first Zionist immigration wave (First Aliya, 1882–1904). Brenner and his characters are of the Second Aliya (1904–1914). Stories such as "Nerves" are responsible for establishing the image of the Second Aliya immigrants as young and idealistic pioneers at an ideological struggle with the more established agricultural class. As Alroey points out, this idealistic group was a minority among the Second Aliya immigrants, but their image formed the basis for the Zionist settlement's self-image in subsequent years. Gur Alroey, *Imigrantim: ha-hagira ha-yehudit le-erets yisra'el be-reshit ha-me'a ha-'esrim* [Immigrants: the Jewish immigration to Erets Yisrael in the early twentieth century] (Yad yitshak ben-tsvi, 2004). On the conflicted cultural relationship between the Hebrew colonies and the Palestinian

2. SCRATCH

population, see Yafah Berlovits, *Lehamtsi erets, lehamtsi 'am: tashtiyot sifrut ve-tarbut ba-yetsira shel ha-'aliya ha-rishona* [Inventing a land, inventing a people] (ha-Kibbuts ha-Me'uhad, 1996), chap. 4.

17. Fredric Jameson, *The Antinomies of Realism* (Verso, 2013), 28. Several critics have argued that Brenner was a modernist writer somewhat *avant la lettre*, among them Todd Hasak-Lowy, *Here and Now: History, Nationalism, and Realism in Modern Hebrew Fiction* (Syracuse University Press, 2008), 45; Shachar Pinsker, *Literary Passports: The Making of Modernist Hebrew Fiction in Europe* (Stanford University Press, 2010), 56–63; Allison Schachter, *Diasporic Modernisms: Hebrew and Yiddish Literature in the Twentieth Century* (Oxford University Press, 2011), 59–60. Their studies highlight the attributes Brenner shares with his European and Russian contemporaries. Nevertheless, I am less concerned with determining whether Brenner should be placed in the "realist" or "modernist" camp. One of the most useful observations in Jameson's *Antinomies* is that the realist canon is rife with what could be identified as modernist techniques and that it is the tension between these "static" techniques and a desire for a "story" that defines realism, rather than matters of mimesis or fidelity of representation.
18. Jameson, *Antinomies*, 28.
19. Brenner, "Nerves," 37.
20. Brenner, "Nerves," 37.
21. Chapter 3 discusses how the tendency to "unsee" the Palestinian villages that are in clear sight persists after they are destroyed and their residents expelled.
22. Fathi Ghanem, *al-Jabal* [The mountain] [1957] (Dar al-Hilal, 1965). Ami Elad notes disagreements on the date of *al-Jabal*'s publication, but according to contemporary reviews, the novel was serialized in the Egyptian weekly *Ruz al-yusuf* in 1957 and was published as a book in 1959. See Muhammad 'Abdallah al-Shafaqi, "Muhawalat naqd, qissat al-jabal" [An attempt at critique: *The Mountain*], *al-Adab* (June 1959): 195; Yusuf al-Sharuni, *Dirasat fi al-adab al-'arabi al-mu'asir* (al-Mu'assasa al-misriyya al-'amma li-l-ta'lif wa-l-tarjama wa-l-tiba'a wa-l-nashr, 1964), 121; Ami Elad, "Ideology and Structure in Fathī Ghānim's *Al-Jabal*," *Journal of Arabic Literature* 20, no. 2 (1989): 168fn3.
23. See Omnia S. El Shakry, *The Great Social Laboratory: Subjects of Knowledge in Colonial and Postcolonial Egypt* (Stanford University Press, 2007), 145–65. On the battle over ancient Egyptian heritage and the creation of an Egyptian Pharaonism, see Colla, *Conflicted Antiquities*.
24. For critical accounts of this episode, see Timothy Mitchell, *Rule of Experts: Egypt, Techno-Politics, Modernity* (University of California Press, 2002), 179–205; Donald M. Reid, *Contesting Antiquity in Egypt: Archaeologies, Museums and the Struggle for Identities from World War I to Nasser* (American University in Cairo Press, 2015), 160–63; Kees Van der Spek, *The Modern Neighbors of Tutankhamun: History, Life, and Work in the Villages of the Theban West Bank* (American University in Cairo Press, 2011).
25. Hassan Fathy, *Architecture for the Poor: An Experiment in Rural Egypt* (University of Chicago Press, 1973), 176.
26. Mitchell, *Rule of Experts*, 187. See also Mitchell's analysis of hygiene and the formation of "the Egyptian character" in Timothy Mitchell, *Colonising Egypt* (Cambridge University Press, 1988), 95–127.

27. On the continuity of economic and class structures across regimes, see El Shakry, *The Great Social Laboratory*, 198–204.
28. Edward W. Said, "Zionism from the Standpoint of Its Victims," *Social Text* 1 (1979): 26–27.
29. Colla, *Conflicted Antiquities*, 14.
30. Lynn Meskell, "Sites of Violence: Terrorism, Tourism, and Heritage in the Archaeological Present," in *Embedding Ethics*, ed. Lynn Meskell and Peter Pels (Routledge, 2005), 123.
31. See Hagar Kotef, *Movement and the Ordering of Freedom: On Liberal Governances of Mobility* (Duke University Press, 2015), 10. Hassan Fathy's cosmopolitan career is a case in point. *Architecture for the Poor*, the book in which he described the civilizing ambitions of New Qurna and disparages the squabbling authorities and the local villagers who had thwarted the project, was published in English rather than Arabic, whereas his allegorical novella on the failed project, "Land of Utopia," was published in French.
32. For recent developments of these spatial logics, see Nasia Anam, "Encampment as Colonization: Theorizing the Representation of Refugee Spaces," *Journal of Narrative Theory* 50, no. 3 (2020).
33. Aamir Mufti elaborates on this analogy in *Enlightenment in the Colony: The Jewish Question and the Crisis of Postcolonial Culture* (Princeton University Press, 2007). Mufti builds on Hannah Arendt's identification of the Jewish minority as always potentially moveable within the nation-state to explore parallel processes of minoritization and displacement in India and Pakistan.
34. Ghanem, *al-Jabal*, 13.
35. Ghanem, *al-Jabal*, 7.
36. Selim, *The Novel and the Rural Imaginary*, 143. Cf. Emily Drumsta on the investigator "clearing space" for the voices of the villagers and for genres other than the novel when learning to disdain the government's mode of producing knowledge, in *Ways of Seeking: The Arabic Novel and the Poetics of Investigation* (University of California Press, 2024), 125–128.
37. Selim, *The Novel and the Rural Imaginary*, 127. For more on the productive ethos in Nasserist Egypt and on *The Mountain*'s conflicted position within it, see Alon, "The Writer Sweating at His Desk."
38. The root f-l-ḥ means to split or cleave and, by extension, to plow, till, and cultivate the land. The Gurnawis subsist by scraping at the mountain, a very different gesture.
39. 'Abd al-Rahman al-Sharqawi, *al-Ard* (Dar al-katib al-'arabi, 1968), 29–30.
40. Ghanem, *al-Jabal*, 66.
41. Selim, *The Novel and the Rural Imaginary*, throughout but especially 20–21.
42. Ghanem, *al-Jabal*, 91.
43. Cf. Yusuf al-Sharuni's claim that the true drama of the novel is not the conflict between the ruling powers and the villagers, since that conflict is quickly resolved when we learn, together with the narrator, to identify with the villagers against the governing power. At the heart of the novel, he claims, is the existential battle between the people of the mountain and the mountain itself. Al-Sharuni, *Dirasat*, 123. Studies of the 1963 film version of *al-Jabal* (dir. Khalil Shawqi) also highlight *kaḥt* as a fatalistic obsession. Cinema scholar Amir al-'Umari reads the mountain

as a tomb in which the bodies of the villagers amass together with the bodies of the ancestors in *al-Sinima al-misriyya wa-l-adab: qissat hubb* [Egyptian cinema and literature: a love story] (Afaq li-l-nashr wa-l-tawziʻ, 2021), 54, 60. On the depiction of "ill-begotten, rather than virtuous" labor in the film, see Joel Gordon, *Revolutionary Melodrama: Popular Film and Civic Identity in Nasser's Egypt* (Middle East Documentation Center, 2002), 178–82. The film does away with the mediating figure of the urban inspector/writer, removing the metafictional aspect of the novel.
44. Ghanem, *al-Jabal*, 109.
45. Ghanem, *al-Jabal*, 134.
46. On Cairo as a center of Afro-Asian solidarity, see Reem Abou-El-Fadl, "Building Egypt's Afro-Asian Hub Infrastructures of Solidarity and the 1957 Cairo Conference," *Journal of World History* 30, no. 1/2 (2019): 157–92.
47. For example, al-Shafaqi, *Dirasat*, 202. See also discussion in Alon, "The Writer Sweating at His Desk."
48. Drumsta, *Ways of Seeking*, 118.
49. El Shakry, *The Great Social Laboratory*, 91.
50. I refer here to Jameson's elaboration of the vanishing mediator as "a catalytic agent, which permits an exchange of energies between two otherwise mutually exclusive terms" in Fredric Jameson, "The Vanishing Mediator: Narrative Structure in Max Weber," *New German Critique* 1 (1973), 78.
51. Ghanem, *al-Jabal*, 176.
52. Sander L. Gilman, *The Jew's Body* (Routledge, 1991). This image was prominent in the Jewish media as well. In popular Jewish and Hebrew publications in the beginning of the century, items on physical diseases were increasingly replaced by discussion of psychic and neurotic ailments, which were believed to be especially prevalent among the Jews. See Hamutal Bar-Yosef, "ha-Heksher ha-dekadenti shel ha-sifrut ha-ʻivrit be-sof ha-meʼa ha-teshaʻesre" [The decadent context of Hebrew literature in the late nineteenth century], *Alpayim* 13 (1996).
53. Much has been written on the New Jew and the New Hebrew body. In addition to Gilman, *The Jew's Body*, see Michael Gluzman, *ha-Guf ha-tsiyoni: leʼumiyut, migdar u-miniyut ba-sifrut ha-yisraʼelit ha-hadasha* [The Zionist body: nationalism, gender and sexuality in the new Israeli literature] (ha-Kibbuts ha-meʼuhad, 2007); Boaz Neumann, *Land and Desire in Early Zionism* (Brandeis University Press, 2011).
54. Dana Olmert, "Geographical and Potential Space: A Reading of Two Early Stories by Y. H. Brenner," *Jerusalem Studies in Hebrew Literature* 19 (2003): 123.
55. Cited in José M. López Pinero, *Historical Origins of the Concept of Neurosis*, trans. D. Berrios (Cambridge University Press, 1983), 46.
56. Pioneer among the critics who used psychoanalysis to read Brenner was Dov Sadan in *Midrash psikhoʼanaliti: prakim ba-psikhologya shel Y. H. Brenner* [A psychoanalytic midrash: studies in Brenner's psychology] (Magnes, Hebrew University, 1996). Hamutal Bar-Yosef published a number of studies on the influence of psychoanalytic and psychopathologic discourses on Hebrew writers, among them Brenner, in *Magaʻim shel dekadens: Byalik, Berdichevski, Brenner* [Touches of decadence: Byalik, Berdichevski, Brenner] (Ben Gurion University Press, 1997); "Psychopatologia ʻivrit kdam freudianit bi-tkufat maʻavar ha-meʼot" [Pre-Freudian Hebrew psychopathology at the turn of the century], *Sadan: Studies in Hebrew Literature* 4 (2000). Olmert, in "Geographical and Potential Space," reads Brenner's London stories in

light of Winnicott's psychological method. Gluzman, in *ha-Guf ha-tsiyoni*, explores melancholia and body image in Brenner's *Breakdown and Bereavement* in the context of his study of Hebrew masculinities.
57. Anita Shapira's biography of Brenner, *Yosef Haim Brenner: A Life*, trans. Anthony Berris (Stanford University Press, 2015) is exemplary of the tendency to read Brenner's literary writing as testimonies to his depression and psychological conflicts.
58. Brenner, "Nerves," 41.
59. Yoseph Haim Brenner, *Kol kitve Y. H. Brenner* [The complete works] (ha-Kibbuts ha-me'uhad: Dvir, 1960), 268.
60. Hayim Nahman Bialik, "Ta'ut ne'ima" [A pleasant mistake], *ha-Shiloah* 19, no. 4 (1908): 380.
61. Julia Kristeva, *Powers of Horror: An Essay on Abjection*, trans. Leon S. Roudiez (Columbia University Press, 1982), 207.
62. Bialik, "Ta'ut ne'ima," 380.
63. Brenner, "Nerves," 41. Italicized in original.
64. Yoseph Haim Brenner, *Breakdown and Bereavement*, trans. Hillel Halkin (Cornell University Press, 1971), 118.
65. The use of the Bible as a "map" of contemporary Palestine was not unique to Zionism but was shared by religious non-Zionist Jews as well as by Christian pilgrims. Zionism, however, read the Bible secularly, as a national history. On the relation between Zionism and the Bible, see Anita Shapira, *ha-Tanakh ve-ha-zehut ha-yisra'elit* [The Bible and Israeli identity] (Magnes, The Hebrew University, 2005); Ilana Pardes, *Agnon's Moonstruck Lovers: The Song of Songs in Israeli Culture* (University of Washington Press, 2013). On the crisis of representation of landscape in the colonial setting, see the introduction to Glenn Hooper, *Landscape and Empire 1770–2000* (Ashgate, 2004).
66. Brenner, "Nerves," 41.
67. Quoted in Anita Shapira, *Brenner: sipur hayim* [Brenner: a life story] (Am oved, 2008), 103.
68. Ariel Hirschfeld, "Retet tsamarot ve-dagim meluhim: 'al ha-milim ve-ha-dvarim be-'atstabim le-Yosef Hayim Brenner," in *Sifrut ve-hevra ba-tarbut ha-'ivrit ha-hadasha*, ed. Yehudit Bar-El and Yig'al Schwartz (ha-Kibbuts ha-me'uhad, 2000), 71–81.
69. Brenner, "Nerves," 35.
70. The repetition compulsion also gives Zionism its narrative structure. What is the Zionist return to Palestine if not a wish, as Freud writes in *Beyond the Pleasure Principle*, to return to "an ancient starting point, which the living being left long ago, and to which it harks back again by all the circuitous paths of development"? Sigmund Freud, *Beyond the Pleasure Principle*, trans. C. J. M. Hubback (Martino, 2009), 48.
71. See, in particular, the debates that came to be known as the Brenner Affair, instigated by Brenner's polemic column from November 24, 1910, "ba-'Itonut u-ba-sifrut" ("From the Press and Literature") in Brenner, *Kol kitve*, 3:476–87. In this text, Brenner provocatively redefines the boundaries of the Jewish nation, rejects its association with Judaism as a religion, and instead grounds it in Hebrew expression, a national group identity, and a locus in Erets Yisra'el. On the outraged

2. SCRATCH

responses to this essay, see Nurit Govrin, *Me'ora Brenner: ha-ma'avak 'al hofesh ha-bituy* [The Brenner affair] (Yad yitshak ben-tsvi, 1985).

72. Hannan Hever, *ha-Sipur ve-ha-leom: keri'ot bikortiyot be-kanon ha-siporet ha-'ivrit* [The story and the nation: critical readings in the Hebrew canon] (Resling, 2007), 52.
73. Cf. Liron Mor's analysis of the literature of *levatim*, or internal struggle with indecision, as a colonial technology that allows the Zionist subject to both distance themself and still participate in the colonial project, in Liron Mor, *Conflicts: The Poetics and Politics of Palestine-Israel* (Fordham University Press, 2024), 90–95.
74. Brenner, "Nerves," 59. Translation modified.
75. The poem cycle first appeared in the journal *ha-Shiloah* in 1906.
76. The Yemenite-Israeli singer Bracha Zfira, who recorded the song in the 1930s, attributed the melody to the Iraqi song "*Qaduk al-mayyas*" ("Your proud figure"), which was popular in Palestine in the 1920s. But the Arabic melody, also known as "*Madāḥ al-qamr*" ("Moon eulogist"), is older and clearly was coupled to the poem soon after its publication. See Bracha Zephira, *Kolot rabim* [Many voices] (Masadah, 1978).
77. Naomi Seidman, *A Marriage Made in Heaven: The Sexual Politics of Hebrew and Yiddish* (University of California Press, 1997).
78. Berdichevsky, "Yehudim," 34.
79. Brenner, "Nerves," 66.
80. One of Brenner's proposed titles for the novel, *'Al saf ha-mirga'a* [On the verge of tranquility], supports this suggestion, given the central place of the unusual word *mirga'a* in "Nerves."
81. Brenner, *Breakdown*, 79.
82. Yoseph Haim Brenner, "Ha'arakhat 'atsmenu bi-shloshet ha-krachim," in *Kol kitve*, 7:235.
83. Brenner, *Kol kitve*, 7:266–67.
84. For a nonteleological reading of the disgusting in Mendele, see Amir Banbaji, *Mendele ve-ha-sipur ha-leumi* [Mendele and the national narrative] (Dvir, 2009), 184–292.
85. Brenner himself notices a different tone in Mendele's book *'Emek ha-bekha*, which, he claims, is more poetic and forgiving. In this book, Mendele no longer engages in wrathful or mocking "evaluation" of the Jews, writes Brenner, but in quiet and assured acceptance. His voice "leisurely merges with static life forms, health, and wholesome restfulness." Brenner, *Kol kitve*, 7:255.
86. Brenner, *Breakdown*, 27.
87. The word *ḥefets* actually has two related meanings. *Ḥefets* is an inanimate object, but the same word can also mean a desire. The name encompasses the two combatting elements of Hefetz's personality, the emphatic, desiring idealist and the impassive scratcher.
88. Brenner, *Breakdown*, 32.
89. William Ian Miller, *The Anatomy of Disgust* (Harvard University Press, 1997), 52. See also, in this context, Julia Kristeva's visceral reaction to the skin on the surface of milk as the abject exemplar in Kristeva, *Powers of Horror*, 2–3.
90. Brenner, *Breakdown*, 308–9.
91. Dimitris Vardoulakis, "Stasis: Beyond Political Theology?," *Cultural Critique* 73 (2009): 129.

3. ROUTINE: THE PRESENT OF REPRODUCTIVE LABOR

1. Sonallah Ibrahim, *That Smell and Notes from Prison*, trans. Robyn Creswell (New Directions, 2013), 31. I cite the English translation throughout with minor modifications when an important aspect of the Arabic original is lost: Sonallah Ibrahim, *Tilk al-ra'iha wa-qisas ukhra*, 3rd ed. (Dar al-huda, 2003). The publication history of the novel is not straightforward. First published in 1966, it was immediately confiscated by the censor, although Ibrahim managed to circulate a few individual copies. It then appeared in 1968 in the Lebanese magazine *Shi'r* and in 1969 in Cairo, although both of these versions were edited and heavily censored. The complete novel appeared in 1971 in Denys Johnson-Davies's English translation. The Arabic original was published in its entirety in 1986, including an introduction in which Ibrahim recounts the history of the novel's composition and publication. See Marina Stagh, "The Limits of Freedom of Speech: Prose Literature and Prose Writers in Egypt Under Nasser and Sadat" (PhD Diss., Stockholm University, 1993), 148.
2. Yeshayahu Koren, *Funeral at Noon*, trans. Dalya Bilu (Steerforth, 1996), 7. I cite this translation throughout with occasional minor modifications. Yeshayahu Koren, *Levaya ba-tsohorayim* [Funeral at noon] (ha-Kibbuts ha-me'uhad, 2008).
3. I discuss Ibrahim's reading of Hemingway later. Koren mentions his debt to Hemingway in "Sone' milim gvohot" ["Hating fancy words"], interview by Sarah Ortal, *Yediot Ahronot*, June 5, 1992, 23.
4. See, for example, Idwar Kharrat's analysis of new literary sensibilities in the aftermath of 1967 in Idwar Kharrat, *al-Hassasiyya al-jadida: maqalat fi al-zahira al-qasasiyya* [The new sensibility] (Dar al-adab, 1993).
5. The distinction between lawmaking and law-preserving violence is Walter Benjamin's. In "Critique of Violence," he famously distinguishes between an originary lawmaking violence, operating before the law or outside politics, and a law-preserving violence, operating legally at the service of the state. Benjamin, "Critique of Violence," in *Walter Benjamin: Selected Writings*, ed. Michael William Jennings and Marcus Paul Bullock, trans. Edmund Jephcott (Belknap, 2004), 1:236–52.
6. For an overview of Anglophone novels, see Gayle Greene, "Mad Housewives and Closed Circles," in *Changing the Story: Feminist Fiction and the Tradition* (Indiana University Press, 1991), 58–85.
7. Michael Douglas Sayeau, *Against the Event: The Everyday and the Evolution of Modernist Narrative* (Oxford University Press, 2013), 39.
8. For an overview of this vast field, see Tithi Bhattacharya, "Mapping Social Reproduction Theory," in *Social Reproduction Theory*, ed. Tithi Bhattacharya (Pluto, 2017).
9. "Our man [Marx] does not see this, [but] consumption presupposes work of some kind," the Italian group Lotta Feminista flatly noted in the early 1970s. "This work is housework. Housework is done by women. This work has never been seen, precisely because it is not paid." Lotta Feminista, "Introduction to the Debate," in *Italian Feminist Thought: A Reader*, ed. Paola Bono and Sandra Kemp (Blackwell, 1991), 261. See also Barbara Ehrenreich and Deirdre English, "The Manufacture of Housework," *Socialist Revolution* 5, no. 26 (1975): 6.
10. "Nothing happens; this is the everyday" is the riddle that Maurice Blanchot posits in his celebrated foundational essay on the everyday, "Everyday Speech," and that

3. ROUTINE

is taken as axiomatic in most subsequent "everyday studies." Maurice Blanchot, "Everyday Speech," in *The Infinite Conversation* (University of Minnesota Press, 1993), 241.
11. Domietta Torlasco, "Philosophy in the Kitchen," in *World Picture* 11 (2016). The video essay converses with Cesare Casarino, "Images for Housework: On the Time of Domestic Labor in Gilles Deleuze's Philosophy of the Cinema," *Differences* 28, no. 3 (2017): 67–92.
12. Olivia Landry and Christinia Landry, "Torlasco's 'Philosophy in the Kitchen': Image, Domestic Labor, and the Gendered Embodiment of Time," *New Review of Film and Television Studies* 17, no. 4 (2019): 468. This contradictory reading emerges from the writers' appeal to citations from Gilles Deleuze's *Cinema 1* and *Cinema 2*, which are included in the voiceover to Torlasco's video essay.
13. Cited in Henri Lefebvre, *Critique of Everyday Life*, trans. John Moore and Gregory Elliott (Verso, 2008), 2:42–43.
14. Lefebvre, *Critique of Everyday Life*, 2:42–43.
15. Donna Haraway's warning is an apt reminder: "Feminists have recently claimed that women are given to dailiness, that women more than men somehow sustain daily life, and so have a privileged epistemological position potentially. There is a compelling aspect to this claim, one that makes visible unvalued female activity and names it as the ground of life. But the ground of life? What about all the ignorance of women, all the exclusions and failures of knowledge and skill?" Donna Jeanne Haraway, *Simians, Cyborgs, and Women: The Reinvention of Nature* (Routledge, 1991), 180–81.
16. Harry Harootunian, "Remembering the Historical Present," *Critical Inquiry* 33, no. 3 (2007): 475.
17. This mode of critique can be traced back to Georg Lukács's notion of class analysis as "rediscovered time" and a means of dismantling the reified present of the everyday. Georg Lukács, *History and Class Consciousness*, trans. Rodney Livingstone (MIT Press, 1971).
18. Cf. Kristin Ross, *Fast Cars, Clean Bodies: Decolonization and the Reordering of French Culture* (MIT Press, 1995), 13.
19. Lauren Gail Berlant, *Cruel Optimism* (Duke University Press, 2011), 66. See also Lauren Gail Berlant, "Thinking About Feeling Historical," *Emotion, Space and Society* 1 (2008): 4–9.
20. I am much indebted in this chapter to the work of Michael Douglas Sayeau, *Against the Event: The Everyday and the Evolution of Modernist Narrative* (Oxford University Press, 2013). See also Liesl Olson, *Modernism and the Ordinary* (Oxford University Press, 2009); Hannah Freed-Thall, *Spoiled Distinctions: Aesthetics and the Ordinary in French Modernism* (Oxford University Press, 2015); Thomas S. Davis, *The Extinct Scene: Late Modernism and Everyday Life* (Columbia University Press, 2016); and Claire Seiler, *Midcentury Suspension: Literature and Feeling in the Wake of World War II* (Columbia University Press, 2020).
21. David Scott, *Omens of Adversity: Tragedy, Time, Memory, Justice* (Duke University Press, 2014), 2.
22. Joel Beinin, *Was the Red Flag Flying There? Marxist Politics and the Arab-Israeli Conflict in Egypt and Israel, 1948–1965* (University of California Press, 1990), 6.
23. Maneuvering between the often-conflicting principles of anticolonial nationalism and socialist commitments, Nasser adopted a state-led capitalist program that

incorporated vastly popular initiatives of public welfare, nationalization, and land reform. As a centralized statist project, Nasserism sought to organize all political and social activity under its authority and actively repressed any organization that could threaten the state's exclusive hold on power. By the late 1950s, the expansive state security apparatus was persecuting many of its allies including prominent feminist activists and members of the Communist Party. See Sara Salem, *Anticolonial Afterlives in Egypt: The Politics of Hegemony* (Cambridge University Press, 2020), 80–118; Omnia S. El Shakry, *The Great Social Laboratory: Subjects of Knowledge in Colonial and Postcolonial Egypt* (Stanford University Press, 2007), 207; Laura Bier, *Revolutionary Womanhood: Feminisms, Modernity, and the State in Nasser's Egypt* (Stanford University Press, 2011); Joel Beinin, "The Communist Movement and Nationalist Political Discourse in Nasirist Egypt," *Middle East Journal* 41, no. 4 (1987): 584.

24. Arwa Salih, *The Stillborn: Notebooks of a Woman from the Student-Movement Generation in Egypt*, trans. Samah Selim (Seagull, 2018), 23.
25. Samah Selim, *The Novel and the Rural Imaginary in Egypt, 1880–1985* (Routledge, 2004), 148.
26. Robyn Creswell, "Translator's Introduction," in *That Smell and Notes from Prison*, 6.
27. Raymond Williams, *Marxism and Literature* (Oxford University Press, 1977), 131.
28. Moreiras uses this term in relation to the collapse of actually existing socialism in 1989, or "the moment when the conflict between the so called First and Second Worlds is revealed as a false dialectic of modernization." Alberto Moreiras, *The Exhaustion of Difference: The Politics of Latin American Cultural Studies* (Duke University Press, 2001), 51.
29. Beinin, *Was the Red Flag Flying There?*, 14.
30. Tom Segev, *1967: Israel, the War, and the Year That Transformed the Middle East* (Metropolitan, 2007), 138–39.
31. On the emergence of a technocratic class that formed the basis for new middle-class consumerism in Egypt, see Ibrahim G. Aoude, "From National Bourgeois Development to Infitah: Egypt 1952–1992," *Arab Studies Quarterly* 16, no. 1 (1994): 1–23.
32. Segev, *1967*, 20–22.
33. The English term *state* has a complex and nonlinear etymology that can be traced back to both the Greek *stasis* and the Latin term *status* (both of which are related to standing or stature). The first meaning of *state* is broad, "a condition or manner of existing." It can be attributed to both material conditions and emotional states ("state of mind"). It is temporally defined, indicating a largely static situation observed in a particular moment in time. The second and more limited meaning of the term *state*, as a political body governing over a geographical territory, developed around the fifteenth century, apparently out of inquiries on the "conditions (or state) of a country" ("State," the *Oxford English Dictionary*). The state is conceived as a snapshot, a momentarily static state of affairs.
34. "Mi-medina le-medina" [From state to state], The Academy of the Hebrew Language, April 22, 2015, https://hebrew-academy.org.il/2015/04/22/%D7%9E%D7%9E%D7%93%D7%99%D7%A0%D7%94-%D7%9C%D7%9E%D7%93%D7%99%D7%A0%D7%94/.
35. Franz Rosenthal, "Dawla," in *Encyclopaedia of Islam*, 2nd ed., ed. P. Bearman et al. (Brill, 1991).

36. Though note Adam Mestyan's study of how the political entities that emerged in the post-World War 1 Middle East recycled imperial formations rather than adopted the nation-state form, in *Modern Arab Kingship: Remaking the Ottoman Political Order in the Interwar Middle East* (Princeton University Press, 2023).
37. Henri Lefebvre, *The Production of Space* (Blackwell, 1991), 21.
38. David Lloyd, *Anomalous States: Irish Writing and the Post-Colonial Moment* (Duke University Press, 1993), 73.
39. Lloyd, *Anomalous States*, 74.
40. There is vast scholarship on writing by, for, and about women in Egypt in this period. See, for example, Beth Baron, *The Women's Awakening in Egypt: Culture, Society, and the Press* (Yale University Press, 1994), 159–61; Beth Baron, *Egypt as a Woman: Nationalism, Gender, and Politics* (University of California Press, 2005). For discussions on Zionist women as homemakers, see Shahar Marnin-Distenfeld, "Al tikni be-'einayim 'atsumot" [Don't shop blindfolded], *Kesher*, no. 51 (2018); Sharon Geva, *ha-Isha ma omeret? Nashim be-yisra'el bi-shnot ha-medina ha-rishonot* [What does the woman say? Women in the first years of Israeli statehood] (Magnes, 2020).
41. Afsaneh Najmabadi, "Crafting an Educated Housewife in Iran," in *Remaking Women*, ed. Lila Abu-Lughod (Princeton University Press, 1998), 94.
42. Sylvie Fogiel-Bijaoui, "Feminism, le'umiyut ve-shinuy hevrati" [Feminism, nationalism, and social change], in *Zman yehudi hadash* (Keter, 2007), 4:242.
43. Bier, *Revolutionary Womanhood*, 62.
44. An important exception is Dvora Baron, who since the late 1920s published Hebrew stories largely concerned with Jewish women's life in Eastern Europe. The 1970 publication of Baron's long novella *ha-Golim* (The exiles), composed of two previously published stories brought together, can be seen as emerging from the new interest in housework routines. Unlike most of Baron's stories, *ha-Golim* takes place among the Jewish community of Jaffa that was exiled to Alexandria during World War I. Orly Lubin writes on the manner in which *ha-Golim* establishes a circular "women's time" in contrast to the masculine linear time of the national subject in "Tidbits from Nehama's Kitchen: Alternative Nationalism in Dvora Baron's The Exiles," in *Hebrew, Gender, and Modernity: Critical Responses to Dvora Baron's Fiction*, ed. Sheila E. Jelen and Shachar Pinsker (University Press of Maryland, 2007).
45. Some of the pioneering texts of "everyday studies" appearing in this period include the collection of essays in Georg Simmel, *Simmel on Culture: Selected Writings* (Sage, 1997); Siegfried Kracauer, *The Mass Ornament: Weimar Essays*, trans. Thomas Y. Levin (Harvard University Press, 1995); Lukács, *History and Class Consciousness*; and Walter Benjamin, *The Arcades Project*, trans. Howard Eiland and Kevin McLaughlin (Belknap, 2002).
46. Henri Lefebvre, *Everyday Life in the Modern World*, trans. Sacha Rabinovitch (Transaction, 1984), 73.
47. See for example Ben Highmore, *Everyday Life and Cultural Theory: An Introduction* (Taylor & Francis, 2002), 10; and Eran Dorfman, *Foundations of the Everyday: Shock, Deferral, Repetition* (Rowman & Littlefield, 2014), 12–13. Michael Sayeau writes: "*Madam Bovary* is, if not the origin of modernism's turn against the event, at least the most significant and influential moment of its early emergence," in *Against the Event*, 55.
48. Bakhtin continues to assert that the abhorrent circular time of the everyday cannot hold an entire novel: "It is a vicious and sticky time that drags itself slowly through

space. And therefore it cannot serve as the primary time of the novel. Novelists use it as an ancillary time, one that may be interwoven with other noncyclical temporal sequences or used merely to intersperse such sequences; it often serves as a contrasting background for temporal sequences that are more charged with energy and event." What is striking about *That Smell* and *Funeral* is that the circular time of the everyday overwhelms and effaces the "noncyclical temporal sequences" in both texts. M. M. Bakhtin, "Forms of Time and Chronotope in the Novel," in *The Dialogic Imagination*, ed. Michael Holquist (University of Texas Press, 1981), 248.

49. Rita Felski, "The Invention of Everyday Life," in *Doing Time: Feminist Theory and Postmodern Culture* (New York University Press, 2000), 81–82.

50. Lesley Johnson and Justine Lloyd, *Sentenced to Everyday Life: Feminism and the Housewife* (Berg, 2004), 151.

51. The vilification of housework is clear in classic texts of second-wave feminism such as Betty Frieden's *The Feminine Mystique*. It is present too, though to a far lesser extent, in the Marxist-feminist tradition; for example, see Angela Y. Davis, *Women, Race and Class* (Random House, 1981), 222. One of the important breakthroughs of the Wages for Housework campaign and its insistence that women's unpaid labor was the condition for the reproduction of all labor was marking a pathway for feminist theory to denounce the gendering of housework without maligning housework itself.

52. These discourses were present in urban centers in Egypt and in the Zionist agricultural settlements. Simone de Beauvoir spoke of women's "life of repetition" as a mode of political oppression in lectures she gave on her visit to Egypt and Israel in 1967. See an overview of the visit in Yoav Di-Capua, *No Exit: Arab Existentialism, Jean-Paul Sartre, and Decolonization* (University of Chicago Press, 2018), 204-5.

53. Jane Elliot makes a similar argument, suggesting that American mainstream feminism, in its popular focus on the figure of the white suburban housewife caught in a monstrous temporality of repetition, has served an ideological and narrative function in the United States in the context of the post-1960s weakening of narratives of inevitable national progress. Jane Elliott, "Stepford U.S.A. Second-Wave Feminism, Domestic Labor, and the Representation of National Time," *Cultural Critique*, no. 70 (2008): 32–62.

54. The term *jīl al-sittīnāt* (the Sixties Generation) commonly refers to a group of literary innovative writers who began publishing in the 1960s and 1970s. Its most prominent members include Gamal al-Ghitani, Muhammad al-Bisati, Baha' Tahir, Ibrahim Aslan, Radwa Ashur, 'Abd al-Hakim Qasim, Yahya Tahir 'Abdallah, and Sonallah Ibrahim. On the politics and aesthetics of the Sixties Generation, see Yasmine Ramadan, "The Emergence of the Sixties Generation in Egypt and the Anxiety Over Categorization," *Journal of Arabic Literature* 43, no. 2–3 (2012); Muhammad Badawi, *al-Riwaya al-jadida fi misr* (al-Mu'assasa al-jami'iyya li-dirasat wa-nashr wa-tawzi', 1993); and Sabry Hafez, "The Egyptian Novel in the Sixties," in *Critical Perspectives on Modern Arabic Literature*, ed. Issa Boullata (Three Continents, 1980).

55. Ibrahim, *That Smell*, 28.

56. Ibrahim, *That Smell*, 72.

57. Adorno argues that the task of immanent critique is to "reliquify" thought movement that has congealed in philosophical concepts, in Theodore Adorno, *Negative Dialectics*, trans. E. B. Ashton (Routledge, 1973), 97. On the limits of critique as a

practice done "with a hammer (or a sledgehammer)" in hand, see Bruno Latour, "An Attempt at a 'Compositionist Manifesto,' " *New Literary History* 41, no. 3 (2010): 475; and Rita Felski, *The Limits of Critique* (University of Chicago Press, 2015).

58. Ibrahim had no access to Hemingway's prose while in prison, but he claims that he read about his techniques in Carlos Baker's foundational study, *Hemingway: The Writer as Artist* (Princeton University Press, 1952). The book was translated into Arabic in Beirut in 1959 as *Ernest Hemingway: dirasa fi fannihi al-qasasi* [Ernest Hemingway: a study of the art of his stories], trans. Ihsan Abbas, ed. Muhammad Yusef Najem (Dar maktaba al-haya, 1959).
59. Ibrahim, *That Smell*, 70.
60. Sonallah Ibrahim, *Dhat: riwaya* (Dar al-mustaqbal al-ʿarabi, 1992). All quotations below are from the English translation: Sonallah Ibrahim, *Zaat*, trans. Anthony Calderbank (American University in Cairo Press, 2001).
61. On these transitions as depicted in the television series based on Ibrahim's novel, see Sara Salem, "Sonallah Ibrahim and Miriam Naoum's *Zaat*: Deploying the Domestic in Representations of Egyptian Politics," *Journal of Middle East Women's Studies* 16, no. 1 (2020): 19–40.
62. Yoav Di-Capua, "The Traumatic Subjectivity of Sunʿallah Ibrahim's *Dhat*," *Journal of Arabic Literature* 43, no. 1 (2012): 80–101.
63. Di-Capua, "Traumatic Subjectivity," 99.
64. Karl Marx, *Capital: A Critique of Political Economy*, trans. Ben Fowkes (Penguin, 1981), 165.
65. Ibrahim, *Zaat*, 5.
66. Lefebvre, in *Le temps des méprises*, as retold in Ross, *Fast Cars, Clean Bodies*, 58.
67. Theodor W. Adorno, *Minima Moralia: Reflections from Damaged Life*, trans. E. F. N. Jephcott (Verso, 1974), 39.
68. Ibrahim, *That Smell*, 35.
69. On parataxis and Marxist critique, see also Anahid Nersessian, *The Calamity Form: On Poetry and Social Life* (University of Chicago Press, 2020), 23–56.
70. Paul Starkey, *Modern Arabic Literature* (Georgetown University Press, 2006), 148.
71. Kharrat, *al-Hassasiyya al-jadida*, 16.
72. Ibrahim, *That Smell*, 70–71.
73. Yasmine Ramadan, *Space in Modern Egyptian Fiction* (Edinburgh University Press, 2020), 39.
74. Sonallah Ibrahim, *Yawmiyat al-wahat* [al-Wahat prison diaries] (Dar al-mustaqbal al-ʿarabi, 2004).
75. Ibrahim, *Yawmiyat al-wahat*, 49–50.
76. Ibrahim, *Yawmiyat al-wahat*, 58–59.
77. Ibrahim, *Yawmiyat al-wahat*, 95–97.
78. Ibrahim, *Yawmiyat al-wahat*, 100.
79. Mahmud Amin al-ʿAlim, *Thulathiyat al-rafd wa-l-hazima: dirasa naqdiyya li-thalath riwayat li-Sonʿ Allah Ibrahim* [The trilogy of refusal and defeat: critical study of three novels by Sonallah Ibrahim] (Dar al-mustaqbal al-ʿarabi, 1985), 38.
80. Slavoj Žižek, *Event: A Philosophical Journey Through a Concept* (Penguin, 2014), 10. Emphasis in the original. "The event" has been the object of extensive philosophical deliberation in recent decades, a debate whose politico-theological contours far exceed the scope of this chapter. Suffice to say that the urgency of theorizing "the

event" stems from a general sense of obstructed history dominated by repetitive cycles of sameness and an anxious desire to articulate the conditions of possibility for the emergence of "something new."

81. Aristotle, *Poetics*, trans. Richard Janko (Hackett, 1987), 14.
82. That texts actively *participate* in a genre rather than passively *belong* to it is a point made by Derrida, who calls this relationship a "a parasitical economy," in Jacques Derrida, "The Law of Genre," trans. Avital Ronell, *Critical Inquiry* 7, no. 1 (1980): 59.
83. Ibrahim, *That Smell*, 62.
84. Hoda El Sadda, *Gender, Nation, and the Arabic Novel: Egypt, 1892–2008* (Syracuse University Press, 2012), 120. Cf. Ramadan, *Space in Modern Egyptian Fiction*, 39–41.
85. As cited in Ibrahim's 1986 introduction, *That Smell*, 67.
86. Ibrahim, *That Smell*, 71.
87. Sianne Ngai, *Ugly Feelings* (Harvard University Press, 2004), 353.
88. Laila Shereen Sakr, *Arabic Glitch: Technoculture, Data Bodies, and Archives* (Stanford University Press, 2023), 1.
89. Sarah Sharma, "A Manifesto for the Broken Machine," *Camera Obscura* 35, no. 2 (2020): 172.
90. Sharma, "A Manifesto," 174.
91. Koren, *Funeral*, 175.
92. See Kfir Lustig Cohen's reading of *Funeral at Noon* as a struggle between individualist and collectivist aspirations in *Makers of Worlds, Readers of Signs: Israeli and Palestinian Literature of the Global Contemporary* (Verso, 2019), 92–120.
93. Lefebvre, *The Production of Space*, 21.
94. Ayman Siksek, "Ta'atu'ei ke'ilu" [Illusions of as-if], *Ha'aretz*, May 8, 2008, www.haaretz.co.il/literature/1.1341183.
95. On the naturalization of the destroyed Palestinian villages as a means of erasing them from Israeli consciousness, see Noga Kadman, *Erased from Space and Consciousness: Israel and the Depopulated Palestinian Villages of 1948*, trans. Dimi Reider (Indiana University Press, 2015).
96. Gil Z. Hochberg, "A Poetics of Haunting: From Yizhar's Hirbeh to Yehoshua's Ruins to Koren's Crypts," *Jewish Social Studies* 18, no. 3 (2012): 65. See also Matti Shmuelof, "Rahok me-ha-pisga" [Far from the top], *ynet*, August 18, 2008.
97. Koren, *Funeral*, 1. Translation slightly modified.
98. See Anne-Lise François, *Open Secrets: The Literature of Uncounted Experience* (Stanford University Press, 2008).
99. Hochberg, "Poetics of Haunting," 56.
100. Idan Landau, "ha-Yif'a ha-shketa hazot" [This silent brilliance], *Ha'aretz*, April 29, 2008.
101. Koren, *Funeral*, 12.
102. Talmud Bavli, Masechet Sanhedrin 75:1.
103. Koren, *Funeral*, 169. The translation has been slightly modified.
104. Koren, *Funeral*, 251.
105. Gershon Shaked, "Rikmat hayim be-seter" [A secret living texture], *Siman kri'a* 5 (1976).
106. Landau, "ha-Yif'a"; Cohen Lustig, *Makers of Worlds*, 95–97, 102.
107. Hochberg, "Poetics of Haunting," 64.

3. ROUTINE

108. Blanchot, "Everyday Speech," 242.
109. Cohen Lustig, focusing on Yiftah's sacrificial role, argues that this is an allegory of Jewish intergenerational continuity. *Makers of Worlds*, 110–11. Given the prevalence of the biblical intertextual puzzle in *Funeral at Noon*, it is surprising that Menachem Peri, Koren's editor, distinguishes Koren's style from S. Y. Agnon's riddle-like, self-conscious mode in which everything is "a sign for something else." Quoted in Maya Sela, "Levaya ba-tsohorayim" [Funeral at noon], *Ha'aretz*, December 5, 2014, https://www.haaretz.co.il/gallery/literature/.premium-1.2501864. As I argue, it is not that Koren is not interested in symbolism and allegories, but that he grounds them in the characters' embodied sensual input.
110. Erich Auerbach, *Mimesis: The Representation of Reality in Western Literature*, trans. Willard R. Trask (Princeton University Press, 1953), 11. The origins of the sweeping thesis presented in *Mimesis* is Auerbach's essay on Madam Bovary, "On the Serious Imitation of the Everyday," which originally appeared in the publications of the Edebiyat Fakultesi (Faculte des Lettres) of Istanbul University in 1937.
111. Auerbach, *Mimesis*, 15.
112. Auerbach, *Mimesis*, 11.
113. Cited in Michael E. Gardiner and Julian Jason Haladyn, *Boredom Studies Reader: Frameworks and Perspectives* (Routledge, 2017), 16.
114. See Elizabeth S. Goodstein, *Experience Without Qualities: Boredom and Modernity* (Stanford University Press, 2005).
115. Cf. Allison Pease, *Modernism, Feminism and the Culture of Boredom* (Cambridge University Press, 2012).
116. François, *Open Secrets*, 72. Frances Ferguson has also argued that the psychological novel has emerged in the context of the incident of rape in heroine-centered fiction because it is a crime whose articulation and persecution requires insight into psychological states; Frances Ferguson, "Rape and the Rise of the Novel," *Representations*, no. 20 (1987): 88–112.
117. Koren, *Funeral*, 14.
118. Karl Schoonover, "Wastrels of Time: Slow Cinema's Laboring Body, the Political Spectator, and the Queer," *Framework* 53, no. 1 (2012): 65–78.
119. Silvia Federici, *Revolution at Point Zero: Housework, Reproduction, and Feminist Struggle* (PM, 2012), 2.
120. Silvia Federici, "The Reproduction of Labour-Power in the Global Economy, Marxist Theory and the Unfinished Feminist Revolution" [2008], in *Revolution at Point Zero*, 99.
121. For an overview of these debates in Egyptian print culture, see Ramadan, "The Emergence of the Sixties Generation." Influential responses to the 1967 defeat include Abdallah Laroui, *The Crisis of the Arab Intellectual: Traditionalism or Historicism?*, trans. Diarmid Cammell (University of California Press, 1976); Sadiq Jalal Azm, *al-Naqd al-dhati ba'da al-hazima* [Self criticism after the defeat] (Dar al-tali'a, 1968); and Qustantin Zurayq, *Ma'na al-nakba mujaddadan* [The meaning of the disaster renewed] (Dar al-'ilm li-l-malayin, 1967).
122. See for example Ibrahim M. Abu-Rabi, *Contemporary Arab Thought: Studies in Post-1967 Arab Intellectual History* (Pluto, 2004); and Elizabeth Suzanne Kassab, *Contemporary Arab Thought: Cultural Critique in Comparative Perspective* (Columbia University Press, 2010). For a critique of the notion of 1967 as an earthquake,

see Anneka Lenssen et al., "The Longevity of Rupture: 1967 in Art and Its Histories," *ARTMargins* 2, no. 2 (2013): 15.
123. Sonallah Ibrahim, *67: riwaya* [67, a novel] (Dar al-thaqafa al-jadida, 2016).
124. See Yoni Livne, "Levaya ba-tsohorayim" [Review of Funeral at Noon], *Yediot ahronot*, August 7, 2008.
125. The "Council for the Coalition of Hebrew Youth," better known as the Canaanite movement, espoused a Hebrew nativist nationalism dissociated from Judaism, spawning from a mythical Hebrew/Semitic nation that supposedly thrived around the Fertile Crescent in the second millennium BC. The Canaanites were as dismissive of Arab nationalism as they were of Jewish nationalism, imagining a regional Pagan-Hebrew culture under which the Palestinians were to be subsumed. On the legacy and influence of the Canaanite movement in Hebrew poetry, see Hannan Hever, "Territoriality and Otherness in Hebrew Literature of the War of Independence," in *The Other in Jewish Thought and History*, ed. Laurence J. Silberstein and Robert L. Cohn (New York University Press, 1994).
126. Yeshayahu Koren, "Yarad geshem halash" [It rained weakly], *Ha'aretz*, March 3, 2008.

4. THRESHOLD: THE LIMIT OF CORRESPONDENCE

1. Ella Elbaz, "Factoring Asymmetry into the Equation: On Juxtaposing Palestinian and Israeli Literatures," *Journal of Arabic Literature* 55, no. 1 (2024): 126–53.
2. On Palestinian and Israeli temporalities of the settler colonial present, see also Nasser Abourahme, *The Time beneath the Concrete: Camp, Colony, Palestine* (Duke University Press, 2025), which came out too late for me to engage in this book. Both Palestinian literature and, to a far lesser extent, Hebrew literature, are written outside or around Palestine/Israel. Furthermore, Palestinian literature, as a national literature in exile, is written in many languages, not only Arabic. Nevertheless, my argument here pertains to texts written from within the geographical space under direct Israeli state control.
3. Kfir Cohen Lustig, *Makers of Worlds, Readers of Signs: Israeli and Palestinian Literature of the Global Contemporary* (Verso, 2019), 5.
4. Mathias Nilges, *How to Read a Moment: The American Novel and the Crisis of the Present* (Northwestern University Press, 2021), 8.
5. Fredric Jameson, *The Seeds of Time* (Columbia University Press, 1994), 17–18.
6. Sami Berdugo's *Sipur hove 'al pney ha-arets* (A present tale upon the land, 2014) exemplifies an attempt to capture the "Israeli condition" in Hebrew literature through an idiosyncratic journey across the country's peripheries.
7. On the interim temporality of the Palestinian National Authority and the way it shapes infrastructural planning, see Sophia Stamatopoulou-Robbins, "An Uncertain Climate in Risky Times: How Occupation Became Like the Rain in Post-Oslo Palestine," *International Journal of Middle East Studies* 50, no. 3 (2018): 383–404.
8. Kareem Rabie, *Palestine Is Throwing a Party and the Whole World Is Invited: Capital and State Building in the West Bank* (Duke University Press, 2021), 16.
9. Liron Mor, *Conflicts: The Poetics and Politics of Palestine-Israel* (Fordham University Press, 2024), 245. As Mor points out, there is nothing essentially new about

the practices of "administering" the occupation through impartial-looking bureaucratic means. But in the early 2000s, *nihul ha-sikhsukh*, or conflict management, became not only a set of practices but an explicit policy.
10. Hoda El Shakry, "Palestine and the Aesthetics of the Future Impossible," *Interventions* 23, no. 5 (2021). On governing Palestinians' futures through the production of uncertainty, see Mark Griffiths and Mikko Joronen, "Governmentalizing Palestinian Futures: Uncertainty, Anticipation, Possibility," *Geografiska Annaler: Series B, Human Geography* 103 no. 4 (2021): 352–66.
11. El Shakry, "Palestine," 6.
12. Daniel Monterescu and Noa Shaindlinger, "Situational Radicalism: The Israeli 'Arab Spring' and the (Un)Making of the Rebel City," *Constellations: An International Journal of Critical and Democratic Theory* 20, no. 2 (2013), 236.
13. Anat Weisman, "Mahshavot be-zman hove" [Thoughts in the present tense], *Zmanim* 68/69 (1999): 122–31.
14. Elana Gomel and Vered Karti Shemtov, "Limbotopia: The 'New Present' and the Literary Imagination," *Comparative Literature* 70, no. 1 (2018): 63.
15. Oded Nir, "How to End an Ending? Moving Beyond Crisis in Israeli Culture," *ASAP Journal* 8, no. 2 (2023): 303.
16. Raef Zreik, "'Al ha-'atsmi she-ba-hagana ha-'atsmit ve-ha-zkhut lehitnagdut" [On the self in self-defense and the right to resist], *Te'orya u-vikoret* 60 (Summer 2024): 9.
17. On the way the present is overtaken by "risk management" or by neoliberal models of managing the future in Hebrew literature in this period, see Shir Alon, "Neoliberal Riskscapes and Preemptive Poetics in Orly Castel-Bloom's *Dolly City*," *Comparative Literature* 71, no. 1 (2019): 1–18.

5. TOUCH: THE PRESENT OF CRISIS ORDINARINESS

1. Ahdaf Soueif, *Fi muwajihat al-madafi': rihla filastiniyya* [Facing the cannons: a Palestinian journey] (Dar al-shuruq, 2004). Citations are slightly modified from the English translation: Ahdaf Soueif, "Palestinian Writers," in *Mezzaterra: Fragments from the Common Ground* (Anchor Books, 2010). A shorter version of "Palestinian Writers" appeared in *The Guardian* in September, 2004.
2. B'Tselem, 2004 Summary Statistics, https://www.btselem.org/statistics/20043112_2004_statistics.
3. Soueif, *Mezzaterra*, 321.
4. See also Shibli's short essay, "Indifférente ou presque" [Indifferent, or almost], *Esprit*, no. 8–9 (2007): 250–51.
5. Soueif, *Mezzaterra*, 321.
6. Adania Shibli, "Adania Shibli on Writing Palestine from the Inside," interview by José García, *Literary Hub*, February 6, 2017, https://lithub.com/adania-shibli-on-writing-palestine-from-the-inside/.
7. Shibli, "Adania Shibli on Writing."
8. Gary T. Marx, *Windows Into the Soul: Surveillance and Society in an Age of High Technology* (University of Chicago Press, 2016), 143–44.
9. Roland Barthes, *The Neutral: Lecture Course at the Collège de France (1977–1978)*, trans. Rosalind E. Krauss and Denis Hollier (Columbia University Press, 2005).

5. TOUCH

10. Suleiman appears as E. S. in a series of films that are often viewed as a trilogy: *Chronicle of a Disappearance* (1996), *Divine Intervention* (2002), and *The Time That Remains* (2009).
11. I thank Ayelet Alon for discussing Odgen's work with me. Traditional psychoanalysis has rejected the cognitive approach to autism spectrum disorder (ASD), viewing it as a psychological, rather than a biological, disorder stemming from maternal deprivation and essentially equivalent to attachment disorder. In recent years, most psychoanalysts have accepted the biological basis of ASD and work to incorporate it into a psychoanalytic practice that recognizes the complexity of neurodiversity. For a discussion of these developments, see Judith Mitrani, "Minding the Gap Between Neuroscientific and Psychoanalytic Understanding of Autism," *Journal of Child Psychotherapy* 36, no. 3 (2010): 240–58; and Susan P. Sherkow and Alexandra M. Harrison, *Autism Spectrum Disorder: Perspectives from Psychoanalysis and Neuroscience* (Rowman & Littlefield, 2013).
12. Thomas H. Ogden, *The Primitive Edge of Experience* (Jason Aronson, 1989), 31.
13. Ogden, *The Primitive Edge*, 32.
14. Eve Kosofsky Sedgwick, *Touching Feeling: Affect, Pedagogy, Performativity* (Duke University Press, 2003), 14.
15. Erin Manning, *The Minor Gesture* (Duke University Press, 2016), 14.
16. Brian Massumi, "Prelude," in Erin Manning, *Always More Than One: Individuation's Dance* (Duke University Press, 2013), xxii.
17. Melanie Yergeau, *Authoring Autism: On Rhetoric and Neurological Queerness* (Duke University Press, 2018); Julia Miele Rodas, *Autistic Disturbances: Theorizing Autism Poetics from the DSM to Robinson Crusoe* (University of Michigan Press, 2018).
18. Yergeau, *Authoring Autism*, 7.
19. Adania Shibli, "Hiwar maʿa / ʿan sinima al-sharq baʿda mushahadat film *Sajl ikhtifaʾ*" [A dialogue with/about the cinema of the Orient after watching *Chronicle of a Disappearance*], *Masharif* 14 (1997): 138–44. Shibli reflected on this first publication a few years later in "al-Kitaba kama al-haya," *Majallat al-dirasat al-filastiniyya* 96 (2013): 167–68.
20. Shibli, "Hiwar," 143.
21. Shibli, "Hiwar," 138.
22. Shibli, "Hiwar," 144.
23. Yergeau, *Authoring Autism*, 10.
24. Caroline Levine, *Forms: Whole, Rhythm, Hierarchy, Network* (Princeton University Press, 2015), 6–11.
25. Helga Tawil-Souri, "Checkpoint Time," *Qui Parle* 26, no. 2 (2017), 401. See also Toine van Teeffelen, "The Waiting Game," *Electronic Intifada*, September 1, 2003, https://electronicintifada.net/content/waiting-game/4753; Laila l-Haddad, "The Quintessential Palestinian Experience," *Electronic Intifada*, April 14, 2009, https://electronicintifada.net/content/quintessential-palestinian-experience/8183; Sousan Hammad "Waiting in Palestine," *Boston Review*, June 17, 2013, http://bostonreview.net/blog/waiting-palestine; Ala Hlehel, "Bloated Time and the Death of Meaning," in *Kingdom of Olives and Ash: Writers Confront the Occupation*, ed. Ayelet Waldman and Michael Chabon (Harper Collins, 2017), 19–28; and Julie Peteet, "Closure's Temporality: The Cultural Politics of Time and Waiting," *The South Atlantic Quarterly* 117, no. 1 (2018): 43–64. For an ethnography of waiting in Palestine, see

5. TOUCH

Livia Wick, "The Practice of Waiting under Closure in Palestine," *City and Society* 23 (2011): 24–44. On waiting as a logic of control, see Mikko Joronen "Spaces of Waiting: Politics of Precarious Recognition in the Occupied West Bank," *Environment and Planning D: Society and Space* 35, no. 6 (2017): 994–1011.
26. Helga Tawil-Souri, "Checkpoint Time," 401.
27. On the normalized violence of the Second Intifada, see Lori Allen, "Getting by the Occupation: How Violence Became Normal During the Second Palestinian Intifada," *Cultural Anthropology* 23, no. 3 (2008): 453–87. On conflict management, see Yaacov Bar-Siman-Tov, ed., *The Israeli-Palestinian Conflict: From Conflict Resolution to Conflict Management* (Palgrave Macmillan, 2007).
28. Raja J. Khalidi and Sobhi Samour, "Neoliberalism as Liberation: The Statehood Program and the Remaking of the Palestinian National Movement," *Journal of Palestine Studies* 40, no. 2 (Winter 2010): 6–25.
29. The term *nakba* was originally not specific to 1948: there were many "catastrophes" preceding it. Nevertheless, over time, it became the commonplace term for the defeat of 1948 and its catastrophic aftermaths, thanks to works like Constantine Zurayk, *Maʿna al-nakba* [The meaning of the catastrophe] (Dar al-ʿilm li-l-malayyin, 1948); and ʿArif al-ʿArif, *al-Nakba: nakbat bayt al-maqdis wa-l-firdaws al-mafqud, 1947–49* [The Nakba: the Nakba of Jerusalem and the lost paradise 1947–49], 6 vols. (al-Maktaba al-ʿasriyya, 1956–1961).
30. Hannan Ashrawi's speech at the Non-Governmental Organizations Panel at the United Nations World Conference Against Racism, Racial Discrimination, Xenophobia, and Related Intolerances, Durban, South Africa (August 28, 2001) was published in *Islamic Studies* 41, no. 1 (2002): 97–104.
31. Joseph Massad "Resisting the Nakba," *al-Ahram Weekly*, May 15–21, 2008, http://weekly.ahram.org.eg/Archive/2008/897/op8.htm#1.
32. Elias Khoury, "al-Nakba al-mustamirra," *Majallat al-dirasat al-filastiniyya* 89 (Winter 2012); "Rethinking the Nakba," *Critical Inquiry* 38, no. 2 (2012): 250–66.
33. Elias Sanbar, "Out of Place, Out of Time," trans. Ruth Morris, *Mediterranean Historical Review* 16, no. 1 (2001): 87–94; Ahmad H. Saʿdi and Lila Abu-Lughod, *Nakba: Palestine, 1948, and the Claims of Memory* (Columbia University Press, 2007), 6.
34. Rabea Eghbariah, "Toward Nakba as a Legal Concept," *Columbia Law Review* 124, no. 4 (2024): 889.
35. Esmail Nashif, "Mawt al-nas" [Death of the text], *Majallat al-dirasat al-filastiniyya*, no. 96 (2013).
36. Palestinian, Arab, and Marxist scholars have all identified Israel as a settler colonial state as early as the 1960s, but what characterizes the recent debates on settler colonialism is their focus on enduring temporalities (a structure, not an event, in Patrick Wolfe's succinct phrase that has become akin to a motto, from "Settler Colonialism and the Elimination of the Native," *Journal of Genocide Research* 8, no. 4 [2006]: 388). The scholarship on settler colonialism in Palestine is by now vast, but see for example the *Settler Colonial Studies* special issue on Palestine and especially the introduction, Omar Jabary Salamanca et al., "Past Is Present: Settler Colonialism in Palestine," *Settler Colonial Studies* 2, no. 1 (2012): 1–8, for a sense of the early emphases of this body of works. Cf. Lila Abu-Lughod's discussion of the uses and limits of the current settler coloial framework in "Imagining Palestine's Alter-Natives: Settler Colonialism and Museum Politics," *Critical Inquiry* 47, no. 1 (2020): 1–27.

5. TOUCH

37. Nora Parr, "What Is 'Trauma' in Arabic," *Politics/Letters*, December 20, 2018, http://politicsslashletters.org/what-is-trauma-in-arabic.
38. Lauren Berlant, *Cruel Optimism* (Duke University Press, 2011), 9–10.
39. Allen, "Getting by the Occupation."
40. Adania Shibli, "al-Talaʿub bi-l-ʿadid min dharrat al-ghubar" [Playing with innumerable specks of dust], *al-Karmil* 70–71 (2002): 300–309. English citations, when available, are from Yasmeen Hanoosh's partial translation "Dust," *The Iowa Review* 37, no. 2 (2007): 93–104. Translations of other sections are my own.
41. Shibli, "al-Talaʿub," 300. My translation.
42. On the checkpoint regime and obstructed mobility, see Yael Berda, *Living Emergency: Israel's Permit Regime in the Occupied West Bank* (Stanford University Press, 2018); Hagar Kotef, *Movement and the Ordering of Freedom: On Liberal Governances of Mobility* (Duke University Press, 2015), 27–29.
43. See Nurith Gertz and George Khleifi, "Palestinian Roadblock Movies," *Geopolitics* 10, no. 2 (2005): 316–34.
44. Shibli, "Dust," 93.
45. Shibli, "Dust," 100.
46. Shibli, "Dust," 95, translation slightly modified.
47. Liron Mor, *Conflicts: The Poetics and Politics of Palestine-Israel* (Fordham University Press, 2024), 230.
48. Shibli, "Dust," 96.
49. Shibli, "Adania Shibli on Writing."
50. Shibli, "Hiwar," 139–40.
51. Laura U. Marks, *Enfoldment and Infinity: An Islamic Genealogy of New Media Art* (MIT Press, 2010), 63.
52. Simon O'Meara, "Haptic Vision: Making Surface Sense of Islamic Material Culture," in *The Routledge Handbook of Sensory Archaeology*, ed. Robin Skeates and Jo Day (Rouledge, 2019), 468.
53. O'Meara, "Haptic Vision," 467.
54. Laura U. Marks, *Touch: Sensuous Theory and Multisensory Media* (University of Minnesota Press, 2002), XII. Cf. Liron Mor's distinction between "colonial vision" and a social, contextual, and ad hoc laborious reading of images in Ronit Matalon's novel *The One Facing Us* [Ze 'im ha-panim eleynu], in Liron Mor, "Reorienting Visual Reading: From Colonial Visions to the Subtexts 'Facing Us,'" *Qui Parle* 31, no. 2 (2022): 189–229.
55. Adania Shibli, *Misas* (Dar al-adab, 2003). Citations are from the English translation unless otherwise noted: *Touch*, trans. Paula Hydar (Clockroot Books, 2010).
56. Shibli, *Touch*, 36.
57. On internal focalization, see Gérard Genette, *Narrative Discourse: An Essay in Method*, trans. Jane E. Lewin (Cornell University Press, 1980), 185–98.
58. Shibli, *Touch*, 35.
59. Shibli, *Touch*, 47–49.
60. Shibli, *Touch*, 7.
61. Manning, *The Minor Gesture*, 14.
62. On the pitfalls of diagnosing neurodiverse literary characters, see Sonya Freeman Loftis, "The Autistic Detective: Sherlock Holmes and his Legacy," *Disability Studies Quarterly* 34, no. 4 (2014): 203–213.

5. TOUCH

63. For readings that focus on the girl's deciphering of an unfamiliar world, see for example Kfir Cohen Lustig, *Makers of Worlds* (Verso, 2019), 233–35; and Amal Eqeiq, "From Haifa to Ramallah (and Back): New/Old Palestinian Literary Topography," *Journal of Palestine Studies* 48, no. 3 (2019): 31.
64. Ogden, *The Primitive Edge of Experience*, 32.
65. Adania Shibli, *Tafsil thanawi* (Dar al-adab, 2017). All citations are from Adania Shibli, *Minor Detail*, trans. Elizabeth Jaquette (New Directions, 2020).
66. Gil Z. Hochberg, *Becoming Palestine: Toward an Archival Imagination of the Future* (Duke University Press, 2021), x. Hochberg contends that the recent archival turn in Palestinian visual and performance art differs from earlier appeals to the archive as a site of historical truth.
67. Aviv Lavie, "Huhlat ve-kuyam: rahatsuha, gazezu seʿara, ansuha ve-harguha," *Haʾaretz*, October 28, 2003, https://www.haaretz.co.il/misc/1.920403; Moshe Gorali, "'Od degel shahor," *Haʾaretz*, October 28, 2003, https://www.haaretz.co.il/misc/1.920418.
68. Shibli, *Minor Detail*, 61.
69. Saidiya V. Hartman, "Venus in Two Acts," *Small Axe* 12, 26, no. 2 (2008): 1–14; Saidiya V. Hartman, *Lose Your Mother: A Journey Along the Atlantic Slave Route* (Farrar, Straus and Giroux, 2008).
70. Hartman, "Venus," 13.
71. Noura Erakat and Marc Lamont Hill, "Black-Palestinian Transnational Solidarity: Renewals, Returns, and Practice," *Journal of Palestine Studies* 48, no. 4 (2019).
72. Hartman, *Lose Your Mother*, 133.
73. Stephen Michael Best, *None Like Us: Blackness, Belonging, Aesthetic Life* (Duke University Press, 2018), 15.
74. Best, *None Like Us*, 22.
75. Shibli, *Minor Detail*, 59.
76. Shibli, *Minor Detail*, 59–60. A version of the story appears in Carlo Ginzburg, *Clues, Myths, and the Historical Method*, trans. John Tedeschi and Anne C. Tedeschi (Johns Hopkins University Press, 1989), 102.
77. Ginzburg, *Clues, Myths, and the Historical Method*, 103. Ginzburg goes on to suggest, hypothetically, that the idea of narration, "as distinct from charms, exorcisms, or invocation," emerged from hunting societies.
78. Cohen Lustig, *Makers of Worlds*, 480.
79. Cohen Lustig, *Makers of Worlds*, 511.
80. Shibli, *Minor Detail*, 55.
81. Shibli, *Minor Detail*, 54.
82. Hartman, "Venus," 11.
83. Hartman, *Lose Your Mother*, 153.
84. Hartman, "Venus," 10.
85. Shibli, *Minor Detail*, 105.
86. In an interview for the 2020 Edinburgh International Book Festival, Shibli comments on the suddenness of this ending. "I just did it to her," she remarks, still seeming to be astonished by the audacity of this move. See https://www.youtube.com/watch?v=2TJ1jpTYQcU, 43:39.
87. Tony Morrison, *Beloved*, cited in Best, *None Like Us*, 69.
88. Sigmund Freud, "The Interpretation of Dreams," in *Standard Edition of the Complete Psychological Works of Sigmund Freud*, ed. and trans. James Strachey (Hogarth,

1995), 517. As Derrida points out, Freud's attempt at a clear taxonomy of resistance inevitably ends up as a list of tangled and overdetermined categories. Jacques Derrida, *Resistances of Psychoanalysis*, trans. Peggy Kamuf, Pascale-Anne Brault, and Michael Naas (Stanford University Press, 1998), 22.
89. This is a small sample from a long and hardly exhaustive list of modes of resistance that Rebecca Comay compiled from Freud's writing. See Rebecca Comay, "Resistance and Repetition: Freud and Hegel," *Research in Phenomenology* 45, no. 2 (2015): 245.
90. Comay, "Resistance and Repetition," 258.
91. Wendy Anne Lee, *Failures of Feeling: Insensibility and the Novel* (Stanford University Press, 2019), 101.
92. Shibli, *Touch*, 68.
93. Barthes, *The Neutral*, 7.
94. Marx, *Windows Into the Soul*, 143–44.
95. For a reading of the politics of invisibility in this scene, see Gil Z. Hochberg, *Visual Occupations: Violence and Visibility in a Conflict Zone* (Duke University Press, 2015), 64.
96. Kirstie Ball, "Exposure: Exploring the Subject of Surveillance," *Information, Communication and Society* 12, no. 5 (2009): 644. Science fiction fantasies of penetrating this realm are becoming reality, with the turn to predictive policing based on algorithmic analysis. See Orr Hirschauge and Hagar Shezaf, "How Israel Jails Palestinians Because They Fit the Terrorist Profile," *Ha'aretz* (May 28, 2017), www.haaretz.com/israel-news/.premium-1.792206.
97. In Suleiman's *Divine Intervention*, E. S. and his lover meet in a car at the checkpoint and spend their time together watching not each other but the surveillance tower.

CONCLUSION: CIVIL WAR

1. Mathias Nilges, *How to Read a Moment: The American Novel and the Crisis of the Present* (Northwestern University Press, 2021), 20–21.
2. Michel Serres, *The Parasite*, trans. Lawrence R. Schehr (Johns Hopkins University Press, 1982).
3. Roland Barthes, cited in Kristin Ross, *Fast Cars, Clean Bodies: Decolonization and the Reordering of French Culture* (MIT Press, 1995), 106.
4. Moishe Postone, *Time, Labor, and Social Domination: A Reinterpretation of Marx's Critical Theory* (Cambridge University Press, 1993), 87.
5. Catherine Gallagher, "The Rise of Fictionality," in *The Novel, Volume 1: History, Geography, and Culture*, ed. Franco Moretti (Princeton University Press, 2006), 356.
6. Édouard Glissant, *Poetics of Relation*, trans. Betsy Wing (University of Michigan Press, 1997), 189–90.
7. My analysis of Khoury's evocation of *ashla'* is also indebted to Nadera Shalhoub-Kevorkian, who in the midst of Israel's genocide in Gaza has begun to theorize *ashlā'*, scattered, wounded, and dismembered flesh, as a colonial technology. See discussion in the final paragraph of the introduction.
8. Much of the scholarly literature on civil war is empiricist, aiming to classify modes of conflict, instigators, and outcomes. My understanding of civil war as a modern

CONCLUSION

political category is indebted to Reinhart Koselleck's study of the semantic slippage between "civil war" and "revolution" in "Historical Criteria of the Modern Concept of Revolution," in *Futures Past: On the Semantics of Historical Time*, trans. Keith Tribe (MIT Press, 1985), 43–57; Nasser Mufti, *Civilizing War: Imperial Politics and the Poetics of National Rupture* (Northwestern University Press, 2017).

9. Nicole Loraux, *The Divided City: On Memory and Forgetting in Ancient Athens* (Zone Books, 2002), 24, 105.
10. See Giorgio Agamben, *Stasis: Civil War as a Political Paradigm*, trans. Nicholas Heron (Stanford University Press, 2015).
11. Elias Khoury, "al-Dhakira al-mafquda," *Mawaqif* 35 (April, 1979), 68. Reprinted in *al-Dhakira al-mafquda: dirasat naqdiyya* [Lost memory] (Dar al-adab, 1990), 25–43.
12. The war was both a regional conflict and an internal Lebanese affair in which conflicts of class, religion, regional alignment, and political ideology intersected and overlapped. Sune Haugbolle divides the war into five main periods: the two-years war, from April 1975 to November 1976, triggered by clashes between the leftist Palestine Liberation Organization–aligned Lebanese National Movement (LNM) and the rightist Christian Lebanese Front (LF); the long interlude of failed peace attempts, Israeli and Syrian intervention, and a host of internal conflicts between November 1976 and June 1982; the Israeli invasion from June 1982 to February 1984; the internal wars or "War of the Camps" of the late 1980s; and finally the intra-Christian wars of 1988–1990. In Sune Haugbolle, "The Historiography and the Memory of the Lebanese Civil War," *Mass Violence & Résistance*, October 25, 2011, http://www.massviolence.org/The-historiography-and-the-memory-of-the-Lebanese-civil-war.
13. Jeffrey Sacks, *Iterations of Loss: Mutilation and Aesthetic Form, Al-Shidyaq to Darwish* (Fordham University Press, 2015), 160.
14. In a conversation with Sonja Mejcher-Atassi, Khoury notes that he wrote *City Gates* while "feeling as if I had gone through a nightmare. It was a personal experience about things that were totally closed and language that was totally destroyed, to a degree that nothing could be seen and said anymore." Elias Khoury, "The Necessity to Forget and Remember," interview by Sonja Mejcher-Atassi, *Banipal* 12 (2001): 10.
15. Nouri Gana, "Formless Form: Elias Khoury's City Gates and the Poetics of Trauma," *Comparative Literature Studies* 47, no. 4 (2010): 513. See also Dalia Said Mostafa, "Literary Representations of Trauma, Memory, and Identity in the Novels of Elias Khoury and Rabī' Jābir," *Journal of Arabic Literature* 40, no. 2 (2009): 208–36.
16. Khoury, *al-Dhakira*, 28.
17. Khoury, *al-Dhakira*, 28.
18. Khoury, *al-Dhakira*, 42–43.
19. Khoury, *al-Dhakira*, 43.
20. Khoury discusses this turn in "The Necessity to Forget and Remember," 12.
21. Khoury, *al-Dhakira*, 73.
22. Sonja Mejcher-Atassi, "Elias Khoury's *Abwab Al-Madina* (Gates of the City): A Modern Version of 'the City of Brass' from *Alf Layla wa-Layla* (the Thousand and One Nights)," in *Reflections on Reflections: Near Eastern Writers Reading Literature*, ed. Angelika Neuwirth and Andreas Islebe (Reichert, 2006), 273–89.
23. This interest is most apparent in Khoury's 1998 novel *Bab al-shams* (*Gate of the Sun*). On the recuperative role of storytelling in *City Gates*, see Nouri Gana, "Formless Form."

24. Khoury, *al-Dhakira*, 74. Khoury does not mention Roland Barthes's famous 1967 essay "The Death of the Author," which he was no doubt familiar with, especially because he had attended some of Barthes's seminars in Paris. Barthes's ideas about the "modern figure of the author" and the replacement of the author by the impersonality of language or "the text" clearly resonates with Khoury's analysis, but Khoury reads the effacement of the author against the particular modern history and present of Arabic literature. While for Barthes the "death of the author" is primarily an imperative for a liberated practice of reading, for Khoury it instigates a guiding principle for writing.
25. Emily Drumsta, *Ways of Seeking: The Arabic Novel and the Poetics of Investigation* (University of California Press, 2024), 113.
26. Khoury, *al-Dhakira*, 76.
27. Khoury, *City Gates*, 22.
28. Khoury, *City Gates*, 24.
29. Eugenie Brinkema, *The Forms of the Affects* (Duke University Press, 2014), 24; Khoury, *City Gates*, 4.

BIBLIOGRAPHY

Abou-El-Fadl, Reem. "Building Egypt's Afro-Asian Hub Infrastructures of Solidarity and the 1957 Cairo Conference." *Journal of World History* 30, no. 1/2 (2019): 157–92.

Abourahme, Nasser. *The Time Beneath the Concrete: Camp, Colony, Palestine*. Duke University Press, 2025.

Abu-Lughod, Lila. "Imagining Palestine's Alter-Natives: Settler Colonialism and Museum Politics." *Critical Inquiry* 47, no. 1 (2020): 1–27.

Abu Rayya, Mahmud. *Adwa' 'ala al-sunna al-Muhammadiyya* [Shedding light on the Sunna]. Dar al-ta'alif, 1958.

Abu-Rabi, Ibrahim M. *Contemporary Arab Thought: Studies in Post-1967 Arab Intellectual History*. Pluto, 2004.

Adorno, Theodor W. *Minima Moralia: Reflections from Damaged Life*. Trans. E. F. N. Jephcott. Verso, 1974.

——. *Negative Dialectics*. Trans. E. B. Ashton. Routledge, 1973.

Adunis. *Al-Thabit wa-l-mutahawwil: bahth fi al-ittiba' wa-l-ibda' 'inda al-'arab* [The mutable and the immutable: a study of creativity and adheration among the Arabs]. Dar al-'awda, 1974.

Agamben, Giorgio. *Stasis: Civil War as a Political Paradigm*. Trans. Nicholas Heron. Stanford University Press, 2015.

Agnon, Shmuel Yosef. "Banquet Speech." Nobel Prize in Literature 1966, Stockholm, Sweden, December 10, 1966.

——. "Hadom ve-kisse" [Footstool and throne]. In *Lifnim min ha-homa*. Schocken, 1975.

——. *Ha-Esh ve-ha-'etsim* [The fire and the wood]. Schocken, 1998.

——. "'Ido ve-'enam" [Edo and Enam]. In *'Ad hena*. Schocken, 1966. Trans. Walter Lever as "Edo and Enam." In *Two Tales by S. Y. Agnon: Bethrothed and Edo and Enam*, ed. Jeffrey Saks. Toby, 2014.

——. *Me-'atsmi el 'atsmi* [From myself to myself]. Schocken, 1976.

Alcalay, Amiel. *After Jews and Arabs: Remaking Levantine Culture*. University of Minnesota Press, 1993.

al-'Alim, Mahmud Amin. *Thulathiyat al-rafd wa-l-hazima: dirasa naqdiyya li-thalath riwayat li-Sun' Allah Ibrahim* [The trilogy of refusal and defeat: a study of three novels by Sunallah Ibrahim]. Dar al-mustaqbal al-'arabi, 1985.

Allan, Michael. *In the Shadow of World Literature: Sites of Reading in Colonial Egypt.* Princeton University Press, 2016.

Allen, Lori. "Getting by the Occupation: How Violence Became Normal During the Second Palestinian Intifada." *Cultural Anthropology* 23, no. 3 (2008): 453–87.

Almog, Shmuel. "Ha-bsora ha-ruhanit shel 'avodat ha-tarbut" [The spiritual message of cultural labor]. In *Tsiyonut ve-historya*. Magnes, 1982.

Alon, Shir. "Neoliberal Riskscapes and Preemptive Poetics in Orly Castel-Bloom's *Dolly City*." *Comparative Literature* 71, no. 1 (2019): 1–18.

———. "The Writer Sweating at His Desk: Labor and Literature in Fatḥī Ghānim's al-Jabal." *Journal of Arabic Literatures* 55, no. 2–3 (2024): 322–48.

Alroey, Gur. *Imigrantim: ha-hagira ha-yehudit le-erets-yisra'el be-reshit ha-me'a ha-'esrim* [Immigrants: the Jewish immigration to Eretz Yisrael in the early twentieth century]. Yad yitshak ben-tsvi, 2004.

Alter, Robert. *The Invention of Hebrew Prose: Modern Fiction and the Language of Realism.* University of Washington Press, 1988.

Amin, Samir. *Accumulation on a World Scale: A Critique of the Theory of Underdevelopment.* Monthly Review, 1974.

Anam, Nasia. "Encampment as Colonization: Theorizing the Representation of Refugee Spaces." *Journal of Narrative Theory* 50, no. 3 (2020): 405–36.

Anderson, Benedict. *Imagined Communities: Reflections on the Origin and Spread of Nationalism.* Verso, 1983.

Anidjar, Gil. *The Jew, the Arab: A History of the Enemy.* Stanford University Press, 2003.

———. *Semites: Race, Religion, Literature.* Stanford University Press, 2008.

Aoude, Ibrahim G. "From National Bourgeois Development to Infitah: Egypt 1952–1992." *Arab Studies Quarterly* 16, no. 1 (1994): 1–23.

Appadurai, Arjun. "Disjuncture and Difference in the Global Cultural Economy." *Theory, Culture and Society* 7, no. 2–3 (1990): 295–310.

Apter, Emily. *Against World Literature: On the Politics of Untranslatability.* Verso, 2013.

Arbel, Michal. *Katuv 'al 'oro shel ha-kelev: 'al tfisat ha-yetsira etsel Shai 'Agnon* [Written on the dog's skin: creation in S. Y. Agnon]. Merkaz heksherim at Ben Guryon University, 2006.

al-'Arif, 'Arif. *al-Nakba: nakbat bayt al-maqdis wa-l-firdaws al-mafqud,1947–49* [The Nakba: the Nakba of Jerusalem and the lost paradise 1947–49]. 6 vol. Al-Maktaba al-'asriyya, 1956–1961.

Aristotle. *Poetics.* Trans. Richard Janko. Hackett, 1987.

Arpaly, Boaz. *Ha-'Ikar ha-shlili* [The negative principle]. Ha-Kibbuts ha-me'uhad, 1992.

Arstila, Valtteri, and Dan Lloyd, eds. *Subjective Time: The Philosophy, Psychology, and Neuroscience of Temporality.* MIT Press, 2014.

Al-Attabi, Qussay. "The Polemics of Iltizām: Al-Ādāb's Early Arguments for Commitment." *Journal of Arabic Literature* 52, no. 1–2 (2021): 124–46.

Auerbach, Erich. *Mimesis: The Representation of Reality in Western Literature.* Trans. Willard R. Trask. Princeton University Press, 1953.

———. *Scenes from the Drama of European Literature.* University of Minnesota Press, 1984.

Avanessian, Armen, and Anke Henning. *Present Tense: A Poetics.* Trans. Nils F. Schott and Daniel Hendrickson. Bloomsbury, 2015.

BIBLIOGRAPHY

Awda, Hisham. "'Adania Shibli: harakat al-kalimat rahina jighrafiyat al-makan" [The movement of words depends on geography]. *al-Dustur*, May 10, 2010. https://www.addustour.com/articles/451926.

Ayoub, Georgine. "Un idiome clair et pur: Le trésor enseveli." In *Cent titres 3: Poésie de langue Arabe*. Centre internationale de poésie, 2002.

al-Azm, Sadiq Jalal. *Al-Naqd al-dhati ba'da al-hazima* [Self criticism after the defeat]. Dar al-tali'a, 1968.

al-Azmeh, Aziz. *The Times of History: Universal Topics in Islamic Historiography*. Central European University Press, 2007.

Badawi, Muhammad. *Al-Riwaya al-jadida fi misr* [The new novel in Egypt]. Al-Mu'assasa al-jami'iyya li-dirasat wa-nashr wa-tawzi', 1993.

Badr, Abd-al-Muhsin Taha. *Al-Riwa'i wa-l-ard* [The novelist and the land]. Al-Hay'a al-misriyya al-'amma, 1971.

———. *Tatawwur al-riwaya al-'arabiyya al-haditha fi misr: 1870–1938* [The evolution of the modern Arabic novel in Egypt, 1870–1938]. Dar al-ma'arif, 1963.

Bakhtin, M. M. "Forms of Time and Chronotope in the Novel." Trans. Caryl Emerson and Michael Holquist. In *The Dialogic Imagination*, ed. Michael Holquist. University of Texas Press, 1981.

Ball, Kirstie. "Exposure: Exploring the Subject of Surveillance." *Information, Communication and Society* 12, no. 5 (2009): 639–57.

Banbaji, Amir. *Mendele ve-ha-sipur ha-le'umi* [Mendele and the national narrative]. Dvir, 2009.

Bar-Siman-Tov, Yaacov, ed. *The Israeli-Palestinian Conflict: From Conflict Resolution to Conflict Management*. Palgrave Macmillan, 2007.

Bar-Yosef, Hamutal. "Ha-Heksher ha-dekadenti shel ha-sifrut ha-'ivrit be-sof ha-me'a ha-tesha'esre" [The decadent context of late nineteenth century Hebrew literature]. *Alpayim* 13 (1996): 173–200.

———. *Maga'im shel dekadens: Byalik, Berdichevski, Brenner* [Touches of decadence: Bialik, Berdichevski, Brenner]. Ben Gurion University Press, 1997.

———. "Psychopatologia 'ivrit kdam freudiyanit bi-tkofat ma'avar ha-me'ot" [Pre-Freudian Hebrew psychopathology at the turn of the century]. *Sadan: Studies in Hebrew Literature* 4 (2000): 37–71.

Barak, On. *On Time: Technology and Temporality in Modern Egypt*. University of California Press, 2013.

Bardaouil, Sam. *Surrealism in Egypt: Modernism and the Art and Liberty Group*. I. B. Tauris, 2016.

Baron, Beth. *Egypt as a Woman: Nationalism, Gender, and Politics*. University of California Press, 2005.

———. *The Women's Awakening in Egypt: Culture, Society, and the Press*. Yale University Press, 1994.

Barthes, Roland. *The Neutral: Lecture Course at the Collège de France (1977–1978)*. Trans. Rosalind E. Krauss and Denis Hollier. Columbia University Press, 2005.

Bashkin, Orit. "The Middle Eastern Shift and Provincializing Zionism." *International Journal of Middle East Studies* 46, no. 3 (2014): 577–80.

Behar, Almog. "Me-Yehuda Halevi le-Yehuda Burla" [From Yehuda Halevi to Yehuda Burla]. In *ha-Piyut ke-tsohar tarbuti*, ed. Haviva Pedaya. Ha-Kibbuts ha-me'uhad, 2013.

Behar, Moshe. "Fusing Arab Nahda, European Haskalah and Euro-Zionism: Eastern Jewish Thought in Late-Ottoman and Post-Ottoman Palestine." *Journal of Modern Jewish Studies* 16, no. 2 (2017): 271–74.

BIBLIOGRAPHY

Beinin, Joel. "The Communist Movement and Nationalist Political Discourse in Nasirist Egypt." *Middle East Journal* 41, no. 4 (1987): 568–84.

———. *Was the Red Flag Flying There? Marxist Politics and the Arab-Israeli Conflict in Egypt and Israel, 1948–1965*. University of California Press, 1990.

Benjamin, Walter. *The Arcades Project*. Trans. Howard Eiland and Kevin McLaughlin. Harvard University Press, 2002.

———. "Critique of Violence." Trans. Edmund Jephcott. In *Walter Benjamin: Selected Writings*, ed. Michael William Jennings and Marcus Paul Bullock. Belknap, 2004.

———. "On Some Motifs in Baudelaire." Trans. Harry Zohn. In *Illuminations*, ed. Hannah Arendt. Schocken, 1968.

Berda, Yael. *Living Emergency: Israel's Permit Regime in the Occupied West Bank*. Stanford University Press, 2018.

Berdichevsky, Dina. "Yehudim, masa'im ve-sh'ar hasrei ha-janer: ha-mikre shel Brenner ve-tkufato" [Jews, essayists, and other genreless types: the case of Brenner and his period]. *Mi-Kan* 20 (2020): 26–46.

Berg, Nancy E. *Exile from Exile: Israeli Writers from Iraq*. State University of New York Press, 2012.

Berlant, Lauren. "Critical Inquiry, Affirmative Culture." *Critical Inquiry* 30, no. 2 (2004): 445–51.

———. *Cruel Optimism*. Duke University Press, 2011.

———. "Thinking About Feeling Historical." *Emotion, Space and Society* 1 (2008): 4–9.

Berlovits, Yafah. *Lehamtsi erets, lehamtsi ʿam: tashtiyot sifrut ve-tarbut ba-yetsira shel ha-ʿaliya ha-rishona* [Inventing a land, inventing a people]. Ha-Kibbuts ha-meʾuhad, 1996.

Bernard, Anna. *Rhetorics of Belonging: Nation, Narration, and Israel/Palestine*. Liverpool University Press, 2013.

Best, Stephen Michael. *None Like Us: Blackness, Belonging, Aesthetic Life*. Duke University Press, 2018.

Best, Stephen, and Sharon Marcus. "Surface Reading: An Introduction." *Representations*, no. 108 (Fall 2009): 1–21.

Bhattacharya, Tithi. "Mapping Social Reproduction Theory." In *Social Reproduction Theory*, ed. Tithi Bhattacharya. Pluto, 2017.

Bialik, Hayim Nahman. "Taʿut neʿima" [A pleasant mistake]. *Ha-Shiloah* 19, no. 4 (1908): 380.

Bier, Laura. *Revolutionary Womanhood: Feminisms, Modernity, and the State in Nasser's Egypt*. Stanford University Press, 2011.

Blanchot, Maurice. "Everyday Speech." Trans. Susan Hanson. In *The Infinite Conversation*. University of Minnesota Press, 1993.

———. *The Space of Literature*. Trans. Ann Smock. University of Nebraska Press, 1982.

Bloom Cohen, Hella. *The Literary Imagination in Israel-Palestine: Orientalism, Poetry, and Biopolitics*. Palgrave, 2016.

Booth, Marilyn. *Classes of Ladies of Cloistered Spaces: Writing Feminist History through Biography in Fin-de-siècle Egypt*. Edinburgh University Press, 2015.

Bou Ali, Nadia. "Collecting the Nation: Lexicography and National Pedagogy in al-nahḍa al-ʿarabiyya." In *Archives, Museums and Collecting Practices in the Modern Arab World*, ed. Sonja Mejcher-Atassi and John Pedro Schwartz. Routledge, 2012.

Brenner, Yoseph Haim. *Breakdown and Bereavement*. Trans. Hillel Halkin. Cornell University Press, 1971.

BIBLIOGRAPHY

——. *Kol kitve Y. H. Brenner* [The complete works of Y. H. Brenner]. Dvir, 1960.
——. "Nerves." Trans. Hillel Halkin. In *Eight Great Hebrew Short Novels*, ed. Alan Lelchuk and Gershon Shaked. New American Library, 1983.
Brinkema, Eugenie. *The Forms of the Affects*. Duke University Press, 2014.
Brinker, Menahem. *'Ad ha-simta ha-tveryanit* [To the Tiberian alley]. Am oved, 1990.
Burla, Yehuda. "Ha-sifrut ha-'aravit" [Arabic literature]. *Ha-Tkufa* 18; 19 (1922).
Butler, Judith. *Parting Ways: Jewishness and the Critique of Zionism*. Columbia University Press, 2012.
Casarino, Cesare. "Images for Housework: On the Time of Domestic Labor in Gilles Deleuze's Philosophy of the Cinema." *Differences* 28, no. 3 (2017): 67–92.
Chakrabarty, Dipesh. *Provincializing Europe: Postcolonial Thought and Historical Difference*. Princeton University Press, 2000.
Cohen Lustig, Kfir. *Makers of Worlds, Readers of Signs: Israeli and Palestinian Literature of the Global Contemporary*. Verso, 2019.
Colla, Elliott. *Conflicted Antiquities: Egyptology, Egyptomania, Egyptian Modernity*. Duke University Press, 2008.
——. "How Zaynab Became the First Arabic Novel." *History Compass* 7, no. 1 (2009): 214–25.
Comay, Rebecca. "Resistance and Repetition: Freud and Hegel." *Research in Phenomenology* 45, no. 2 (2015): 237–66.
Connor, Steven. *The Book of Skin*. Cornell University Press, 2004.
Cossery, Albert. *Laziness in the Fertile Valley*. Trans. William Goyen. New Directions, 2013.
Creswell, Robyn. "Translator's Introduction." In Sonallah Ibrahim, *That Smell and Notes from Prison*. New Directions, 2013.
Darwish, Mahmoud. *The Butterfly's Burden*. Trans. Fady Joudah. Copper Canyon, 2007.
——. *La ta'atadhir 'amma fa'alta* [Don't be sorry for what you have done]. Riad El-Rayyes, 2004.
Davis, Angela Y. *Women, Race and Class*. Random House, 1981.
Davis, Kathleen. *Periodization and Sovereignty: How Ideas of Feudalism and Secularization Govern the Politics of Time*. University of Pennsylvania Press, 2008.
Davis, Thomas S. *The Extinct Scene: Late Modernism and Everyday Life*. Columbia University Press, 2016.
de Beauvoir, Simone. *The Second Sex*. Trans. H. M. Parshley. Vintage, 1989.
De Man, Paul. "Literary History and Literary Modernity." *Daedalus* 99, no. 2 (1970): 384–404.
Derrida, Jacques. *Dissemination*. Trans. Barbara Johnson. University of Chicago Press, 1981.
——. *Of Grammatology*. Trans. Gayatri Chakravorty Spivak. Johns Hopkins University Press, 1976.
——. "The Law of Genre." Trans. Avital Ronell. *Critical Inquiry* 7, no. 1 (1980): 55–81.
——. *Resistances of Psychoanalysis*. Trans. Peggy Kamuf, Pascale-Anne Brault, and Michael Naas. Stanford University Press, 1998.
Di-Capua, Yoav. "Changing the Arab Intellectual Guard: On the Fall of the Udaba', 1940–60." In *Arabic Thought Against the Authoritarian Age: Toward and Intellectual History of the Present*, ed. Max Weiss and Jens Hansen. Oxford University Press, 2018.

———. *No Exit: Arab Existentialism, Jean-Paul Sartre, and Decolonization.* University of Chicago Press, 2018.

———. "The Traumatic Subjectivity of Sunʿallah Ibrahim's *Dhat.*" *Journal of Arabic Literature* 43, no. 1 (2012): 80–101.

Dorfman, Eran. *Foundations of the Everyday: Shock, Deferral, Repetition.* Rowman & Littlefield International, 2014.

Dotan, Keren. "Likhtov moderniyut mi-mizrah" [Writing modernity from the East]. *Mi-Kan* 17 (2017): 122–62.

Drumsta, Emily. *Ways of Seeking: The Arabic Novel and the Poetics of Investigation.* University of California Press, 2024.

Eghbariah, Rabea. "Toward Nakba as a Legal Concept." *Columbia Law Review* 124, no. 4 (2024): 887–991.

Ehrenreich, Barbara, and Deirdre English. "The Manufacture of Housework." *Socialist Revolution* 5, no. 26 (1975): 5–40.

Einboden, Jeffrey. "The Genesis of *Weltliteratur*: Goethe's *West-Östlicher Divan* and Kerygmatic Pluralism." *Literature and Theology* 19, no. 3 (2005): 238–50.

El Sadda, Hoda. *Gender, Nation, and the Arabic Novel: Egypt, 1892–2008.* Syracuse University Press, 2012.

El Shakry, Hoda. *The Literary Qurʾan: Narrative Ethics in the Maghreb.* Fordham University Press, 2020.

———. "Palestine and the Aesthetics of the Future Impossible." *Interventions* 23, no. 5 (2021): 669–90.

El Shakry, Omnia S. *The Great Social Laboratory: Subjects of Knowledge in Colonial and Postcolonial Egypt.* Stanford University Press, 2007.

Elad, Ami. "Ideology and Structure in Fatḥī Ghānim's *al-Jabal.*" *Journal of Arabic Literature* 20, no. 2 (1989), 168–86.

El-Ariss, Tarek, ed. *The Arab Renaissance: A Bilingual Anthology of the Nahda.* Modern Language Association of America, 2018.

———. *Trials of Arab Modernity: Literary Affects and the New Political.* Fordham University Press, 2013.

Elbaz, Ella. "Factoring Asymmetry into the Equation: On Juxtaposing Palestinian and Israeli Literatures." *Journal of Arabic Literature* 55, no. 1 (2024): 126–53.

El-Haddad, Laila. "The Quintessential Palestinian Experience." *Electronic Intifada*, April 14, 2009. https://electronicintifada.net/content/quintessential-palestinian-experience/8183.

Elliott, Jane. "Stepford U.S.A. Second-Wave Feminism, Domestic Labor, and the Representation of National Time." *Cultural Critique*, no. 70 (Fal 2008): 32–62.

Elmarsafy, Ziad. *Sufism in the Contemporary Arabic Novel.* Edinburgh University Press, 2012.

Eqeiq, Amal. "From Haifa to Ramallah (and Back): New/Old Palestinian Literary Topography." *Journal of Palestine Studies* 48, no. 3 (2019): 26–42.

Erakat, Noura, and Marc Lamont Hill. "Black-Palestinian Transnational Solidarity: Renewals, Returns, and Practice." *Journal of Palestine Studies* 48, no. 4 (2019): 7–16.

Fakhreddine, Huda J. *The Arabic Prose Poem: Poetic Theory and Practice.* Edinburgh University Press, 2022.

———. *Metapoesis in the Arabic Tradition: From Modernists to Muḥdathūn.* Brill, 2015.

Fanon, Frantz. *The Wretched of the Earth.* Trans. Richard Philcox. Grove, 2004.

BIBLIOGRAPHY

Fathy, Hassan. *Architecture for the Poor: An Experiment in Rural Egypt.* University of Chicago Press, 1973.
Federici, Silvia. *Revolution at Point Zero: Housework, Reproduction, and Feminist Struggle.* PM Press, 2012.
Felski, Rita. "The Invention of Everyday Life." In *Doing Time: Feminist Theory and Postmodern Culture*, 77–98. New York University Press, 2000.
———. *The Limits of Critique.* University of Chicago Press, 2015.
Ferguson, Frances. "Rape and the Rise of the Novel." *Representations*, no. 20 (1987): 88–112.
Fogiel-Bijaoui, Sylvie. "Feminism, le'umiyut ve-shinuy hevrati" [Feminism, nationalism, and social change]. In *Zman yehudi hadash.* Keter, 2007.
François, Anne-Lise. *Open Secrets: The Literature of Uncounted Experience.* Stanford University Press, 2008.
Freed-Thall, Hannah. *Spoiled Distinctions: Aesthetics and the Ordinary in French Modernism.* Oxford University Press, 2015.
Freud, Sigmund. *Beyond the Pleasure Principle.* Trans. C. J. M. Hubback. Martino, 2009.
———. *Standard Edition of the Complete Psychological Works of Sigmund Freud.* Ed. and trans. James Strachey. Hogarth, 1995
Friedman, Susan Stanford. "Periodizing Modernism: Postcolonial Modernities and the Space/Time Borders of Modernist Studies." *Modernism/Modernity* 13, no. 3 (2006): 425–43.
———. "Planetarity: Musing Modernist Studies." *Modernism/Modernity* 17, no. 3 (2010): 471–99.
Fritzsche, Peter. *Stranded in the Present: Modern Time and the Melancholy of History.* Harvard University Press, 2004.
Furani, Khaled. *Silencing the Sea: Secular Rhythms in Palestinian Poetry.* Stanford University Press, 2012.
Gallagher, Catherine. "Formalism and Time." In *Reading for Form*, ed. Susan J. Wolfson and Marshall Brown. University of Washington Press, 2006.
———. "The Rise of Fictionality." In *The Novel, Volume 1: History, Geography, and Culture*, ed. Franco Moretti. Princeton University Press, 2006.
Gana, Nouri. "Formless Form: Elias Khoury's *City Gates* and the Poetics of Trauma." *Comparative Literature Studies* 47, no. 4 (2010): 504–32.
Gardiner, Michael E., and Julian Jason Haladyn, eds. *Boredom Studies Reader: Frameworks and Perspectives.* Routledge, 2017.
al-Garibi, Khalid. *Jadaliyat al-asala wa-l-muʿasara fi adab al-Masʿadi* [The dialectics of authenticity and contemporaneity in al-Masʿadi's writings]. Samid lil-nashr wa-l-tawziʿ, 1994.
Gasper, Michael Ezekiel. *The Power of Representation: Publics, Peasants, and Islam in Egypt.* Stanford University Press, 2009.
Genette, Gérard. *Narrative Discourse: An Essay in Method.* Trans. Jane E. Lewin. Cornell University Press, 1980.
Geva, Sharon. *Ha-Isha ma omeret? nashim be-yisra'el bi-shnot ha-medina ha-rishonot* [What does the woman say? Women in the first years of Israeli statehood]. Magnes, 2020.
Geyer, Michael, and Charles Bright. "World History in a Global Age." *The American Historical Review* 100, no. 4 (1995): 1034–60.

BIBLIOGRAPHY

Ghanem, Fathi. *Al-Jabal* [The mountain]. [1957]. Dar al-hilal, 1965.
Gifford, James. *Personal Modernisms: Anarchist Networks and the Later Avant-Gardes.* University of Alberta Press, 2014.
Gilman, Sander L. *The Jew's Body.* Routledge, 1991.
Ginzburg, Carlo. *Clues, Myths, and the Historical Method.* Trans. John Tedeschi and Anne C. Tedeschi. Johns Hopkins University Press, 1989.
Glissant, Édouard. *Poetics of Relation.* Trans. Betsy Wing. University of Michigan Press, 1997.
Gluzman, Michael. *Ha-Guf ha-tsiyoni: le'umiyut, migdar u-miniyut ba-sifrut ha-yisra'elit ha-hadasha* [The Zionist body: nationalism, gender and sexuality in the new Israeli literature]. Ha-Kibbuts ha-me'uhad, 2007.
Goldberg, Leah. *Avedot (mukdash le-antonya)* [Losses (dedicated to Antonia)], ed. Giddon Ticotsky. Sifriyat ha-poalim, 2010.
——. *Ha-Ometz le-hulin* [Mundane bravery], ed. A. B. Jaffe. Sifriyat ha-poalim, 1976.
Gomel, Elana, and Vered Karti Shemtov. "Limbotopia: The "New Present" and the Literary Imagination." *Comparative Literature* 70, no. 1 (2018): 60–71.
Goodstein, Elizabeth S. *Experience Without Qualities: Boredom and Modernity.* Stanford University Press, 2005.
Gorali, Moshe. "'Od degel shahor" [Another black flag]. *Ha'aretz*, October 28, 2003. https://www.haaretz.co.il/misc/1.920418.
Gordon, Joel. *Revolutionary Melodrama: Popular Film and Civic Identity in Nasser's Egypt.* Middle East Documentation Center, 2002.
Govrin, Nurit. *Brener: Oved'etsot u-more derekh* [Brenner: drifter and guide]. Tel-Aviv University, 1991.
——. *Me'ora Brenner: ha-ma'avak 'al hofesh ha-bituy* [The Brenner affair: the battle for free speech]. Yad yitshak ben-tsvi, 1985.
Greene, Gayle. *Changing the Story: Feminist Fiction and the Tradition.* Indiana University Press, 1991.
Griffiths, Mark, and Mikko Joronen. "Governmentalizing Palestinian Futures: Uncertainty, Anticipation, Possibility." *Geografiska Annaler: Series B, Human Geography* 103, no. 4 (2021): 352–66.
Hafez, Sabry. "The Egyptian Novel in the Sixties." In *Critical Perspectives on Modern Arabic Literature*, ed. Issa Boullata. Three Continents, 1980.
Hainge, Greg. *Noise Matters: Towards an Ontology of Noise.* Bloomsbury Academic, 2013.
Halabi, Zeina G. "The Literary Lives of Umm Kulthūm: Cossery, Ghali, Negm, and the Critique of Nasserism." *Middle Eastern Literatures* 19, no. 1 (2016): 77–98.
Halperin, Liora. *Babel in Zion: Jews, Nationalism, and Language Diversity in Palestine, 1920–1948.* Yale University Press, 2015.
Hammad, Sousan. "Waiting in Palestine." *Boston Review*, June 17, 2013. http://bostonreview.net/blog/waiting-palestine.
Hamori, Andras. "An Allegory from the Arabian Nights: The City of Brass." *Bulletin of the School of Oriental and African Studies* 34, no. 1 (1971): 9–19.
Hanssen, Jens, and Max Weiss, eds. *Arabic Thought Beyond the Liberal Age: Towards an Intellectual History of the Nahḍa.* Cambridge University Press, 2016.
Haraway, Donna Jeanne. *Simians, Cyborgs, and Women: The Reinvention of Nature.* Routledge, 1991.

BIBLIOGRAPHY

Harootunian, Harry. "Remembering the Historical Present." *Critical Inquiry* 33, no. 3 (2007): 471–94.
Harshav, Benjamin. *Language in Time of Revolution.* University of California Press, 1993.
Hartman, Saidiya V. *Lose Your Mother: A Journey Along the Atlantic Slave Route.* Farrar, Straus and Giroux, 2008.
——. "Venus in Two Acts." *Small Axe* 12, no. 2 (2008): 1–14.
Hartog, François. *Regimes of Historicity: Presentism and Experiences of Time.* Trans. Saskia Brown. Columbia University Press, 2015.
Hasak-Lowy, Todd. *Here and Now: History, Nationalism, and Realism in Modern Hebrew Fiction.* Syracuse University Press, 2008.
Haugbolle, Sune. "The Historiography and the Memory of the Lebanese Civil War." *Mass Violence and Résistance*, October 25, 2011. http://www.massviolence.org/The-historiography-and-the-memory-of-the-Lebanese-civil-war.
Hawwari, Ahmad Ibrahim. *Naqd al-riwaya fi al-adab al-ʿarabi al-hadith fi misr* [Novel criticism in modern Arabic literature in Egypt]. Dar al-maʿarif, 1978.
Hayot, Eric. *On Literary Worlds.* Oxford University Press, 2012.
Hayot, Eric, and Rebecca L. Walkowitz. *A New Vocabulary for Global Modernism.* Columbia University Press, 2016.
Henig, Roni. *On Revival: Hebrew Literature Between Life and Death.* University of Pennsylvania Press, 2024.
Hever, Hannan. "Guru lakhem min ha-galitsaʾim: safrut galitsya ve-ha-maʾavak al ha-kanon ba-siporet ha-ʿivrit." *Teʾorya u-vikoret* 5 (1994): 55–77.
——. *ha-Sipur ve-ha-leom: kriʾot bikortiyot be-kanon ha-siporet ha-ʿivrit* [The story and the nation: critical readings in the Hebrew literary canon]. Resling, 2007.
——. "Territoriality and Otherness in Hebrew Literature of the War of Independence." In *The Other in Jewish Thought and History*, ed. Laurence J. Silberstein and Robert L. Cohn. New York University Press, 1994.
——. "Yitzhak Shami: Ethnicity as an Unresolved Conflict." *Shofar* 24, no. 2 (2006): 124–39.
Highmore, Ben. *Everyday Life and Cultural Theory: An Introduction.* Taylor & Francis, 2002.
Hill, Peter. *Utopia and Civilisation in the Arab Nahda.* Cambridge University Press, 2020.
Hirschauge, Orr, and Hagar Shezaf. "How Israel Jails Palestinians Because the Fit the Terrorist Profile." *Haaretz*, May 28, 2017. www.haaretz.com/israel-news/.premium-1.792206.
Hirschfeld, Ariel. "Retet tsamarot ve-dagim meluhim: ʿal ha-milim ve-ha-dvarim be-ʿatstabim le-Yosef Hayim Brenner." In *Sifrut ve-hevra ba-tarbut ha-ʿivrit ha-hadasha*, ed. Yehudit Bar-El and Yigʿal Schwartz. Ha-Kibbuts ha-meʾuhad, 2000.
Hochberg, Gil Z. *Becoming Palestine: Toward an Archival Imagination of the Future.* Duke University Press, 2021.
——. *In Spite of Partition: Jews, Arabs, and the Limits of Separatist Imagination.* Princeton University Press, 2010.
——. "A Poetics of Haunting: From Yizhar's Hirbeh to Yehoshua's Ruins to Koren's Crypts." *Jewish Social Studies* 18, no. 3 (2012): 55–69.
——. *Visual Occupations: Violence and Visibility in a Conflict Zone.* Duke University Press, 2015.

Hoffman, Adina. "In Search of Yitzhaq Shami." *Raritan* 28, no. 3 (Winter 2009): 1–8.
Hoffmann, E. T. A. "The Sandman." Trans. R. J. Hollingdale. In *Tales of Hoffmann*. Penguin, 2004.
Holt, Elizabeth M. *Fictitious Capital: Silk, Cotton, and the Rise of the Arabic Novel*. Fordham University Press, 2017.
Hooper, Glenn. *Landscape and Empire 1770–2000*. Ashgate, 2004.
Hoshen, Dalia. *'Agnon: sipur (ena) sugiya ba-gemara* [Agnon: a story is (not) a Talmudic question]. Reuven Mas, 2006.
Hunt, F. V. "Acoustic vs Acoustical." *Journal of the Acoustical Society of America* 27, no. 5 (1955): 975–76.
Ibrahim, Sonallah. *67: riwaya*. Dar al-thaqafa al-jadida, 2016.
———. *Dhat*. Cairo: Dar al-mustaqbal al-'arabi, 1992. Trans. Anthony Calderbank as *Zaat*. American University in Cairo Press, 2001.
———. *Tilk al-ra'iha wa-qisas ukhra*. 3rd ed. Dar al-huda, 2003. Trans. Robyn Creswell as *That Smell and Notes from Prison*. New Directions, 2013.
———. *Yawmiyat al-wahat* [Wahat prison diaries]. Dar al-mustaqbal al-'arabi, 2004.
'Id, Husayn. *Fathi Ghanim, al-haya wa-l-ibda'* [Fathi Ghanem, life and creation]. Al-Hay'a al-'amma li-qusur al-thaqafa, 1995.
Jabiri, 'Ali Husayn. *Ma'sat al-hallaj bayna Masinyun wa-l-bahithin al-baghdadiyin, 1908–1998* [The passion of al-Hallaj between Massignon and the Baghdadi scholars]. Dar ninawa, 2008.
al-Jabiri, Muhammad 'Abid. *Al-Khitab al-'arabi al-mu'asir: dirasa tahliliyya naqdiyya* [Contemporary Arab discourse: critical and analytic studies]. Dar al-tali'a, 1982.
Jabra, Jabra Ibrahim. "Modern Arabic Literature and the West." *Journal of Arabic Literature* 2, no. 1 (1971): 76–91.
Jacquemond, Richard. *Conscience of the Nation: Writers, State, and Society in Modern Egypt*. Trans. David Tresilian. American University in Cairo Press, 2008.
Jameson, Fredric. *The Antinomies of Realism*. Verso, 2013.
———. *The Political Unconscious: Narrative as a Socially Symbolic Act*. Cornell University Press, 1981.
———. *Postmodernism, or, the Cultural Logic of Late Capitalism*. Duke University Press, 1991.
———. *The Seeds of Time*. Columbia University Press, 1994.
———. *A Singular Modernity: Essay on the Ontology of the Present*. Verso, 2002.
———. "The Vanishing Mediator: Narrative Structure in Max Weber." *New German Critique* 1 (1973): 52–89.
Johnson, Lesley, and Justine Lloyd. *Sentenced to Everyday Life: Feminism and the Housewife*. Berg, 2004.
Joronen, Mikko. "Spaces of Waiting: Politics of Precarious Recognition in the Occupied West Bank." *Environment and Planning D: Society and Space* 35, no. 6 (2017): 994–1011.
Kadman, Noga. *Erased from Space and Consciousness: Israel and the Depopulated Palestinian Villages of 1948*. Trans. Dimi Reider. Indiana University Press, 2015.
Kassab, Elizabeth Suzanne. *Contemporary Arab Thought: Cultural Critique in Comparative Perspective*. Columbia University Press, 2010.
Kaufman, Eleanor. *Deleuze, the Dark Precursor: Dialectic, Structure, Being*. Johns Hopkins University Press, 2012.

BIBLIOGRAPHY

Kendall, Elisabeth. *Literature, Journalism and the Avant-Garde: Intersection in Egypt.* Routledge, 2006.

Khalidi, Raja J., and Sobhi Samour. "Neoliberalism as Liberation: The Statehood Program and the Remaking of the Palestinian National Movement." *Journal of Palestine Studies* 40, no. 2 (Winter 2010): 6–25.

Kharrat, Idwar. *Al-Hassasiyya al-jadida: maqalat fi al-zahira al-qasasiyya* [The new sensibility: essays on the literary phenomenon]. Dar al-adab, 1993.

Khoury, Elias. *Abwab al-madina* [City gates]. Dar al-adab, 1990. Trans. Paula Haydar as *City Gates*. Picador, 1993.

———. *Al-Dhakira al-mafquda: dirasat naqdiyya* [Lost memory]. Dar al-adab, 1990.

———. "Memory of the City." *Grand Street* 54 (Autumn 1995): 137–42.

———. "The Necessity to Forget and Remember." Interview with Sonja Mejcher-Atassi. *Banipal* 12 (2001): 8–14.

Kilito, Abdelfattah. *Thou Shalt Not Speak My Language*. Trans. Waïl S. Hassan. Syracuse University Press, 2008.

Kimmerling, Barukh. *Mehagrim, mityashvim, yelidim* [Immigrants, settlers, natives]. Am oved, 2004.

Klemm, Verena. "Different Notions of Commitment (Iltizam) and Committed Literature (Al-Adab Al-Multazim) in the Literary Circles of the Mashriq." *Arabic and Middle Eastern Literatures* 3, no. 1 (2000): 51–62.

Koren, Yeshayahu. *Levaya ba-tsohorayim*. Ha-Kibbuts ha-me'uhad, 2008. Trans. Dalya Bilu as *Funeral at Noon*. Steerforth, 1996.

———. "Sone' milim gvohot" [Hating fancy words]. Interview by Sarah Ortal. *Yediot ahronot*, ha-musaf le-shabat, June 5, 1992, 23.

———. "Yarad geshem halash" [It rained weakly]. *Ha'aretz*, March 3, 2008. https://www.haaretz.co.il/literature/2008-03-03/ty-article/0000017f-efe1-dc28-a17f-fff7cdc40000.

Koselleck, Reinhart. *Futures Past: On the Semantics of Historical Time*. Trans. Keith Tribe. MIT Press, 1985.

Kotef, Hagar. *Movement and the Ordering of Freedom: On Liberal Governances of Mobility*. Duke University Press, 2015.

Kracauer, Siegfried. *The Mass Ornament: Weimar Essays*. Trans. Thomas Y. Levin. Harvard University Press, 1995.

Kramnick, Jonathan, and Anahid Nersessian. "Form and Explanation." *Critical Inquiry* 43, no. 3 (2017): 650–69.

Kristeva, Julia. *Powers of Horror: An Essay on Abjection*. Trans. Leon S. Roudiez. Columbia University Press, 1982.

Kurzweil, Baruch. *Masot 'al sipure shai 'agnon* [Essays on S. Y. Agnon's stories]. Schocken, 1962.

Lagji, Amanda. *Postcolonial Fiction and Colonial Time: Waiting for Now*. Edinburgh University Press, 2022.

Landau, Idan. "Ha-Yif'a ha-shketa hazot" [This quiet brilliance]. *Ha'aretz*, April 29, 2008.

Landry, Olivia, and Christinia Landry. "Torlasco's 'Philosophy in the Kitchen': Image, Domestic Labor, and the Gendered Embodiment of Time." *New Review of Film and Television Studies* 17, no. 4 (2019): 456–80.

Laroui, Abdallah. *The Crisis of the Arab Intellectual: Traditionalism or Historicism?* Trans. Diarmid Cammell. University of California Press, 1976.

———. *L'ideologie arabe contemporaine: essai critique*. François Maspero, 1977.

Latour, Bruno. "An Attempt at a 'Compositionist Manifesto.'" *New Literary History* 41, no. 3 (2010): 471–90.
Lavie, Aviv. "Huhlat ve-kuyam: rahatsuha, gazezu se'ara, ansuha ve-harguha." *Ha'aretz*, October 28, 2003. https://www.haaretz.co.il/misc/1.920403.
Lee, Wendy Anne. *Failures of Feeling: Insensibility and the Novel*. Stanford University Press, 2019.
Lefebvre, Henri. *Critique of Everyday Life*. Trans. John Moore and Gregory Elliott. 3 vols. Verso, 2008.
———. *Everyday Life in the Modern World*. Trans. Sacha Rabinovitch. Transaction, 1984.
———. *The Production of Space*. Blackwell, 1991.
Lenssen, Anneka, Dina Ramadan, Sarah A. Rogers, and Nada Shabout. "The Longevity of Rupture: 1967 in Art and Its Histories." *ARTMargins* 2, no. 2 (2013): 14–18.
Lesjak, Carolyne. "Reading Dialectically." *Criticism* 55, no. 2 (2013): 233–77.
Levine, Caroline. *Forms: Whole, Rhythm, Hierarchy, Network*. Princeton University Press, 2015.
Levy, Lital. "The Nahḍa and the Haskala: A Comparative Reading of 'Revival' and 'Reform.'" *Middle Eastern Literatures* 16, no. 3 (2013): 300–16.
———. "Partitioned Pasts: Arab Jewish Intellectuals and the Case of Esther Azhari Moyal (1873–1948)." In *The Making of the Arab Intellectual*, ed. Dyala Hamzah, 128–63. Routledge, 2012.
———. *Poetic Trespass: Writing Between Hebrew and Arabic in Israel/Palestine*. Princeton University Press, 2014.
Librett, Jeffrey S. *Orientalism and the Figure of the Jew*. Fordham University Press, 2014.
Litvak, Olga. *Haskalah: The Romantic Movement in Judaism*. Rutgers University Press, 2012.
Livne, Yoni. "Levaya ba-tsohorayim" [Funeral at noon]. *Yediot ahronot*, August 7, 2008.
Lloyd, David. *Anomalous States: Irish Writing and the Post-Colonial Moment*. Duke University Press, 1993.
Loftis, Sonya Freeman. "The Autistic Detective: Sherlock Holmes and His Legacy." *Disability Studies Quarterly* 34, no. 4 (2014).
Loraux, Nicole. *The Divided City: On Memory and Forgetting in Ancient Athens*. Zone, 2002.
Lorenz, Chris, and Berber Bevernage, eds. *Breaking Up Time: Negotiating the Borders Between Present, Past and Future*. Vandenhoeck & Ruprecht, 2013.
Lotta Feminista. "Introduction to the Debate." In *Italian Feminist Thought: A Reader*, ed. Paola Bono and Sandra Kemp. Blackwell, 1991.
Lubin, Orly. "Tidbits from Nehama's Kitchen: Alternative Nationalism in Dvora Baron's the Exiles." In *Hebrew, Gender, and Modernity: Critical Responses to Dvora Baron's Fiction*, ed. Sheila E. Jelen and Shachar Pinsker. University Press of Maryland, 2007.
Lukács, Georg. *History and Class Consciousness*. Trans. Rodney Livingstone. MIT Press, 1971.
Manning, Erin. *Always More Than One: Individuation's Dance*. Duke University Press, 2013.
———. *The Minor Gesture*. Duke University Press, 2016.
Mao, Douglas, and Rebecca L. Walkowitz. "The New Modernist Studies." *PMLA* 123, no. 3 (2008): 737–48.
Marks, Laura U. "Arab Glitch." In *Uncommon Grounds: New Media and Critical Practices in North Africa and the Middle East*, ed. Anthony Downey. I.B. Tauris, 2014.

BIBLIOGRAPHY

———. *Enfoldment and Infinity: An Islamic Genealogy of New Media Art*. MIT Press, 2010.
———. *Touch: Sensuous Theory and Multisensory Media*. University of Minnesota Press, 2002.
Marnin-Distenfeld, Shahar. "Al tikni be-ʿeinayim ʿatsumot! Yitsugey ʿakeret ha-bayit be-pirsomot mi-tkufat ha-mandat" [Don't shop blindfolded! Representations of the homemaker in mandatory Palestine]. *Kesher*, no. 51 (2018): 111–21.
Martin, Theodore. *Contemporary Drift: Genre, Historicism, and the Problem of the Present*. Columbia University Press, 2017.
Marx, Gary T. *Windows Into the Soul: Surveillance and Society in an Age of High Technology*. University of Chicago Press, 2016.
Marx, Karl. *Capital: A Critique of Political Economy*. Trans. Ben Fowkes. Penguin, 1981.
al-Masʿadi, Mahmud. *Al-Aʿmal al-kamila* [Complete works]. 4 vols. Dar al-janub, 2012.
———. *Haddatha abu hurayra qal*. Al-Dar al-tunisiyyah li-l-nashr, 1973.
———. "Interview with Mahmud al-Masʿadi." By Mohamed-Salah Omri. *Comparative Critical Studies* 4 no. 3 (2007): 435–40.
Massad, Joseph. "Resisting the Nakba." *Al-Ahram*, May 15–21, 2008. http://weekly.ahram.org.eg/Archive/2008/897/op8.htm#1.
Massignon, Louis. *Essay on the Origins of the Technical Language of Islamic Mysticism*. Trans. Benjamin Clark. University of Notre Dame Press, 1997.
———. *Testimonies and Reflections: Essays of Louis Massignon*, ed. and trans. Herbert Mason. University of Notre Dame Press, 1989.
Massumi, Brian. "Prelude." In Erin Manning, *Always More Than One: Individuation's Dance*. Duke University Press, 2013.
Masuzawa, Tomoko. *The Invention of World Religions, or, How European Universalism Was Preserved in the Language of Pluralism*. University of Chicago Press, 2005.
Mejcher-Atassi, Sonja. "Elias Khoury's *Abwab Al-Madina* (Gates of the City): A Modern Version of 'the City of Brass' from *Alf Layla Wa-Layla* (the Thousand and One Nights)." In *Reflections on Reflections: Near Eastern Writers Reading Literature*, ed. Angelika Neuwirth and Andreas Islebe. Reichert, 2006.
Meskell, Lynn. "Sites of Violence: Terrorism, Tourism, and Heritage in the Archaeological Present." In *Embedding Ethics*, ed. Lynn Meskell and Peter Pels. Routledge, 2005.
Mestyan, Adam. *Modern Arab Kingship: Remaking the Ottoman Political Order in the Interwar Middle East*. Princeton University Press, 2023.
Miller, William Ian. *The Anatomy of Disgust*. Harvard University Press, 1997.
Mintz, Alan L., and Anne Golomb Hoffman. "Introduction." In S. Y. Agnon, *A Book That Was Lost: Thirty-Five Stories*, ed. Alan L. Mintz and Anne Golomb Hoffman. Toby, 1995.
Mitchell, Timothy. *Colonising Egypt*. Cambridge University Press, 1988.
———. *Rule of Experts: Egypt, Techno-Politics, Modernity*. University of California Press, 2002.
Mitrani, Judith. "Minding the Gap Between Neuroscientific and Psychoanalytic Understanding of Autism." *Journal of Child Psychotherapy* 36, no. 3 (2010): 240–58.
Monterescu, Daniel, and Noa Shaindlinger. "Situational Radicalism: The Israeli 'Arab Spring' and the (Un)Making of the Rebel City." *Constellations: An International Journal of Critical and Democratic Theory* 20, no. 2 (2013): 40–65.
Montgomery, James E. "The Empty Ḥijāz." In *Arabic Theology, Arabic Philosophy: From the Many to the One, Essays in Honor of Richard M. Frank*, ed. James E. Montgomery. Peeters, 2006.

Mor, Liron. *Conflicts: The Poetics and Politics of Palestine-Israel*. Fordham University Press, 2024.

———. "Reorienting Visual Reading: From Colonial Visions to the Subtexts 'Facing Us.'" *Qui Parle* 31, no. 2 (2022): 189–229.

Moreiras, Alberto. *The Exhaustion of Difference: The Politics of Latin American Cultural Studies*. Duke University Press, 2001.

Moretti, Franco. *The Bourgeois: Between History and Literature*. Verso, 2013.

———. "Conjectures on World Literature." *New Left Review* 1 (2000): 54–68.

Mufti, Aamir. *Enlightenment in the Colony: The Jewish Question and the Crisis of Postcolonial Culture*. Princeton University Press, 2007.

———. *Forget English! Orientalisms and World Literatures*. Harvard University Press, 2016.

———. "Orientalism and the Institution of World Literatures." *Critical Inquiry* 36, no. 3 (2010): 458–93.

Mufti, Nasser. *Civilizing War: Imperial Politics and the Poetics of National Rupture*. Northwestern University Press, 2017.

Muhyi al-Din ʿAbd al-Hamid, Muhammad. *Al-Tuhfa al-saniyya bi-sharh al-muqaddima al-ajurrumiyya* [A Commentary on al-ajurrumiyya]. Dar ibn kathir, 2018.

Murphet, Julian, Helen Groth, and Penelope Hone, eds. *Sounding Modernism: Rhythm and Sonic Mediation in Modern Literature and Film*. Edinburgh University Press, 2017.

Mostafa, Dalia Said. "Literary Representations of Trauma, Memory, and Identity in the Novels of Elias Khoury and Rabīʾ Jābir." *Journal of Arabic Literature* 40, 2 (2009): 208–236.

al-Muwaylihi, Muhammad. *Hadith ʿIsa ibn Hisham aw fitra min al-zaman*. Muhammad al-kutubi, 1923.

Najmabadi, Afsaneh. "Crafting an Educated Housewife in Iran." In *Remaking Women*, ed. Lila Abu-Lughod. Princeton University Press, 1998.

Napolin, Julie Beth. *The Fact of Resonance: Modernist Acoustics and Narrative Form*. Fordham University Press, 2020.

Nashif, Esmail. "Mawt al-nas" [Death of the text]. *Majallat al-dirasat al-filastiniyya*, 96 (2013): 96–117.

Nersessian, Anahid. *The Calamity Form: On Poetry and Social Life*. University of Chicago Press, 2020.

———. *Utopia, Limited: Romanticism and Adjustment*. Harvard University Press, 2015.

Neumann, Boaz. *Land and Desire in Early Zionism*. Brandeis University Press, 2011.

Ngai, Sianne. *Ugly Feelings*. Harvard University Press, 2004.

Nichanian, Marc. *Mourning Philology: Art and Religion at the Margins of the Ottoman Empire*. Trans. G. M. Goshgarian and Jeff Fort. Fordham University Press, 2014.

Nilges, Mathias. *How to Read a Moment: The American Novel and the Crisis of the Present*. Northwestern University Press, 2021.

Nir, Oded. "How to End an Ending? Moving Beyond Crisis in Israeli Culture." *ASAP journal* 8, no. 2 (2023): 301–23.

———. *Signatures of Struggle: The Figuration of Collectivity in Israeli Fiction*. SUNY Press, 2018.

North, Michael. *What Is the Present?* Princeton University Press, 2018.

Ogden, Thomas H. *The Primitive Edge of Experience*. Jason Aronson, 1989.

Olender, Maurice. *The Languages of Paradise: Race, Religion, and Philology in the Nineteenth Century*. Harvard University Press, 1992.

BIBLIOGRAPHY

Olmert, Dana. "Geographical and Potential Space: A Reading of Two Early Stories by Y. H. Brenner." *Jerusalem Studies in Hebrew Literature* 19 (2003): 123–41.
Olson, Liesl. *Modernism and the Ordinary*. Oxford University Press, 2009.
O'Meara, Simon. "Haptic Vision: Making Surface Sense of Islamic Material Culture." In *The Routledge Handbook of Sensory Archaeology*, ed. Robin Skeates and Jo Day. Routledge, 2019.
Omri, Mohamed-Salah. *Nationalism, Islam and World Literature: Sites of Confluence in the Writings of Mahmud Al-Mas'adi*. Routledge, 2006.
Oron, Michal. "Smalim u-motivim kabaliyim ba-sipur 'ido ve-'enam le-Shai 'Agnon" [Kabbalistic symbols and motifs in Agnon's Edo and Enam]. *Ba-Seminar* (1977): 160–72.
Ozick, Cynthia. "Agnon's Antagonisms." *Commentary* 86 (1988): 43–48.
Pagis, Dan. *Milim nirdafot: shirim* [Synonyms: poems]. Ha-Kibbuts ha-me'uhad, 1982.
Pannewick, Friederike, Georges Khalil, and Yvonne Albers, eds. *Commitment and Beyond: Reflections on/of the Political in Arabic Literature since the 1940s*. Reichert Verlag, 2015.
Pardes, Ilana. *Agnon's Moonstruck Lovers: The Song of Songs in Israeli Culture*. University of Washington Press, 2013.
Parikka, Jussi. "Mapping Noise: Techniques and Tactics of Irregularities, Interception, and Disturbance." In *Media Archaeology: Approaches, Applications, and Implications*, ed. Erkki Huhtamo and Jussi Parikka. University of California Press, 2011.
Parr, Nora. "What Is 'Trauma' in Arabic." *Politics/Letters*, 2018. http://politicsslashletters.org/what-is-trauma-in-arabic.
Pease, Allison. *Modernism, Feminism and the Culture of Boredom*. Cambridge University Press, 2012.
Peteet, Julie. "Closure's Temporality: The Cultural Politics of Time and Waiting." *South Atlantic Quarterly* 117, no. 1 (2018): 43–64.
Pinero, José M. López. *Historical Origins of the Concept of Neurosis*. Trans. D. Berrios. Cambridge University Press, 1983.
Pinsker, Shachar. *Literary Passports: The Making of Modernist Hebrew Fiction in Europe*. Stanford University Press, 2010.
Pollock, Sheldon I. *The Language of the Gods in the World of Men: Sanskrit, Culture, and Power in Premodern India*. University of California Press, 2006.
Postone, Moishe. *Time, Labor, and Social Domination: A Reinterpretation of Marx's Critical Theory*. Cambridge University Press, 1993.
Prendergast, Christopher, ed. *Debating World Literature*. Verso, 2004.
Rabie, Kareem. *Palestine Is Throwing a Party and the Whole World Is Invited: Capital and State Building in the West Bank*. Duke University Press, 2021.
Radhakrishnan, R. "Why Compare." *New Literary History* 40, no. 3 (Summer 2009): 453–71.
Ramadan, Yasmine. "The Emergence of the Sixties Generation in Egypt and the Anxiety over Categorization." *Journal of Arabic Literature* 43, no. 2–3 (2012): 409–30.
———. *Space in Modern Egyptian Fiction*. Edinburgh University Press, 2020.
Ramazani, Jahan. "Modernist Bricolage, Postcolonial Hybridity." *Modernism/Modernity* 13, no. 3 (2006): 445–64.
Ray, Sangeeta. *Gayatri Chakravorty Spivak: In Other Words*. Wiley-Blackwell, 2009.
Raz-Krakotzkin, Amnon. "Exile, History and the Nationalization of Jewish Memory: Some Reflections on the Zionist Notion of History and Return." *Journal of Levantine Studies* 3, no. 2 (2013): 37–70.

———. "The Zionist Return to the West and the Mizrachi Jewish Perspective." In *Orientalism and the Jews*, ed. Ivan Davidson Kalmar and Derek J. Penslar. Brandeis University Press, 2005.

Reid, Donald M. *Contesting Antiquity in Egypt: Archaeologies, Museums and the Struggle for Identities from World War I to Nasser*. American University in Cairo Press, 2015.

Rodas, Julia Miele. *Autistic Disturbances: Theorizing Autism Poetics from the DSM to Robinson Crusoe*. University of Michigan Press, 2018.

Rosenthal, Franz. "Dawla." In *Encyclopaedia of Islam*, 2nd ed., ed. P. Bearman, T. Bianquis, C. E. Bosworth, E. van Donzel and W. P. Heinrichs. Brill, 1991.

Ross, Kristin. *Fast Cars, Clean Bodies: Decolonization and the Reordering of French Culture*. MIT Press, 1995.

Ryding, Karin C. *A Reference Grammar of Modern Standard Arabic*. Cambridge University Press, 2005.

Sacks, Jeffrey. *Iterations of Loss: Mutilation and Aesthetic Form, Al-Shidyaq to Darwish*. Fordham University Press, 2015.

———. "The Philological Present: Reading the Arabic Nineteenth Century." *Journal of Arabic Literature* 47, no. 1–2 (2016): 169–207.

Sadan, Dov. *Midrash psikho'analiti: prakim ba-psikhologya shel Y. H. Brenner* [A psychoanalytic midrash: studies in Y. H. Brenner's psychology]. Magnes, Hebrew University Press, 1996.

Sa'di, Ahmad, and Lila Abu-Lughod. *Nakba: Palestine, 1948, and the Claims of Memory*. Columbia University Press, 2007.

Said, Edward W. "Arabic Prose and Fiction After 1948." In *Reflections on Exile*. Harvard University Press, 2000.

———. *Orientalism*. Pantheon, 1978.

———. "Zionism from the Standpoint of Its Victims." *Social Text* 1 (1979).

Sajdi, Dana. *The Barber of Damascus: Nouveau Literacy in the Eighteenth-Century Ottoman Levant*. Stanford University Press, 2013.

Sakr, Laila Shereen. *Arabic Glitch: Technoculture, Data Bodies, and Archives*. Stanford University Press, 2023.

Salamanca, Omar Jabary, Mezna Qato, Kareem Rabie, and Sobhi Samour. "Past Is Present: Settler Colonialism in Palestine." *Settler Colonial Studies* 2, no. 1 (2012): 1–8.

Salem, Sara. *Anticolonial Afterlives in Egypt: The Politics of Hegemony*. Cambridge University Press, 2020.

———. "Sonallah Ibrahim and Miriam Naoum's *Zaat*: Deploying the Domestic in Representations of Egyptian Politics." *Journal of Middle East Women's Studies* 16, no. 1 (2020): 19–40.

Salih, Arwa. *The Stillborn: Notebooks of a Woman from the Student-Movement Generation in Egypt*. Trans. Samah Selim. Seagull, 2018.

Sammud, Nur al-Din. *Mahmud al-Mas'adi wa-kitabuhu al-sudd* [Mahmud al-Mas'adi and his book The Dam]. Al-Dar al-tunisiyya li-l-nashr, 1973.

Sanbar, Elias. "Out of Place, Out of Time." Trans. Ruth Morris. *Mediterranean Historical Review* 16 no. 1 (2001): 87–94.

Sandywell, Barry. "The Myth of Everyday Life: Toward a Heterology of the Ordinary." *Cultural Studies* 18, no. 2–3 (2004): 160–80.

Sayeau, Michael Douglas. *Against the Event: The Everyday and the Evolution of Modernist Narrative*. Oxford University Press, 2013.

BIBLIOGRAPHY

Schachter, Allison. *Diasporic Modernisms: Hebrew and Yiddish Literature in the Twentieth Century.* Oxford University Press, 2011.

———. "Orientalism, Secularism, and the Crisis of Hebrew Modernism: Reading Leah Goldberg's *Avedot*." *Comparative Literature* 65, no. 3 (2013): 345–62.

Scholem, Gershom. *Pirke yesod be-havanat ha-kabala u-smaleha* [Fundamentals of the kabbalah and its symbols]. Mosad bialik, 1980.

Schoonover, Karl. "Wastrels of Time: Slow Cinema's Laboring Body, the Political Spectator, and the Queer." *Framework* 53, no. 1 (2012): 65–78.

Schwartz, Yigal, and Joseph Zernik. "Yad 'anakim zdona u-botahat" [A giant steady hand]. In Yitzhaq Shami, *Tahanat ha-hayim*. Kinneret zmora bitan, 2015.

Scott, David. *Omens of Adversity: Tragedy, Time, Memory, Justice.* Duke University Press, 2014.

Sedgwick, Eve Kosofsky. *Touching Feeling: Affect, Pedagogy, Performativity.* Duke University Press, 2003.

Segev, Tom. *1967: Israel, the War, and the Year That Transformed the Middle East.* Metropolitan, 2007.

Seidman, Naomi. *A Marriage Made in Heaven: The Sexual Politics of Hebrew and Yiddish.* University of California Press, 1997.

Seiler, Claire. *Midcentury Suspension: Literature and Feeling in the Wake of World War II.* Columbia University Press, 2020.

Sela, Maya. "Levaya ba-tsohorayim" [Funeral at noon]. *Ha'aretz*, December 5, 2014.

Selim, Samah. *The Novel and the Rural Imaginary in Egypt, 1880–1985.* Routledge, 2004.

———. *Popular Fiction, Translation and the Nahda in Egypt.* Palgrave Macmillan, 2019.

Serres, Michel. *The Parasite.* Trans. Lawrence R. Schehr. Johns Hopkins University Press, 1982.

al-Shafaqi, Muhammad Abdallah. "Muhawalat naqd, qissat al-jabal" [An attempt at critique: The Mountain]. *Al-Adab* (June 1959): 195–203.

Shaked, Gershon. "Rikmat hayim be-seter" [A secret texture of life]. *Siman kri'a* 5 (1976): 455.

Shalash, 'Ali. *Nash'at al-naqd al-riwa'i fi al-adab al-'arabi al-hadith* [The origins of novel criticism in modern Arabic literature]. Maktabat gharib, 1992.

Shalhoub-Kevorkian, Nadera. "Ashlaa' and the Genocide in Gaza: Livability Against Fragmented Flesh." *Hot Spots, Fieldsights*, October 31, 2024. https://culanth.org/fieldsights/ashlaa-and-the-genocide-in-gaza.

Shami, Yitzhaq. "Ha-sofrim ha-'aravim" [The Arab writers]. In *Tahanat ha-hayim*, ed. Joseph Zernik. Kinneret zmora bitan, 2015.

Shannon, Claude Elwood, and Warren Weaver. *The Mathematical Theory of Communication.* University of Illinois Press, 1949.

Shapira, Anita. *Brener: sipur hayim.* Am oved, 2008. Trans. Anthony Berris as *Yosef Haim Brenner: A Life.* Stanford University Press, 2015.

———. *Ha-Tanakh ve-ha-zehut ha-yisra'elit* [The Bible and Israeli identity]. Magnes, the Hebrew University, 2005.

Sharma, Sarah. "A Manifesto for the Broken Machine." *Camera Obscura* 35, no. 2 (2020): 171–79.

al-Sharqawi, 'Abd al-Rahman. *Al-Ard* [The land], 3rd ed. Dar al-katib al-'arabi, 1968.

al-Sharuni, Yusuf. *Dirasat fi al-adab al-'arabi al-mu'asir* [Studies in modern Arabic literature]. Al-Mu'assasa al-misriyya al-'amma li-l-ta'lif wa-l-tarjama wa-l-tiba'a wa-l-nashr, 1964.

Sheehi, Stephen. *Foundations of Modern Arab Identity*. University Press of Florida, 2004.
Sherkow, Susan P., and Alexandra M. Harrison. *Autism Spectrum Disorder: Perspectives from Psychoanalysis and Neuroscience*. Rowman & Littlefield, 2013.
Shibli, Adania. "Adania Shibli on Writing Palestine from the Inside." Interview by José García. *Literary Hub*, February 6, 2017. lithub.com/adania-shibli-on-writing-palestine-from-the-inside/.
———. "Hiwar ma'a/'an sinima al-sharq ba'da mushahidat film sajl ihtifa" [A conversation with/about the cinema of the Orient after watching *Chronicle of Disappearance*]. *Masharif* 14 (February 1997): 138–44.
———. "Indifférente, ou presque." *Esprit*, no. 8–9 (Aug-Sep 2007): 250–51.
———. "Al-Kitaba kama al-haya" [Writing is like life]. *Majallat al-dirasat al-filastiniyya* 96 (2013): 167–68.
———. *Misas*. Dar al-adab, 2003. Trans. Paula Hydar as *Touch*. Clockroot, 2010.
———. *Tafsil thanawi*. Dar al-adab, 2017. Trans. Elizabeth Jaquette as *Minor Detail*. New Directions, 2020.
———. "Al-Tala'ub bi-l-'adid min dharrat al-ghubar" [Playing with countless specks of dust]. *Al-Karmel* 70–71 (2002): 300–9. Partially translated by Yasmeen Hanoosh as "Dust." *The Iowa Review* 37, no. 2 (2007): 93–104.
Shmuelof, Matti. "Rahok me-ha-pisga" [Far from the top]. *ynet*, August 18, 2008. https://www.ynet.co.il/articles/0,7340,L-3582075,00.html.
Shumsky, Dmitry. *Beyond the Nation-State: The Zionist Political Imagination from Pinsker to Ben-Gurion*. Yale University Press, 2018.
Siksek, Ayman. "Ta'atu'ei ke'ilu" [Illusions of as-if]. *Ha'aretz*, May 8, 2008. www.haaretz.co.il/literature/1.1341183.
Soueif, Ahdaf. *Fi muwajiha al-madafi': rihla filastiniyya* [Facing the cannons: a Palestinian journey]. Dar al-shuruq, 2004.
———. *Mezzaterra: Fragments from the Common Ground*. Anchor, 2010.
Spivak, Gayatri Chakravorty. "Echo." *New Literary History* 24, no. 1 (1993): 17.
———. "Subaltern Studies: Deconstructing Historiography." In *The Spivak Reader: Selected Works of Gayatri Chakravorty Spivak*, ed. Donna Landry and Gerald MacLean. Routledge, 1996.
Stagh, Marina. "The Limits of Freedom of Speech: Prose Literature and Prose Writers in Egypt under Nasser and Sadat." PhD Diss., Stockholm University, 1993.
Stamatopoulou-Robbins, Sophia. "An Uncertain Climate in Risky Times: How Occupation Became Like the Rain in Post-Oslo Palestine." *International Journal of Middle East Studies* 50, no. 3 (2018): 383–404.
Starkey, Paul. *Modern Arabic Literature*. Georgetown University Press, 2006.
Steyerl, Hito. "In Defense of the Poor Image." *e-flux Journal* 10, no. 11 (2009). https://www.e-flux.com/journal/10/61362/in-defense-of-the-poor-image/.
Stewart, Kathleen. *Ordinary Affects*. Duke University Press, 2007.
Tageldin, Shaden M. *Disarming Words: Empire and the Seductions of Translation in Egypt*. University of California Press, 2011.
Tamari, Salim. "Ishaq al-Shami and the Predicament of the Arab Jew in Palestine." *Jerusalem Quarterly*, no. 21 (August 2004): 10–26.
Tawil-Souri, Helga. "Checkpoint Time." *Qui Parle* 26, no. 2 (2017): 383–422.
Teeffelen, Toine van. "The Waiting Game." *Electronic Intifada*, September 1, 2003. https://electronicintifada.net/content/waiting-game/4753.

BIBLIOGRAPHY

Thompson, Levi. *Reorienting Modernism in Arabic and Persian Poetry*. Cambridge University Press, 2022.
Torlasco, Domietta. "Philosophy in the Kitchen." In *World Picture* 11, http://worldpicturejournal.com/WP_11/Torlasco_11.html, 2016.
al-ʿUmari, Amir. *Al-Sinima al-misriyyah wa-l-adab: qissat hubb* [Egyptian cinema and literature: a love story]. Afaq li-l-nashr wa-l-tawziʿ, 2021.
Van der Spek, Kees. *The Modern Neighbors of Tutankhamun: History, Life, and Work in the Villages of the Theban West Bank*. American University in Cairo Press, 2011.
Vardoulakis, Dimitris. "Stasis: Beyond Political Theology?" *Cultural Critique* 73 (Fall 2009): 125–47.
Viswanathan, Gauri. *Masks of Conquest: Literary Study and British Rule in India*. Columbia University Press, 1989.
Waardenburg, Jacques. "Louis Massignon (1883–1962) as a Student of Islam." *Die Welt des Islams* 45, no. 3 (2005): 312–42.
Wasserstrom, Steven M. *Religion after Religion: Gershom Scholem, Mircea Eliade, and Henry Corbin at Eranos*. Princeton University Press, 1999.
Weisman, Anat. "Mahshavot be-zman hove: tarbut ha-zman be-yisraʾel" [Present thoughts: the culture of time in Israel]. *Zmanim* 68/69 (1999): 122–31.
Weiss, Tzahi. "Ladaʿat mibli ladaʿat" [Knowing without knowing]. *Reshit* 1 (2009): 261–77.
Weiss, Yfaat. *Nesiʿa u-nesiʿa meduma: Leʾa Goldberg be-germanya, 1930–1933* [A journey and an imaginary journey: Leah Goldberg in Germany, 1930–1933]. Merkaz zalman shazar, 2014.
———. "A Small Town in Germany: Leah Goldberg and German Orientalism in 1932." *Jewish Quarterly Review* 99, no. 2 (2009): 200–229.
Wick, Livia. "The Practice of Waiting Under Closure in Palestine." *City and Society* 23 (Spring 2011): 24–44.
Williams, Raymond. *Marxism and Literature*. Oxford University Press, 1977.
Wolfe, Patrick. "Settler Colonialism and the Elimination of the Native." *Journal of Genocide Research* 8, no. 4 (2006): 387–409.
Wollaeger, Mark A., and Matt Eatough. *The Oxford Handbook of Global Modernisms*. Oxford University Press, 2012.
WRec, Warwick Research Collective. *Combined and Uneven Development: Towards a New Theory of World-Literature*. Liverpool University Press, 2016.
Yergeau, Melanie. *Authoring Autism: On Rhetoric and Neurological Queerness*. Duke University Press, 2018.
Zephira, Bracha. *Kolot rabim* [Many voices]. Masada, 1978.
Žižek, Slavoj. *Event: A Philosophical Journey Through a Concept*. Penguin, 2014.
Zreik, Raef. "'Al ha-ʿatsmi she ba-hagana ha-ʿatsmit ve-ha-zkhut lehitnagdut" [On the self in self defense and the right to resist]. *Teʾorya u-vikoret* 60 (Summer 2024).
Zurayk, Constantine. *Maʿnat al-nakba* [The meaning of the catastrophe]. Dar al-ʿilm li-l-malayyin, 1948.
———. *Maʿnat al-nakba mujaddadan* [The meaning of the catastrophe, once again]. Dar al-ʿilm li-l-malayyin, 1967.

INDEX

abjection, 72, 88, 98–99
Abramovich, Sholem Y. (Mendele Mocher Sforim), 96–97, 211n85
absolute song, 40, 65
abstraction, 19, 86–87, 183, 186
Abu al-ʿAtahiyya (poet), 42–44, 201n22
Abwab al-madina (*City Gates*) (Khoury), 34, 182–87
accumulation, 71, 144, 170
Adonis (Syrian poet), 12, 40–41, 201n12
aesthetics, 4, 17, 38, 53, 92–93, 96–97, 123, 151, 183; exteriority and, 182; modernist, 22, 178; negative, 98; static, 102
aesthetic theory, 4, 28, 98, 193n26
affect, affectivity and, 17–19, 34, 74, 110, 136, 157–62, 170
affective experiences, 34, 39–40, 135, 187, 187n 191n7
affective present, 4, 16–21, 107, 154, 184
affective structure, 23, 111, 125, 191n7
Agamben, Giorgio, 182, 197n66
agency, 150–51, 153–54, 158, 160–61, 165, 181; bodies and, 136–37
Agnon, Shmuel Yosef, 30–31, 34, 37–42, 65–68, 200n8, 204nn60–61, 219n109. *See also specific works*; Nobel prize for, 55–56
agricultural settlements, 72–75, 91–92, 206n16, 216n52
aḥādīth. *See ḥadīth*
ahistoricity, ahistoricism and, 33, 39–40, 42, 46–49, 110, 120–21, 130–31, 185
Alf layla wa-layla (A Thousand and One Nights), 185–86
alienation, 16, 54, 105, 109–10, 117, 120–21, 181

ʿ*aliya* (ascendance) story, 73–74
allegory, national 32, 135, 204n66
al-Sharqawi, ʿAbd al-Rahman, 79–80
ambivalence, 21, 68, 94
Amir, Aharon, 140–41
anachronism, 31, 37–39, 48, 56–57, 67
anonymity, 186–87
anti-colonialism, 26, 44, 69, 79, 112
anti-evental mechanisms, 107, 125
Antinomies of Realism, The (Jameson), 18, 74, 207n17
antisemitism, 26, 96–97
Arab cultural revival (*nahḍa*), 7–9, 12–13, 16, 26–28, 184–85, 198n79
Arabic language, 94, 113–14, 155, 183–85, 192n15, 212n1; Classical grammar, 1–3, 49, 191n4, 196n64; tenses, 13, 194n33
Arabic literature, 5–6, 16, 22, 38–41, 116, 178. *See also specific works*; Hebrew press on, 7–8, 27; modernity and, 26, 44–46, 54–55, 182, 187; poetry, 1–4, 42–43, 49, 64, 185, 199n84; Said on, 16–17
"Arabic Prose and Fiction After 1948" (Said), 16, 195n46
Arab-Jewish identity, 192n15
Arab modernity/modernism, 12, 16, 26–27, 183–84
Arab nationalism, 139
Arab present, 8–9, 16, 20, 24
Ard, al- (*The Land*) (al-Sharqawi), 79–80
Arendt, Hannah, 104, 208n33
ASD. *See* autism spectrum disorder
ashlaʾ (dismembered body parts), 34–35, 182, 186–87, 226n7

INDEX

Atlantic slave trade, 169–70
"'Atsabim" ("Nerves") (Brenner), 31, 71–75, 86–90, 97, 100–101, 179–80
Auerbach, Erich, 135–36, 219n110
authenticity, 12, 14, 16, 176, 185, 192n10, 202n33; cultural, 41–42, 84; desire for, 68; national, 49; orality and, 47; Shibli on, 152
autism, autistic perception and, 34, 147, 150–54, 166–68, 175
autism spectrum disorder (ASD), 150, 222n11
Avedot (*Losses*) (Goldberg), 36–37, 200nn1
'*avodat erets israel* (labor of/for the Land of Israel), 28
Awakening of Egypt, The (*Nahḍat Maṣr*) (statue), 69–70

Bab al-maftuh, al- (*The Open Door*) (al-Zayyat), 116
Bakhtin, Mikhail, 117, 215n48
Baron, Dvora, 215n44
Barthes, Roland, 149, 163, 175–76, 180, 228n24
Beloved (Morrison), 174
Benjamin, Walter, 11, 15–16, 195n43, 212n5
Berdugo, Sami, 220n6
Berlant, Lauren, 14, 18, 110, 157, 191n7
Beyond the Pleasure Principle (Freud), 210n70
Bialik, Hayim Nahman, 88, 94, 132–33
Bible, 42, 64, 89–91, 98, 135–36, 210n65, 219n109
birdsong, 31, 65–68
Blanchot, Maurice, 135, 212n10
bodies, 87, 100, 109, 123, 134, 138, 165, 167, 175, 181; agency and, 136–37; *ashla'* and, 34–35, 182, 186–87, 226n7; autonomy and, 150; bodily fluids from, 126–28; dirt and, 153; dust and, 159–61; the present and, 17, 74
borders, 106, 115, 132–35, 140
boredom, 113, 117–18, 136–39
Breakdown and Bereavement (*Shkhol ve-khishalon*) (Brenner), 31, 71–73, 87, 89, 95, 97–98, 101–3
Brenner, Yoseph Haim Brenner, 31–32, 179–80, 193n26, 207n17, 210n57, 210n71, 211n80. See also specific works; on Abramovic, 96–97, 211n85; Bialik on, 88; in *ha-Poʻel ha-tsaʻir*, 9–10; in Palestine, 73, 90–93; psychoanalysis and, 87, 209n56; translation by, 22
Buber, Martin, 28–29
Burla, Yehuda, 27–29, 199n84

Cairo Trilogy (Mahfouz), 116
Canaanite movement, 220n125

capitalism, 12, 15, 26, 110, 120–22, 184, 195n39, 213n23; alienation and, 117; globalized, 172; modernist, 28, 109, 180
censorship, 118–19, 212n1
Children of the Ghetto (*Awlad al-ghitu*) trilogy (Khoury), 170
Christianity, 42, 50–51, 203n46
Chronicle of a Disappearance (*Sajl ikhtifa'*) (film), 149, 152, 163, 176
circular time, 132, 215n48
City Gates (*Abwab al-madina*) (Khoury), 34, 182–87
civil war, 21, 182–83, 227n8; Lebanese Civil War, 34–35, 182–86, 227n12
cleaning, cleanliness and, 105, 108–9, 152, 179–81
Cold War, 144
colonialism, 26, 41, 45–46, 182, 202n30, 202n33, 206n16. See also Nakba; settler colonialism, Zionist; modernity and, 16, 77–78, 202n28; Said on, 77–78; settler, 8–10, 28–30, 156, 179–80, 223n36; technology and, 35, 211n73, 226n7; time, temporality and, 16, 159
communication theory, 19–20
compulsion, compulsivity and, 5, 32, 91, 98, 102
concrete rhetoric, concreteness and, 134–38
conflict resolution, conflict management and, 145, 154
consumption, consumerism and, 106–7, 110–11, 113, 120–22, 144
contemporaneity, 14, 16, 38–39, 55, 64–65, 67
Cossery, Albert, 31, 69–71, 205n1
crisis ordinary, crises and, 127, 157, 159, 162, 172
Critique of Everyday Life (Lefebvre), 108–9

daily life, the everyday and, 15–16, 108, 121–23, 213n15, 213n17; housework and, 115–18, 215n44, 216n51; repetition and, 133–34; routines and, 5, 17, 32–33, 93, 104–7, 116, 124–25, 157; temporality and, 109–10
Darwish, Mahmoud, 1–4, 191n1
dawla (state), 114
death, 59, 65, 91, 104, 132, 164; murders and, 66–67, 125, 168–71, 173–74, 180
"Death of the Author" ("Mawt al-muʾallif") (Khoury), 185–86
decolonization, 16, 145
De Man, Paul, 14
denarrativization, 112, 123
depersonalization, 137
Derrida, Jacques, 194n29, 196n64, 218n82, 225n88

INDEX

"Dhakira al-mafquda, al-" ("The Lost Memory") (Khoury), 12–13, 183–85
Dhat (*Zaat*) (Ibrahim), 120–22
"Dialog with/About the Cinema of the Orient After Watching *Chronicle of a Disappearance*, A" (Shibli), 152–53
diaspora, 29; Jewish, 73, 91, 96–97; Palestinian, 156
dirt, 19–20, 101, 107–8, 123, 153, 179–81
disembodiment, 35, 66, 153
disillusionment, 74, 110–11, 124, 127
displacement, 4, 155–56. *See also* Nakba
Divine Intervention (*Yad ilahiyya*) (film), 149, 158–59, 226n97
domestic labor, 116, 118, 127, 129–30
dust, 159–60, 171, 180

"Edo and Enam" ("'Ido ve-'enam") (Agnon), 31, 40, 55–62, 65–67
Egypt, 8, 26, 28–29, 139, 144, 168; Cairo, 69–70; gender and, 115–16, 118; Israel and, 111–13; Nasser and, 77, 84–85, 105, 111–12, 213n23; nationalism in, 69–71, 79; novels from, 6–7, 31, 69–86, 106–7, 118–26, 192n10; Sixties Generation, 118, 216n54; tourism and, 76–80, 83
emasculation, 127
embodiment, 149, 151, 154, 161; affect and, 32, 137, 162; habits and, 19, 181; present and, 3, 13, 22
empty time, 15–16, 108, 195n43
episodic structures, 16–17, 43, 47, 164–66, 192n25
eroticism, sensuality and, 92–94, 99–101
essentialism, strategic, 67–68
ethnic cleansing, 149, 156, 180
Eurochronology, 37–38, 40, 200n6
everyday life. *See* daily life, the everyday and
exegesis, 37, 47–48, 58, 60–63
"Exercises in Practical Hebrew" ("Targilim be-'ivrit shimushit") (Pagis), 3, 191n6
experienced present, 17–18, 178–81
exteriority, 163, 182, 187

Fathy, Hassan, 76–77, 208n31
feelings, structures of, 17–19, 142, 149. *See also* affect
feminism, 66, 107–9, 116–18, 128, 213n15, 216n51, 216n53
FISD. *See* free indirect somatic discourse
free indirect somatic discourse (FISD), 165, 168
Freud, Sigmund, 11, 15–16, 63, 91, 175, 196n64, 210n70, 225n88

Funeral at Noon (*Levaya batsohorayim*) (Koren), 33, 104–7, 123, 129–40
le futur antérieur ("prior future"), 11–12, 23, 174, 194n29
the future, 15–16, 18, 70, 82, 126, 144–45, 178; labor for, 28–29; modernity and, 12–14; the past and, 74, 174
future perfect, 11–12, 23, 174, 194n29

Gaza, 24, 35, 139–40, 144–45, 147, 149, 154–56, 226n7
gaze, 8, 66, 72–73, 75–76, 126, 152, 164, 176–77
gender, 31, 58–61, 64, 94, 100, 125, 213n15, 216n52. *See also* sexual violence; crisis of masculinity and, 80–81, 87, 127–29; housewives and, 32, 104, 106–7, 115–17, 120–22, 129–30; housework and, 20, 32–33, 105–10, 115–18, 138–41, 215n44, 216n51; labor and, 107–8, 115–16; in *The Mountain*, 80–81; routine and, 105, 179; temporality and, 114–15, 215n44
genocide, 24, 156, 226n7
Ghanem, Fathi, 31–32, 71, 75–78, 102–3, 179, 207n22
Ginzburg, Carlo, 171–72, 225n77
Glissant, Édouard, 182
globalization, 25, 106–7, 143, 155, 172, 195n39
Goldberg, Leah, 30, 36–37, 200nn1–2
Gouri, Haim, 113
grammar: Classical Arabic, 1–3, 49, 191n4, 196n64; Hebrew, 3, 56–57, 97–98, 194n33
grammatical tenses, 11–16, 194n33. *See also* specific tenses

Haddatha Abu Hurayra qal (*Thus Spoke Abu Hurayra*) (al-Mas'adi), 30–31 42–44, 40, 47–53, 55, 64–67
ḥadīth (account of the prophet), 47–48, 202n35
"ha-Janer ha-erets yisra'eli veavizarehu" ("The Land of Israel genre and its accoutrements") (Brenner), 9–10, 87–88, 92
Hallaj, Mansur al- (Islamic mystic), 50–52
ha-Po'el ha-tsa'ir (The Young Worker) journal, 7, 9–10, 192n14
hapticity, 134, 149, 151–54. *See also* touch; haptic reading and, 163–67; resistance to reading and, 175–77
haptic poetics, 151, 162, 170, 174, 176
ḥarb ahliyya. *See* civil war
Hartman, Saidiya, 169–70, 173–74
haskala (Jewish enlightenment), 25–28
Haykal, Mohammed Hussayn, 6–7, 192n10

INDEX

Hebrew, 8, 13, 22, 36, 113–14, 183; culture, 37, 142, 145, 192n14; grammar, 3, 56–57, 97–98, 194n33; present, 20, 24; revivalism, 10, 25–26, 37, 90–91
Hebrew literature, 36–42, 56–62, 70, 143, 178, 192n15, 220n6. *See also specific works*; gender in, 116; periodization and, 22
Hemingway, Ernest, 22, 105–6, 119, 124, 212n3, 217n58
heterosexuality, 80–81
historical present, 15, 17, 110, 157
historicity, 17, 24, 45, 110, 114, 146, 202n28
historiography, 106, 139–40, 149, 155–56, 197n76, 198n79, 200n6
"Hiya jumla ismiyya" ("A Noun Sentence") (Darwish), 1–2
Hoffmann, E. T. A., 63
homoeroticism, 81, 100
housework, 20, 33, 105, 108–10, 118, 138–41, 214n44, 216n51; housewives and, 32, 104, 106–7, 115–17, 120–22, 129–30, 132, 136
humanism, 31, 37–39, 41, 50, 53, 55, 61–62, 186
Hussein, Taha, 53, 76, 203n50, 205n5
hygiene, personal, 105, 115, 127–28, 153, 179–80

Ibn Khaldun, 114
Ibrahim, Sonallah, 22, 33, 104, 176, 217n58. *See also specific works*; arrest of, 111–12, 122–24; censorship of, 118–19; Hemingway and, 105–6, 119, 124
IDF. *See* Israel Defense Forces
idleness, 71–72, 97–98, 100–103, 107
"'Ido ve-'enam" ("Edo and Enam") (Agnon), 31, 40, 55–62, 65–67
Idris, Yusuf, 79, 119
illegibility, 182, 184–85
iltizām (committed literature), 53, 70–71, 205n5
immanent critique, 181, 216n57
immediacy, 14, 19, 74–75
immobility, 5, 17, 21, 101, 157–58
impassivity, 176–77, 181
imperialism, 27, 111, 140–41, 170, 174, 215n36
indigenous peoples, 72–73, 75, 77–78
Indo-European languages, 42, 203n46
inertia, 98, 102, 137, 181. *See also* impassivity
intentionality, 20, 151–52, 181. *See also* involuntariness
interiority, interiorities and, 20, 149, 153–54, 176–77, 181–82
intertextuality, 47, 52, 62, 133, 135, 219n109
involuntariness, 151–53. *See also* intentionality
irony, 39, 56, 77, 89, 94

Islam, Islamic history and, 43–47, 203n46; Islamic mysticism, 44, 50–52, 203n46; Islamic visual culture, 163–64; premodern Arab-Islamic culture, 9, 45–46, 48–55, 163–64, 202n28
Israel, State of, 35, 115–18, 130, 192n19, 226n7. *See also* Zionism, Zionist settlements and; Egypt and, 111–13; Erets Yisrael, 73–74, 86–90, 193n19, 206n16, 210n71; establishment of, 16, 26, 28–29, 155; Second Intifada and, 144–45; Six-Day War, 139–40; surveillance by, 144–45, 148, 155, 158, 160; United States and, 142–43
Israel Defense Forces (IDF), 147, 154, 158–59, 168, 174, 176
Israeli literature, 25, 143–44

Jabal, al- (*The Mountain*) (Ghanem), 31, 71–73, 75–86, 100–103, 180, 207n22, 208n43
Jabra, Jabra Ibrahim, 53–54, 204n55
Jameson, Fredric, 18, 20, 22, 74, 102–3, 196n54, 207n17, 209n50
jīl al-sittīnāt (the Sixties Generation), Egypt, 118, 216n54
Judaism, Jewish history and, 9, 24, 31–32, 36–37, 61, 112, 143–44, 219n109, 220n125; diaspora, 73, 91, 96–97; migration to Palestine, 28–29, 73–74, 86–95

Kabbalah, 61, 204n66
Kafr Qasim Massacre, 168
Kharrat, Idwar, 122, 212n4
Khoury, Elias, 12–13, 16, 226n7, 227n14, 228n24. *See also specific works*; Lebanese Civil War and, 34–35, 183–86; on Ongoing *Nakba*, 155
Klein, Melanie, 150
Koren, Yeshayahu, 22, 33, 104–6, 129, 140–41, 219n109. *See also specific works*
Kristeva, Julia, 88
Kulluna ba'id bi-dhat al-miqdar'an al-hubb (*We Are All Equally Far from Love*) (Shibli), 162

labor, 79–86, 93, 101, 126, 143; daily, 139, 181; domestic, 116, 118, 127, 138–39; gendered, 107–8, 115–16; physical, 70, 134; of the present, 28–29, 180; productive, 70–73, 75, 83–84, 107, 109, 118, 127; reproductive, 32–33, 104–9, 129–30, 138
Land, The (*al-Ard*) (al-Sharqawi), 79–80
"Land of Israel genre and its accoutrements, The" ("ha-Janer ha-erets yisra'eli veavizarehu") (Brenner), 9–10, 87–88, 92

INDEX

Laroui, Abdallah, 11–12, 194n29
Laziness in the Fertile Valley (*Les Fainéants dans la vallée fertile*) (Cossery), 31, 69–70
Lebanese Civil War, 34–35, 182–86, 227n12
Lefebvre, Henri, 108–9, 114, 117, 121
"Lefi ha-tza'ar ha-sakhar" ("The Reward Is in Accordance with the Pain") (Agnon), 57
Les Fainéants dans la vallée fertile (*Laziness in the Fertile Valley*) (Cossery), 31, 69–70
Levaya batsohorayim (*Funeral at Noon*) (Koren), 33, 104–7, 123, 129–40
liberalism, 26, 118, 155
linearity, 16, 113–15, 117–18, 171–72, 180, 215n44
literary forms, prose and, 4, 16–17, 23–24, 40–41, 53–54, 107, 124, 176. *See also* reverb; routine; scratch; touch; affective present and, 4, 16–21
lived experience, 4, 110
Lose Your Mother (Hartman), 169, 173
Losses (*Avedot*) (Goldberg), 36–37, 200nn1
"Lost Memory, The" ("al-Dhakira al-mafquda") (Khoury), 12–13, 183–85

Madame Bovary (Flaubert), 117, 215n47, 219n110
madness, 160–61, 212n6
Mahfouz, Naguib, 116
Manning, Erin, 151, 166–67
maqāmā (Arabic episodic genre), 43, 47, 192n25
Marks, Laura, 163–64
marriage, 105, 120, 126, 129, 132–34
Marxism, 108–12, 117–18, 156, 216n51
Massignon, Louis, 44, 50–51, 203n41, 203nn45–46
masturbation, 126–28
Mas'adi, Mahmud al-, 30–31, 34, 37–55, 65–68, 200n8, 203n38, 203n50
materiality, 20, 82, 109, 137–38, 186
Mawaqif (journal), 12–13, 183
"Mawt al-mu'allif" ("Death of the Author") (Khoury), 185–86
medina (state), 113–14
melancholic historicism, 174–75
memory, 12–13, 16, 155–56
Mendele, Mocher Sforim (Sholem Y. Abramovich), 96–97, 211n85
middle class, 110–13
Middle East, 6, 24–30, 139
Mi-kan u-mi-kan (*From Here and There*) (Brenner), 9–10
milḥemet aḥim (fraternal war), 183. *See also* civil war
mimesis, 66–67, 96, 119–20, 138, 163

Minor Detail (*Tafsil thanawi*) (Shibli), 143, 167–69, 171–75, 179–80
Misas (*Touch*) (Shibli), 162, 164–66, 172, 175
Mitchell, Timothy, 77
modernity, modernism and, 14, 124, 192n15, 195n39, 197n68, 207n17, 215n47. *See also* revival modernity; Adonis on, 40–41; aesthetics and, 22, 178; Arab, 12, 16, 26–27, 183–84; Arabic literary, 26, 182, 187; Benjamin on, 11; capitalist, 28, 109, 180; colonial, 16, 77–78, 202n28; European, 27, 38, 53–54; experience of, 18, 23; global, 22–24, 29; Jameson on, 23; Laroui on, 11–12
modernization, 4, 12, 17, 23, 27, 37–38, 110, 214n28; Egyptian, 76–77; housewives and, 115, 118; Jewish, 25–26, 28, 31–32; *nahḍa* and, 26
modern present, 4, 14–16, 187
Morrison, Tony, 174
Mountain, The (*al-Jabal*) (Ghanem), 31, 71–73, 75–86, 100–103, 180, 207n22, 208n43
Mukhtar, Mahmoud, 69
mundane, mundanity and, 95, 124, 135–36, 139, 148–49, 158, 167
murder, 66–67, 125, 168–71, 173–74, 180
Mutable and the Immutable, The (*al-Thabit wa-l-mutahawwil*) (Adonis), 40–41

nahḍa, Arab (cultural revival), 7–9, 12–13, 16, 26–28, 184–85, 198n79
Nahḍat Maṣr (*The Awakening of Egypt*) (statue), 69–70
Nakba (Palestinian catastrophe), 16, 26, 33, 131, 223n29; Ongoing, 34, 145–46, 149, 155–57, 162, 169, 173
nakba al-mustamirra, al- (Ongoing Nakba), 34, 145–46, 149, 155–57, 162, 169, 173
naksa, al- (the setback), 139, 156
narrators, narration and, 52, 57–59, 61–63, 65–66, 225n77; in *City Gates*, 183; first person, 79, 105, 122; in *Minor Detail*, 168–69, 171–74; in *The Mountain*, 80–84; narrative voice and, 165, 186; in "Nerves," 74–75, 91; in "Playing with Innumerable Specks of Dust," 157–62, 165; in *That Smell*, 105, 112, 124–26, 128–29; third person, 121, 137, 164–65; in *Touch*, 164–67
Nasser, Gamal Abdel, 77, 84–85, 105, 111–12, 213n23
nationalism, 24–26, 98, 111; Arab, 139, 220n125; Egyptian, 69–71, 79; Hebrew nativist, 9, 220n125
national productivity, 32, 102, 107
nation-states, 12, 26, 38, 111, 114, 182, 215n36

INDEX

negative globality, 23
neoliberalism, 17, 142–43, 145, 155, 172
"Nerves" ("'Atsabim") (Brenner), 31, 71–75, 86–90, 97, 100–101, 179–80
neuroses, psychic ailments and, 86–87, 95, 209n52
neutrality, 159–61, 175–76
neutralization, 148–49, 152, 162, 175–77
"New Jew," 86, 209n53
Ngai, Sianne, 72–73, 128
Nichanian, Marc, 40, 41, 204n58
noise, static, 20, 149, 171, 196n58
nonproductivity, 32, 72–73, 79–86, 97–98, 100–101, 105, 179–80
"Noun Sentence, A" ("Hiya jumla ismiyya") (Darwish), 1–2
novels, 11, 48–49, 132, 205n1, 208n43, 216n48. *See also specific novels*; Egyptian, 6–7, 31, 69–86, 106–7, 118–26, 192n10; historical, 8–9, 47; modern, 14, 20, 54, 74; psychological, 136, 219n116; temporality and, 16, 178, 192n9
novelty, 11, 23, 38, 44, 63–64, 110, 183

objectivity, 11, 105–6
Ogden, Thomas, 150–51, 167
Ongoing *Nakba* (*al-nakba al-mustamirra*), 34, 145–46, 149, 155–57, 162, 169, 173
opacity, 17, 34, 157, 163, 177, 181–82
Open Door, The (*al-Bab al-maftuh*) (al-Zayyat), 116
orality, 170–71, 186
Orientalism, Orientalist studies and, 5, 8, 27, 30–31, 36–38, 40, 44–47, 200n2; Agnon and, 56; philology, 39, 41–42, 59; typologies, 64–65
Oslo Accords, 144–45, 154, 197n76
Ottoman empire, 26, 114, 192n15

PA. *See* Palestinian Authority
Pagis, Dan, 3, 191n6
Palestine, 30, 72, 169, 193n19, 206n16, 225n66. *See also Nakba*; Zionism, Zionist settlements and; ethnic cleansing in, 149, 156, 180; Gaza, 24, 35, 139–40, 144–45, 147, 149, 154–56; genocide in, 24, 226n7; Israeli occupation of, 16–17, 26, 143, 149, 154–58, 172; Jewish migration to, 28–29, 73–75, 86–95; *Nakba*, 16, 26, 33–34, 223n29; Palestinian literature, 25, 143–44, 220n2; Second Intifada, 144–45; suspended present in, 145–46, 155, 167; West Bank, 106, 139, 145, 147, 149, 154–55, 158

Palestinian Authority (PA), 144, 154–55
Parasite, The (Serres), 180
parasites, parasitism and, 19–20, 31, 40, 66, 76–77, 98, 180, 196n58
passive, passivity and, 99, 136, 148, 150
the past, 13–16, 18, 49–50, 130, 185; the future and, 74, 174; Jewish, 37, 90; Palestinian, 156–57; the present and, 64–65, 168–69, 171, 173–74
past tense, 14, 168–69, 194n33
periodization, 22, 30–31, 41, 45–47, 54–55, 65
philology, 37, 40, 58, 60–62, 204n58; Orientalist, 39, 41–42, 59
physical labor, 70, 134
"Playing with Innumerable Specks of Dust" ("al-Tala'ub bi-l-'adid min dharrat al-ghubar") (Shibli), 157–62, 165
Poetics (Aristotle), 125
Poetics of Relation (Glissant), 182
poetry, 36–37, 101, 197n71, 201n12; Arabic, 1–4, 42–43, 49, 64, 185, 199n84
political violence, 54, 112, 123, 128
postcolonial theory, postcolonialism and, 5, 16, 32, 110–11, 202n30, 202n33
premodern Arab-Islamic culture, 45–46, 48–55, 163–64, 202n28
present, 5, 13–16, 69–74, 195n39, 195n45, 213n17; absent, 6–7, 13, 30, 36–40; Arab, 8–9, 16, 20, 24; affective, 4, 16–21, 107, 154, 184; continuous, 43–44, 145–46; crisis of, 185; embodiment and, 3, 13, 22; experience and, 17–18, 22, 178–81; Hebrew, 20, 24; historical, 15, 17, 110, 157; Israeli, 143; labor of the, 28–29, 180; modern, 4, 14–16, 187; Palestinian, 143, 155, 167, 170; as the past, 167–75; the past and, 64–65, 168–69, 171, 173–74; of philology, 40–42; of reproductive labor, 104–7; suspended, 145–46, 155, 167; timeless, 34, 43–44, 55, 180; urban, 10–11, 192n25
present tense, 2–3, 168–69, 194n33
prior future (*le futur antérieur*), 11–12, 23, 174, 194n29
productive labor, 70–73, 75, 83–84, 107, 109, 118, 127
productivity, national, 32, 102, 107
psychoanalysis, 66, 86–87, 150, 146, 175, 209n56, 222n11
psychological novels, 136, 219n116

qaṣṣ, al- (fiction), 147–48
Qur'an, 47–49

INDEX

racialization, racial hierarchies and, 5, 26, 30
rape, 66, 168, 180, 219n116
Raz-Krakotzkin, Amnon, 26, 28
reading, 55, 57–68, 175–77; haptic, 163–67; literary practice of, 56, 61, 200n5; surface, 19, 206n12
realism, 7, 11, 39, 79, 106, 118–19, 207n17
repetition, 5, 81–82, 100, 110, 114–15, 124, 174–75; housework and, 109, 118, 129–30, 139; routines and, 104–6
reproductive labor, 32–33, 104–9, 129–30, 138
resistance, 155–56, 175–77, 225n88; Freud on, 175; illegibility as, 182; passive, 148
reverb (static form), 5, 17, 30–31, 38, 40, 62–68, 179
revival modernity, revivalism and, 12, 15, 23–24, 27–29, 33–34, 39, 42, 65, 142, 182–83; Egypt and, 69–70; Hebrew, 10, 25–26, 37, 90–91; modernization and, 46; *nahḍa*, 7–9, 12–13, 16, 26–28, 184–85, 198n79
revulsion, 107, 127, 139
"Reward Is in Accordance with the Pain, The" ("Lefi ha-tzaʿar ha-sakhar") (Agnon), 57
routine, 108, 113, 119–23, 130–34, 136–37, 141, 179; daily, 5, 17, 32–33, 93, 104–7, 115–18, 124–25, 157; housework, 20, 122, 126–27, 215n44; temporality of, 109, 129, 139; violence, 148–49, 159

Said, Edward, 16–17, 50, 77, 82, 86, 195n46
Sajl ikhtifaʾ (*Chronicle of a Disappearance*) (film), 149, 152, 163, 176
Sartre, Jean-Paul, 205n5
scratch (static form), scratching and, 17, 31–32, 72–73, 95–103, 107, 179
Second Intifada (2000), 144–45, 154
second-wave feminism, 109
secularism, 9, 15, 37–38, 45–46, 192n15
Sedgwick, Eve Kosofsky, 150, 196n56, 206n12
senses, 137, 151, 163, 165–67, 186–87
settlements, 76–90, 93–99, 102–3. *See also* Zionism, Zionist settlements and; agricultural, 72–75, 91–92, 206n16, 216n52; surface, 100–101
settler colonialism, Zionist, 9–10, 26, 28–29, 140, 179–80, 223n36; Brenner on, 31–32; violence of, 24, 155–56, 170; in the West Bank, 154–55
sexual deviance, 132–33
sexuality, 80–81, 87, 91, 100
sexual violence, 66, 67–68, 104, 168, 180, 219n116
Shami, Yitzhaq, 7–11, 192nn14–15, 193n26, 199n84

Shibli, Adania, 33–34, 143, 177, 179–80, 225n86. *See also specific works*; hapticity employed by, 152; Nakba and, 167–68; Ongoing Nakba and, 157–58; Soueif and, 147–48; Suleiman and, 149, 152–53, 163–64
Shkhol ve-khishalon (*Breakdown and Bereavement*) (Brenner), 31, 71–73, 87, 89, 95, 97–98, 101–3
Sipur hove ʿal pney ha-arets (*A present tale upon the land*) (Berdugo), 220n6
Six-Day War, 139–40
Sixties Generation (*jīl al-sittīnāt*), Egypt, 118, 216n54
social reproduction, 107, 180
song, 51–52, 57–60, 62, 93–94, 100; absolute, 40, 65; birdsong, 31, 65–68
Soueif, Ahdaf, 147–48
sovereignty, 143, 154, 185; political, 45–46, 114, 144–46; state, 106, 182
spatiality, 23–24, 72, 113–14, 133
Spivak, Gayatri, 31, 66–68
stagnation, 119, 144, 146, 149, 173–74
stasis, static and, 5, 19–20, 34, 42–46, 68, 179, 182; etymology of, 21, 101; of global modernism, 22–24
state, 5, 21, 84, 182. *See also* Israel, State of; etymology, 113–14, 214n33; maintenance, 111, 140; Palestinian, 144, 154; time, 33, 106, 111–15, 118, 123, 130–32, 139; violence, 33, 106–7, 114, 128–29, 140–78
statehood, 111, 130, 139–40
statelessness, 33, 182
static forms, 5, 22–23, 30–35, 41, 71, 179–81. *See also* reverb; routine; scratch; touch; affective present and, 4, 16–21
statism, 29, 84, 112, 184
strategic essentialism, 67–68
structures of feelings, 17–19, 142, 149. *See also* affect
subjectivity, 26, 161, 167, 184, 186–87
subjunctive mood, 173–74
Suez crisis (1957), 111–12
Sufism, 44, 47–48, 50–52, 203n46
Suleiman, Elia, 22, 33–34, 177, 226n97. *See also specific works*; films by, 149, 152–53, 158–59, 163
surface reading, 19, 206n12
surfaces, 72, 86–95, 100–101
surveillance, 126, 176–77; Israeli, 144–45, 148, 155, 158, 160

Tafsil thanawi (*Minor Detail*) (Shibli), 143, 167–69, 171–75, 179–80

INDEX

"Tala'ub bi-l-'adid min dharrat al-ghubar, al-" ("Playing with Innumerable Specks of Dust") (Shibli), 157–62, 165

Tanturiyya, al- (*The Woman from Tantoura*) (Ashour), 170

"Targilim be-'ivrit shimushit" ("Exercises in Practical Hebrew") (Pagis), 3, 191n6

technology, 15, 19, 41, 128, 144; colonial, 35, 211n73, 226n7; surveillance, 148, 176

temporality, temporal orders and, 1–5, 11–16, 48, 194n29, 195n37, 195n43, 215n48. *See also specific grammatical tenses*; Arabic literature and, 45; of consumption, 113; cyclical, 118, 129, 131–32; gender and, 114–15, 117, 215n44; hierarchies and, 28; nonsynchronous, 28; novels and, 109–10, 178, 192n9; parallel, 24; postcolonialism and, 110; of the present, 178–79; psychoanalytic, 156; reproductive, 32, 130; of routine, 109, 129, 139; settler colonialism and, 223n36; stagnation and, 144, 173; of statelessness, 33; of trauma, 170–71; violence and, 33–34, 158

Thabit wa-l-mutahawwil, al- (*The Mutable and the Immutable*) (Adonis), 40–41, 201n12

That Smell (*Tilk al-ra'iha*) (Ibrahim), 33, 104–7, 112–13, 118–20, 122–26, 138–40, 212n1

third person narration, 105, 121, 137, 164–65

t'hiya (Jewish revival), 25–26

Thousand and One Nights, A (*Alf layla wa-layla*), 185–86

Thus Spoke Abu Hurayra (*Haddatha Abu Hurayra qal*) (al-Mas'adi), 30–31 42–44, 40, 47–53, 55, 64–67

Tilk al-ra'iha (*That Smell*) (Ibrahim), 33, 104–7, 112–13 122–26, 113, 118–20, 138–40, 212n1

time, 154, 159. *See also* temporality, temporal orders and; circular, 132, 215n48; empty, 15–16, 108, 195n43; state, 33, 106, 111–15, 118, 123, 130–32, 139

timelessness, 5, 15, 30–31, 39, 41–53, 55, 57–58, 64–66, 72

timeless present, 34, 43–44, 55, 180

touch (static form), 5, 17, 137–38, 149, 167–75, 179; haptic reading and, 163–67

Touch (*Misas*) (Shibli), 162, 164–67, 172–75

translation, 1–2, 26–27, 57, 155, 167, 212n1

transmission, 19–20, 31, 47

transparency, 182

trauma, 11, 120–21, 156–57, 170–71, 184

typology, literature as, 62–65. *See also* reading

United States, 142–44, 178, 216n53

urban present, 10–11, 192n25

Vardoulakis, Dimitris, 101–2

verbs, 1–4, 191n4

violence, 16–17, 29–30, 147–50, 157, 169, 182, 212n5; military, 154–55; normalization of, 33–34, 145, 149, 154–55; political, 54, 112, 123, 128; routine, 148–49, 159; sexual, 66–68, 104, 168, 180, 219n116; state, 33, 78, 106–7, 114, 128–29, 140; temporality and, 33–34, 158; of Zionist settler colonialism, 24, 155–56, 170

virginity, virginal and, 64, 180

vision, haptic, 163–64

Wahat Diaries, The (*Yawmiyat al-wahat*) (Ibrahim), 124

waste management, 105, 180

We Are All Equally Far from Love (*Kulluna ba'id bi-dhat al-miqdar'an al-hubb*) (Shibli), 162

West Bank, 106, 139, 145, 147, 149, 154–55, 158

Williams, Raymond, 17–19, 195n51

witnesses, bearing witness and, 13, 35, 47–48, 51, 59, 158, 177; Massignon on, 64; narrators as, 61, 63

Woman from Tantoura, The (*al-Tanturiyya*) (Ashour), 170

women, 104–8, 215n44, 216n52. *See also* gender; housework and, 20, 32–33, 105–10, 115–18, 138–41, 215n44, 216n51

Woolf, Virginia, 124

world literature, 44–45, 54, 61–62, 204n55

Yad Ilahiyya (*Divine Intervention*) (film), 149, 158–59

Yawm ba'da yawm (*Day After Day*) (Sadiq), 116

Yawmiyat al-wahat (*The Wahat Diaries*) (Ibrahim), 124

Yergeau, M. Remi, 151–53

Yiddish, 10, 94

Zaat (*Dhat*) (Ibrahim), 120–22

Zaydan, Jurji, 8–9

Zaynab (Haykal), 6–7, 192n10

Zionism, Zionist settlements and, 26, 192nn14–15, 199n84, 206n16, 210n65, 210n70. *See also* settler colonialism, Zionist; advent of, 28–29; agricultural settlements, 72–75, 91–95, 206n16, 216n52; Brenner and, 86–93; gender and, 115–17

GPSR Authorized Representative: Easy Access System Europe, Mustamäe tee
50, 10621 Tallinn, Estonia, gpsr.requests@easproject.com

www.ingramcontent.com/pod-product-compliance
Lightning Source LLC
Chambersburg PA
CBHW022046290426
44109CB00014B/997